The Blue Parade

Thomas A. Reppetto

THE FREE PRESS
A Division of Macmillan Publishing Co., Inc.
NEW YORK

Collier Macmillan Publishers
LONDON

To My Parents

The Free Press
A Division of Macmillan Publishing Co., Inc.
866 Third Avenue, New York, N.Y. 10022

Collier Macmillan Canada, Ltd.

Library of Congress Catalog Card Number: 78–53080

Printed in the United States of America

printing number

1 2 3 4 5 6 7 8 9 10

Library of Congress Cataloging in Publication Data

Reppetto, Thomas A
  The blue parade.

  Bibliography: p.
  Includes index.
    1. Police--United States--History. 2. Law
  enforcement--United States--History. I. Title.
  HV8138.R46   363.2'0973   78-53080
  ISBN 0-02-926360-3

Excerpts from *The Autobiography of Lincoln Steffens*, copyright, 1931, by Harcourt Brace Jovanovich, Inc.; copyright, 1959, by Peter Steffens. Reprinted by permission of the publisher.

Excerpts from *Gem of the Prairie*, by Herbert Asbury, copyright 1942, by Alfred A. Knopf, Inc. Reprinted by permission of the publisher.

Excerpts from *The Illinois Crime Survey*, by The Illinois Association for Criminal Justice, copyright 1929. Reprinted as Publication No. 9, Patterson Smith Series in Criminology, Law Enforcement, and Social Problems (Montclair, N.J.), 1968. Used by permission of Patterson Smith Publishing Corp.

Contents

Photographic inserts appear following pages 118 and 246.

Preface and Acknowledgments

In the past ten to fifteen years the police have become a subject of great concern to many segments of American society. Politicians from the President on down frequently praise or criticize them; they are a major interest of television and print journalism and a favorite research topic for academics. Indeed, individual police officers and organizations have participated in political campaigns, often with considerable success; some cops have blossomed forth into print or have been the subjects of television productions depicting their careers; others have taken up the professor's role.

Given the high level of attention paid to it, one would expect that knowledge of policing would be both wide and deep. On the contrary, it is likely that most Americans still view police work in the cop-show, detective-story image of complex investigations and heroic deeds performed in relation to dramatic crimes. Even dramatizations and reports that have dealt with the police in a less sensational way tend to present only a limited portion of the story. In part this may be attributed to the methods of research commonly used by scholars and journalists. In the first instance there is a strong tendency to emphasize the present. This may simply reflect the predilections of many Americans, including some of the best educated, to assume that anything that took place in the dim period before the 1960's cannot be of any relevance. Secondly, there is a tendency to draw evidence from a single locale or level of government. Since American police are among the most fragmented and localized of institutions it is very risky to attempt to generalize about them on the basis of observations of one or two municipal departments, or even of a number of forces in a single region of the country. Very few studies have attempted to perform a comparative analysis across a wide span of years and locales.

The present work approaches the subject with the conviction that real understanding will come from a broad-gauged study. It therefore traces the development of American policing from its eighteenth-century European antecedents to its various facets in the mid-twentieth century in different regions of the country and at several levels of government. It strives for breadth by examining elements of the political, social, and economic contexts within which the police operate, and for depth by devoting several individual chapters to particular locales.

I was aided in my research by the staffs of the New York Public Library, The New-York Historical Society, The Museum of the City of New York, The New York Municipal Reference Library, The Harvard University Library, The Boston Public Library, The Library of Congress, The Bancroft Library, and the Library of the John Jay College of Criminal Justice, as well as by Detective Alfred Young, historian of the New York City Police Department. I am grateful to them all.

All of the manuscript or portions of it have been read by Christa Carnegie, Milton Loewenthal, Donal E. J. MacNamara, William Preston, and Philip John Stead, who offered many helpful comments. I must also record my debt to the staff of The Free Press, especially Gladys Topkis and George Rowland, and to manuscript editor Hunt Cole, who were responsible for various phases of the production of this book. I have benefited greatly from their criticisms and their publishing expertise.

My principal assistant in compiling the manuscript was Carol Campolo Pane. Portions were also typed by Jean McQuillan and Diana Penny Tyson. My thanks to all of them for their patience.

Introduction

This is a book about the development of American police administration, even though it does not rely on organization charts and task descriptions. Indeed, a major theme is that police administration is not applied mechanics, but a living, breathing organism shaped by the political, social, and economic trends of time and place. In particular, the book takes the view that public policy is formed by a struggle of interest groups. As a 1937 Brookings Institution study of law enforcement observed:

> ... public policy in a democracy is a crude compound of the demands and assumed needs either of the population as a whole or of particular self-conscious and articulate groups. Each group—the largest embracing the whole of society—has its own ideas of what should be done to promote its material and cultural interests. ... Sometimes the demand is for subsidies or services directly to members of the group; but not infrequently it is for the regulation or suppression of other competing groups. Consequently, [police]administrative organization is a reflection of the social structure, a somewhat impressionistic and distorted reflection because the political power of a group in a democracy is not always an accurate measure of its social significance or a fair means of determining the priority of its claims.
>
> Administrative organization, however, is more than a reflection; it is a functioning integral part of the social structure. Here are the potent economic groups, ... and here, in a dark but rather ample corner, is the underworld.[1]

There are many ways by which a competing group may put forth its claims to power, status, and other rewards. Perhaps the ultimate method is to project, successfully, its position as morally superior to that of opponents. As Joseph Gusfield has observed, "The public support of one conception of morality at the expense of another enhances the prestige and self-esteem of the victors and degrades the culture of the losers."[2] This method is particularly effective in policing, where, as this study will argue, the prime task is to express the moral values of the society the police force serves. Thus my inquiry focuses to a great extent on the images of morality that surround the struggle for control of the police.

With the police, as, one suspects is the case with practitioners of other disciplines, there is little new, and the controversies of a hundred years ago are still alive. In a way, the progress of police administration can be seen as a parade. Various individuals and organizations march past the reviewing stand, bands play lustily, and by turns the crowd cheers, boos, or displays indifference. When the parade is long, the viewer is struck by repetitiveness. One marching group, leader, or blaring band tends to look and sound very much like twenty others. At the end, one feels he has witnessed a colorful, even exciting, spectacle yet is puzzled by its meaning.

It is the chief purpose of this work to identify the key actors, organizations, and events in American policing. It will further attempt to answer two questions: "What is the essence of policing?" and "How are police controlled?" It will try, in effect, to determine the meaning of the ongoing march of law-enforcement personnel and phenomena that I call "the blue parade."

A brief discussion of method seems in order. In researching this study, as I consulted a growing number of books, articles, and reports, it became increasingly apparent that *all* sources are inaccurate to some degree. Because of this fact, and others related to it, the reader should be aware of the various problems my study has sought to overcome.

First there is the problem of numbers, particularly in dealing with questions regarding the rates and volumes of crime. Indeed, a variety of myths in the police field rest on incorrect perceptions of the nature and extent of crime. Even in this age of sophisticated computers, criminal justice statistics are in woeful shape. So seemingly simple a task as determining the number of robberies in a city during a particular year presents manifold problems. When such analyses move backward in time, the difficulties grow in a geometric progression. A study of police early in the century revealed that in 1913 New York City coroners' records reflected 323 homicides, though the police file showed but 261. Two years later, across the continent in San Francisco, out of 71 homicides the police recorded but 50.[3] Since murder is a relatively rare crime and a difficult one to conceal, the problems of recording more numerous and commonplace crimes can only be imagined. As the English writer Josiah Stamp put it:

> The government is very keen at amassing statistics. They collect them, add them, refer them to the *n*th power, take the cube root, to prepare wonderful diagrams. But you must never forget that every one of these figures comes in the first instance from the [village watchman], who just puts down what he damn pleases.[4]

Thus, while quantitative data have been utilized where appropriate, I have made a deliberate choice to avoid substituting bad data for other more informative but less quantitative sources. More importantly, public policy in the area of police administration, as elsewhere, is most often based not on a close analysis of records and statistics, but rather on impressions and opinions, so that frequently it matters less what is objectively true than what people think is true.

If one turns to less formal documents such as memoirs and biographies, different problems arise. Many individuals connected with events tend to enhance their own role and diminish that of others. A ready example is the case of Prohibition Agent Eliot Ness, a minor participant in the successful prosecution of the gangster Al Capone. Years after the case, Ness published a book, *The Untouchables*, which magnified his role. Still later, a popular TV series converted him into an FBI man engaged in a wholesale extermination of organized crime!

Of course, a number of possible tools exist to counter various distortions. One might, for example, conclude that, where several accounts are in agreement, the facts are correct. However, this may also mean that everyone has consulted the same basic source. Thus a number of books on the English police "borrow," often without attribution, from the classic 1901 study *A History of Police in England*, by Captain W. L. Melville-Lee. Another possibility is to consult works presenting diametrically opposed views of the same incident. But while this alerts one to possible omissions and distortions, it also puts one in the position of judging what is true or false.

This book does not attempt to unravel mysteries, but to look at the obvious; it seeks to present what appears to be incontrovertible facts rather than judge which is the truthful side in the great disputes. Therefore, I do not offer a definitive opinion as to, for example, who threw the bomb in the Chicago Haymarket, or the identity of the Lindbergh kidnapper. Instead, I report what others determined, and the impact of those findings on police administration.

Various accounts of at least somewhat questionable authenticity are presented herein as legendary, apocryphal, or according to so-and-so. While it might be argued that such material is best left out, omission would severely weaken my presentation, dealing as it does with the myths and imageries of police administration—often more powerful than its truths. For example, as we shall see, Al Capone was brought down because federal agents believed a fictitious story about an encounter between the gangster and President Hoover.

Hoping that by ending well before contemporary times I could avoid being drawn into current conflicts of issues and personalities, I chose to conclude this study with the era that encompassed World War II. Most of the events I discuss are now largely forgotten, as are all but two of the individuals involved: Earl Warren and J. Edgar Hoover. In the case of the former, the controversy that surrounds him relates to his role as Chief Justice rather than as a California prosecutor, and it is his earlier position that I refer to. The problem is more severe with Mr. Hoover. I originally gave some thought to leaving him out of the book, but since he played a major role in police administration prior to World War II, such an omission would have been essentially dishonest, given the scope of my reportage. I hope the distance afforded by my ending this inquiry where I have will provide an extra measure of objectivity in any consideration of the perennial problems of the members of the blue parade.

1

Great Britain: The New Urban Society (1748-1890)

On June 2, 1780, Lord George Gordon, president of a so-called "Protestant Association," organized a mass march on Parliament to present a petition demanding repeal of the Catholic Relief Act. To the ruling elite the law was a matter of no consequence, an innocuous measure which had been passed unanimously two years earlier, primarily to permit the enlistment of Catholics in the army, which was then hard pressed by the American rebels. But when Parliament rejected their petition, the mob, estimated at some 60,000 people, began to riot. Over the next few days they destroyed Catholic chapels and the houses of government officials, attacked public buildings including the Bank of England, and set fire to several prisons, releasing the inmates.

Despite the fact that London was a great imperial city, the protection of the capital was entrusted to a motley collection of constables and watchmen. In a typical instance during the rioting, "In the glare of the flames was seen a single, ludicrously pathetic figure of a watchman, ... with lantern and rattle calling the hour as in a time of profound tranquility." The next recourse was the army. However, the troops could act only at the direction of the civil authorities. Under the riot act of 1714, when a crowd of twelve or more was, in the judgment of a justice of the peace or magistrate, an unlawful assembly, that official could read the riot act,* and upon failure to

* "Our sovereign lord the King chargeth and commandeth all persons, being assembled, immediately to disperse themselves and peaceably to depart to their habitations, or to their lawful business, upon the pains contained in the Act made in the

1

disperse within one hour, individual mob members could be treated as felons. The justices could then order the military to disperse them by any means, including deadly force. In this instance, though, after the houses of several magistrates were destroyed, other judicial officers found it convenient to disappear, and at the height of the riot the troops had to stand by while the mob looted and burned.

On the 8th of June, King George III demanded that the military be permitted to shoot on their own initiative. The majority of his advisers argued that this was unconstitutional, but the stubborn monarch threatened to ride into the streets and personally give the order to fire. The Attorney General sided with his sovereign, and a message was dispatched to the military commander, Lord Jeffery Amherst: "In obedience to an order of the King in Council, the military to act without waiting for directions from the Civil Magistrates, and to use force for dispersing the illegal and tumultuous assemblies of the People." Upon receipt of this message the troops killed outright or fatally wounded some three hundred persons and ended the riot.[1]

One of the world's greatest cities had suffered a week of terror and destruction over a relatively unimportant cause. The Gordon Riots were not the first or the last such affairs in Georgian London, but in the reign of Victoria they would gradually fade out and under her successors be virtually unknown. At the time of the riot there were pressures for the creation of a professional police force. In the aftermath of 1780, these pressures would grow, although, in the quaint manner that is reputed to characterize British society, it would take another half century before the goal was achieved.

SUSPENDED TERROR

In eighteenth-century England the term "police" was practically synonymous with the general powers of civil government. Not until the nineteenth century would it take on its present meaning—a body of civil officers who enforce law and maintain order.[2] Whatever the title, however, the law and order function had been carried out by a variety of means for centuries. In Saxon times, the system of pledge required groups of families to swear responsibility for their members, with collective punishment meted out for individual breaches. In the Norman period, powerful sheriffs were appointed to exercise royal governing authority over whole counties. In 1285, the Statute of Winchester provided for town watchmen. In the next century, law enforcement was placed in the hands of parish constables, chosen for a year, and justices

first year of King George, for preventing tumults and riotous assemblies. God Save the King."

of the peace, who combined the duties of minor judge and police administrator. Both offices were part-time and unsalaried, with the justices drawn from the squire class and the constables from the yeomen or small tradesmen.

In the predominantly agricultural society which existed into the eighteenth century each villager knew his neighbors, and social control was maintained by peer pressure. Strangers, who were easily identified as such, were kept under close watch. When a sheriff or constable needed assistance, he invoked either the *posse comitatus*—"power of the county"—or the "hue and cry," and all able-bodied men were required to join the "posse" in pursuit of the offender.[3]

In London, the system was less effective. There, in addition to the parish constables, unarmed watchmen chosen by lot patrolled the streets at night. But in the impersonal conditions of urban life, recognizing strangers was more difficult and the prospect of support from one's neighbors dubious. To raise the hue and cry was likely to bring to the scene only friends of the accused. By the seventeenth century the urban constable-watchman task had devolved upon hired substitutes, and under Charles II (1660 to 1685), the number of watchmen was increased. The "Charlies" were also required to perform other duties of municipal housekeeping such as lighting lamps, calling the time, and reporting unsanitary conditions.

Since the watch was poorly paid, it was frequently made up of the aged and infirm, or persons moonlighting from their regular employment. Standards of performance were low, and accounts of the time usually mentioned the watchmen unfavorably. Henry Fielding, in his novel *Amelia*, portrays them as

> . . . chosen out of those poor old decrepit people who are, from their want of bodily strength, rendered incapable of getting a living by work. These men, armed only with a pole, which some of them are scarce able to lift, are to secure the persons and houses of his majesty's subjects from the attacks of gangs of young, bold, stout, desperate and well-armed villains. . . . If the poor old fellows should run away from such enemies, no one I think, can wonder. . . .[4]

The watch was also organized on a basis of parish or neighborhood control, so that performance levels varied greatly between adjacent areas and criminals could escape arrest by simply stepping across the street into another jurisdiction.*

Though the watch was clearly inadequate, it was not called into seri-

---

* The most effective forces were those employed by the City of London (the square-mile enclave consisting of the oldest section of the metropolis) and the wealthier parishes of St. James and Marylebone, where Chelsea Pensioners (ex-soldiers) were utilized.[5]

ous question until British society underwent drastic changes. Between 1700 and 1800 the population of London doubled, reaching nearly 1 million.* As the country's leading port, most important consumer market, and world center of international trade, insurance, banking and finance, eighteenth-century London became the largest and most important city of the western world.[7] In the nineteenth century, the full impact of the Industrial Revolution would further increase the city's importance and accelerate the process of national urbanization, so that by 1861, 60 percent of the population of Britain would reside in urban areas.[8] The creation of an urban industrial society rendered obsolete policing arrangements of the Middle Ages.

Each generation defines the nature, extent, and origin of its problems. In the process there is often considerable debate, and even when consensus is achieved, one generation's wisdom is frequently disputed by another's. In eighteenth-century London the prevailing view was that crime and disorder were rampant and posed major threats to life and property. The validity of this is by no means certain. "Crime" is a term which can describe many differing phenomena—assaults, theft, treason, official corruption, business fraud, and a myriad of other acts or omissions. In similar vein, disorder may range from mass riot to laughing too loudly. One person's *joie de vivre* is to another disturbing the peace. In its most elemental definition crime is conduct which governmental authority has legally forbidden and for which punishment can be exacted.

Most recorded assessments of eighteenth-century crime came from commentators of middle- or upper-class origin, and their concerns tended to relate to the safety of their own persons and property from attack by the lower classes or to the supposed immoral conduct of the latter. To the upper classes the lower were frequently synonymous with the "mob" or the "dangerous" and "criminal" elements.[9] This definition generally included not only the poor but also working class groups such as the apprentice boys who were always a source of rowdy behavior in the manner of present-day youth gangs.[10]

The tone of the criticism of lower-class life can be grasped in the satirical paintings of Hogarth or the plays and novels of Henry Fielding. In fact Fielding did more than write; he was also a major criminal jus-

---

* London is a name with different meanings. At one time it referred to the old city within the walls. By the eighteenth century, it also included the City of Westminster and urbanized areas of the counties of Middlesex and Surrey. In the nineteenth century, it meant the Metropolitan Police district established in 1829 and enlarged in 1840 to about 700 square miles. Later a portion of the metropolitan area was included within a newly created County of London. The population of greater London is estimated as follows:

1600—200,000	1700—575,000	1801—900,000
1650—400,000	1750—675,000	1820—1,275,000

In 1700 one-third to one-fourth of the population resided in the old City of London; by 1800, only about one-sixth did.[6]

tice reformer. Born in 1707, he became a preeminent dramatist before he was thirty, and then was driven from the London stage because of his attacks on the Prime Minister, Robert Walpole. Afterward he shifted to writing novels. In 1748 he accepted appointment as a magistrate and turned to the serious study of crime. In his *Enquiry into the Causes of the Late Increase in Robbers* (1751), he noted that

> [Due to the] great increase of robberies within these few years . . . I make no doubt, but that the streets of this town, and the roads leading to it, will shortly be impassable without the utmost hazard. . . .[11]

A contemporary sometime crime victim and frequent viewer with alarm was Fielding's bitter enemy Horace Walpole, son of the Prime Minister and himself a distinguished man of letters. In November 1749, Walpole reported that he had been attacked by two highwaymen in Hyde Park and that the pistol of one of them had gone off accidentally, grazing the skin under Walpole's eye.[12] In September of 1750, he recorded:

> I was sitting in my own dining-room on Sunday night, the clock had not struck eleven, when I heard a loud cry of "Stop thief!" A highwayman had attacked a post-chaise in Piccadilly, within fifty yards of this house; the fellow was pursued, rode over the watchman, almost killed him, and escaped.[13]

In Walpole's colorful imagery, London life was carried on in a virtual state of siege. "One is forced to travel, even at noon, as if one were going to battle." "Going to a friend's house for dinner is as dangerous as going to the relief of Gibraltar."[14]

As crime victim and concerned citizen, it was natural that Walpole should take an interest in the administration of justice. He was especially distressed over the inefficiency of magistrates, relating how two wealthy young friends had dragged a servant to Fielding's Bow Street office to charge him with attempted murder and found Fielding neglecting his duties by having dinner with "a whore, a blind man, and three Irishmen." (The blind man was Fielding's brother John, "the whore" his wife, and the Irishmen were probably actors from the surrounding theater district.)[15]

Literary men were not the only prominent crime victims. In the 1780s the Prince of Wales and his brother, the Duke of York, were held up in broad daylight in Berkeley Square.[16] In 1795 the magistrate and police reformer Patrick Colquhoun described London as "the general receptacle for the idle and depraved of almost every country."[17]

But the actual extent of crime is difficult to estimate. The nineteenth-century crime historian Luke Pike suggested that London was probably safer in the eighteenth century than at any previous time. He noted, for example, that the national murder rates had declined steadily since the fourteenth century, when they were about eighteen times higher than in the nineteenth century. He suggested that complaints about crime simply reflected how the security of life and property was acquiring a higher value with each generation.[18]

In fact, the most prevalent type of crime in the eighteenth century was directed against property rather than life. Of 678 executions between 1749 and 1771, only 87 were for murder; of 97 executions in 1785, 43 were for burglary, 31 for robbery—only 1 for murder.[19] And given the great increase in commercial prosperity and therefore in items worth stealing, it is not surprising that property crime was common. Indeed, foreign travelers often remarked on the great extent of property crime and the low incidence of murder.[20]

A further complication in assessing eighteenth-century accounts is the difficulty in separating fear of crime from disapproval of conduct deemed immoral or alarm at public disorder. Starting about 1725, gin was introduced to England and rapidly became a staple of the lower classes, who had previously drunk low-potency beer. Gin provided a cheap and powerful substitute, and the London poor became much more violent and dangerous. In 1750 there was one public house for every fifteen homes in the City of London; the ratio was one to four in slum parishes, such as St. Giles, though after mid-century the number of drinking establishments stabilized.[21]

This was also a period when upper-class violence in the form of dueling and drunken brawling was high. Nor were upper-class youth gangs uncommon. A contemporary journal described one such, the Mohocks:

> They attacked the watch in Devereux Court and Essex Street, made them scower. They also slit two persons noses and cut a woman in the arm with a penknife that she is lam'd. They likewise rowled a woman in a tub down Snow Hill, . . . set other women on their heads, misusing them in a barbarous manner.[22]

Thus it is likely that the lower classes were no more violent than the upper.

There were recurrent riots throughout the eighteenth century.* While the actual rioters were usually members of the lower class, their leaders or supporters were often members of the middle class who

---

* The causes of riots were varied: high versus low church (1715–16), anti-Irish feeling (1736), sailors robbed in a bawdy house (1749), political conflict between classes (Wilkes Riots, 1760s), and anti-Catholicism (Gordon Riots, 1780).

wished to embarrass the governing aristocracy.* John Wilkes, a London alderman, member of Parliament and later Lord Mayor, led several riots in the 1760s but commanded troops during the Gordon Riots of 1780. Usually, the mob leaders sought a redress of grievances rather than overthrow of the government, and thus were using riot as a political tactic. More simple folk were moved by the spirit of fun and the prospect of loot, so that London mobs were usually not homicidal, and generally the only deaths were occasioned by troops firing volleys.

The many facets of eighteenth-century London's fear of crime and disorder illustrate the complexity of such problems in any age, including our own. Despite the prevalence of property crimes, it is likely that the actual risk to well-off citizens of eighteenth-century London was not as great as it was perceived to be. In any age, however, it is not what is true but what influential people think is true that motivates policy, and in this respect, the circumstances of time and place contributed greatly to the perception of danger.

The eighteenth and early nineteenth centuries, during which England was transformed into an urban society, erased most of the familiar landmarks for several generations of Englishmen. The seemingly quiet, orderly village life, with green fields and trees all around and a social system characterized by the refrain

> God bless the squire and his relations
> And keep us in our proper stations

was replaced in London, and later in other cities, by anonymous masses, endless buildings, and dirty streets. To a Londoner of 1800, contrasting the new urban reality to the perhaps idealized rural past,** crime and disorder would loom larger than they would to later generations better acclimated to urban life.

Size also made for distortion. In a rural community of 500, two robberies in a year were not alarming. In a city parish of 10,000, the same rate would yield forty robberies per year, nearly one a week. Thus crime would appear more prevalent in the city.

A third distorting factor, not present in later generations of city life, was the social integration of eighteenth-century London. As a 1748 newspaper noted:

* Throughout most of the eighteenth century the city merchants were in opposition to the national Parliament dominated by landowners, though after the destruction caused by the Gordon Riots, there was less merchant support for the mobs.[23]

** For example, rural riots over such causes as bread or grazing land were known from time immemorial.

> If we look into the Streets, what a Medley of Neighborhood do we see! Here lives a Personage of high Distinction; next Door a Butcher with his stinking Shambles! A Tallow-Chandler shall front my Lady's nice Venetian Window; and two or three brawny naked curriers in their Pits shall face a fine Lady in her back Closet and disturb her spiritual Thoughts.[24]

The result was that lower-class street disorder was highly visible to the better-off.

The eighteenth century was also a time of political unrest characterized by great fear of Jacobites, Papists, Irish rebels, and French spies who were often imagined to be behind various riots.[25] Thus crime and disorder tended to be viewed as threats to the existing social and political system. Sir Leon Radzinowicz recounts the mood of the mid-eighteenth century:

> Although the [Jacobite] rebellion of 1745 had been crushed, a feeling of anxiety and insecurity persisted. Deep apprehension was felt in many quarters that a renewed attack against the established institutions was still a possibility calling for constant vigilance. The position was further aggravated by the existence in London of a vast and unruly mob, always ready to take advantage of any incident to create disorder and endanger public safety. The strength of the nation was being undermined by widespread alcoholism which also engendered a general relaxation of manner.[26]

Clearly, many of the perceived problems of eighteenth-century London arose from its very strength. Its size and wealth created opportunities for a considerable volume of crime while fostering the impression that crime was more widespread than objective measures might indicate. The city's relative political and social freedom provided the opportunity for economic development and individual advancement as well as license and disorder. Thus, while well-off Londoners of the eighteenth and early nineteenth centuries clearly felt great insecurity, it is not certain whether this reflected reality or an overreaction to an environment that appeared more menacing than it was.* But real or exaggerated, the menace of crime and the problem of how to deal with it increasingly came to occupy the attention of prominent Englishmen as the eighteenth century wore on.

A system of crime prevention and/or control (the two concepts are not the same)** usually rests implicitly or explicitly on the prevailing

---

* In our own time researchers have noted the difference between fear of crime, i.e., of one's own victimization, and concern about crime as a social problem.[27]

** "Prevention" usually refers to efforts to forestall the commission of a crime, while "control" relates to measures, such as arrest and prosecution, taken after a crime has been committed.

theories of crime causation. Throughout history various explanations have vied in popularity. In the Middle Ages it was fashionable to ascribe individual criminal behavior to metaphysical causes such as possession by the devil. More recent explanations have suggested the possibility of mental or physical defects. Sometimes the individual criminal is seen as a product or victim of broad social and economic forces. In contrast to these deterministic theories are explanations that see the criminal as an immoral individual who freely chooses the path of crime. It is the latter view, of course, that underlies the criminal justice system, with its notion of punishment.

Eighteenth-century commentators such as Fielding, Walpole, and Colquhoun were concerned not so much with explaining individual crime as with determining why crime suddenly seemed so prevalent. In general, there was recognition that the creation of an urban society with a large concentration of dispossessed poor was at the heart of the problem. By 1800, approximately 7 or 8 percent of the population of England was on welfare, and many more were engaged in begging.[28] However, the meaning of this was unclear. Fielding attributed the increase of crime to the idleness and debauchery of the lower class and the development of professional criminals who wanted money for high living. As he argued:

> I think that the vast torrent of luxury which of late years has poured itself into this nation, hath greatly contributed to produce among many others, the mischief I here complain of.... It reaches the very dregs of the people, who aspiring still to a degree beyond that which belongs to them, and not being able by the fruits of honest labor to which their industry would entitle them; and abandoning themselves to idleness, the more simple and poor-spirited betake themselves to a state of starving and beggary, while those of more art and courage become thieves, sharpers, and robbers.[29]

Some people saw crime as a result of the way in which the poor were treated:

> The heartless, selfishness of the upper classes, their disgraceful ignorance of, and indifference to the brutal degradation in which they suffer the poor to lie, is the primary cause of almost all the crime in the country.[30]

Despite such views as the latter, there was little effort to alleviate the depressed condition of the London poor. In the eighteenth century the poor law of Elizabeth I (1601), which provided for parish relief, was still the basic guide. This permitted the authorities to ship paupers back to their native parishes after forty days on relief. Welfare was not popular with the local ratepayers, and there were continual complaints that recipients preferred relief to work and spent their money on drink. In 1834 the law was amended so as to deny relief to the able-bodied.[31]

Other explanations of crime focused on specific groups such as soldiers and sailors, large numbers of whom were periodically demobilized after the imperial wars. Walpole observed:

> You will hear little news from England but of robberies; the numbers of disbanded soldiers and sailors have all taken to the road, or rather to the streets; people are almost afraid of stirring after it is dark.[32]

One hypothesis about ex-soldiers' and ex-sailors' involvement in crime was roughly similar to the present-day argument that a portion of our crime problem is a result of the effect on individuals of state-sanctioned violence. But since a large portion of the army and navy were recruited via the press gang, many were already troublesome before they put on the uniform. Accused criminals were often sent to the military by magistrates; while sometimes the local squire or craftmaster might suggest to the commanding officer of the press gang that there were certain employees who would never be missed.[33]

There was even a forerunner of some of our current urban design theories about crime, in the argument that London building practices had created a physical environment which facilitated criminal opportunity. As early as 1593 attempts had been made to limit urban growth because of fears that it would become impossible to control disease and disorder.[34] Until the fire of 1666, it had been the practice to stretch chains across the streets to prevent criminals or roving bands of apprentice boys from entering certain areas.[35] In an effort to halt growth, new construction was forbidden in central London, so it became common simply to add on to existing buildings, with the result that they became mazes of courtyards, structures, and cellars. This and the poorly lit streets provided a crime-conducive environment. Henry Fielding said the alleys, courts, and lanes in London were like a "vast wood or forest, in which a thief may harbor with as great security as the wild beasts do in the deserts of Africa or Arabia."[36]

Other explanations of crime focused on foreigners, such as the large Irish population; the breakdown of family controls; the labeling of individuals as criminals, thus forming their antisocial identity; and the need for excitement in the lives of young boys.[37] And indeed, if one substitutes other groups for the Irish, all of the eighteenth-century English explanations have many supporters in twentieth-century America.

If a theory of crime causation is to form the basis of public policy, it must be in tune with the predominant sentiments of the age and must be capable of implementation without major economic or social dislocation. Explanations of crime that related it to poverty, urban development, or militarism could hardly provide suitable foundations for improved crime control in eighteenth-century London. Redistribution of wealth, reduction of the size and density of the capital, and renunciation of military force were unthinkable, given the social, economic, and political realities of the time, and family discipline was largely beyond state control. However, an explanation of the crime rate in terms of the deliberate acts of individuals seeking economic gain by illegitimate means was both politically and technically feasible as a policy guide. It offered no offense to the dominant groups and provided for a means of crime control via the criminal justice system, a much more pliable entity than the social, economic, or political structure of the country.

Thus, as the eighteenth century wore on, the view that criminal behavior was rational and could be repressed by state sanctions gained in favor. By the nineteenth century it was the conventional wisdom. As Captain W. L. Melville-Lee, the most prominent Victorian commentator on police, described it:

> The desire to acquire wealth without working for it—"to live idly yet to fare well"—is the main incentive that makes men criminal and experience proves that if those who live by their wits are sufficiently harassed, they soon show their wit by returning to the humdrum path of honesty until such time as their vigilance of their enemies is relaxed. . . . [T]he normal criminal is anything but a creature of impulse; his calculations may not be shrewd but they are undoubtedly deliberate . . . it is almost the unanimous opinion of those best qualified to judge that the bulk of the offenses committed in this country are perpetrated by those who enter upon a criminal career because it appears to them that it is easy and profitable. . . . It is obvious, therefore, that an effective police by making the profession of dishonesty difficult and precarious can remove the principal incentive that makes men criminal.[38]

As agreement grew that crime could be repressed by the criminal justice system, the chief problem of eighteenth-century thinkers was to create an effective system.

Given the relative ineffectiveness of the magistrate, constable, and watchman arrangements, a type of private detective system had developed as a supplement. One profession was that of "thief taker," practiced by private individuals who for a fee or public reward would apprehend criminals—40 pounds for a robber down to 1 pound for a simple deserter.[39] Similar services were provided by some constables who served as magistrates' assistants. For a fee they would undertake to recover stolen property or apprehend offenders. Because of the cost, this system was available only to the well-off.

During the period 1715–1725 the leading thief taker, one Jonathan Wild, was actually the directing force of most of the theft activity in

London. Wild, who styled himself "Thief Taker General," would receive reports from crime victims at his "office of lost property," then retrieve the filched items from one of his warehouses of stolen goods and return it for a fee. Wild also provided a degree of discipline and organization for the London underworld. Those who violated his rules were delivered to justice, and Wild was responsible for the hanging of a number of thieves by the authorities. When he himself went to the gallows because of the jealousy of a magistrate, some argued that however great a rogue he was, his services were invaluable since he had done more harm to the criminal element than all the forces of law and order. Among Wild's more notable victims were the highwayman and burglar Jack Sheppard, who made several daring escapes from prison, and Sheppard's lieutenant "Blueskin" Blake, who in his anger at betrayal attempted to cut off Wild's head in front of the Old Bailey courthouse.[40] Wild's career and the legends that surrounded it were exploited by many writers to exemplify the "honest" crook against the dishonest cop. Defoe, Swift, and others depicted him as an arch villain, while they made Sheppard, Blueskin, and the later highwayman Dick Turpin heroes to generations of boys.

Corruption also affected the unsalaried magistrates, who frequently collected fees for protection from prostitutes, gamblers, and thieves. While rural justices came from the squire class, many of their city compatriots were brothel owners and the like, so that by the eighteenth century few men of quality would accept the post. In his play *The Coffeehouse Politician*, Fielding brought out most of the habits of London's magistrates in the character of Justice Squeezum. Squeezum took bribes, detained innocent persons in custody, forcing them to pay for their discharge, suborned witnesses to give perjured evidence and juries to give false verdicts, examined attractive young women privately, and sold his protection to keepers of gaming houses and brothels.[41] Of course, the corruption of the criminal justice system simply reflected the common practices of the larger society, where bribery and favoritism were rampant.

Ultimately, however, crime control rested not on justices, constables, watchmen, thief takers, and reward seekers, or the press gang, but on a policy of severe punishment. The number of hanging offenses was in the vicinity of 300, and public executions were frequent, running as high as 100 per year nationally. Such occasions offered exciting spectacles for the multitudes as the prisoner was drawn through the streets en route to Tyburn Hill. Nor was hanging the only capital punishment. In December 1742 Thomas Rounce was sentenced "to be hanged but cut down before he is dead, his privities to be cut off, his bowels taken out, and then to be quartered, which quarters are to be put up where

His Majesty shall appoint."[42] But the latter refinements were usually reserved for those, like Rounce, found guilty of treason. Those who escaped hanging were sentenced to "transportation" to one of His Majesty's colonies or penal servitude aboard a prison hulk.

Countering the policy of terror was the leniency of the criminal justice system. Not only was corruption the norm but many judges were reluctant to impose severe penalties, so defendants were often acquitted on technicalities. Thus "Tyburn or transportation" tempered by leniency—or, as Radzinowicz has characterized it "suspended terror"[43]—was the essence of English criminal justice.

THE MAN IN BLUE

One remedy proposed for London crime was a body of professional police, like the system in effect in Paris, which was generally thought to be a much safer and more orderly city than London. As the English writer Philip Stead has recently noted:

> There is no doubt . . . that Paris was safer for the individual than was London in the eighteenth century. Travelers found the English capital much more thronged with beggars and street-women and law enforcement was generally poor.
>
> . . . While the policing of London was being performed by parish constables, watchmen with pole and lantern, and a few magistrates' officers, Paris had a numerous, armed, professional police under central direction.[44]

While the French police system provided greater security than London had, it too relied to a large extent on detection, apprehension, and punishment after the fact rather than prevention. It was also independent of the law. If a suspect was released by the courts, he could still be imprisoned by a royal *lettre de cachet*.

Another well-policed city was Munich under the rule of Count Rumsford, favorite minister of the Bavarian Elector.* In 1788, when Rumsford took office, the streets of the city resembled those of London, but the minister was a man to be reckoned with.

---

* Despite his name Rumsford was an American, born Benjamin Thompson in Massachusetts. He served as a British colonel during the Revolution and was knighted for his services. After the Tory defeat, he joined the Bavarian Army and then became Minister of War and Police. He was also a noted scientist who endowed a chair of physics at Harvard. His second wife was the widow of the chemist Lavoisier.

New Year's Day was a traditional time for bands of street beggars to be out in force, even invading church services, but for New Year's of 1790 Rumsford planned a surprise. He arranged secretly for military units to be brought into the city, where they seized and imprisoned 2,600 mendicants (about 5 percent of the population of Munich) and compelled them to labor in workhouses. After this success, the troops were kept on regular police patrol as in Paris. In 1795, Rumsford went to London to argue for the adoption of a police system in that city similar to that of Munich. His arguments were given special force by the fact that upon arrival he was held up and his papers stolen.[45]

Despite the effectiveness of French or German police, the prospect of arbitrary power led to great opposition in Britain to the creation of a police system of the type utilized on the Continent. British history had witnessed a long struggle between Crown and landed gentry which by the eighteenth century had essentially been resolved in favor of the latter who had no wish to strengthen the forces of the King. Occasionally, though, when riot and crime appeared out of hand, it was proposed that the military be utilized for police duties. In 1745, at the time of the Jacobite rising led by Bonnie Prince Charlie, 10,000 militia had stood guard over London streets for several months, with a noticeable decline in crime.[46] But memories of the Stuart kings and Cromwell's military regime made the politically dominant gentry distrustful of the army as an internal force.

English reformers, however, envisioned a police system as primarily a preventive rather than a punishing force, as on the Continent. They drew support from the utilitarian ideas of philosophers such as Cesare Beccaria and Jeremy Bentham, who advocated certainty of apprehension rather than severity of punishment.[47] Although popular myth credits Sir Robert Peel with establishing a professional police force of the modern variety, in fact many individuals and events are associated with the creation of the "London model" of policing.

The first police reformer of note was Henry Fielding, during his tenure as magistrate at Bow Street. With his appointment in 1748 the police era may be said to have begun. When he died in 1754, his work was carried on by his blind half-brother John (known to the underworld as "the blind beak"), who served an additional twenty-six years as a magistrate. The Fieldings created a force which became the premier organization of its kind. The Bow Street Runners, as they came to be called, constituted a body of officers who served metropolitan rather than parochial interests and, although paid partly out of fees, also received funds from the treasury. Under the direction of conscientious magistrates the Runners were a much more reliable body than the constables or thief takers, and although their worth was often the subject of controversy,* they were, in fact, Britain's first professional police. In 1782 to the Runners was added a foot patrol in central London, supplemented in 1805 by a mounted force for patrol of the highways. Thus the Runners became the antecedents of modern tactical squads or anti-crime units. However, their total strength never exceeded 160, so that London still relied primarily upon the constable-watchman system.

The Gordon Riots spurred renewed demands for the creation of a police system, but until well into the nineteenth century these were not heeded. Even the younger Pitt as Prime Minister was forced to withdraw a police improvement bill in 1785 because of the traditional opposition of London merchants. In 1798 Patrick Colquhoun, successor to the Fieldings as London's most prominent police reformer, was able to establish a marine police to protect commerce on the Thames, but was unable to extend the concept to the metropolis.[49]

The French Revolution and Industrial Revolution helped to change opinion. The nineteenth century saw the rise of an industrial proletariat and the spread of revolutionary "French" ideas. By 1812, the economic disasters caused by the Napoleonic embargoes led to serious internal disorder in which the military again had to shoot on their own initiative. Even English intellectuals such as Southey, Wordsworth, and Coleridge, who had hailed the French Revolution, now feared its implications. Nor did the defeat of Bonaparte provide surcease. Disorders continued at home. Riots at St. Peter's Field outside Manchester in 1819 claimed fifteen lives. The yeomanry—a type of militia cavalry made up of gentry and tradespeople who supplied their own horses and weapons—failed to disperse the crowd and had to be rescued by regular troops.

Indeed, the militia was highly unreliable. The infantry was composed of the classes who were rioting, and the cavalry of the classes being rioted against. Nor were the upper classes particularly eager to confront the mob. After the Manchester Riots (derisively named the Battle of "Peterloo") many of the yeomanry received threats on their lives.[50] In 1820, even the elite Royal Guards staged a mutiny in London. In any event, soldiers were not a particularly efficient tool for crime control. Most criminals did not operate in large bodies but as individuals and in small groups. Thus, to be effective, the troops would have to be dispersed, but this would negate their military effectiveness.

Throughout the eighteenth and early nineteenth centuries, the secret intelligence service also played an important role in combating dis-

* Charles Dickens for one asserted, "To say the truth, we think there was a vast amount of humbug about these worthies.... As a Preventive Police they were utterly ineffective, and as a Detective Police were very loose and uncertain in their operations.[48]

order. The so-called "King's Messengers" participated in arrests and heavily infiltrated antigovernment organizations, but their efforts were resented even more than those of the military. (See pp. 27–28.)

To many observers a professional police system seemed to offer the prospect of improving on the patchwork of justice, constable, watchman, hangman, spy, and militia system without requiring an extreme military solution, although the difference between police and military was not clear to everyone, and many continued to see the establishment of a police force as a disguised military regime. In 1829 Sir Robert Peel, as Home Secretary in the Tory government of the Duke of Wellington, carried through Parliament a bill creating a Metropolitan Police for London in place of the watch system. It was this body that provided the model of professional policing which continues to this day.

The London Police are the pride and joy of many English and American writers, and accounts of their birth often draw forth the extravagant praise otherwise reserved for the Founding Fathers in Philadelphia or Lord Nelson at Trafalgar. One version is that their creation was some sort of democratic boon to improve public safety for the average citizens of the capital, who were mostly poor.[51] Given a century of upper-class fear of the "mob," this seems counter to the evidence, although in time it did have that effect. Rather, the basic motive appears to have been improved security for the dominant groups through means that would preserve the constitutional system and permit the new economic order to flourish. As Wellington had urged after the Guards mutiny in 1820:

> In one of the most critical moments that ever occurred in this country, we and the public have reason to doubt in the fidelity of the troops, the only security we have, not only against revolution but for the property and life of every individual in the country who has anything to lose. . . . The Government ought, without the loss of a moment's time, to adopt measures to form either a police in London or a military corps, which should be of a different description from the regular military force, or both.[52]

And as Disraeli recalled a generation later:

> Then arose Luddite mobs, Meal mobs, farm riots, riots everywhere; and all the ugly sights and rumors which made young lads, 30 or 40 years ago believe (and not so wrongly) that the "masses" were their natural enemies, and that they might have to fight any year or any day, for the safety of their property and the honor of their sisters.[53]

While dismissing the more flowery claims for the creation of police, it would be equally simplistic to see them as simply a tool to preserve the status quo in the interest of the ruling classes. Despite the police system (or perhaps because of it) the ruling class and status quo have changed considerably since 1829, with power shifting among the landed aristocracy, the commercial interests, and, in time, the industrial prole- tariat and intellectuals of the Labor party.

Similarly, the attempts to regulate lower-class behavior can be seen from differing perspectives. There is the obvious argument that tighter police control will produce a sober, industrious, and docile working class. This view sees crime and disorder as political attacks on the ex- ploiters by the exploited. It ignores the well-known fact that the poor are disproportionately victimized by their fellows or that crime and vice could in fact be seen as "pacification" programs. In the eighteenth cen- tury, for some energetic members of the lower classes like Jonathan Wild, organized crime offered a route to economic improvement. But success required the unofficial permission of the authorities. For others, drink and debauchery might produce occasional violence and crime but also led to withdrawal, illness, and death. Thus crime could provide an obstacle or an alternative to political revolt. It is also important to recall that the police as a preventive force were definitely a humane and civilizing instrument which made it unnecessary to rely on bar- barous punishments to deter crime.

Thus it would appear to be more accurate to see the creation of the police, like that of the civil bureaucracy, as an inevitable product of the modern industrial state. Both provide for the orderly administration of affairs but do not in themselves guarantee the perpetuation of a particular elite.* Even modern socialist states have found it necessary to maintain police organizations similar to the English model.

In its organization and methods, the Peelian police force was mili- tary in the sense that recruits were expected to be of an age and phy- sique similar to army men (at least 5'7", under thirty-five), and many were in fact former members of the armed forces, including one of the commissioners, Colonel Charles Rowan, a veteran of Waterloo who had been recommended by Wellington. Like members of the army too, its members were uniformed and organized in a hierarchical chain of command with central control and a military type of discipline. Many later writers have been critical of this aspect of the Metropolitan Po- lice, but given the personnel available, only a military discipline would ensure that constables actually walked beats and enforced the law on the dark and dangerous streets, something the nonmilitary watchmen had failed to do.

On the other hand, there were differences from the army. Some were cosmetic, such as the use of civil titles (inspector, superintendent,

---

* For example, it was always assumed that the British civil service could not function under a socialist regime, but when the Labor party came into power in 1945, the bureaucracy gave it loyal cooperation.[54]

commissioner) beyond the rank of sergeant and the adoption of blue uniforms, copper buttons, and top hats in an age when soldiers wore red coats, brass buttons, and helmets; not until 1864 would the force dare to adopt the helmet which has become its symbol. Other differences were fundamental. The police were not provided with firearms,* and the rank and file were made responsible to the ordinary civil law rather than the articles of war. Thus a police constable held an individual legal office with limited authority. As the eminent nineteenth-century English jurist Sir James Fitzjames Stephen explained:

> The police in their different grades are no doubt officers appointed by law for the purpose of arresting criminals, but they possess for this purpose no powers that are not also possessed by private persons. . . . A policeman has no other right as to asking questions or compelling the attendance of witnesses than a private person has; in a word, with a few exceptions, he may be described as a person paid to perform as a matter of duty acts, which if he so minded, he might have done voluntarily.[55]

If charged with unlawful conduct, the constable could not offer the defense of obedience to orders.** In this way the police were restrained from too slavish an obedience to the executive. The government also declined to create a military-style officer corps, so that British police leadership, except for the highest posts, was drawn from the ranks, thus avoiding the possibility of social ties with the armed forces and the aristocracy.*** To serve as a check on Colonel Rowan, a second commissioner was appointed—Mr. Richard Mayne, barrister at law.

Another important feature was the beat system, in which police constables were assigned to relatively small permanent posts and were expected to become familiar with them. Beats differed from patrols of the type maintained in Paris or by the Bow Street organization, which permitted periodic roving surveillance of areas but did not encourage a close familiarity with a particular territory. In Paris, the police patrols were never assigned to the same area on successive nights.[57] Thus, the effectiveness of the patrol, usually a small detachment, depended on the chance of its detecting a crime in progress, while the beat system provided for the continuing presence of a policeman as part of neighborhood life. In the beat system, the constable became known to the public and was in a position to become aware of potential criminal

---

* Inspectors did carry pocket pistols, and constables were provided with truncheon, staff, and rattle. On night patrol they were also authorized to carry a cutlass, though in time even these weapons were dispensed with.

** The army too was liable to civil punishment for any excesses, but the doctrines of military command provided greater defense.

*** According to Peel, "subordinate [command] positions in the police were better given to men who had not the rank, habits or station of gentlemen."[56]

activity. A citizen with information was more likely to convey it to a familiar figure than a strange one, and a criminally inclined individual was more apt to be constrained by the knowledge that he was under the surveillance of a local officer than by the relatively remote possibility of being interdicted by a passing patrol.

In effect, the beat system recreated some of the elements of social control present in village life by organizing the metropolis into communities known as police beats. On the other hand, to avoid the excessive localism which characterized the parish watch system, the beat constables were placed under sergeants who reported to inspectors, etc., up to the commissioners. The commissioners in turn were appointed by and responsible to the Home Secretary, and ultimately the cabinet, rather than local authorities in London, and traditionally the bulk of the force have been non-Londoners at the time of their appointment. As a later commissioner remarked, "We like to take them right from the plow."*[58]

In retrospect, the creation of the London Metropolitan Police solved many of the security problems of nineteenth-century London. It gave the government the strength and efficiency of an army but was subject to the restraints of civil law; it provided a degree of localism but was under ultimate national authority.

In the early years, the main jobs of the new police were suppressing mob disorder, winning public support, and creating a disciplined force. On September 29, 1829, the force held a muster of its first 1,000 recruits. It was a rainy day, and some of the men broke out very unmilitary umbrellas, while others, carrying on the quite military habit of hard drinking, showed up intoxicated.[60] The umbrella problem was eliminated by an order issued that day, but drinking was not so easily handled. In the first eight years, 5,000 members of the force had to be dismissed and 6,000 resigned. After four years only 15 percent of the 3,400 original recruits were left.[61]

Nor was the task of the constables a light one. They were at first resented and occasionally murdered. In 1833 a police constable was stabbed to death when he and his comrades attempted to disperse a meeting of the National Political Union of Working People at Cold Bath Fields. A coroner's jury ruled it justifiable homicide because the police had charged without first having the riot act read by a magistrate; the verdict was set aside by the government.[62] As late as 1848 it was thought necessary to swear in over 150,000 special constables to protect

---

* Given the physical standards it was not surprising that the recruits frequently were from the farm. By the pre-World War I era, they had to be 5'9". In an era when the minimum height for the army was 5', the requirements for police service were well beyond the average man.[59] Thus few residents of the hungry and diseased urban working classes were likely to qualify.

the capital against the Chartists' march on London. In the face of police strength six to eight times greater than the demonstrators' the march turned out to be peaceful, or in the words of Lord Palmerston, "the Waterloo of peace and order"[63]—that is, Waterloo from the British, not the French, perspective.

Although this was the last of the great disorders, it was necessary on several subsequent occasions to deploy the army in London, and in some respects there was truth to the popular saying that "the success of the man in blue is based on the backing of the man in red."* However, the commissioners did not make the mistake of attempting to turn the blue coat into a red coat, recognizing the fundamental difference between the two. Indeed, the commissioners were at pains to ensure restraint; for example, in their first set of orders they advised:

> [The constable] must remember that there is no qualification more indispensable to a police officer than a perfect command of temper, never suffering himself to be moved in the slightest degree by any language or threats that may be used: if he do his duty in a quiet and determined manner, such conduct will probably induce well-disposed bystanders to assist him should he require it.[65]

In time, as the personnel became more disciplined and the threat of riot lessened, the influence of Colonel Rowan declined. After his retirement in 1850 a replacement was appointed, but primacy passed to Sir Richard Mayne, so that in 1855 the government dispensed with a second commissioner. Within a generation the police became widely accepted and Parliament mandated the creation of similar forces in other English cities and counties. Outside London the national government did not exercise direct control, nor did the historic City of London ever join the Metropolitans, creating instead its own similar force.

The British police system was also copied in both Europe and America. Even Paris adopted many of the British practices. In 1854 the government of Napoleon III, himself a former London special constable (in 1848, while in exile in England), installed the British beat system, necessitating a tripling of the existing forces.[66]

By the end of the century, the image of the calm, courteous "bobby" had become a national symbol and London was seen as a relatively safe city thanks to its police. Though mid-nineteenth-century social commentators such as Mayhew, Greenwood, and Booth still found much crime in London,[67] Pike, writing in the 1870s, declared:

---

* Major riots occurred in 1855 over Sunday closing laws, in 1868 over the political reform movement, and in 1886–87 as a result of political meetings in Trafalgar Square. Between 1869 and 1910 troops were called out in Britain twenty-four times and opened fire twice.[64]

... it may with little fear of contradiction be asserted that there never was, in any nation of which we had a history, a time in which life and property were so secure as they are at present in England ... and it is in marked contrast to the sense of insecurity which prevailed at the beginning of the present century.[68]

A generation later, Captain Melville-Lee provided a more balanced assessment:

It is of course impossible to estimate with any degree of accuracy to what extent this diminution of crime and this increased security of recent years are due to the exertions of our modern constabularies; enough has been said to make it abundantly clear that the amelioration is real, and that it is progressive in its tendency. ... There is no doubt that the spread of education and the labors of religious and philanthropic bodies have done much to civilize the masses; it is certain also that an improved prison system and a reformed penal code have reacted beneficially on the criminal classes; but if we believe in the teachings of history we shall put our trust in no combination of influences directed toward the maintenance of the peace that does not at least include a good preventive police force.[69]

To the list of crime deterrents the author might have added the general rise in the standard of living which occurred throughout the century, the effect on national morale of the various imperial triumphs of the Victorian era, the widespread adoption of street lights, and the destruction of old slums by a type of urban renewal. But in sum, the sense of security in London at the end of the nineteenth century was much greater than in earlier times, and although many factors were present, the police contribution would appear to have been a major one.

How, then, was this contribution achieved? The first and most obvious answer is the repressive effect of a continued police presence which the beat system provided. Criminals and the disorderly were restrained by the prospect of arrest by the omnipresent police. Commissioner Mayne, for example, argued that in the first years of the force burglars were caught openly carrying their tools, whereas later they learned to conceal them.[70] However, with the rise of the police, transportation and execution for property crimes ceased and imprisonment declined. When Queen Victoria came to the throne in 1837, 43,000 of her subjects were convicts; when she died in 1901, only 6,000 were, despite a doubling of the population. In 1834, two-thirds of convicted burglars received life sentences; by 1886, 70 percent got less than one year.[71] Thus the apparent decline in nineteenth-century crime rates cannot simply be attributed to repression.

Indeed, notwithstanding today's laments for the "good old days," Victorian jurists could be as erratic as any others, and "hanging" judges sat alongside "bleeding hearts." In the 1880s, the judge of Assizes, the higher court in tough, slum-ridden Liverpool, was Mr. Justice Day, noted for his harsh punishments—"Day of Judgment," the magazine *Vanity Fair* called him. In addition to long prison terms he would impose twenty to thirty lashes with the cat before *and after* the defendant served his time, the latter to impress the convict's friends when he returned to society. In the same city, though, the recorder, or lower court judge, Mr. Hopwood, was noted for awarding short sentences or probation even for serious offenses such as robbery. Needless to say, criminals much preferred to appear before Mr. Hopwood. As a bit of popular doggerel phrased it:

> Oh, Mr. Hopwood, what shall I do?
>   They've sent me to Assizes,
> And I wanted to go to you,
>   For though I may only get the sentence of a "Day,"
> Oh, Mr. Hopwood, the cat may spoil my stay.[72]

Perhaps a greater contribution to the reduction in crime was the "moral" model that the new police provided. The patrolling constables' superiority to the decrepit watchmen was readily apparent and reassuring to the more solid Londoners. Whereas the watchmen tended to slink away before crime and disorder, the bobby quickly appeared to assert the values of the prevailing social order. As Captain Melville-Lee explained:

> . . . the term "police" . . . also embraces all the various expedients employed by society to induce its members to acquiesce in the arrangements that tend to promote public security. . . . In this latter sense the object of police is not only to enforce compliance with the definite laws of the land, but also to encourage a general recognition of the unwritten code of manners which makes for social progress and good citizenship.[73]

The English social scientist Geoffrey Gorer has asserted:

> On the basis of the evidence available to me, . . . I should consider that the most significant factor in the development of a strict conscience and law-abiding habits in the majority of urban Englishmen and women was the invention and development of the institution of the modern English police force.

He further argues that the bobby became the model of what a man should be, competing with the image of Jack Sheppard, Blueskin, and Dick Turpin.[74]

The achievement of the police was even more notable when one realizes that the caliber of personnel was no higher than the level of ordinary laborers or enlisted men in the armed forces, since conditions of service were very difficult. Bobbies worked twelve to fourteen hours a day with but two days off per month, and discipline was strict. Not surprisingly, many took bribes or drank on duty. Certain derelictions may have helped to establish friendly relations on the beat. For example, policemen often received regular stipends for waking people up, since alarm clocks were not generally available.[75] In 1872 and 1890 there were brief strikes by some members of the London Metropolitan Police, and between 1897 and 1906 thirty-two members of the force were found guilty of taking bribes or cooperating with gamblers.[76] (See Chapter 3.) The corruption was never systemic, however, nor did it reach the commissioner's level.

Even the higher ranks were badly treated. In the early years of the force one superintendent was dismissed because he forwarded a woman's rape complaint against an inspector to the commissioners rather than a magistrate. Even though the superintendent acted in accordance with prevailing regulations, the government refused to support him in the face of a judicial complaint. Similarly, the Home Secretary, Lord Melbourne, had ordered the police to suppress the 1833 Cold Bath political meeting but neglected to take the responsibility when criticism arose.[77] The fact that most senior officers were not drawn from the educated classes allowed the government to use them as scapegoats whenever necessary. If the officers had been "gentlemen," such a policy would have been impossible, since many formal and informal means of redress would have been available, not the least of which would have been for an officer to issue a challenge to his superior to meet him in a duel.

THE WEARING OF THE GREEN

The English have always taken great pride in the restraint of their police, particularly when comparing them to their American counterparts. However, that restraint has not been so apparent in Ireland. Contemporaneous with the creation of the London Metropolitan Police a very different body of police was created for service in the Irish portion of what was constitutionally a single United Kingdom. While Parliament acted to avoid the imposition of military repression on Englishmen, it imposed no such restraints in Ireland.

In the seventeenth century, the British had completed their conquest and established a small English elite to rule over the vast majority of Catholic Irish, outside of the northern province of Ulster, where a substantial Scottish Protestant population was in residence. Thus was created a situation in Ireland that was fundamentally different from the state of things in England, where rioters generally sought not to overthrow the government, but to redress various grievances. Always there were large numbers of English citizens ready to support the authorities by providing information or enrolling as militia or special constables. Without strong citizen support, based on a moral consensus, the London model of community policing could not have existed.

In Ireland, outside of Ulster, most people desired the overthrow of British rule, and few would stand up for the government. Throughout the eighteenth century, political unrest was manifested in terror and occasional revolt which the rural police system could not begin to deal with. So a large military garrison was maintained. As in England, though, the difficulty of utilizing soldiers for police duty was apparent. The army could shoot down the mobs but was of little use against bands of criminals or terrorists who could disappear into ordinary life.

From 1807 on, the British were confronted by a mass opposition led by Daniel O'Connell. In 1814, while Sir Robert Peel was Chief Secretary for Ireland, a military-type "peace preservation" force was created.* In 1822, four provincial police forces were established, organized by counties, with a strength of over 5,000. Finally, in 1836, Parliament created an Irish Constabulary (after 1867 known as the Royal Irish Constabulary or RIC) of 8,500 men to police all the country outside of Dublin, the latter maintaining a London-type force.

The constabulary was armed with carbines and pistols and stationed in barracks distributed throughout the countryside. Its officers were mostly Englishmen or Anglo-Irish similar in social standing to their army counterparts. A good many, in fact, transferred in from the lesser-paid regular officer corps. The rank and file were Irish, including a preponderance of Catholics.** All ranks were subject to a military type of discipline. In effect, the Irish Constabulary was like an army regiment which had been broken into small units to patrol certain specific geographical areas. As one of its officers noted:

> To readers unacquainted with the corps, I may say that it is a military police peculiar to Ireland, and officered in much the same way as the army. . . . I may say that the Royal Irish Constabulary depot differs in no respect from an army infantry barracks. . . .[79]

* As a result of Peel's connection with the creation of both the modern Irish and English police, the former were known as "peelers" and the latter as "bobbies," thus adding to the magnification of Peel's role in the development of modern policing.

** By 1900, approximately half of the officer corps came from the ranks, while the percentage of Catholic rank and file was estimated at 70 to 80 percent.[78]

As might be expected the British officers had the usual army of occupation attitudes. A City of London police commissioner, Sir William Nott-Bower, reviewing his days as a subaltern in the RIC, circa 1875, remembered the people as "wild and lawless" but was comforted by the fact that "one out of three was a traitor" to his own people.[80] As late as World War I, the force was advised in a confidential handbook that its duty was to punish as well as arrest.[81]

It seems clear that in creating the Royal Irish Constabulary the British government recognized that no reforms it was prepared to make could satisfy the Irish population to such an extent that they could be policed in the same manner as Britain. Even liberal politicians such as Lord Morley concurred in this view; he noted in 1886, "If Kerry was treated as Northumberland, Kerry must control her police, and if Kerry controlled her police there was an end of law and order."[82]

While the force, grown to 13,000 by the 1850s, was predominantly military, the utilization of a beat system adapted to the rural environment provided many of the same advantages the beat system gave to the London Police. However, the paramilitary mission of the RIC was always paramount. Riots and so-called "outrages," i.e., acts of violence swept the country from time to time, and to some observers violence and crime in Ireland appeared to be at a higher level than in any other area in Western Europe.[83]

In 1867 the constabulary crushed an abortive revolution and was rewarded by receiving the prefix "Royal" and a harp-and-crown insignia from Queen Victoria. In the 1880s the country was again in a revolutionary mood; an estimated 10,000 evictions of tenants and 2,500 "outrages" climaxed in 1882 with the murder of the Chief Secretary and Undersecretary in Phoenix Park, Dublin. Again the RIC was able to maintain control.* Given its success, the force was the model for British colonial police in India and elsewhere and its officers were frequently seconded to lead these forces.** [84]

In the twentieth century, the RIC was caught up in the general administrative malaise which characterized the regime of "Gussie" Bir-

* The Phoenix Park murderers were eventually apprehended by detectives of the Dublin Metropolitan Police.

** Since the higher officers of the English police were mainly drawn from the ranks, their education was usually limited to a few years of grammar school. As late as 1880, the chief constable of Liverpool reported that "a great portion" of the force was illiterate.[85] There was also no formal training for men promoted to higher rank. In contrast, RIC officers were frequently from Eton, Harrow, or other public schools and graduates of the Royal Military College at Sandhurst. In addition, they were required to complete a six-month course at headquarters in Dublin. Thus RIC superior officers were much better qualified than their British counterparts, and consequently a number of them were chosen to head British as well as colonial forces.

rell, the lighthearted liberal politician who served as Chief Secretary for Ireland. In the years just prior to World War I, the Ulster Protestants and southern Catholics each built up private armies with little interference from the constabulary. As Birrell laughingly explained, the police spent most of their time fishing.[86] After the 1916 Easter uprising, the tide of Irish rebellion rose and the RIC collapsed, so that in 1919 it was largely superseded by a hastily recruited auxiliary force including the "Black and Tans." This body made no pretense of being any kind of police organization but instead operated as a type of commando unit in what was in fact a civil war. After 1922, the traditions of the RIC were carried on by the Royal Ulster Constabulary (RUC).

THE POWERS THAT PREY

The London Metropolitan Police and the RIC represented quite different models of policing. Contemporaneously with these two organizations came a third model—the detective force. When the London Metropolitan Police was created, it was principally concerned with beat patrol activities, and the Bow Street Runners remained in existence. For a time the two organizations were rivals, though the Runners generally took the lucrative cases such as jewel thefts, leaving the murders to the new police.[87]

At least three broad categories of crimes may be of concern to detectives. The first are routine offenses such as street robberies, petty thefts, and assaults. Frequently those are perpetrated by low-skill offenders who reside in or frequent areas near the scene of the crime. Most such cases require little investigative talent and are best handled by ordinary beat patrolmen, who because of their detailed knowledge of a particular territory are likely to be familiar with local troublemakers. If such investigations are prolonged, however, the patrolman must neglect his routine duties. In the early years of the Metropolitan force constables were temporarily relieved from patrol to investigate crimes on their beats. In 1842, a regular detective branch was opened at police headquarters in Scotland Yard superseding the Bow Street forces.* [88]

A second category is crime committed by skilled, organized, and mobile criminals such as safecrackers, confidence men, highway robbers,

---

* Scotland Yard was the name of the grounds upon which the original police headquarters was located, having once served as a residence of visiting kings of Scotland. In the vernacular the term came to stand for (1) the headquarters building, (2) the administrative headship of the police, and (3) the detective branch. The last is the usage of fiction; the official name is the Criminal Investigation Division (CID).

or in some instances vice entrepreneurs. In this instance, territorial knowledge is not especially useful; rather, the investigators must be familiar with the criminal underworld or some segment of it, such as receivers of stolen property. This was the type of work the Bow Street Runners specialized in with such success that some amassed personal fortunes of 20,000 to 30,000 pounds.[89]

A third category of crime is political crimes against the state such as treason or subversion. These are not usually perpetrated by ordinary criminals; therefore, the normal constable or detective knowledge is of little use. The investigation of political crimes is also controversial in a way that the investigation of conventional crime is not. While there are disputes over methods used in normal criminal investigation such as interrogation procedures or search and seizure, the basic legitimacy of pursuing conventional criminals is presumed by the creation of a police department. In contrast, in a constitutional state which recognizes some restraint on executive power, political policing is a questionable undertaking. While it is conceded that the state may defend itself from violence, it is often difficult to determine if individuals or groups are, in fact, violent without commencing an investigation. However, if mere suspicion is enough to legitimize police inquiry, then many innocent persons will be subject to government surveillance and inhibited from exercising their rights.

Britain maintained a secret service to conduct foreign espionage from Elizabethan times and frequently it was utilized to deal with domestic subversion.* In the seventeenth and eighteenth centuries, it reported to the Privy Council and in appropriate cases enjoyed virtually unlimited power of arrest, search, and seizure. In the eighteenth century, the Bow Street magistrates, including the Fieldings, were apparently paid out of the secret service funds, and at times the magistrate was, in effect, chief of the political police. In 1745, at the time of Bonnie Prince Charlie's landing, Fielding's predecessors rounded up suspects throughout the kingdom. During the Napoleonic wars and their aftermath, the magistrates again oversaw counterintelligence.[90] As the conduct of the military produced outrage at Peterloo, so too the secret service had its scandal. In 1817 the activities of the agent provocateur "Oliver" in luring men into subversive acts so that they could be caught and hanged provoked outrage.[91]

In the early years of the London force, police were detailed to spy on dissident groups, and in 1833 another scandal arose when it was learned that one Sergeant Popay had infiltrated the radical National Political Union of Working People, the same group involved in that

---

* The term "secret service" is employed to denote agencies of the state which collect political intelligence at home or abroad. In the contemporary United States this would include the CIA, FBI, and certain other Federal, state, and local agencies.

year's Cold Bath Fields riots.* Popay, a former schoolteacher, was clever, and in the guise of a radical artist he managed to acquire a leadership post in the Union. From his inside position he argued for violence and supplied swords for military training. When a member of the Union happened to observe Popay performing uniformed police duties, the latter was unmasked. A Parliamentary investigation followed, and the sergeant was dismissed; pulling back from supporting his men as he did after the Cold Bath meeting, Lord Melbourne omitted to mention that the infiltration was undertaken at his direction.[93]

The methods of the detectives also provided a contrast with the uniformed police. In the world of fiction, investigation is often seen as a deductive process applied to specific crimes. In contrast, the real-world detective tends to concentrate on criminals rather than crimes, and his work is more patient craftsmanship than a brilliant intellectual exercise. Most conventional crime is directed against property by individuals who engage in such behavior on at least an occasional basis. Vice offenses are usually carried on by organized groups. Therefore, rather than spend his time moving from case to case, the practical detective found it sensible to get to know the thieves and vice operators. Usually this took the form of frequenting their haunts and maintaining direct contacts with them, a practice common with the Bow Street Runners. As one writer noted of the Runners:

> The qualifications most needed by them were those social gifts which commanded the largest acquaintance among the most lawless of mankind. One day they would be drinking and roaring out an obscene ditty amidst the applause of their boon companions in a "flashhouse"; the next they would return in their official capacity to carry those very companions off to gaol; they would go for their prey as gentlemen to their preserves for game.[94]

And indeed, the head of the Sûreté, the contemporary French detective force, Eugene Francois Vidocq, was himself a former criminal whose maxim was "It takes a thief to catch a thief."**

The newly created London detective branch continued the practices of the Runners by ordering detectives to mix with thieves.[96] As a mid-nineteenth-century writer complained:

> ... the sort of odd intimacy that commonly exists between the thief and his natural enemy, the detective policeman, is very remarkable; the latter is as well acquainted with the haunts of the former as he is with the

---

* One manifestation of its radicalism was its practice of parading under the stars and stripes.[92]

** Eugene Francois Vidocq (1775–1857) served as chief of the Sûreté from 1811 to 1827. Later he worked as a private detective.[95]

abodes of his own friends and relatives.... When the crisis arrives, and the thief is "wanted," he is hailed as Jack, Tom, or Bill and the capture is effected in the most comfortable and business-like manner imaginable.[97]

This, of course, was similar to the practice of the beat constables who familiarized themselves with the local residents, but the detectives' beat was not so much territorial as it was a slice of the underworld. Further, in the patrolman's case most citizens were law-abiding and his contacts relatively open, whereas the detective's clientele were mostly criminal and his contacts necessarily furtive. Detective and thief were, in fact, fellow craftsmen who shared a great many of the same perceptions and values. Both recognized that criminal behavior was normal in some milieus and viewed arrest and punishment as part of the game. Given the intimacy and shared values, it was inevitable that deals would be struck, ranging from outright corruption to the exchange of information for favors.* Indeed, most policemen and some judges believed without such deals the detectives could not function.[98]

The public, however, could not be told that the detectives worked through informers and deals, since in many cases these skirted the law and public morality. Thus detectives themselves often helped to foster the view that their work was largely a deductive process. Also, since they were ultimately responsible to nondetective administrators such as the commissioners, there was continued tension between the needs of their craft and the dictates of government policy. Under the regime of Commissioner Mayne the detective force numbered no more than sixteen men, and its operations were restricted by Mayne's distrust of clandestine methods. When in 1867 Irish rebels blew up a wall of Clerkenwell Prison, killing four people and injuring forty, the detective branch was criticized for its failure to act in response to prior warnings of the event. Mayne himself escaped dismissal only because of his long service, but he died shortly afterward.

In 1868, as a result of the Clerkenwell incident, the number of headquarters detectives was increased to approximately 40, and an additional 180 detectives of all ranks were assigned to the various local division headquarters. The latter were in effect beat constables permanently relieved of patrol duty, while those in the headquarters squad continued in succession to the Runners' function as a major crimes unit.

In 1877, three of the four chief inspectors of the headquarters detectives were convicted of accepting bribes.** A formal investigation was

---

* The practices described relate to property crime rather than such "nonprofessional" conduct as murder.

** The government and public were somewhat relieved by the fact that the chief culprit had a most un-English surname. "Nat" Druscovich, of Polish origin, had been brought in as a detective without constable experience because of his superior education, particularly in languages. Unfortunately, he succumbed to the induce-

undertaken by a government commission and the following year the Criminal Investigation Division (CID), under a civilian director, was created and placed in charge of both headquarters and division detectives.

The first CID director, Howard Vincent, was a twenty-nine-year-old lawyer and former army officer who had achieved little success in either career. Ambitious and aggressive, he was determined to make a large reputation for himself. When he learned that an investigating commission had been appointed, he hurried to Paris to study the French Sûreté, whose detectives routinely employed clandestine methods against both political and criminal suspects and retained a large number of spies. Vincent then made a report of his findings to the Home Secretary and talked himself into appointment to the well-paid directorship.

Under his regime the CID was severely criticized for utilizing "French" methods. As his superior, Police Commissioner Sir Edward Henderson, wrote:

> There are many and great difficulties in the way of a detective system; it is viewed with the greatest suspicion and jealousy by the majority of Englishmen and is, in fact, entirely foreign to the habits and feelings of the Nation.[100]

But Vincent did not bother to consult his superior, preferring to deal directly with the Home Secretary, and the "French" methods continued. In 1880, a grand jury indicted three of his detectives and a police matron for having entrapped a druggist who sold abortion fluids, even though the druggist had been convicted and imprisoned. The reactions of the CID to the various criticisms and prosecutions was best summed up by Captain Melville-Lee:*

> The self-constituted censors who are so ready to lament the alleged incompetence of our detectives would be the foremost to complain should a measure of State protection, equal to that enjoyed by foreign police functionaries, be conferred on any such agent at home. The traditional love of liberty which in this country, has always opposed espionage with so much resolution, is all together admirable; but like everything else that is pre-

---

ment of confidence men engaged in turf frauds and received two years in prison. During the trial his partner, Detective Sergeant Charles Von Tornow, was also accused of accepting bribes though he was exonerated.[99] One can imagine the merry scenes at Scotland Yard when English thieves named Smith and Jones were hauled in by the team of Druscovich and Von Tornow.

* Like Howard Vincent, Captain Melville-Lee (1865–1955) was both an army officer and a barrister. Like Vincent too, he hoped to obtain appointment to a high police post, but a polo injury proved an insurmountable barrier. During World War I he served in a counterintelligence post.

cious, it has to be purchased at a price, and in this case the price is the dangerous latitude conceded to "the powers that prey."[101]

In this instance, the government backed its agents and the prosecution failed.[102]

The early years of the CID were also a time of great activity by the Irish nationalists. With revolution in Ireland blocked by the RIC and the army, the rebels turned to a terror campaign in England. The years 1883–1885 saw bombings of railroads, subways, the Tower of London, and even Scotland Yard itself. Confronted with the threat, the government turned to its most reliable antiterrorist force and brought in detachments of the RIC to London to guard public buildings and cabinet ministers.

The presence of the green-uniformed, carbine-carrying Irishmen was a blow to the pride of the Metropolitan Police, and it quickly sought to recover lost ground. In 1883, a special Irish squad was formed to work in conjunction with Robert Anderson of the secret service. Detectives of this squad, which came to be called the "Special Branch" of the CID, even struck at the nationalist base of support in America, enlisting the aid of the United States Secret Service. The government also invoked special powers to open mail despite Parliamentary criticism. In 1887, detectives managed to intercept an Irish-American terrorist and break up a plot to plant a bomb in Westminster Abbey during Queen Victoria's jubilee ceremony, after which the movement receded.[103]

The Special Branch remained in existence investigating various groups, turning from Irish revolutionaries to other foreigners. It was the constant complaint of foreign ambassadors and police officials that London was a hotbed of assassins and terrorists plotting against crowned heads.[104] As one chief of the CID complained:

> ... we are inundated with the scum of other countries ... Nihilists from Russia, Advanced Socialists from Germany and Communists from France (to say nothing of a large contingent of knifing Neapolitans).[105]

Typical of the troublesome foreigners was Johann Most, born in Germany in 1846, whom a childhood facial operation left with a "hideous" appearance.[106] He became a socialist and in 1869 led a demonstration before the Austrian House of Parliament for which he received a sentence of five years, although he was released after one. Expelled from Austria, he became editor of a socialist paper in Germany and was elected to the Reichstag. In 1874 he was sentenced to eighteen months for a revolutionary speech. Afterward, as a result of Bismarck's antisocialist laws, he emigrated to London.

Most was a strong advocate of violence against the ruling class, and in 1881 he published an article celebrating the assassination of Czar Alexander II. As a result, he was arrested by the CID, convicted, and given sixteen months' hard labor. Again Vincent was criticized because, it was alleged, he had turned over to foreign police evidence seized in Most's apartment which led in turn to the arrest of radicals in Vienna and elsewhere. But again the Liberal government of Gladstone defended the police practices.[107]

Three years later, in 1884, Howard Vincent resigned as the head of the CID. Although he felt frustrated in his efforts to introduce continental methods, his resignation stemmed from the fact that having married a wealthy woman he no longer needed the salary. Given his new resources, Vincent switched from the Liberals (because they were not sufficiently strong for imperialism), entered Parliament as a Tory, and was knighted. For many years he served as an elder statesman of policing, although, despite his financial means and experience in a variety of fields, in twenty years of Parliamentary service he never went beyond the back bench.

Curiously, the man who would benefit the most personally from the creation of a strong detective branch was a young Irish Catholic, Patrick Quinn, who left his home in County Mayo in 1873, at nineteen, to join the London Police. Within five years he was promoted to sergeant. When the special Irish squad was created, he was assigned to it, and from then until his retirement in 1918 he served in that unit, heading it from 1903 onward. In this capacity, Quinn guarded most of the crowned heads of Europe and received numerous foreign decorations. He was also the bodyguard and intimate companion of that merry monarch Edward VII. In World War I, he was a key figure in British counterintelligence and was the one who sealed the fate of the Irish revolutionary leader Sir Roger Casement. When Casement was convicted of treason for his part in the 1916 Easter uprising, there was strong American pressure to save his life. But Quinn discovered and circulated Casement's purported diary, revealing its author to be a homosexual. This revelation silenced many supporters of clemency, and Casement was executed. Upon Quinn's retirement he was knighted, becoming the first policeman from the ranks to be so honored.[108]

A TIME OF TROUBLE

The scandals of the late '70s and the terrorist activities of the '80s were not the only troubles to descend on the police in those decades. In 1886 riots erupted after a political meeting in Trafalgar Square and mobs rampaged through the fashionable West End smashing shop windows, in one instance while a police detachment a block away stood immobile through a misunderstanding of orders. Most embarrassing of all, the superintendent in charge, a seventy-four-year-old gentleman, had his pocket picked. In the aftermath, both he and the commissioner were replaced. Truly, the state of public order had changed greatly from the days of Lord George Gordon. In 1780 only the prospect of the actual destruction of the city moved the authorities, whereas in 1886 a few broken windows and gentlemen's top hats sent flying were the occasion for a cabinet crisis.

The new commissioner was Major General Charles Warren, fresh from governing various African tribes. Prior to his appointment, commissioners had maintained a feeling of mutual respect between themselves and the force. Warren, however, was imperious and short-tempered. Later, during the Boer War, he proved an incompetent field commander as well. Winston Churchill, recalling his service as a lieutenant with Warren, wrote, "I was genuinely sorry for him. I was also sorry for the Army."[109]

In October of 1887 a number of radical demonstrations took place in London, outraging public opinion by incidents such as unfurling the red flag under Nelson's column. Commissioner Warren responded quickly by forbidding any political meetings in Trafalgar Square, though this was of doubtful legality. On "Bloody Sunday," November 13, 1887, the police, with the assistance of the army, forcibly dispersed crowds attempting to meet in the square. Among the arrested radical leaders was John Burns, who would later serve in the cabinet of his defense attorney, Herbert H. Asquith, when Asquith became Prime Minister.[110]

Warren's tenure saw the Jack the Ripper murders, a case which is still the subject of enormous controversy. The generally agreed facts are that between August and November 1888, five East End prostitutes were murdered by a single individual. The murder of prostitutes or other slum dwellers was not unusual in London, but the number of victims in a short space of time and their savage mutilation created paroxysms of fear. Even so, at first glance these events would hardly seem the catalyst for mass terror. But since the creation of the new police, most Londoners had developed a strong sense of personal security. Therefore, the continued failure to apprehend the killer shook public confidence.

The crime also exposed the helplessness of the detectives when faced with a real mystery. Methods and sources of information successful against local offenders or professional thieves were useless against a lone, "nonprofessional" stranger. The murders took place within a quarter-square-mile area and the killer was able to disappear quickly, suggesting that he might have had a refuge in the neighborhood. The detective put in charge of the case, Inspector Frederick Abberline, though a headquarters man, was given the assignment because of his experience as a divisional detective in the East End.

Neither General Warren nor Robert Anderson, now head of the CID, came off with much credit. The commissioner personally destroyed evidence in the case,* while his plan, to use bloodhounds to pursue suspects, raised doubts about his essential grasp of urban crime. (When tested, the bloodhounds ran away.) Anderson chose to vacation in Switzerland at the height of the investigation, though as a concession he removed himself to Paris to be "closer" to the action. Also, despite his absence he issued public announcements which gave the impression that the murdered prostitutes were receiving just punishment for their wicked lives.

The crime was not solved at the time or later. Suspects have ranged from a royal duke to a Russian barber. Some have thought the murders were a plot by Czarist agents to discredit Russian anarchists living in the East End. The weight of opinion, if not evidence, placed responsibility upon a failed barrister who drowned himself in the Thames in December of 1888, after which the murders ceased.[111]

Commissioner Warren was forced to resign before the last murder, though his resignation was in large part a result of the criticism he had drawn in repressing various demonstrations. In the aftermath of the case, the CID was raised to a strength of 700, although the case did not lead to the appointment of officials of the vigor and flamboyance of Howard Vincent or a new infusion of "French" methods of investigation.

THREE MODELS OF POLICING

In the two decades following the Clerkenwell explosion, the detective branch grew over fiftyfold, becoming by 1890 a police department within a police department and exercising national and even international jurisdiction. While it was technically part of the regular Metropolitan force, the CID was actually highly autonomous, the full embodiment of the detective force model of policing, existing alongside the community and constabulary forces represented by the London police and the RIC.

These three diverse models of police service that arose in nineteenth-

---

* Some writings chalked on the wall at one of the crime scenes were thought to suggest that the killer was a Jew or a Mason. Warren alleged it was the former and that by erasing them he was avoiding the dangers of anti-Semitic riots. Others noted Warren's membership in the Masons and drew different conclusions. As with all famous cases, numerous legends, controversies, and theories surround every aspect of the Jack the Ripper case.

century Britain all were centrally controlled and composed of full-time professional public servants in place of the amalgam of part-time functionaries and private employees which had preceded them. But there were significant differences among the three. The London-style community force dealt with ordinary crime and disorder in an open and visible fashion. While certain features of this model were military, the force was essentially a civilian body dependent on close integration with and support from the community it policed, though its ultimate allegiance was to an authority beyond the local community.

The RIC, a military body, was created to deal with the levels of violence greater than ordinary crime but less than all-out rebellion. Such a force, while visible and territorially integrated into the community, was much less so than the London police and could expect less support from the citizenry. This type of organization frankly was established to serve a government which was deemed repressive by a large segment of the population. Indeed, the creation of such a force was a clear acknowledgment of this state of affairs. As Sir Charles Jeffries, Under Secretary in the Colonial Office, explained:

[The RIC] provided what we should now call a "paramilitary" organisation or gendarmerie, armed, and trained to operate as an agent of the central government in a country where the population was predominantly rural, communications were poor, social conditions were largely primitive, and the recourse to violence by members of the public who were "agin the government" was not infrequent.[112]

The third force was a type of domestic secret service exemplified by the headquarters detectives of Scotland Yard, who dealt with extraordinary crime by covert methods. In its purest form, a classic secret service is meant to counter substantial threats against the security of the state. While this mission was clear in the case of the Special Branch, the detectives also worked against swindlers, forgers, and other master thieves who if unchecked, posed a threat to the economic system. This mission was also apparent in sensational cases such as the Ripper murders, which caused widespread fear that threatened to paralyze normal life and destroy confidence in the government.

A young Irishman of modest origins, like Patrick Quinn, had a choice of three police careers. He could join the RIC and live the life of a trooper in a colonial (albeit his own) country; but, as in the army, his prospects for promotion to officer rank were limited. A second choice was to join a London-type force as a patrolman, serving amid a basically friendly populace. Finally, such a young man could, after brief service in the patrolman capacity, enter the detective branch and operate in the nether world of informants, plots, and counterplots. In either of the latter two careers, there was the possibility of promotion to all but the very highest posts.

For an upper-middle-class young man like Howard Vincent, an officer's commission in the RIC was available as an equivalent to the army, but no similar opportunity existed in the English police. The few men of his background who served there came in at the top level, usually after a previous career in the law, army, or higher civil service.*

The British police system developed as a response to political, social, and economic conditions. On the European continent, most major cities had a police department similar to that of London and a quasi-military constabulary force which patrolled the rural areas, particularly where banditry or guerrilla activity was rife. There also were detective forces, including specialized political squads, utilizing clandestine methods. The continental forces, however, exercised greater control over individual freedom and continued to reflect a broader definition of policing by undertaking a variety of administrative duties which Anglo-Saxon officials would view as civil in nature.**

Another important difference between Britain and the continent was in the relationship between police and the judiciary. In Britain, after 1842 the detective branch was removed from direct control of the magistrates. This meant that decisions to undertake an investigation, conduct a search and seizure, or effect an arrest were made by policemen operating independently of judicial authority. The magistrates did not become involved until the prisoner appeared before them. On the continent, detectives continued to work under magisterial direction, and the judiciary oversaw criminal investigations. To the English, the separation of functions meant that judicial authority would be impartial as between police and suspects, while under the French system the accused and his lawyer would be made aware that a criminal investigation was under way.

Continental police also followed the military system of an officer corps, and individuals with appropriate higher education (mostly in law and government) could enter the service in commissioned ranks. Continental forces were also more likely to apply scientific methods to criminal investigation, although the difference was largely one of degree.

---

* In Vincent's time, only the commissioner and ten or twelve assistant commissioner and chief constable posts of the Metropolitan Police were reserved for educated "gentlemen," and as time went on even this number decreased.

** In 1914, the Berlin Police Department controlled the health and building departments and supervised public markets. In Paris, the police force was responsible for health, hospital inspections, and the Bureau of Public Assistance (welfare).[113] When American police complain of being burdened with "nonpolice" duties, meaning non-law-enforcement duties, in the historical sense their use of the term "nonpolice" is incorrect.

Detectives the world over, whether working on crime or political matters, relied primarily on informants and extralegal arrangements.

Finally, the police of continental countries did not normally enjoy public favor, as did their English counterparts. The level of internal unrest was always much higher on the continent, and the constabulary and political police were frequently employed against the populace, creating resentments which carried over to regular police duties.

In general, American observers were impressed with the integrity and competence of European forces, particularly admiring the courtesy and restraint of British bobbies. However, they would frequently miss the subtleties and culture-bound features of European police administration, with the result that American adaptations were often impractical.

New York: The New World (1845–1913)

On an autumn afternoon in 1846 the packet *Henry Clay* sailed into New York Harbor with its cargo of Irish immigrants fleeing from the poverty of their famine-ridden land. As the vessel neared the shore, one of them lifted his three-year-old son to his shoulders and, pointing with his finger, said, "Look, Dick—New York, 'tis New York." Many immigrants were to come to the city in the next seventy-five years, a period in which New York came to rival, then surpass London as the queen city of the western world. For some, life in the new land would be at least as hard as in the old, for others it would be considerably better, and to a lucky few would come fame and fortune in the full realization of the American dream. One of the latter was the three-year-old immigrant boy; in time, as boss of Tammany Hall, Richard "Dick" Croker would be the ruler of New York. His life and the events which surrounded it would, in an ironic way, sum up many of the great truths of America, not the least of which were those pertaining to its police.[1]

LITTLE OLD NEW YORK

In 1846 New York was the leading city in America in terms of population and commercial importance. Its growth had been phenomenal. In

1790, with a population of 33,000, it stood second to Philadelphia. In 1820, it had 100,000 people. By the time of Croker's arrival twenty-six years later, it contained a half-million souls. At that time the city included only Manhattan Island, with most of the population confined to the lower portion. In 1898, at the height of Croker's power, the State Legislature combined Manhattan, Brooklyn, Queens, the Bronx, and Staten Island into a single city of nearly 4 million inhabitants, and by the time of his death in 1922 this figure had almost doubled. Because of its size and prominence the trends of urban development would manifest themselves first in New York, and the city would set the pattern for the rest of the country.

The growth and prosperity of New York stemmed from its suitability as a port linking Europe and America. This was also the basis of many of its problems. Given its accessibility to Europe it became the main port of entry for immigrants, and because of its location on a long narrow island, expansion could be only in a vertical direction. As commerce and population grew, they had to be lodged in taller buildings or in new neighborhoods "uptown." In Croker's youth there was no mass transportation, and workers, who typically labored fourteen to sixteen hours a day, had to live within walking distance of their place of employment. The crowded tenement buildings, providing an intensive cost-effective use of valuable land, became the predominant housing type. Those who could afford the time and expense of a carriage ride to work preferred to live in the "nicer" neighborhoods beyond the commercial districts. However, these too were frequently overrun by the expansion of commerce and tenements. Thus there was a continued instability of neighborhood life as new immigrants poured in on the old and the old upon the more established middle class, a process which was to continue throughout Croker's time. As early as 1857 it was well recognized, and a committee of the State Legislature noted:

> As our wharves became crowded with warehouses, and encompassed with bustle and noise, the wealthier citizens . . . transferred their residences to streets beyond the din; compensating for remoteness from their counting houses, by the advantages of increased quiet and luxury. Their habitations then passed into the hands . . . of industrious poor, whose employment in workshops, stores, and about the wharves and thoroughfares, rendered a near residence of much importance. . . . This state of tenantry comfort did not, however, continue long; for the rapid march of improvements speedily enhanced the value of property in the lower wards of the city, and as this took place, rents rose, and accommodations decreased in the same proportion . . . those who were able to do so, followed the example of former proprietors, and emigrated to the upper wards. The spacious dwelling houses then fell before improvements or languished . . . as tenant

houses of the type which is now the prevailing evil of our city.... They soon became filled from cellar to garret, with a class of tenantry living from hand to mouth, loose in morals, improvident in habits, degraded or squalid as beggary itself.[2]

A generation later the journalist and social reformer Jacob Riis, himself an immigrant, was to declare, "The tenements *are* New York," since by 1890 three-quarters of the population resided in them.[3] The instability and crowding in both streets and dwellings meant intense competition for living space amid strangers, often of alien culture. For the poor, the only solution to the war of all against all was to group together—the young in street gangs and the adults in political clubs—and give blind obedience to bosses and bitter hostility to rival groups.

In the 1830s, New York began to experience the same fears of crime and disorder which had manifested themselves in London a century before. Following the British precedent, colonial New York had employed the constable-watch system, and as in the mother country, the new problems were beyond its capability, though the city's high constable, Jacob Hays, was a man of Bunyanesque reputation who according to legend could suppress riots singlehandedly.* Indeed, in some respects social conditions in nineteenth-century New York were even worse than those of the old country. In the 1880s sections of the East Side had nearly 300,000 people per square mile, compared with half that number in the slums of London.[4]

The most feared district was the Five Points, a collection of short streets in the lower Broadway area which by the 1840s was generally thought to be the worst slum in America.** Until it was destroyed in 1852, its leading landmark, the Old Brewery, converted to a tenement, enjoyed a reputation as the most violent building in the city. It housed about 1,000 persons, mostly Irish and Negroes, and according to popular legend experienced a murder a night, though this appears highly doubtful. Charles Dickens reported on a visit to the Five Points:

> This is the place: these narrow ways, diverging to the right and left, and reeking everywhere with dirt and filth. Such lives as are led here, bear the same fruits here as elsewhere. The coarse and bloated faces at the doors, have counterparts at home, and all the wide world over. Debauchery has made the very houses prematurely old.[5]

---

* Hays, born in 1772, was a member of a prominent New York family. He served as high constable from 1802–1844. In 1935 a descendant, Arthur Hays Sulzberger, became publisher of *The New York Times*.

** The Five Points district included the area bounded by Broadway, Canal, the Bowery, and Park Row. The actual Five Points was the intersection of Cross, Anthony, Little Water, Orange, and Mulberry Streets.

Equally bad slums existed in the Bowery cabaret district and the Fourth Ward along the East River docks. Riots were common and exacerbated by the rivalries between ethnic gangs such as the largely Irish-Catholic Dead Rabbits of the Five Points and the native American Bowery Boys.

New York also had its "sensational" crimes. In 1841 the murdered body of a young girl named Mary Rogers was found in the river. This dramatic incident served both politics and literature as an example of the dangers of urban life. Governor William Seward cited it in a message to the Legislature urging the creation of a police force,[6] and Edgar Allan Poe, transporting the crime to Paris, produced an early detective story, *The Mystery of Marie Roget*.* The Legislature acted on Seward's request, and in 1845 New York became the first American city to establish a London-type police department. Chicago followed in 1851, and Boston and Philadelphia in 1854.

While the new police resembled the London model, there were differences. It was a decade before the American cops would consent to wear a uniform, since it was regarded as a symbol of servility;** however, within a generation of their founding, the Americans would carry firearms. The most important difference, though, was the system of control. In general, American police were subordinated to local government, down to the lowest level. Despite the fact that there was but a single New York City Police Department, appointment to a patrolman's position required approval of the local alderman. Each ward had its own police station, and a policeman normally lived and worked in the same ward. If his aldermanic sponsorship was withdrawn, an officer was not reappointed. In 1849 George Walling, a young patrolman who was later to serve as chief of police, lost favor with the alderman of the Third Ward but managed to establish a new connection in the Eighteenth Ward and transferred to its station.[9] Even after aldermanic appointment was formally discontinued, local politicians continued to exercise de facto control.

Compared with that of the London bobby, a New York policeman's job was definitely desirable. Patrolmen were paid higher wages than skilled mechanics, and though the hours were long (nine hours patrol, seven hours reserve per day), discipline was lax and graft readily available.[10] Thus, throughout the nineteenth century it was common practice

---

* Poe attempted to reconstruct the crime and in fact identified the supposed murderer (a U.S. naval officer), but the New York police thought the man innocent.[7]

** In 1853 James Gerard, a wealthy New Yorker, wore an expensively tailored London bobby uniform to a police ball and attracted such admiration that many of the regular cops decided to follow his example.[8]

for policemen to pay or otherwise importune politicians to procure appointment, transfers, promotions, and other favors.

New York was also the first city to develop a powerful political machine—in Democratic Tammany Hall, which would serve as a model for the rest of the country. In 1854 Tammany's man, Fernando Wood, was elected mayor, and he soon organized corruption on a scale previously unequaled, a key element of the machine being the Municipal police force, which, in addition to its power to collect graft, also controlled elections.

The success of Tammany, with its growing Irish-Catholic base, outraged the moral sensibilities of the nativist element and the political sensibilities of Republican politicians denied a share of the graft. Moral indignation and the competition for power were to intertwine in the struggle between new and old immigrants. Out of this fundamental conflict in American urban politics police administration would be shaped in a pattern which would persist to the present day. The British propertied classes' fear of the "mob" would reappear in America, heightened by differences of religion, language, and race. But the American elite did not possess the resources and prestige of the British gentry, so that the lower classes could not be so easily suppressed, and in time, at least in local politics, they would constitute a rival power elite.

In the mid-nineteenth century, the principal antagonists in the cities were the Anglo-Saxon Protestants, on one side, and the Irish Catholics and Germans, on the other. Their differences were deep and bitter. Indeed, the two groups could not agree on the nature of Sunday. Native Americans of Anglo-Saxon background viewed the Lord's day as a time for prayer and meditation. Immigrants were used to the continental Sunday of sport, drinking, and music.[11] The question of whether Sunday was to be the occasion for turning inward or outward was usually settled by the nativist political strength, which passed "blue" laws forbidding most activities.

Gradually, the immigrants came to dominate the cities while the nativists remained a strong minority whose values continued to predominate in state government. The police were caught between the two forces. As Frank Goodnow, a leading nineteenth-century authority on American government, commented:

There has never been invented so successful a "get-rich-quick" institution as is to be found in the control of the police force of a large American city. Here the conditions are more favorable than elsewhere to the development of police corruption, because the standard of city morality which has the greatest influence on the police force, which has to enforce the law, is not the same as that of the people of the state as a whole which puts the law upon the statute book. What the state regards as immoral the city regards as innocent. What wonder then if the city winks at the selling by police of the right to disobey the law which the city regards as unjustifiable.[12]

Thus a cycle of WASP-inspired reform would be followed by a return to immigrant control. In time the identity of some of the actors changed, but always there was conflict. By the twentieth century, the Germans and many of the Irish adopted the values of the native groups, and the "foreign" threats came from Italians, Slavs, and Jews. In the post-World War II era, blacks and Hispanics came to be viewed as the source of urban crime and disorder.

The Metropolitans

As in London, the elite elements of New York society perceived that local control of the police meant that they would be ineffective in regulating lower-class behavior. Thus, in 1857, the rural-dominated Legislature moved to establish a Metropolitan police department encompassing Manhattan, Brooklyn, Staten Island, and Westchester County, under a Board of Commissioners appointed by the governor. This was a two-edged blow to Tammany, since it would deprive the machine of an institution for patronage and graft and in addition would mean that the nativist, Protestant, Republican state authorities would be able to harass the Catholic, foreign-born Democratic city dwellers. Mayor Wood declared the scheme illegal and threatened to fire any policeman who accepted state jurisdiction; only 300 of 1,100 did. There followed episodes of drama, comedy, and ultimate tragedy which made the New York Police Department a stage upon which the moral dilemmas of urban America were acted out but not resolved. In policing, as in the more conventional theater, New York would generally be first in the sophistication of its drama and the renown of its leading players.

The first act began in June 1857, when a city official obtained a warrant for Mayor Wood's arrest on a charge of illegally obstructing the appointment of a street commissioner. On the 17th, George Walling, who had resigned as a Municipal captain to accept a similar rank in the Metropolitan force, attempted to serve the warrant. Big, rugged, and personally popular, he was allowed into City Hall, but Wood refused to submit and Walling was ejected. He then joined fifty more Metros who were also attempting to gain entry against the resistance of several hundred Municipal cops and their sympathizers. The two groups fought savagely, and the outnumbered Metros were badly beaten.

Now bugles and drums were heard as the New York National Guard's Seventh Regiment marched down Broadway to take ship for Boston to participate in a patriotic celebration. The regiment was halted by the Metropolitan police commissioners and, in the great Anglo-

Saxon tradition, summoned to the aid of the civil authorities.* Just how the troops sorted out the legal question of which was the legitimate party was not clear, since the New York State Court of Appeals did not decide the issue for several months. However, the commander, General Charles Sanford, was a prominent Republican politician, and the regiment was 100 percent native American, so perhaps the path of duty was an obvious one. In any event, at the sight of bayonets Wood submitted to arrest.

For several weeks both Metros and Municipals patrolled the streets, often attempting to free persons arrested by the rival force. In the fall, the courts declared the continued maintenance of the Municipals illegal and they were disbanded. In addition, several Metro officers who were severely injured in the June riot successfully sued Mayor Woods, who passed the bill on to the taxpayers.[13]

The introduction of the Metros had important implications for slum neighborhoods. The new cops not only would be stricter on saloons but would curtail the autonomy of the street gangs. From their inception, both practical and legal reasons had dictated that the police concentrate on control of the streets, since they could not normally enter buildings without a warrant or permission. The streets were also the turf of the gangs. Friction between the two groups was inevitable, though given Tammany dominance over the police, accommodations could be reached. The Metro force lacked the close integration with the community that the thoroughly politicized Municipals had enjoyed. The latter had been tied individually and organizationally to the corrupt local neighborhood politics which was, in turn, closely allied with the gangs of young toughs, who provided a source of votes and Election Day muscle in return for patronage and protection.**

The gangs were not slow to take advantage of the struggle between the Metros and the Municipals. On the 4th of July, 1857, open warfare broke out between the Dead Rabbits and the Bowery Boys. The two groups battled for two days at a cost of at least eight dead and a hundred injured while the Municipals ignored them and the Metros hung back on the periphery. Again, Sanford's troops had to save the day.[14]

In the aftermath of this event, the Metros took steps to control gang disorder. As early as 1853 Captain Walling had formed a strong-arm

---

* Throughout the nineteenth century the New York militia (known as the National Guard in honor of Lafayette, who had commanded the National Guard of Paris) provided support to the police authorities in the same manner as the royal Guards in London.

** One major group of young toughs was the volunteer fire companies, who often fought each other while the fire burned on. Thus there is an element of truth in the ancient joke between municipal uniformed services that the police were created to control the firemen.

squad, consisting of a half-dozen husky young patrolmen who operated in civilian clothes. They employed a "slug on sight" strategy, beating up known gang members every time they were seen even if they were not violating the law at the moment.[15] This became a standard means of dealing with gangs, although it could not be used against politically powerful ones. The Metros also developed their formal discipline and riot control tactics, so that in 1863, when they faced the greatest riot in American history, they emerged victorious, hailed by the wealthy as saviors of the city.

At the beginning of the Civil War, half of New York's 800,000 inhabitants were foreign-born, including about 200,000 Irish. To the older residents the existence of the large foreign population appeared to pose three separate menaces to public safety—crime, vice, and revolution. The foreigners, who lived under conditions of extreme hardship in an uncertain economy, were disproportionately involved in ordinary crime, constituting 80 percent of the 58,000 persons convicted of criminal offenses in 1860.[16] Given the difficulties of life, they frequently sought the solace of liquor, gambling, and prostitution, although these pursuits were also attractive to other citizens, including those rural visitors who after returning home would denounce the morality of the city. Finally, there was the danger of political revolt of the type Europe had experienced in 1848, since the city seemed full of men who had been Irish rebels, Garibaldi redshirts, German radicals, or English Chartists.[17]

As in the case of eighteenth-century London, it is difficult to determine the reality of the various threats. Arrest figures may simply reflect greater police action against minorities. As in London, too, the extent of crime and vice may well have been proportionately no greater than in other cities, but the volume would make it appear more menacing, particularly to those of rural background. The possibility of the various revolutionary groups (whose numbers were conjectural) uniting in common cause would appear remote, yet it was this last which underlay the fears of many. As early as 1830 the visiting French magistrate Alexis de Tocqueville had observed:

> The lower ranks which inhabit these cities constitute a rabble even more formidable than the populace of European towns. . . . I look upon the size of certain American cities, and especially on the nature of their population, as a real danger which threatens the future security of the democratic republic of the New World; and I venture to predict that they will perish from this circumstance.

He continued, as if in anticipation of the creation of the New York Metropolitan police, unless the government succeeds in creating an armed force which, while it remains under the control of the majority of the nation, will be independent of the town population and able to repress its excesses.[18]

Later, in the 1880s, the British scholar James Bryce would voice similar concerns:

[T]he government of the cities is the one conspicuous failure of the United States. . . . For in great cities we find an ignorant multitude, largely composed of recent immigrants. . . . In New York they have revealed themselves on the largest scale . . . gross as a mountain, monstrous palpable.[19]

The Metros, as representatives of nativist and Republican sensitivities, opposed vice, crime, and revolution, while the Tammany politicians, the former and future masters of the police, had a somewhat different perspective. To them, attempts to regulate morality were futile, since in their opinion the vast majority of the population wanted illicit pleasure. Thus their practice throughout the nineteenth century would be to permit a wide-open town and "to hell with the reformers." On the issue of conventional crime, Tammany bosses, like most of the immigrants, deplored it. But the neighborhood gangs were an integral part of city life and local politics, so that it was necessary to extend political protection to individual hoodlums. Also, the line between vice and conventional crime was not always clear. A saloon which stayed open after hours and permitted prostitution was also a good place to fence stolen goods.

Finally, although important elements of the Democratic party opposed the Union cause in the Civil War, political revolution never commended itself to the Tammany bosses. They were mostly men who had begun as poor immigrants and rose to wealth (via graft), so that in their hearts they shared the same view of the goodness of America's political system as their opponents. Tammany or Republican, the New York cops were repeatedly to prove their ability to control the urban masses, although most of the time their efforts were less violent than the final drama of the Metropolitan era.

In July 1863, at the height of the Civil War, the Irish population of the city rioted in protest at the draft law and proceeded to rampage through much of Manhattan, burning, looting, and lynching Negroes. The 2,400-man police department was a special enemy, being seen as a tool of the Republican federal government; and indeed the police were so strong for the Union that detectives had ranged as far as Ohio to arrest Confederate sympathizers.[20] Despite the fact that their superintendent, John Kennedy, was beaten and left for dead in the opening skirmishes, the cops, half of whom were Irish-Catholics, displayed remarkable ability in street fighting. Armed mostly with clubs, time and again they scattered mobs which allegedly outnumbered them fifty or a hundred to one. In a typical incident, Captain Walling led eighty cops in dispersing 2,000 rioters, and later in the day personally clubbed a man to death.[21]

The regular and militia forces were also active, although the riot coincided with the Battle of Gettysburg and a number of regiments had been dispatched to the front. Thus the police and understrength military held on in the city for several days until reinforced. While the police used clubs and a few revolvers, the soldiers relied on mass volleys and point-blank artillery fire to quell the riot. Despite the fierceness of the fighting, only three policemen were killed, though legend holds that hundreds, even thousands of rioters were killed. It is likely that many of the reports of the riot were distorted in an effort to make the mob look worse and the authorities more heroic;* but in estimating the rioters' temper, account should be taken of the verified incidents where Negroes were lynched, the colored orphans' asylum burned, and wounded soldiers mutilated.[23]

The Spirit of Tammany

> Tammany, Tammany
> Swamp 'em, swamp 'em
> Get the wampum
> Taammanee!
> [old song]

In 1870, the Democratic-dominated Legislature returned police control to the city and the Metropolitan district was dissolved. But even though Boss Tweed's Tammany Hall took control of the force, for individual policemen life remained much the same. In 1864 the Board of Commissioners had been made bipartisan, ensuring that the Metros would accommodate themselves to some of the local values. The astute George Walling was to be appointed police superintendent, or chief, in 1874 and would serve for eleven years.

From 1870 to 1894, the city was ruled by various factions of the Democratic party, principally Tammany Hall. While the police board contained two Republicans, they were usually of the "friendly" type. Each commissioner had his share of the patronage; appointments, assignments, and promotions depended upon the favor of the commissioners, who were usually responsive to neighborhood politicians such as aldermen and Tammany district leaders. Such men were frequently ex-gang boys, noted for their physical prowess in brawls. Not surprisingly, they

---

* A modern analysis suggests that the number of rioters may have been as low as 3,000 and the number of deaths between 100 and 120, including three regular policemen, one volunteer, a fireman, and seven soldiers.[22]

were not innately "law and order" men, though as they rose in the world they generally became more contemptuous of gangsters and sought respectability.

Young Dick Croker, a blacksmith's son, was typical. He grew up in the "Gashouse" district of the East Side and became a member of the Fourth Street Tunnel gang. Short and powerfully built, he was a noted fighter, a skill which served him in his duties as a Tammany vote hustler. On Election Day, 1874, his get-out-the-vote crew collided with a rival group and in the resulting fight a man was shot; before dying he named Croker as his assailant.* The incident was particularly embarrassing because at the time Croker was serving as New York coroner. Although political influence brought him acquittal, he was cast into limbo, since murderers could not be party leaders. In this respect, Tammany was as circumspect as its opponents, despite the fact that the latter might portray Tammany as a bunch of cutthroats. In time, Croker worked his way back into the fold and a good deal of social respectability, and in 1885 became the boss of Tammany Hall.

From 1868, the headquarters, or "wigwam" (the "hall" of Tammany Hall) had been located on 14th Street near Union Square. In the post-Civil War era, the street was the accepted boundary between the middle-class citizens to the north and the lower classes "downtown," and the hall's location was symbolic of the role its occupants played in mediating the class and tribal wars of the city. In 1871, forty-nine lives were lost when troops fired on a Catholic mob attempting to break up an Orange (Protestant) parade. In 1872, Tammany proved its police could be as reliable in defense of order as the Metros. In the spring of that year, some 70,000 men (out of a population of 1 million) had struck to demand that employers comply with an 1870 state law mandating the eight-hour day. The employers resisted, arguing in essence that wages would then exceed productivity. The police worked long hours without any extra compensation to smash the strike, thus winning the praises of respectables like *The New York Times*, which happily described one incident where police evicted strikers who had seized a plant:

> [T]he strikers quailing beneath the shower of blows from the officers' batons broke and ran toward Third Avenue in wild disorder [where they encountered another detachment of police]. Caught between two fires, their demoralization was complete. . . . [A] number of the strikers were knocked down, trampled upon and severely injured.[25]

In 1874 came another moment of glory. Organized labor staged a mass rally in Tompkins Square, in the heart of lower Manhattan. The

---

* It is generally believed that Croker did not fire the fatal shots.[24]

authorities forbade the meeting, and 500 police, under Inspector William Murray, were assembled to enforce the order. Murray, a Civil War hero, did not wait for the crowd to engage in any overt act (and in fact, most observers doubted that they would). Instead, he ordered a club-swinging charge. The mob was completely dispersed and Murray became the toast of Wall Street as "the man who blocked the Communist revolution."[26] In 1885, he succeeded Walling as superintendent of police. Despite an exceptionally long tenure in the top post, Walling took his ouster badly and in his memoirs denounced political interference in police administration, thus setting a pattern for ex-police chiefs, who, contented enough when political influence is used in their behalf, become outraged when it is used against them.

Where earlier threats were from relatively unorganized street mobs, in 1886 Croker had to face an organized political campaign. Henry George, the apostle of a single tax, welded together a left-wing coalition and ran for mayor on the Working Man's ticket. The Republicans nominated a young state legislator named Theodore Roosevelt, and the County Democracy, Tammany's bitter party rivals, put up Abraham Hewitt, a millionaire businessman. Without Tammany support of Hewitt, George would be the mayor. Croker reversed the policy of his predecessor, "Honest John" Kelly, and presented a united Democratic front. The wigwam also contributed plenty of money and muscle in the poorer areas, and Hewitt was elected. As William Allen White wrote:

> [M]en who have surrendered their citizenship to Tammany might do far worse with it. In all their ignorance, and greed and mendacity they might use that citizenship. If the time ever comes when they do use it unrestrained by the intervening agency of Croker, or his heirs, or assigns, heaven protect wealth and social order in New York City! Take away the steel hoops of Tammany from the social dynamite, and let it go kicking around under the feet of any cheap agitators, and then look out for fireworks. . . .
>
> With all the mold of feudalism which Tammany preserves, the Tammany-made citizen is more trustworthy than the citizen the red anarchists would make. . . . For Tammany preaches contentment, it tolerates no Jeremiahs.[27]

While Tammany was an efficient vehicle for protecting uptown from the radical agitators downtown, in other respects it was less successful. Prior to the Civil War, vice activities had been located south of 14th street. In the 1870s, the main center of night life moved to the area from 14th to 42nd Streets between Fourth and Seventh Avenues, which featured a concentration of vice resorts where virtually anything was available for a price. So lucrative were the pickings that when in 1876 Police Captain Alexander Williams heard that he was to be transferred there, he declared, "All my life I've never had anything but chuck steak, now I'm going to get me some tenderloin,"[28] thus providing a name for the district.*

Another problem was the gangs. In the post-Civil War era, the Whyos, from Mulberry bend just north of the Five Points, were the most vicious group. Many of the worst thugs and murderers of the city belonged, and were by turns hanged in the Tombs prison. Individual members of the gang were available for hire, and one even handed out a price list:

Punching—$2.00
Both eyes blacked—$4.00
Nose and jaw broke—$10.00
Jacked out [knocked out with a blackjack]—$15.00
Ear chawed off—$15.00
Leg or arm broke—$19.00
Shot in leg—$25.00
Stabbed—$25.00
Doing the big job—$100.00 and up.[29]

Jacob Riis reported an encounter with the Whyos:

Turning a corner in the small hours of the morning, I came suddenly upon a gang of drunken roughs ripe for mischief. The leader had a long dirk-knife with which he playfully jabbed me in the ribs. . . . I knew them—the Why-os—the worst cutthroats in the city charged with a dozen murders, and robberies without end. A human life was to them, in the mood they were in, worth as much as the dirt under their feet, no more. At that instant, not six feet behind their backs. Captain McCullagh—the same who afterward became Chief—turned the corner with his precinct detective. I gathered all my strength and gave the ruffian's hand a mighty twist that turned the knife aside. I held it out for inspection. "What do you think of it, Cap?" Four brawny fists scattered the gang to the winds for an answer.[30]

Probably no one knew the seamy side of New York better than Riis. As a young immigrant he spent a night as a police "lodger," that is, a tramp allowed to sleep in a precinct station, where he was robbed by another tramp. When he protested to the desk sergeant, Riis was thrown out, and during the ruckus a policeman killed his pet dog. Though bitter, Riis blamed the system, not the individuals who did it.[31]

As a reporter on the police headquarters beat, Riis was a loner, re-

* In 1894 the police commander of the Tenderloin testified that the precinct was worth *at least* $8,000 per year to the commanding officer. Considering inflation and tax rates it would probably take a 1970s salary in the vicinity of $100,000 a year to equal Williams's "real" income.

fusing to cooperate with the pool by depending upon the handouts
from official sources. Instead, he worked long hours to dig out his own
stories and scoop the competition. Naturally this did not make him
popular and wandering the streets was dangerous, so that the Whyo
encounter was not his only close call:

> [A] cry of murder had lured me down Crosby Street into a saloon on the
> corner of Jersey Street, where the gang of the neighborhood had just
> stabbed the saloonkeeper in a drunken brawl. He was lying in a chair
> surrounded by shrieking women when I ran in. On the instant the doors
> were slammed and barred behind me, and I found myself on the battle-
> field with the battle raging unabated. Bottles were flying thick and fast,
> and the bar was going to smash. As I bent over the wounded man, I saw
> that he was done for. The knife was even then sticking in his neck, its
> point driven into the backbone. The instinct of the reporter came upper-
> most, and as I pulled it out and held it up in a pause of the fray, I asked
> incautiously:—
> "Whose knife is this?"
> A whiskey bottle that shaved within an inch of my head, followed by
> an angry oath, at once recalled me to myself . . . the racket rose and the
> women shrieked louder with each passing moment. Through the turmoil
> I strained every nerve to catch the sound of policemen's tramp. It was
> three minutes' run to the stationhouse, but time never dragged as it did
> then. Once I thought relief had come; but as I listened and caught the
> wail of men being beaten in the street, I smiled wickedly in the midst of
> my own troubles, for the voices told me that my opponents [newsmen]
> from headquarters, following on my track, had fallen among the thieves;
> half the gang were then outside. At last . . . the doors fell in with a crash;
> the reserves had come. Their clubs soon cleared the air and relieved me.[32]

The corrupt relationships between police and vice operators posed
a dilemma for Riis as well as other citizens. To be for the police was to
ignore corruption. To be against them was to threaten the organization
which successfully controlled disorder by gangs and riotous mobs. In
the late nineteenth century, it was relatively easy for the well-off to
ignore the gangs, now mostly confined to the slum districts, but the
Tenderloin was astride the city's main thoroughfare—a visible reminder
to the upper-class citizens of the moral degradation which they blamed
upon immigrants and their politics. Most galling of all was the police
department, meant, like the London Metropolitan force, to serve and protect the "good" citizens, not the Tenderloin riff-raff. Thus the police
were crooks or heroes or both depending upon individual perspective.

Another police reporter who saw both sides was Augustine Costello,
a former Irish revolutionary. Despite his background he was a warm
admirer of the police. By the 1880s the police department was a well-
established institution, and in spring every available officer was assem-

bled for one of the city's great spectacles, the annual police parade. Each unit, under its commander, would march proudly down Broadway as hundreds of thousands of New Yorkers cheered "the Finest"—a term whose common use dates from that time. In a country with no royal guard for its great metropolis, the New York police force provided some of the pomp and ceremony which the Life Guards, Uhlans, and Cossacks did elsewhere. Every year the parade would serve as a powerful display of the unity of the men in blue and their acceptance by the public.

In 1885 Costello published *Our Police Protectors*,[33] an admiring study of the police department including sketches of its most prominent personalities. While Superintendent Murray enjoyed the top spot, he was not the premier policeman or the most colorful. The real leader was Inspector Thomas Byrnes, commanding officer of the Detective Bureau; and by far the most colorful was Captain "Clubber" Williams, commander of the Tenderloin. These two symbolized major elements of American police administration.

As in London, the New York detectives had begun as a small adjunct unit to the patrol force, and as late as 1863 they constituted only 1 percent of the department. American detectives were originally recruited directly from civilian life, often from the criminal underworld. Not surprisingly, they were frequently involved in scandal. In consequence, it became the practice to draw detectives from the plodding ranks of the uniformed patrol force, and until Inspector Byrnes took charge in 1880, New York detectives had not established a significant reputation.

By the 1870s the growth of commerce and industry and the new railroads had greatly enhanced the activities of professional criminals. Pickpockets, safecrackers, and confidence men traveled from city to city and maintained ties to others of their kind. When a burglar came into a new town, he would go to a local bar or pool hall known to be a rendezvous for thieves. There he could make the necessary arrangements to operate—for instance, get tips on likely targets and places to fence goods and make arrangements for bail and legal defense if arrested. In some instances he would be required to pay fees for the right to work, including graft to police and politicians.[34] When a town got too hot, an offender could move on. Fingerprint records were not yet in use, and photographs were not taken routinely, so a crook picked up in one town could deny any previous offenses in another. Given the ineffectiveness of local detectives, major investigations were carried out mostly by private agencies such as the Pinkertons.

Byrnes, born in Ireland in 1842, had come to America as a boy, served in the Union Army, and joined the police department in 1863.

By 1870 he was a captain, and in 1879, he solved a 3-million-dollar bank burglary in his precinct. As a result, in 1880, he was appointed commanding officer of the Detective Bureau. Two years later he succeeded in having all detectives placed under his command, but the precinct captains found this intolerable and in 1884 the headquarters-precinct separation of detectives was restored. The precinct captains needed their pair of so-called "wardmen" to collect graft from the vice resorts, a task made easier when the public could not readily identify the collectors as officers. In contrast, Byrnes's headquarters detectives concentrated on professional criminals and major crimes, an arrangement which provided for a formal differentiation of function between criminal investigation and vice control. In 1888, Byrnes's primacy was recognized by his appointment as chief inspector, the number two post in the force, ranking immediately below superintendent.

Other American municipal detectives, such as Francis Tukey in Boston and Jack Nelson in Chicago,[35] had made individual reputations long before Byrnes, but the New Yorker was the most imaginative and by far the most successful. He began to assemble a rogues' gallery containing pictures of known offenders from throughout Europe and America and established a daily lineup of arrested thieves so that masked detectives and victimized citizens could look at them. He also established working regulations for criminals. For example, he drew a dead line at Fulton Street, north of the Wall Street district, and forbad any criminal to enter the district on pain of physical punishment, and he required crooks new in town to check in at headquarters. As a result of his contacts detectives were able to recover stolen goods with remarkable speed—a feat which won admiration from prominent citizens.

None of these were particularly innovative techniques. Tukey of Boston, not to mention the Fieldings in London, had employed lineups. Continental police made criminals register, and Philadelphia had a flourishing rogues' gallery before the Civil War. But Byrnes was able to back up his informal rules with a force beyond any law. He was a noted practitioner of the third degree, utilizing both physical beatings and psychological tortures like the sweat box, a small room where the prisoner would be kept for days with no human contact, being fed by an unseen hand. He also utilized acting techniques such as pretending to a prisoner that his confederates had confessed. Such methods were laughed at by the professionals like Langdon Moore, the famous Boston burglar, but they were effective against the corner-boy gang leaders like Mike McGloin of the Whyos, whose confession sent him to the gallows. With professionals it was necessary to make business deals—freedom for one crook if he squealed on another. Byrnes's greatest weapon, though, was his own power and standing with business and political leaders. It was difficult to bring pressure to bear on behalf of a suspect; thus Byrnes could do what the precinct captains could not—get tough with the crooks who overstepped the bounds.

In essence, Byrnes used muscle and deals to rout the gangs and personal publicity and favors to the mighty to ensure his own position. In microcosm, he fostered the same feelings of ambivalence among knowledgeable observers as the larger police department. Jacob Riis was impressed with his accomplishments—"a big man" was his description—while he struck the young reporter Lincoln Steffens as "simple, no complications at all—a man who would buy you or beat you as you might choose, but get you he would."[36]

Chief Walling had no love for his popular subordinate. To Walling, the detectives were public relations men and Byrnes's office a "star chamber," which emphasized revenge and restitution rather than prevention.[37] In fact, the rise of the detectives was largely based on civilian support over the opposition of the uniformed cops.

Byrnes, in effect, was a combination of the Bow Street Runners, Jonathan Wild, and Scotland Yard's CID, but like the last, though he could master the professional criminals, he was much less successful when confronted with a more complex case involving out-of-the-ordinary offenders. In 1888, when Jack the Ripper was terrorizing London, Byrnes publicly dared him to come to New York. Shortly after, a female barfly known as "Shakespeare" was cut to pieces in a waterfront resort. Although a character named "Frenchie" was sent up for it, underworld gossip maintained that it was a Ripper murder and that Frenchie had been framed to preserve the honor of the police. Whatever the truth, Byrnes was instrumental in securing Frenchie's release after a few years, indicating some uncertainty in his own mind.[38]

Byrnes also took a lead from Superintendent Murray and was strong in warning of the danger of the Communist movement. As Finley Peter Dunne sneered:

> Inspector Byrnes' ... fortune was made by scaring millionaires into the belief that there was about to be an uprising of anarchists and assembling an army of cops to surround a few hundred garment workers in Union Square who had gathered to hear a squeaky little tailor rant in Yiddish against the tyranny of Capital.[39]

Indeed, Byrnes was another policeman who was the toast of Wall Street, an intimate of Jay Gould, and a very successful "investor" who amassed a fortune of $350,000 on a salary of $2,000 a year.*

---

* The relative value of Byrnes's fortune becomes apparent when it is noted that the wealthy aristocrat Theodore Roosevelt at the time had a personal fortune of only $200,000.[40]

Whether New York was safer because of Byrnes or only thought it was is conjecture. Some criminals gave the city a wide berth; others simply made a deal and worked steadily. A later commissioner, commenting on Byrnes's work, told the apocryphal story of a prominent citizen who complained that his watch had been stolen while he was walking across the Brooklyn Bridge. Byrnes allegedly called in his best detective, gave him the serial number, and ordered the watch recovered and brought back to his office within twenty-four hours. At the appointed time the detective returned crestfallen, saying, "Chief, I made every thief in town show me all the watches he stole on Brooklyn Bridge the other day, and none has that serial number."[41]

If Byrnes the detective was a man of system and method and despite his persistent brogue and fractured grammar* was smooth and skilled, an intimate of the mighty, Alexander Williams, the premier patrol commander, was an individualist, flamboyant and controversial, at home only with the roughest elements. Williams was born in Canada in 1839. He spent a number of years as a ship's carpenter and in 1866 became a New York patrolman. He was extremely powerful physically and soon earned the sobriquet "Clubber." While derogatory, the nickname was actually a tremendous boost. Physical prowess was as important to a successful police career of the day as it was to a career in politics. In the hard world of the time, where most men worked with their hands, anyone who could not back up his words with deeds commanded little respect and could not lead other men. Like Williams, most police officers of the period were big men physically, and many were not native New Yorkers. Men who grew up in the tenements tended to be small. In the 1890s the average gang member was 5'3" and 120 to 130 pounds.[43] In contrast, New York cops were usually brawny lads from the farms of Ireland, Germany, or rural America, and their answer to a challenge was delivered with their fists or clubs.

Cops like Captains John H. McCullagh and Williams quickly won attention as rookies by invading gang lairs and manhandling the local hoodlums. McCullagh went into Hell's Kitchen to investigate a theft, knocked out three gangsters, threw them in a cart, and hauled them to the station. Williams, on his first day on the job, picked a fight with the two toughest thugs in the neighborhood, clubbed them unconscious, and pitched them through the plate-glass window of a saloon, bringing forth six of their buddies, who met the same fate.[44]

This strategy was not always successful. Dennis Sullivan, a young

---

* When Brynes lost his temper he would lapse into the Irish slang of his youth. As police chief he once admonished his inspectors thus: "Gentlemen, . . . did not I command you last Monday on this very spot in this same office to enforce to the letter the laws regulating the saloons in this city, and—and to close them one and all at the legally fixed hours for closing? . . . Well, and what I want to know now is: did youse did it?"[42]

patrolman of the Charles Street station, was in the process of making a great reputation by smashing the drug-using Hudson-Duster gang of Greenwich Village when it was decided, with the approval of local politicians, that he must be taught a lesson. One night the gang pounced on him, took his coat, nightstick, shield, and revolver, and badly beat him with stones and blackjacks. When he had been knocked unconscious, he was rolled over on his back, and four of the gangsters ground their heels in his face, inflicting permanent damage. The attack upon Patrolman Sullivan became a legend, and the rival Gophers of Hell's Kitchen formally congratulated the Hudson-Dusters. One Lung Kean, the TB-ravaged bard of the West Side gangs, contributed a poem for the occasion:

> Says Dinny "Here's me only chance to gain meself a name;
>   I'll clean up the Hudson-Dusters and reach the Hall of Fame!"
> He lost his stick and cannon, and his shield they took away,
>   It was then that he remembered every dog has got his day.[45]

Williams was luckier. In 1872 he was made captain of the Gashouse district, and in 1876 his famous transfer to the Tenderloin took place. He served there until 1887 except for two years' leave while he filled the lucrative post of superintendent of street cleaning. From 1887 on, he was an inspector in charge of a group of precincts on the East Side. In 1894, in testimony before a legislative committee, he would admit to a personal fortune of $300,000 and an estate in Cos Cob complete with a private steam yacht, again demonstrating that in America a poor immigrant could rise to great wealth.

Even as an administrator, Williams continued to prowl the streets, making free with his club. He was brought up on charges before the Board of Commissioners on 358 occasions and fined 224 times, but he was never dismissed. Within his domain he was the absolute king. As a demonstration to reporters one day, he hung his watch on a lamppost while a number of local denizens looked on. Men had been murdered for less valuable items, but the watch was still there when Clubber and party returned from a walk around the block. On another occasion, he consented to referee a Madison Square Garden prizefight in full uniform with his club in hand.[46]

Unlike Byrnes, Williams had no defenders among the "better" elements. The detective chief worked in the back rooms of headquarters or the hidden world of professional crime, while the Tenderloin and Williams's nightstick were very much in the open. Even Augustine Costello held no brief for Williams, and the feeling was mutual, since Costello had been the source of the story of how Williams gave the Tenderloin its name, for which Williams paid him back by a taste of the club. Even after publishing his laudatory book, Costello was dragged to the station, cursed by Williams, and beaten with brass knuckles by a captain whose promotion Costello had helped to secure.[47]

Despite his flamboyance, Williams was only the beat cop writ large. In the conditions of the time, cops were expected to be rough. In '63, '72, and '74, clubs were trumps as the better citizens cheered the men in blue. The political fix system also discouraged cop or citizen from relying on the courts for justice. The philosophy of the stationhouse, as a sergeant explained it to a rookie, was what later came to be called "street court":

> Now, let me tell you something. They may beat you in court, the complainant may not show up, they may jump their bail, politicians may interfere, there are several ways they can beat you, but this (and he pointed to the [prisoner's] marks and bruises), they've got, and make no damned mistake about it.[48]

Williams remarked, "There is more law in a policeman's nightstick than the Supreme Court." This philosophy was hardly original with him and in fact was subscribed to by many of loftier station. The precepts of restraint that Commissioners Rowan and Mayne had urged on London bobbies could no more have prevailed with American police in the post-Civil War era than the Duke of Wellington's ideas of regular army discipline could have been imposed on the volunteers of the Union Army. At a fire in midtown Manhattan Jacob Riis saw a policeman turn back a curious spectator with a sharp club rap across the back, causing the man to meekly withdraw chomping on a large cigar. The officer was panic-stricken when Riis informed him that his victim was former President Ulysses S. Grant.[49] But no complaint followed. The old soldier knew well the weaknesses of the ordinary American in uniform.

DOWN WITH THE POLICE: THE CRUSADERS

As the 1890s dawned, the Tammany Tiger rode fat and arrogant. In 1888, Croker had been able to put in his own man as mayor. As a result, machine dominance of city government, and particularly the police department, was nearly complete. The president of the Board of Commissioners was a Tammany district leader, and the Republican members were, as usual, of the friendly variety. Yet Croker's power meant that he could safely ignore the rival Democratic factions and the state Republican machine, headed by Senator Tom Platt, as well as the various reform and good-government types like Theodore Roosevelt. The reformers, especially, had almost no chance of coming to power. Not only did both Croker and Platt despise them, but even more importantly, the city's voters, now increasingly immigrants as Eastern and Southern Europeans flowed in to join the Irish and Germans, were unlikely to establish a reform administration. For them, Tammany softened the harsh life of the slums, with the district leaders playing the role of village chieftain.

But the urban masses were also susceptible to a form of propaganda beyond the direct appeal of the local ward boss, saloonkeeper, or ethnic leader. This was the daily newspapers, now competing for circulation under swashbuckling publishers like William Randolph Hearst and Joseph Pulitzer. The key to profit was to hold a mass audience whose members were interested not so much in the problems of Europe or debates on the tariff as in the dramas of their own environment; crime stories, for example, like those about murdered blondes and kidnapped children, were incidents that the half-literate public could fix on. In the 1870s, Thomas Nast's cartoons of the Tammany Tiger had been a major factor in arousing public opinion against Boss Tweed. Inspector Byrnes's ability to capture favorable publicity had made him and his bureau popular heroes, but it had a reverse twist, since police scandals were as interesting as major crimes.

The press also fed on the mass advertising of the important commercial interests such as department stores. Merchant prince and publishing czar were similar not only in wealth and prestige but also in their reverence for the source of these—the city and its economic and social health—which the political machines with their graft seemed to threaten. Thus the press was a formidable vehicle for attacks on Tammany, particularly the highly visible and intrinsically interesting police department. The power of the press was amply demonstrated when the *Sun* compelled Superintendent Walling to permit reporter Jacob Riis to interview a murderer despite Inspector Byrnes's vehement disapproval. Riis later recollected how Byrnes stood by throughout, speechless and black with rage.[50]

It was no surprise, then, that when the Reverend Charles Parkhurst of the fashionable Madison Square Presbyterian Church preached a sermon attacking police corruption, he received front-page attention, and the stage was set for great events. Parkhurst was not an ordinary clergyman. As president of the New York Society for the Prevention of Crime, he represented the native American Protestant elite whose anti-foreign bias was best exemplified by Parkhurst's immediate predecessor as president of the Society, the Reverend Howard Crosby. Crosby declared:

We prefer that our politics should have an American flavor. This country is not Ireland or Germany, however much we welcome hither the Irish and the Germans, and we do not wish our political atmosphere to smell either of whiskey or of beer. We have institutions that we cherish as our own distinctively. They are American, and not European, and we do not intend to surrender them to arrogant and impudent foreigners who abuse our hospitality by their insulting effrontery.[51]

Under Crosby, who held office from 1878 to 1891, the Society was, in the words of Heywood Broun, "a nice, namby-pamby organization."[52] Under Parkhurst it became a major force.

Born in Massachusetts in 1842, and an Amherst graduate, Parkhurst was typical of American reformers, combining intense moral indignation and intolerance of opposition with a love for publicity.* To Parkhurst, his opponents were "drunks" or "brutes," evil and depraved men, although the mature Richard Croker was in fact a polished gentleman. Croker's family had been landowners in Ireland, but had fallen on hard times. With his new-found wealth, Croker was able to carry on the life style of a duke, spending a great deal of time at his Irish estates or at English racetracks, hobnobbing with the Prince of Wales, later Edward VII; and although he was to enjoy many a political triumph, none was so thrilling as his horse's victory in the English Derby of 1907. Croker, in fact, ruled Manhattan with as much aloofness as his aristocratic friends displayed in ruling their own estates in Ireland. In the larger perspective the Parkhurst versus Croker battle was the struggle of the native American elite against the lower classes, but in the narrow and more personal sense it was a battle of bourgeois puritan against Tory lord, with perhaps more than a touch of envy on the part of the former. Later, Theodore Roosevelt, who was to benefit the most from what became known as the "Parkhurst Crusade," was to characterize the Reverend Doctor as a "dishonest lunatic."[54]

It is noteworthy that in the previous twelve years of his New York pastorate Parkhurst had not found the vice situation worthy of a sermon. Not until he assumed the presidency of the Society for the Prevention of Crime did he begin his attack. Perhaps Parkhurst had noted the publicity and importance which accrued to Anthony Comstock, president of the rival Society for the Suppression of Vice and the most prominent crusader against obscenity in American history.[55] In any event, Parkhurst tipped off a reporter for Joseph Pulitzer's *World* that the sermon on February 14, 1892, would be newsworthy.

The immediate press reaction to Parkhurst's charges of corruption

---

* In 1885, he attempted to turn the funeral of General George B. McClellan into a vehicle for personal publicity, and even his strong supporter, Lincoln Steffens, noted the Reverend Doctor's love for the limelight.[53]

was largely unfavorable, and he was invited to appear before a grand jury. Since he had no evidence, his appearance produced more ridicule. Undaunted, he retained one Charles Gardner, a freelance private detective, to accompany him and a young parishioner on a tour of the city's vice dives. Gardner later admitted having danced and played leapfrog with naked women in a bordello while Parkhurst looked on. The revelations of Parkhurst's midnight rambles drew criticism from Comstock and others on the grounds that this was highly improper behavior for a minister. In the Tenderloin the less respectable folks sang a new version of "Ta-Ra-Ra-Boom-De-Ay":

> Dr. Parkhurst on the floor
>   Playing leap frog with a whore,
> Ta-ra-ra-boom-de-ay,
>   Ta-ra-ra-boom-de-ay[56]

—though it was Gardner who was the actual frog. In any event Parkhurst now had evidence, and his next sermon on the subject gave names and locations where vice flourished. The resultant newspaper publicity forced Tammany on the defensive, and the "great detective," Inspector Byrnes, replaced Murray as superintendent in April of 1892. His first act was the classic response of embattled police administrators, namely to transfer almost all the precinct captains, although, as Parkhurst pointed out, it was unlikely that a man who was crooked in one place would be honest in another.[57]

The "Parkhurst Crusade" became part of American folklore often cited as proof that one honest man can singlehandedly defeat the powers of organized corruption. According to the legend, someone such as Parkhurst suddenly becomes aware of a particular evil and shouts it to the heavens whereupon the multitudes rally around and turn the rascals out. The truth was somewhat less inspiring. The "Crusade" was a model of the kind of "investigation" which is now so much a part of American government, containing timing, drama, brilliant acting, the right cast, and, most importantly, powerful backing. At any time and place there are those who are prepared to undertake the risks and rewards of a moral crusade. To be successful, they must have substantial support from powerful interests in the media and public office. Clergymen as prominent as Henry Ward Beecher and the Methodist Bishop Matthew Simpson had decried vice conditions in New York in the '60s, and '70s,[58] and one of the sharpest exposés of the Tenderloin had been contained in Chief Walling's memoirs published five years before Parkhurst's sermon. However, in these other cases the time had not been right. Most people regarded prostitution, liquor, and gambling as necessary evils and even safety valves to allow people to work off the pressures of nineteenth-century urban industrial life. It is possible that if vice had really been suppressed, the urban proletariat might have rallied stronger for Henry George than for Dick Croker, a prospect the native elite might not have liked.

In the '90s, though, Tammany's very success ensured powerful opposition. Platt's Republicans were denied their share of the spoils, and even some of the vice operators were disgruntled at the exorbitant gouging by the police department. Immigrant families loyal to Tammany feared their daughters might be pressed into prostitution, a prospect brought home by lurid tales of "white slavery." Even many cops were disgusted at the arrogance of the system. A patrolman on station reserve duty noted a wardman who prayed before going to bed and scornfully remarked that it must be for "better collections."[59]

"Down with the police" became Parkhurst's slogan, a sentiment heretofore more likely to emanate from Johann Most, who after expulsion from Britain had made New York his home base. In 1887, when Most denounced the police after the Haymarket bombing trial in Chicago, Inspector Byrnes had him arrested, and Most received a year in jail. But Parkhurst was no revolutionary; his fight was with Tammany, not the police as an institution. He had cleverly grasped that the Tammany cops had become so corrupt and arrogant that it would not take much to bring them down. His ultimate mistake was failing to realize that the public would tire of rule by his type much faster than Tammany, but that was in the future.

Throughout 1892–93 Parkhurst skirmished with the police department. In December 1892, detective Gardner was arrested by Captain William Devery, a precinct commander in Clubber Williams's division, on a charge of attempting to extort money from a madam. Parkhurst alleged a frame-up, and three prominent lawyers, John Goff, Frank Moss, and William Travers Jerome, defended Gardner. Even Parkhurst, though, was shocked when Gardner was remarried (after divorcing his first wife) in a ribald ceremony at the Statue of Liberty. He served eleven months in jail before the charge was dismissed, left town, and spent the rest of his life in trouble with the law.[60]

Finally, in 1894, the Republican-dominated State Legislature appointed an investigating committee under the chairmanship of Senator Clarence Lexow. To assist the probe, wealthy businessmen provided private funds, since the legislative appropriation was insufficient. But while the moral reformers and the press generated the enthusiasm, the real initiator was Boss Platt, since the probe provided an opportunity to embarrass Tammany. The driving force of the investigation was its counsel, Goff, an Irish immigrant and revolutionary who spent his time fighting both of Richard Croker's loves—Tammany Hall and the British aristocracy. Among his projects was the arming of an American expedition to free some Irish rebel prisoners.[61] Goff's appointment was a clever move; an Irish Catholic set out to attack Tammany Hall as a means of countering charges of ethnic and religious hostility on the part of the WASP elite who were the political and financial backers of the investigation. Before the ruthless Goff and his colleagues Moss and Jerome could be given free rein, however, it was necessary to ease out the committee's original counsel, W. H. Sutherland, a lawyer from Western, New York, who Parkhurst thought was "not sufficiently acquainted with New York conditions"[62]—i.e., would not turn the investigation into an inquisition.

Under Goff and company, witnesses found it useful to cooperate. Captain Timothy Creedon, a respected officer and Civil War hero, admitted having paid $15,000 for a promotion, but the big break came when Captain Max Schmittberger admitted to being Clubber Williams's collector, or bagman. Schmittberger was persuaded (in the slang of the day) to "peach" by Goff's assurance of immunity from prosecution. In effect, the committee used Byrnes's methods to defeat the police department. The smartest dive owners became informers for the committee and were allowed to continue to operate.[63] Williams, in contrast, denied accepting graft, claiming that his wealth was based upon real estate speculation in Japan, an area then as remote as the moon. While the committee found this incredible, it was more willing to accept Superintendent Byrnes's explanation that his wealth had been garnered through investments recommended by Jay Gould.[64]

In the end, though there was a flurry of criminal prosecutions and firings, including Captain Devery's, none stood up on appeal. The investigation was halted at the end of 1894, when it began to come close to Republican politicians. It had already served the purpose of embarrassing Tammany and promoting the individual reformers. Goff received a lucrative judgeship, Jerome eventually became district attorney and Moss president of the Board of Police Commissioners, and Parkhurst gained worldwide fame and installation as doyen of the reform movement for a generation.

Meanwhile, in November 1894, a fusion party of Independents, Republicans, and anti-Tammany Democrats elected William Strong as mayor. Under his administration a new Board of Police Commissioners was installed with Theodore Roosevelt as its president. The Police department was about to be reformed for the first time in nearly forty years.

Roughriding Commissioner

While the reformers had yet to develop comprehensive statements of what they desired from police administration, the general outlines could be ascertained. First, they wished to centralize authority in the executive head of the police so his subordinate commanders, normally beholden to ward bosses, could be brought under control. They also wished to protect the police from machine dominance by affording a tenure of office for the chief and civil service protection to the rank and file.* Finally, they sought the appointment as chief of an educated, "nonpolitical" administrator and in the lower ranks of men who could pass written tests and a background investigation. In effect, they argued for a rational-legal bureaucracy, impersonal, tightly controlled, and dedicated to efficiency and integrity. And for a brief time, the Roosevelt regime was to see all these goals achieved. Of course, such a system would negate the power of a political machine in favor of an authoritarian chief, who, given the qualifications outlined, was likely to have internalized the values of the native elite. Even the proposals for formal examinations would work to the disadvantage of immigrants in favor of the better-educated native Americans.

Theodore Roosevelt was a complex man, and no brief description can capture the essence of his life. During his Presidency, he was described by the British Ambassador (a personal friend) as being "about seven years old."[65] As President, while attending the Harvard commencement, he surprised Harvard President Charles William Eliot by setting a pistol on the table,[66] and in 1912 the staid *New York Times* carried an article by a noted psychiatrist questioning Roosevelt's sanity.[67] But whatever his mental state or personal idiosyncrasies, he was an enormously popular and successful politician.

Roosevelt was born in New York in 1858 into a family so aristocratic that they were among a group which refused membership in the New York Opera to the upstart Rockefellers and Vanderbilts, requiring them to build the Metropolitan for themselves. As a Harvard undergraduate he studied science but had a literary flair. Unlike others of his social class, he was eager for the combat of city politics. Elected to the State Assembly at twenty-three, he unsuccessfully sought the speaker's post the next year, and at twenty-eight he was defeated for mayor. In 1884 he headed a state legislative commission to investigate the police department, and in 1889 he became the first United States Civil Service Commissioner.

When he arrived at police headquarters he was thirty-seven, already well known as a writer and politician and discussed among the knowledgeable as a potential President, although no one expected it would occur so quickly. Roosevelt was also attuned to the importance of public relations. During his regime, Jacob Riis and Lincoln Steffens

---

* The New York City police had been placed under civil service in 1884, but given Tammany control over the machinery, this was more form than substance.

of the *Sun* and *Post*, respectively, were de facto deputy commissioners. Among his other literary friends were the novelists Owen Wister, Hamlin Garland, and Stephen Crane.

The last named was something of an embarrassment. Crane became enamored with prostitutes and gallantly defended them from police abuse. In one such incident, in September 1896, he tangled with Charles Becker, a burly, aggressive young Tenderloin precinct detective (wardman) and charged him with brutality. At the departmental hearing, Crane's alleged opium use and liaison with prostitutes were as much an issue as Becker's conduct, and the latter was exonerated. The Roosevelt regime was cracking down on Tenderloin vice, and TR himself praised Becker as a good cop. Crane, whose life style was unconventional, was thereafter the subject of considerable police attention and found it convenient to leave the city.[68]

Though TR was only one of four commissioners, he acted as though he had supreme power, dismissing Byrnes and replacing him with a dull career man, thus neatly avoiding any upstaging. Clubber Williams, too, departed the scene,* but Schmittberger was retained because Steffens persuaded Roosevelt that the Big Dutchman had reformed. Schmittberger became a famous clean-up man, praised by various commissioners, and eventually rose to chief inspector. He was a big, handsome cop whom the politicians had put on the force without requiring a payoff because they admired his looks. As a rookie on the elite Broadway squad, he won more accolades. Throughout his career his straightforward manner impressed people, and he evinced sincerity and contrition when defending graft charges. The police reformers, like other moralists, always had a liking for the reformed sinner. The wise-guy cops like Becker were less certain of Schmittberger's position as a latter-day saint, nor would they forgive him for peaching, and when Tammany came back, they took revenge by refusing him permission to march in the annual police parade.

Roosevelt embarked on his own midnight rambles, as the press described them, looking for derelictions of duty, summoning offenders to his office the following morning, and providing good copy for the papers. Sometimes amusing incidents would occur, as once when he accosted an officer talking in a friendly way to a prostitute. The annoyed cop inquired of the lady, "Should I fan [club] him, Mame?" When she replied affirmatively, TR identified himself, whereupon the two fled into the night.[69] The commissioner also enjoyed a good laugh;

---

* In the following year, Williams ran for the State Senate, but despite the efforts of enthusiastic supporters like Charley Becker, he was rejected by the district of which he had been the uncrowned king. Byrnes went into the insurance business. In 1906, millionaire Thomas Fortune Ryan attempted to persuade the mayor to make Byrnes police commissioner but to no avail.

he allowed a notorious anti-Semite to speak but provided a detail of forty Jewish cops as bodyguards.[70] Roosevelt's more systematic reforms were the upgrading of civil service tests and the concurrent opening of recruitment to the entire state. This, of course, permitted more cops from the better-educated native American upstate population and in combination with background investigations—TR refused to appoint anyone who had worked in a liquor establishment—led to the majority of appointments in his administration going to native Americans.[71]

Roosevelt's biggest problem was enforcement of the Sunday closing law, particularly in the German areas of the city. Also, his fellow commissioners, including Frederick T. Grant, son of the former President, resented his one-man operation and came into increasing public conflict with him. Even Riis and Steffens found some of his tactics annoying. When TR announced a reduction in crime—the records of the time were so primitive that no real determination could be made—they printed every crime story they could find under black headlines announcing a crime wave until TR shut off access to the station records.[72] But finally the opposition of the liquor interests, his fellow commissioners, and Boss Platt as well as difficulty in getting firm control of the force, convinced Roosevelt that he could do little more for the police or himself, and in 1897 he executed what his contemporaries described as a "glorious retreat" to the post of Assistant Secretary of the Navy. His place on the board was filled by Frank Moss, the Lexow assistant counsel.

The following year, the Spanish-American War broke out and Roosevelt accepted a post as lieutenant colonel of the first United States volunteer cavalry regiment, known as the "Roughriders," under Colonel Leonard Wood. The Roughriders along with other regiments participated in the battle known as San Juan Hill. The importance of the battle and the precise role of all parties are subject to dispute, but the press hailed the Roughriders and their leaders. Roosevelt returned to New York, made his peace with Boss Platt, was elected governor, and subsequently advanced to Vice President and President.*

Roosevelt was a man of dash and vigor, but his influence on the police, like his military career, was more form than substance, and things soon returned to normal, although, as one New York paper wrote,

---

* Wood subsequently became Governor General of Cuba, Army Chief of Staff, and in 1920, according to legend, lost the presidency in the famous smoke-filled room in Chicago. Wood, a regular army medical corps captain, had been serving as President McKinley's White House physician, and his qualifications to command a line regiment seemed dubious. To shore them up, he was awarded the Congressional Medal of Honor for an incident twelve years earlier, when, fresh from Harvard Medical School, he left his post to join an unsuccessful expedition in pursuit of Geronimo—though some argued that such conduct deserved a court martial rather than the highest medal.

... the section-room in a police station is a great place for traditions. There walk the ghosts of men notorious in their time, whom the town has forgotten absolutely, and the stories about them affect the manner of grip with which the policeman swings his club, or the temper in which he blackmails disorderly women.[73]

In this tradition some thought that stories of the "square commissioner" would have a positive impact on police behavior for a long time to come. And in his two-year regime Roosevelt appointed 1,700 cops, four times as many as were appointed in the previous two years, and promoted 130, more than the total for the previous six years.[74] Thus many New York cops of the next generation were "Roosevelt" men.

Honest Graft: A Time of Uncertainty

In 1897 the Legislature provided that effective January 1, 1898, Manhattan, the Bronx, Queens, Staten Island, and Brooklyn would become a single city. Thus the winner of the 1897 mayoral election (the Legislature had extended the reform administration a year) would control a kingdom, and Dick Croker himself came home from Europe to direct the fight. He had sensed that the reformers had no real cohesion or program and that Commissioner Roosevelt's tough law enforcement would produce a backlash. Croker's judgment was vindicated when Tammany won an overwhelming triumph.

The new Board of Police Commissioners chose for superintendent William Devery, the precinct captain who several years back had arrested the Reverend Parkhurst's aide, detective Gardner. Devery was a 250-pound giant whom Steffens had described as a "lovely villain."[75] In May of 1898 Tammany's triumph was complete as Devery on horseback led the annual police parade, with Clubber Williams and Dick Croker occupying places of honor on the reviewing stand and Schmittberger nowhere in sight.

Devery was the third man of prominence and wealth whom the force produced during this period. Fired in 1894 as a result of Lexow disclosures, he was returned to duty by court order two years later. The Devery appointment appalled the reformers. Parkhurst declared:

I know him as a man knows a serpent by studying the trail where a serpent has crawled past. Devery's precinct was a moral cesspool. Under the name of captain he was sneakingly disporting himself as the guardian angel of vice and depravity. ... The Lexow investigation had its direct origin in the damnably vicious condition of the precinct that was captained by a man who has just been made the responsible head of the biggest police force in America.[76]

Like Williams and Byrnes, Devery was a tough, colorful individual. Unlike his two great contemporaries, he was a native New Yorker who had delivered his father's lunch pail when the elder Devery was laying the bricks of Tammany Hall; thus allegiance to the machine was bred into him. He was also something of a nonbureaucratic administrator who avoided formality. His real headquarters was in front of a saloon where he held court each night until 2 or 3 in the morning. Like Walling, Devery had little use for detectives, sharing a common view of the uniformed force that the plainclothes boys were phony publicity hounds. Once, when he expressed displeasure over leaks of confidential information from his office, it was suggested that he assign detectives to trace the source. "Detectives hell," he replied, "I need a plumber," thus anticipating the complaint of another more prominent man of the future.[77] Such behavior made him a great favorite with the working press if not their editors.

Where Williams and Byrnes had been Republicans who cooperated with Tammany in their own interest, Devery's guiding principle was to do whatever would advance the cause of his political masters. The problem was to determine who they were. Dick Croker now saw police graft as "dirty" and opted for restraint. In his opinion, the policy of a wide-open town was no longer viable in the age of municipal reform, since a roaring Tenderloin presided over by a Clubber Williams provided too easy a target for reformers. Croker even appointed his own antivice commission.[78] Somewhat along the same lines, other Tammany bosses began to make a distinction between dirty and "honest" graft. In the words of one of them, George Washington Plunkitt:

> Everybody is talkin' these days about Tammany men growin' rich on graft, but nobody thinks of drawin' the distinction between honest graft and dishonest graft. . . . Yes, many of our men have grown rich in politics. I have myself. I've made a big fortune out of the game, and I'm gettin' richer every day, but I've not gone in for dishonest graft—blackmailin' gamblers, saloonkeepers, disorderly people, etc.—and neither has any of the men who have made big fortunes in politics. . . .
>
> Just let me explain by examples. My party's in power in the city, and it's goin' to undertake a lot of public improvements. Well, I'm tipped off, say, that they're going to lay out a new park at a certain place. I see my opportunity and I take it. I go to that place and I buy up all the land I can in the neighborhood. Then the board of this or that makes its plan public, and there is a rush to get my land, which nobody cared particular for before. Ain't it perfectly honest to charge a good price and make a profit on my investment and foresight? Of course it is. Well that's honest graft. . . .[79]

Croker's desire for restraint was not shared by all of his constituents, though; many district leaders, not to mention gangsters, did not yet have estates and racing stables, and their access to "honest" graft was limited.

At the turn of the century, the gangs controlled most of lower Manhattan and the West Side, and while Tammany was still dominated by the Irish, the street gangs were not. In the Five Points, the leader was Paul Kelly (born Paolo Vaccarelli), who ran the New Brighton Dance Hall saloon on Great Jones Street. On the East Side, the Kelly gang's arch rivals were the Eastmans, named for their leader, Edward "Monk" Eastman (born Osterman), a Jewish boy from Brooklyn. Short and husky, "Monk" had begun as a teenage bouncer at the Paradise Dance Hall in the Bowery, where he boasted gallantly that he had never hit a woman—without first taking off his brass knuckles. His flamboyant dress, language, and style served as a model for his peers.[80] Kelly, equally tough, was modest in speech and manner. Then as now, slumming was a popular sport of the rich, and many wealthy persons toured the vice dens with police escorts. On one such foray, a society woman accompanied by a headquarters detective stopped in at the New Brighton, where she chatted pleasantly with a polite young man. Later, asked how she liked the tour, she said her only regret was that she had not seen the awful Paul Kelly, whereupon the detective informed her that she had just spent half an hour in his company.[81]

Over this scene presided Big Tim Sullivan, Tammany leader of the Bowery, state senator, sometime Congressman (actually a minor job in the eyes of Tammany), and unofficial boss of most of the districts south of 14th Street. Born in a Five Points tenement in 1863, Sullivan was a former crony of the Whyos and early became a Tammany lieutenant. In 1889, Inspector Byrnes urged the Legislature to pass a law permitting the police to arrest known criminals on sight. When Sullivan spoke against it, Byrnes denounced him as an associate of criminals and accused him of attempting to persuade a detective to fix a case. Later, as a state senator, Sullivan continually pushed legislation to take away policemen's clubs and blackjacks.[82] In 1890 Croker himself picked him to be leader of the Bowery because of his ability to work with and control the Italians and Jews.*[83] "The Big Feller," as some called him, had his hand in many operations, including prizefighting, racing, and the Broadway theater. He was much beloved in his district. When he was a ten-year-old urchin, a kindly lady teacher had brought him a pair of shoes. Later, as a boss, he would distribute thousands of pairs of free shoes each year on the anniversary of the incident. The youthful

* Big Tim wore the yarmulke at Jewish services and introduced a bill to make Columbus Day a holiday.

experience was also thought to underlie his ardent support of feminist issues; for years he was the only senator to support women's suffrage.[84]

Sullivan and his allies* had no intention of obeying Croker's directions, and Devery was much more responsive to Sullivan than to Croker. As one criminal observed:

> He [Croker] might order the town shut, and it might stay shut for a night; but if the boys thought that his nibs was in earnest they'd turn him down. Croker is boss on the strength of understandin' that [New] York is to be opened and that Tammany is to get the benefit of the political graft. If he should go back on his promises to the boys he won't remain boss a week.[85]

Thus the same rackets went on as before Lexow, but with more centralized control. Under Devery, gambling and vice were overseen by a "commission" which included Big Tim and Devery's business partner, the gambler Frank Farrell.**[86]

One thorn in Big Tim's side was the Second Assembly District, the same area as the old Fourth Ward along the East River. Unlike most other areas south of 14th Street this was still a solidly Irish community, under the control of Paddy Divver, saloonkeeper and former magistrate. The district was a stable slum area, and Paddy was more responsive to family and church sentiment than to the gangster's desire for additional houses of prostitution. In 1901, Big Tim put up Tom Foley, a downtown saloon operator, to contest Paddy's leadership post. Under the slogan "Don't vote the Red Lights into the Old Fourth Ward," Paddy fought back, appealing to his friend Croker, but Sullivan warned the boss that he would brook no interference, and any help from Croker had to be covert.

On the night before the election, members of Paul Kelly's gang crossed over from the Five Points and formed a human chain around each polling place. The move was not unexpected, and as the polls opened, husky Irish lads charged the line. All day the battles raged. Generally, the Irish had the advantage of size, but the Italians had blackjacks and greater organization. Among the interested spectators were Devery's police, most of them Irish, who watched passively as their kinsmen were slugged to the ground by the despised "dagos." The Second District passed to Tom Foley.[87] Having won the leadership against the will of the better element of the district, Foley was careful

---

* The allies, known as "the Sullivans," included among others his two half-brothers and his first cousin, "Little" Tim Sullivan, president of the Board of Aldermen.

** Devery and Farrell were owners of the New York Highlanders baseball team, later the Yankees; in 1915 they sold it to Colonel Jacob Ruppert.

to run clean candidates for office, and in the next election he brought forth a young man named Al Smith to run successfully for the State Assembly.

In 1899–1900 another state investigating commission, under Assemblyman Robert Mazet with Frank Moss as counsel, conducted a Lexow-type probe which made the same findings as the original. This time even Croker had to testify, with embarrassing results.* As a result, the Republican Legislature put the police department under control of a single commissioner appointed to a five-year term by the mayor and removable by him or the governor. Any hopes that the revised system would eliminate Devery were dashed, however, when the new commissioner, Colonel Michael Murphy, another Irish revolutionary, appointed him as his first deputy. The excesses of Sullivan and Devery thus paved the way for the election of another fusion mayor, the wealthy Seth Low, businessman president of Columbia University, and a reform district attorney, William Travers Jerome.

Jerome (first cousin of Jenny Jerome, mother of Winston Churchill) was a superb orator and showman. His family was close to Tammany, and he had received appointment as an assistant district attorney thru Dick Croker, but he had tired of the dull routine and linked up with the reform movement as an assistant to Goff in the Lexow investigation. As a reward he was given a minor judgeship, where he chafed at the success of Theodore Roosevelt, who had done nothing in the Parkhurst Crusade. Jerome noted TR's successful exploitation of the anticorruption issue and his concurrent failure through overrigid enforcement of Sunday closings. Jerome proposed to go after the big boys, not the corner saloon. He began his activity by summoning police captains into his court and interrogating them about gambling and prostitution. Next, he personally led raiding parties against gambling joints, relying on the dubious legality of John Doe warrants, that is, warrants which did not describe specific persons. With an ax in his hand and a Bible in his pocket, Jerome, with his crew, would chop down the door of a gambling joint to gain entrance. Inside, a few shots would be fired, after which the judge would leap on a crap table, produce his Bible, swear the witnesses, and hold court.[89] In effect, Jerome reverted to the old police magistrate tactics of the Fieldings. How defendants could receive a fair trial from the man who was arresting them did not trouble Jerome, though it did occur to others.

The election campaign was, in fact, a contest between Jerome and Devery, with Devery giving as good as he got. Low and the Tammany ticket were ignored. When Jerome charged corruption, Devery responded by questioning Jerome's sanity. If Devery had been one to rely on

---

* Moss got Croker to admit that he was "always working for my pocket."[88]

detectives, he might have had more juicy items, since Jerome was a bit of a drinker and kept a mistress, but these facts would not be made known until some years later when the reformers themselves tired of him and spread the word. With Low's inauguration in January 1902, the Devery regime ended and Dick Croker retired.* His successor, "Boss" Charles Murphy, was equally unable to control the Sullivans.

Devery, the loyal Tammanyite, ran for district leader. To his great surprise, the party opposed him. Like the other king of police corruption, Clubber Williams, Devery found out that once he was out of power the machine had no use for him. It even sent Monk Eastman's gunmen into his district, where twenty of them piled on a man they mistook for Devery. The ex-chief knew how to deal with their type, and, amidst a few broken heads, he won the election. However, Boss Murphy refused to recognize the results. Furious, Devery denounced Murphy as a dope user, brothel owner, and grafter. Only reformers like Lincoln Steffens and Carrie Nation felt sorry for Devery and lent their endorsement.[90]

While a single-commissioner plan was expected to produce strong central control over the police department, it did not work out that way. No New York City police commissioner ever survived a change of administration. As one commissioner remarked, "commissioners are mere birds of passage: they fly so fast and remain on the perilous perch for so short a time that their species can hardly be determined."[91] Thus the pattern of police control in the twentieth century was quite different from that in the nineteenth. In the nineteenth century, actual power was shared among the Tammany ward bosses but remained continuous, so that figurehead chiefs such as George Matsell (1845–1857), Walling (1874–1885), and Murray (1885–1892) enjoyed relatively long tenure. The twentieth century saw the centralization of power, but with such rapid rotation of administrators it could hardly be exercised.** Contrary to expectation it became more difficult to determine who ran the New York City Police Department. In 1890, a citizen with a grievance could see the ward boss or precinct commander and be reasonably assured he was directing his complaint to the right source. In later years, many pockets of power existed and sometimes it appeared as though no one controlled the cops.

Though administrative arrangements changed, the key problem of

---

* After his political fall, he suffered a number of tribulations. One son died in an auto accident, another from drug overdose. His wife sued him, and after her death so did his children. In 1914, at seventy-one, he married a twenty-three-year-old circus performer. Even the British aristocracy shunned him, and Croker switched to the cause of Irish freedom. When he died, the IRA mounted a guard of honor at the funeral.

** In the seventy-seven years of its operation to date, the system has produced thirty-two commissioners, an average of one every 2 1/2 years. During one decade, 1965–1974, there were six incumbents.

the department, the unending conflict over morality and power, did not. This necessitated varying approaches to administration. As the new century began, two conflicting philosophies emerged in the leadership of the police-politics-vice alliance. Croker and his successor Boss Murphy favored discretion, particularly in the Tenderloin (now in the process of moving to the area from 42nd to 52nd, along Broadway). For them, the ideal vice resort was Canfield's, a plush gambling joint next door to Delmonico's, run by gentleman gambler Richard Canfield. Its clientele included many of the wealthiest and most prominent people in New York City. Canfield himself, who posed as a Harvard graduate, was a prominent art connoisseur and friend of artists such as James McNeill Whistler. His establishment operated quietly and paid off graft handsomely. Thus the "Canfield crowd," as the gentlemen gamblers of Broadway were called, were rarely raided by the police.[92]

On the other hand, politicians like Sullivan and Foley were sponsors for Tenderloin dives and for hoodlums like Kelly and Eastman. Their ideal place was Big Tim's Hesper Club, where the East Side gamblers hung out. A contemporary account described a St. Patrick's Day celebration at the Hesper:

> The streets of the Tenderloin lie vacant of its women; the eyes of the city detective force are focused on the great dancing hall—stuffed to the doors with painted women and lean faced men. In the center box . . . sits the "Big Feller." . . . Around him sit the gathering of his business and political lieutenants . . . he leads through the happy mazes of the grand march a thousand pimps and prostitutes to the blatant cry of the band "Sullivan, Sullivan, a damn fine Irish man!"[93]

The kind of police favored by Boss Murphy and the Canfield crowd were semipolitical bureaucrats like Byrnes and Schmittberger—cops who developed skill in the technical side of their work whether investigation or patrol, catered to the demands of the elite, and if they took graft did it in a quiet, gentlemanly way from other gentlemen, not from every loudmouth gambler or madam likely to squeal to an investigating commission. In contrast, wholly political cops like Devery and Williams cared little for the technical aspects of their job—the badge was a license for graft, the club a tool to enforce discipline. Their political allies, the Sullivans, felt that when they had the votes there was no need to bow before a bunch of "Goo Goos" (good-government reformers) whose own morality, personal and public, the Sullivans considered below that of district leaders, many of whom did not smoke or drink. Nor, this line of thought continued, did the Tammany bosses work young children in sweatshops or cheat widows and orphans as they supposed the insurance companies did.

On the reform side of the fence, the great vice crusader William Travers Jerome, as district attorney, was embarassed by the existence of Canfield's gambling joint. Though the place was reportedly closed, the press did not believe it and throughout Jerome's first year in office demanded action. The new DA found it easier to expose than to suppress vice, and despite his brave words, he was not eager to tangle with the Canfield crowd. But Jerome was to be a victim of his own creation. As a judge and investigator, he had cooperated with the Parkhurst type of civic reform groups. However, such organizations relied on private detectives who were often disreputable.* In December 1902, a private detective employed by the Citizen's Union, another Parkhurst-type reform group, announced that he had secured evidence against Canfield's by gaining entrance in the guise of a wealthy Arab potentate. Jerome reluctantly procured a warrant and, assisted by Deputy Police Commissioner Alexander Piper of Seth Low's temporarily reformed police department, led a surprise raid. Unfortunately, no gambling was found in progress despite the fact that the raiding party smashed through doors and walls causing considerable damage. Instead, they found Canfield and his attorneys waiting patiently for them. Eventually, the detective admitted perjury and was sentenced to a year in Sing Sing. Finally, after two years of plea bargaining and threats to subpoena wealthy patrons, Canfield accepted a minimum fine and retired with 12 million dollars, while the Canfield crowd continued relatively unmolested.[95]

The raid illustrated the problems of controlling illicit activities. Any individual could hire private detectives and expose vice in order to discredit even honest officials. There was a solution, however; the police could adopt a policy of strict adherence to the law. As Brooklyn Supreme Court Justice William Gaynor declared, in overturning Judge Goff's conviction of one of Devery's collectors for failing to detect and arrest the keeper of a house of ill fame:

> [The charge] contains such empty accusations as that the defendant did not "repress" or "suppress" the said house. What this means I do not know. . . . The law does not commit the supreme folly of making them the custodians or guardians of the private morals of the community. . . . So long as the house on my block is so decorous and orderly in the windows

---

* For example, Sidney Conkling, who worked for Parkhurst's Society for the Prevention of Crime. Prior to his employment with the Society, Sidney had been dismissed from the police department, fire department, and parks department. Naturally, his standing as a witness was somewhat dubious, and defense attorneys were quick to discredit him. In one instance Sidney was cross-examined as follows: "Have you ever been arrested?" "Yes twice." "What for?" "The *Sun* said that I discharged a revolver one night, killing one man, wounding another, and wounding a horse, all at one shot. That's what the *Sun* said I did."[94]

and on the stoops that I am not able to see a single thing wrong with it I am willing to go by and leave it alone and I want the police to do the same.[96]

Later in an article he expanded:

If an officer should without a warrant enter the residence of that Judge of the Court of General Sessions of the Peace of the County of New York who is called by the ancient name of Recorder [Goff] . . . and say "I suspect this is a house of ill-fame, or a gambling-house, and am going to search it," and should search it by force, the dangerous lawlessness of his act, not merely against an individual and the public peace, but against free government, would be manifest to all, and would be loudly denounced. And yet such acts committed against the influential and the great would be no more lawless, and not half so dangerous to the endurance of free government, as when committed generally, or against the humble, the weak and the unfortunate, who should be the first to receive the good-will and protection of government. To say that a "suspicious" or "bad" place should be entered and searched without a warrant, would be to beg the whole question. Who is to say that it is suspicious or bad, whether it be the Recorder's house or some other house? The "law of the land" does not leave the decision of the matter to any police authority, however high, but requires that it be submitted in advance on sworn testimony showing facts, to a magistrate or court.

The principal duty of the police is to preserve the public peace and keep outward order and decency. . . . Societies and private enthusiasts for the "suppression of vice" should read history, and learn the supreme danger of trying to do all at once by the policeman's club what can be done at all only gradually by the slow moral development which comes principally from our schools and churches.

Then, turning to the raid on Canfield's:

All accounts agree as to the particulars of it. . . . The house invaded was said to be a place of private gaming. A large posse of policemen suddenly surrounded it and violently attacked it. They smashed in a window by means of some heavy weapon, and entered pell mell by the breach, thus made, some of them flourishing revolvers and others armed with axes. After entering, the same course of lawless violence was continued. They had a search warrant from a magistrate, but did not act under it in getting in. . . .

The "raid" as it is aptly called (for a lawless word best describes a lawless act), was according to all accounts, planned and led by the District Attorney of New York County [Jerome] in person—the chief officer elected by the people to guard their rights and liberties, and maintain law and order in the community; but this seems quite incredible. . . .

There seems also to be a considerable number of persons whose vague understanding is, that the prohibitions under Anglo-Saxon law and tradition against arrests and house invasions without warrants, and which are expressed in our laws and fundamental instruments of government everywhere, in this country, are meant only for the protection of "good" people, with whom they of course class themselves; and that therefore they need not trouble themselves about such things. They do not seem to understand that it is not for the prosecuting officers or the police to determine that a given individual is guilty. Some also seem to think that such prohibitions may be suspended when we have a "good" District Attorney or a "good" Commissioner of Police in office. They do not seem to realize that what "good" police officials and prosecuting officers assume to do will be done by their "bad" successors. . . .

When a prosecuting attorney, or a police official, says, "I can't detect crime, I can't discover gamblers or wayward women, in their privacy, by keeping within the law," the emphatic answer of the law is, "Then don't."[97]

Despite such advice, however, a policy of legality was almost impossible to implement. Even Dick Croker and Chief Walling were shocked at the open way in which prostitutes operated in London, since the police could not make arrests except upon a citizen's complaint that he had been solicited. Both proudly declared that such a thing could not happen in New York, where streetwalkers were shoved around by cops like Charley Becker. Walling, like many other American observers, was somewhat selective in his observations. After his ouster from office he was very antipolitician and pointed out how a New York ward heeler, angry because a police officer temporarily blocked his carriage during a parade, struck the officer and then had him transferred as a punishment. He contrasted this with London, where an aristocratic captain of the Coldstream Guards had behaved in a similar fashion and as a result was sentenced to jail despite a plea to the Queen.[98] Of course, Walling failed to connect the American police handling of prostitutes and the assault on the policeman as parallel examples. Cops who could illegally manhandle a prostitute were establishing a climate in which they, in turn, could be brutalized by politicians.

The dilemma posed by the vice problem made it necessary for cops to choose an individual course. For them, there was no such thing as "clean," or "honest," graft. A Tammany leader could accept legal fees, insurance business, and stock market tips, all of which were euphemistically described as "conflicts of interests," but a detective had no similar alibi. Cops who chose not to take graft had to immerse themselves in areas of policing where they did not need to deal with vice—quiet precincts or special units such as the homicide squad—and ignore any corruption they saw. To be a squealer in a predominantly Irish police force was a fate worse than death. As one commissioner remarked in 1906:

Not long ago I was talking to an otherwise thoroughly honest and up-right policeman and I said to him: "Now suppose you knew a man in your precinct was a crook and taking bribes; yes, suppose you caught him at it. I know that you yourself would not take a bribe, not only from what I see of you but from what I hear from others; but under these circumstances would you tell on him?"

"Commisioner," he said, "I wasn't born in Ireland, but my father and mother were, and thank God! none of my name were ever informers either in the old country or in this. I would be ashamed to look my children in the face if I turned informer." ... My father was 90 years of age when he died and he used to tell us children of the fate that followed informers in Ireland—the devil would sometimes claim their bodies even before they got to the graveyard and to the tenth generation ill-luck misfortune and a curse went with them." Did you ever hear of any good happening to a policeman who informed? "Show me a 'squealor' ... and if you will let me tell you, I will show you a fella who had a heart of a coward and a disgrace to the police."[99]

Arthur Carey, a detective trained under Byrnes, made a career in homicide work, serving intermittently in the squad from 1907 to 1928, becoming its head, and rising to inspector. Carey's memoirs, largely dealing with major murder cases, decry the periodic "shake-ups," i.e., vice scandals, when it was necessary for him to leave headquarters and go to a Brooklyn precinct. While he is never explicit, throughout is the plaintive theme "Let me alone to investigate murders, I don't want to know about vice."[100] Other cops felt gambling of the Canfield variety did no harm and accepted the fiction of "clean" money from "right guys" but would never take "dirty" money from whores, drug peddlers, or gunmen. For the more political cops life was much simpler. All of their actions were based on self-interest, the essence of policing was common sense, not a technical skill to be acquired, and the job existed as either a sinecure for the lazy or a license to steal.

Thus in the first decades of the twentieth century many contradictory elements were present in the New York City Police Department. Fusion mayors like Low or reform DAs such as Jerome would launch short-lived clean-up campaigns followed by a return to Tammany mayors like George B. McClellan, Jr. (1904–1909). Between 1901 and 1914 nine men served as police commissioner, coming from such diverse fields as law, politics, and the military. The military was especially popular, in line with British practices of the time; Mayor Robert Van Wyck utilized Colonel Murphy; Mayor Low, General Francis Green and Colonel John Partidge; and Mayor McClellan, General Theodore Bingham.

As in London, the department also employed deputy commissioners from civil life. In 1907, General Bingham appointed Arthur Woods, a former English instructor at Groton, to head the Detective Bureau. Today such an appointment would seem ludicrous, but at the time the requirements of high command were beyond the poorly educated career force, many of whom could barely read or write. And in fact the first police commissioner to be both a career officer *and* a college graduate was not appointed until 1955. Woods, born in Boston in 1870, was from a solid WASP background. After graduation from Harvard and post-graduate work at German universities, he settled down for ten years at Groton, where he taught Teddy Roosevelt's sons. Through this connection he became a *New York Sun* reporter and was introduced to Bingham, Roosevelt's former military aide. Realizing his lack of detective knowledge, Woods made a quick trip to study European departments and upon his return introduced the concept of specialized squads.

Another young civilian who became active in police administration was Raymond Fosdick, brother of the Reverend Harry Emerson Fosdick and protégé of Princeton President Woodrow Wilson. Mayor McClellan, son of the Union Army general and 1864 Democratic presidential candidate, drew away from Tammany in the later stages of his administration and established an investigating arm of city government, the Bureau of Accounts, headed by ambitious young John Purroy Mitchell, grandson of an Irish revolutionary leader. In 1905, the mayor received an honorary degree at the Princeton commencement. Fosdick, the class orator, had been much impressed by Jacob Riis's *How the Other Half Lives*, and, in the fashion of youth, chose to deliver a speech on the wickedness of the older generation and the corruption of society, singling out New York City government as an example. Instead of being angry, McClellan told Fosdick to come and see him.[101] In 1907 he did and became a city investigator under Mitchell, assisting in probes which caused the removal of the borough presidents of Manhattan and the Bronx.

Despite the goings on at City Hall, the police department at the precinct level was still responsive to the Sullivans, though fear of the reformers was to have repercussions even in the bad lands south of 14th Street. In September 1903, the Kelly and Eastman gangs fought a gun battle on the lower East Side in which three men were killed and seven wounded before the reserves from several precincts managed to clear the streets, arresting Eastman and twenty others. Compared to the Dead Rabbit–Bowery Boys riot of 1857, the Kelly-Eastman affair was relatively tame, lasting only two hours instead of two days, and no militia was required. Nevertheless, Inspector Schmittberger and his men were sent into the area to break gangster heads,[102] and word went out from the politicians that if there was a repeat of the incident, protection would be permanently withdrawn and the police strong-arm squads turned loose with a vengeance.[103]

In the half century since the Dead Rabbits fought the Bowery Boys the police had grown stronger, since the cops had what the hoodlums did not, the legal right to use deadly force. Since 1857 the cops had been armed. In 1911, gangsters were even further inconvenienced by the State Legislature's enacting Big Tim's bill to ban the carrying of concealed weapons. A hoodlum who violated the "Sullivan" law by carrying a gun faced seven years in prison. Of course, as with any other law, its enforcement depended on the cops. Thus any gangster on the outs with politicians or police was well advised not to carry a gun. Indeed, some hoods who found themselves in such a position took to wearing pocketless suits, lest someone drop a gun on them.[104]

In the early years of the century the politicians like Big Tim controlled the cops, who in turn controlled organized crime. By the Prohibition era, top gangsters would amass so much wealth and so many ties to respectables that the arrangement would be broken, but in 1903 the gangs were low man on the political-police-gangster totem pole and the Eastmans and Kellys knew it. Thus they reverted to the dueling code, and it was arranged for the two leaders to fight bare-knuckled at a private location. They did, to a draw, and the stalemate continued.[105] Eventually Tom Foley patched up a truce, but both gang chieftans were shortly to succumb.

Monk Eastman's downfall came about ludicrously from the very fact that he was half ganglord and half street-corner tough. One night in February 1904, while cruising through midtown Manhattan, he observed an obviously affluent young man drunkenly lurching along while being tailed by two burly characters who Monk assumed were about to rob the sucker. Never one to pass up an opportunity, Eastman decided to strike first. In the next generation no mob boss would have dreamed of such a caper—indeed, many might have offered an escort to the young man. Alas for Monk, he was right about the younger man, wrong about the older ones, who turned out to be Pinkerton detectives assigned by a wealthy family to guard their roaming offspring. The detectives opened fire as they pursued Monk, who ran straight into a policeman and was clubbed unconscious with a nightstick.[106] When he woke up he was in the 30th Street precinct charged with robbery. True to their word, the politicians withdrew protection, and Monk spent the next five years in Sing Sing. In 1912, he went back to prison for drug dealing. Later, though past forty, he enlisted for World War I. At his physical the doctor looking at his lead-filled body asked what wars he had been in. "A lot of little wars around New York," Monk replied. A genuine hero at the front, on his return to New York he received a pardon from Governor Al Smith. But it was too late; he could not muster the skills required for organized crime in the postwar era and was shot to death in a dispute with a federal agent who allegedly had personal dealings with Monk.[107]

As for Paul Kelly, in 1905 a man was shot to death in his saloon, dying under a large picture of Big Tim Sullivan. Though charged with murder, Kelly was acquitted, but afterward withdrew from open activity in the Five Points in favor of labor organizing, in which he rose to vice president of the International Longshoreman's Union.[108]

The departure of Eastman and Kelly meant fewer headlines, but the shooting continued on the East Side.

Civil Rights and Strong-arms

In 1909, Judge Gaynor was a strong prospect for mayor. Not so coincidentally, he took the opportunity to write Commissioner Bingham regarding a young Brooklyn boy, George Duffy, who had been picked up, photographed, and charged with disorderly conduct as part of a routine drive against street-corner toughs. Bingham refused Gaynor's request that Duffy's photo and records be destroyed, and the judge complained publicly to Mayor McClellan; if only he "had the Power," he said, cops would not abuse citizens' rights.* Bingham, whom Gaynor referred to as "the White House butler," refused to back down, and McClellan dismissed him. When Bingham departed, Deputy Commissioner Woods resigned in protest.[109] Tammany supported Gaynor for mayor against William Randolph Hearst and he was elected. John Mitchell became president of the Board of Aldermen, and Fosdick succeeded him as commissioner of accounts.

The new administration was eagerly awaited by many people. As one writer observed, "We shall see whether an aggressive campaign against the forces of evil can be waged within the Constitution."[110] Gaynor's first act was to invite citizens to bring to him personally their complaints about the cops. One group who did were Owney "the Killer" Madden and his pals in the Gophers gang of Hell's Kitchen, who were clubbed in a skirmish with the police there, after which Gaynor issued an order forbidding promiscuous use of clubs. He also put into practice his policy of legality regarding vice raids and abolished the police rogues' gallery and lineups.[111]

The new mayor was what might be termed an old-fashioned American who believed in a literal interpretation of the Bill of Rights. Indeed, as a judge Gaynor had even declared police regulation of traffic unconstitutional, although the higher courts reversed him. To Gaynor the greatest threat to civil liberties came from overzealous reformers such as Parkhurst and Jerome. When millionaire Jay Schifflein, the financial angel of reform, followed his usual practice of providing unsolicited advice to mayors on how to run the city, Gaynor did not fall on his knees,

---

* Despite Gaynor's help, young Duffy continued his misadventures and eventually was sent to prison.

but curtly wrote, "I have no desire to hear from you on any subject now or in the future."[112]

While Gaynor apparently acted out of the purest libertarian motives, the result of his orders was a slackening of police efforts against the downtown gangsters, who now began to move into the Tenderloin—taking advantage of the new availability of autos to branch out. The influx of East Side hoodlums into their preserves angered the Canfield crowd, and they blamed Big Tim and his "Bowery methods" of allowing anyone to operate who could pay off.[113] But even Big Tim became alarmed at the boldness of the gangsters. He refused to go near the Hesper Club, and he hurriedly rammed his antigun law through the Legislature.

Within a few months of his inauguration Gaynor was under heavy attack led by the usual personal vituperation of the Hearst press, and in September 1910 he was shot by a city employee who had been discharged as a result of a probe by Fosdick's bureau.* The bullet in Gaynor's head could not be removed, and the injury affected both his health and, in the opinion of many, his grip on city affairs.

In 1911 Gaynor, having already gone through two police commissioners, moved thirty-four-year-old Rhinelander Waldo from fire commissioner to the police department. Waldo, a member of an old family well ensconced in the social register, was a West Pointer and had served in the Philippines. In 1906 General Bingham had made him a deputy commissioner. Waldo was an apparently well-meaning, naive individual whom cartoonists of the time liked to portray in a Boy Scout uniform. But whatever his other qualifications, Waldo knew about strong-arm squads, forming three of them, each under a lieutenant. One of the new squad commanders was a veteran clean-up man, "Honest" Dan Costigan; another was Charley Becker, a tough cop whom Waldo, as deputy commissioner, had used for "Internal Affairs" or "shoefly" work (i.e., spying on other cops). In this capacity, Becker's most notable catch was Inspector Schmittberger, who was brought before the police trial board on charges of corruption. However, he was acquitted, to the congratulations of reformers like Goff.[115]

Charley Becker had come to New York from upstate Sullivan County to work as a baker, then as a Bowery saloon bouncer, noted for his pugilistic skills. In 1893 he joined the police department and became a precinct detective. Becker's public and private lives had their ups and downs. His first wife died shortly after his marriage, and his second divorced him. (She later married his brother, also a policeman.) In 1896

---

* In the aftermath the Hearst press was widely criticized, since it had previously urged the shooting of President McKinley and a California prosecutor, after which both were in fact shot (see pages 231, 267), though no real proof was found that the mayor's assailant had been influenced by reading the Hearst paper.[114]

occurred the contretemps with Stephen Crane, and in the same year Becker and his partner accidentally killed a bystander while shooting at a burglar. The incident was made worse when they attempted to claim that the bystander was a burglar. When the investigation disproved the claim, Becker was suspended but not fired. He was also embarrassed when a man he had saved from drowning alleged that Becker had paid him to stage the incident. In 1903 he was promoted to sergeant and in 1907 to lieutenant, and luck finally smiled on Becker's personal life with his marriage to Helen Lynch, a public school teacher of handicapped children. The burly Broadway tough guy and the schoolteacher were by all accounts a devoted couple whose marriage was a continuous love affair.[116]

As commander of a strong-arm squad, Becker branched out to gambling raids, his usual procedure being to chop up the premises and rough up the dealers. Of course, gamblers who had the political OK and paid off were not molested. As one city official characterized the operation, "It was money or the ax."[117] In the spring of 1912 Becker was on top of the world. The graft was good, his marriage was a storybook tale, he hobnobbed with wealthy people who allowed him the use of a chauffeured limousine, and his superiors, Gaynor and Waldo, trusted him. Indeed so trusting were they that when they received letters detailing Becker's graft, they forwarded them to him for investigation. A typical letter read:

> Dear Sir:
>
> I would like to let you know that a gambling house is run wide open under the protection of Jack Rose, Becker's collector, No. 145 West 45th Street, run by Herman Rosenthal.

It was quite possible that many such letters came from cops or rival gamblers. For example, the following:

> Dear Sir:
>
> At no 2334, 8th Avenue, between 125th and 126th Streets, over a barber shop, there is a crap and stuss game running for some time. I wrote to you about this place and begged of you to close it up, but as yet nothing has been done to my sorrow. Can you close this place up? If not, I will make it my business to have a society close it up. My son informs me that a man they call Doty claims to have paid your Inspector (Sweeney) the sum of $500.00 for protection. Now show me, by your actions, how far that protection goes. I will not write you any more, but will wait developments.
>
> A WOMAN[118]

Obviously "A Woman" was a remarkably knowledgeable lady. By presentation of the letters to the accused, the writer could often be identified and taken care of by threats or concessions. In the context of later events, such letters tend to confirm that Becker was much disliked by the police-politics-crime alliance.

Becker had a press agent and a clique of reporters who followed him around, and one day his civilian public relations man killed an unarmed faro dealer and was indicted for murder. More trouble came when the gambler mentioned in the complaining letter, Herman Rosenthal, fell out with the police and began speaking openly of payoffs to Becker. He even threatened that if the pressure did not cease, he was going to talk to the district attorney. Letters were one thing, but talking to the DA was serious business.

Herman Rosenthal, a former president of the Hesper Club, did in fact talk to Herbert Bayard Swope, star reporter and later managing editor of Pulitzer's *New York World*. Swope then referred the case to District Attorney Charles Whitman, and in July 1912 Rosenthal gave a statement detailing his charge against Becker. Then, on the night of July 15, the gambler was lured to a hotel in midtown Manhattan (owned by Big Tim Sullivan). Rosenthal's presence was not unnoticed, and a number of people later testified to a feeling of impending doom. At 1:50 A.M., he was called outside, where, despite the presence of nearby police officers, he was shot to death from an automobile with several men in it which sped away.[119] The crime was an immediate sensation and in the center was the district attorney, Charles Whitman, whose witness now was dead.

Whitman, born in Connecticut in 1868, was the son of a Congregationalist minister. A Phi Beta Kappa from Amherst, he worked his way through New York University Law School. His law practice was at first slim, and he spent his time defending minor criminals in Manhattan. It was clearly unsuitable for a moralistic Yankee to be operating before Tammany magistrates, and Whitman's stubborn arrogance did not help. He almost always lost his case but garnered a reputation as a gadfly. When Seth Low was elected mayor, he appointed Whitman an assistant corporation counsel. Then he became a city magistrate. Like Jerome, instead of waiting for cases, Whitman roamed the street at night raiding after-hours saloons. In 1906 he raided fashionable Healy's for serving drinks beyond closing time, although according to observers the magistrate himself appeared to have drunk too much. At forty he married a social worker who was later vice president of the Daughters of the American Revolution (DAR).[120]

By 1909, the reformers had tired of District Attorney Jerome. Both Hearst and Pulitzer combined to attack him for his failure to prosecute Wall Street figures with the same zeal he displayed toward Tammany bosses or Harry K. Thaw. Jerome's efforts against Thaw, the slayer of architect Stanford White, had been so personally vindictive that even Parkhurst had rebuked him. When Jerome publicly admitted he had shaken dice for drinks, the press was able to destroy his moralistic image, and his career was permanently finished. The reformers then turned to Charles Whitman as their new hope, and in 1910 he took office as district attorney.

Upon assuming the prosecutor's post, Whitman acquired Frank Moss as his assistant, but even with the help of the veteran corruption fighter he was at a loss as to how to proceed. The police-crime-political alliance was a closed fraternity, nor was Whitman able to create public demand for a Lexow-type investigation, since newspapers such as the *World* were supporting the Gaynor administration. Whitman even failed to successfully prosecute the proprietors of the Triangle Shirtwaist factory, where a fire killed 146 people, many of whom had been locked in by management. Thus Rosenthal was a godsend because he provided inside information and juicy publicity, although Whitman, now busy social-climbing at Newport with the Belmonts and Vanderbilts and being put up for the right clubs by police commissioner Waldo, was slow to recognize the value. It was Swope who laid out the plan to go after police corruption for the dubious Whitman, who finally agreed when promised "all the help in the *World*."[121]

Whitman was also persuaded by the recent careers of two New York Republicans. Theodore Roosevelt, after gaining good publicity as police commissioner (and better as a war hero), had been elected governor in 1898, and a few years later was in the White House. Charles Evans Hughes, counsel for a state investigating commission which had conducted a headline-making probe of the insurance industry, had been elected governor shortly afterward in 1906, and now, on the U.S. Supreme Court, was much discussed as a presidential prospect. In contrast, the Republican candidate in the recent gubernatorial election of 1910, United States Attorney Henry Stimson, who had run a very circumspect office, refusing to play for the headlines, had been rejected by the voters in favor of a Tammany hack.

Supreme Court Justice Felix Frankfurter, then a young assistant to Stimson, contrasted his boss to Whitman. Stimson rejected even Theodore Roosevelt's request to speed up a certain investigation:

> I'll never forget the excitement in me to hear Mr. Stimson tell the President of the United States, "This is what I'm going to do. If you don't like it, you can do what you want to do."
>
> For contrast, there was a fellow in New York who afterwards became governor named Charles S. Whitman. He was the antithesis to Stimson. He was a politically minded district attorney—one of the great curses of America. There was a Triangle fire—that awful holocaust in which hun-

dreds of young women lost their lives. . . . Whitman called in the head of the homicide division and said, "What's happening in the Triangle case?"

This was only a few days after it happened. "Well, boss, we're not finished with the investigation, but very soon we'll have the case before the grand jury." "Well, get an indictment! We can always *nol pros* it. Here, look at it!" and he held up an editorial in the Hearst *New York American*. "You go and get an indictment. We can *nol pros* it if we can't maintain it. You can always *nol pros*."

Whitman was getting indictments because Hearst's *American* was shouting blue murder![122]

Whitman proceeded to conduct a very open "secret" investigation of the Rosenthal slaying, utilizing the grand jury leak as his principal public relations device. Whitman, like Becker, had his coterie of press supporters, but where Becker had low-status reporters such as Bat Masterson (of Dodge City fame), sports editor of the *Telegram*, Whitman had lords of the media like war correspondent Richard Harding Davis. Becker also had the dubious benefit of public support from Clubber Williams, now past seventy and frequently drunk.

Taking a leaf from Goff, Whitman took preliminary depositions from his witnesses and was able to release their testimony before it was time for them to take the stand. He was also helped by $200,000 from private business sources, led by Jay Schifflein, which permitted him to hire the William Burns Detective Agency to assist his investigation. Becker, an obvious suspect, denied all knowledge of the Rosenthal murder, though within a few weeks several gamblers had confessed to arranging the crime on his instructions. They and the alleged trigger men, four young hoodlums known as "Gyp the Blood," "Whitey Lewis," "Lefty Louie," and "Dago Frank," were jailed, and on July 29 Becker himself was indicted. Now the case became an international sensation, and the entire police–politics–organized crime alliance shook. Still another investigating committee under Alderman Henry Curran began looking into the police department.[123]

Waldo and Gaynor reacted with fury to the criticism. The commissioner, who had been summoned back from a police chiefs' convention where he was presenting a paper on "How to Wipe Out Police Graft," sued three newspapers for a total of $750,000, while Gaynor, in reference to the fact that most of the defendants (excepting only Becker and Dago Frank) were Jewish, characterized the whole thing as the work of "degenerate foreigners." Both actions only increased the criticism. Even more unwisely, the erractic Gaynor ordered a crackdown on the ritzy Broadway spots, so that the Tenderloin was treated to the spectacle of the strong-arm squads throwing society folks in evening dress headfirst into the street. This was not stopped until Whitman and Richard

Harding Davis, drinking after hours in Healy's, led a society "mob" in mass resistance and the cops backed off.[124]

The guilt or innocence of Becker is still unsettled. He admitted to being a grafter, but the circumstances of the murder were so incredible as to raise serious question of a possible frame-up. First, according to the prosecution, Becker had organized the murder through half a dozen gamblers, who then hired four hit men. Thus at least ten people were involved. Second, the car used had belonged to the former heavyweight boxing champion John L. Sullivan, and after him a well-known gangland figure who had survived an ambush in which the car had been shot up, so that the getaway vehicle was a Broadway landmark, particularly in a time when cars were still a novelty. Third, the murder took place in Times Square on a hot summer's night with many witnesses present, and several people were able to take down the car license number, which was immediately traced. Further, many of the witnesses expected the murder, and one was even able to do a classic Runyonesque bit by walking up to the dying man and saying, "Hello Herman, goodbye Herman."[125] One would expect that an experienced detective like Becker would not have involved half the underworld, used an easily identifiable getaway vehicle, or had the act carried out in such public circumstances.

The trial was something less than a model of justice. The judge was none other than John Goff, the Lexow counsel whose career on the bench had caused one lawyer to characterize him as "the cruelest, most sadistic judge we have had in New York in this century." Another lawyer said, "He had the most odious vice which is found in human nature, a delight in misery merely as misery."[126] The assistant prosecutor was Goff's old Lexow sidekick Frank Moss. Goff consistently ruled for the prosecution and against the defense. Though Becker was convicted, the Court of Appeals reversed the verdict, citing Judge Goff's highly prejudicial behavior. A second trial under the very political though more cautious Judge Samuel Seabury produced a similar verdict, and Becker was sentenced to death. While his lawyers appealed, he was removed to the deathhouse in Sing Sing.

Throughout 1913–14 the case remained in the headlines. Mayor Gaynor died in the midst of a reelection campaign. The Curran Committee uncovered more graft in the police department, leading to the conviction of a captain and four inspectors, but Curran's investigation lacked the drama of the Becker case and did not greatly advance his career.

In November 1913, a fusion party elected John Mitchell as mayor. A year later, District Attorney Whitman was elected governor of New York. In 1915 the last of Becker's appeals was turned down and a date for execution was set. There was but one hope for his life—a commutation of sentence by the governor, now Charles Whitman, who, to say the least, was an interested party in the case. In a personal interview with the governor, Mrs. Becker pleaded on her knees, but it was to no avail and on July 30, 1915, the execution was carried out.* Possibly Whitman felt it was his duty not to yield, or perhaps he feared the future, since a live Becker and his supporters would never cease to deny the murder charge and hound Charles Whitman. Mrs. Becker purchased a headstone saying "Charles Becker ... murdered July 30, 1915, by Governor Whitman," but was persuaded that the governor would prosecute her for criminal libel if she used it. Throughout his ordeal, Becker had the loyal support of his old friend Inspector Williams, and at the funeral the most prominent floral piece was from the Clubber, reading simply "In respect for Charlie." Becker was buried in a Bronx cemetery, where two years later both Williams and Schmittberger would join him.

Whitman was not to reach the White House. He was defeated in 1918 by Al Smith and never again held elective office, failing even in a bid for his old post as district attorney.

Through the years the debate over Becker's guilt or innocence has continued.[127] Such speculations beg the real issue. As a squad commander he had failed to stop the downtown thugs from moving in on the respectable gamblers of the Tenderloin. His fall strengthened the Canfield crowd. Symbolically, his death also was the execution of Clubber Williams and that type of reckless flamboyant cop—a vindication of both the moral reformers and the bosses like Croker and Murphy who urged restraint. Tammany did not even try to save Becker; indeed, the Murphy element helped Whitman by furnishing defense lawyers who urged the gamblers to talk, and the district attorney was careful not to go beyond the police department in his investigation. Later he blocked Frank Moss from succeeding him, further pleasing Tammany. Though they lost a couple of elections, the Murphy crowd came back.

In contrast, the Sullivan faction was hard hit. Big Tim was so mentally disturbed that he could not return to the State Senate in 1912, having to settle for a seat in Congress.** However, he never went to Washington. Committed to a private asylum, he escaped from his keepers, was run over by a train, and lay in Bellevue morgue for ten days until a policeman recognized him and went screaming through the wards, "It's Big Tim! Lord God, it's Big Tim!" The king was dead and the wise guys wondered how accidental it was.[129]

Sullivan's successor as Tammany chief of Lower Manhattan, Tom

---

* Becker also won the backing of Sing Sing Warden Thomas Mott Osborne, a wealthy prison reformer. Shortly after the execution, Osborne himself was ousted by Whitman and tried on charges of homosexual relations with the prisoners.

** Sullivan's illness was described as "a disease which threatened mental as well as physical breakdown."[128]

Foley, spent most of his time pushing the career of Al Smith. The new boss of the underworld was to be a smooth Tenderloin gambler named Arnold Rothstein, who despite his East Side origins moved in the circle of gentlemen. Herbert Bayard Swope, a Tenderloin habitué himself, had been best man at Rothstein's wedding in 1909,[130] and one of Rothstein's lieutenants, Nicky Arnstein, had married the reigning Broadway queen, Fanny Brice. It was a time and place where another Rothstein pal, jockey Tod Sloan, who had thrown the English Derby while riding the King's horse, could be made into a national hero by George M. Cohan as Little Johnnie Jones, the Yankee Doodle Dandy.

While politicians and gangsters solved their organizational problems, the police department did not. In the twenty years from Parkhurst's sermon to Rosenthal's murder, the New York City Police Department had been turned inside out several times over the moral issues the larger society was unable to solve. Some cops had gotten rich and some had been disgraced. Of course, the vast majority experienced neither fate, but all lived in a world of violence, intrigue, and uncertainty crowned by the execution of one of their superior officers. Ordinary citizens and police alike wondered whether a better system could be contrived.

Boston: Europe in America
(1854–1943)

In the spring of 1891, President Benjamin Harrison journeyed to Bennington, Vermont, to dedicate a monument to the state's war heroes. Fifteen thousand people gathered for the occasion amidst bands and pageantry. After an opening prayer by a then obscure New York clergyman, the Reverend Dr. Charles Parkhurst, Harrison delivered the ritual speech praising the sons of Vermont who fought in the Revolution and the late "War of the Rebellion," the last term being appropriate in the heartland of Yankee Republicanism. As the leader of the party the President knew well the self-image of his audience. Continuing his eulogy, he spoke of "the love for social order and respect for laws which has characterized your communities, has made them safe and commemorably abodes for young people." One young person in the audience, an eighteeen-year-old boy, looked on entranced at the majesty of the ceremony and the man in whose person reposed the glory and dignity of the United States and wondered how it felt to bear so much responsibility. Someday he would know. Twenty-eight years later, in another shrine of Yankeedom, the social order and respect for laws would appear threatened by those to whom its protection had been entrusted. This rebellion too would be crushed by Yankee heroes, and as a result, John Calvin Coolidge would be embarked on the road to the Presidency.[1]

NEW WORLD AND OLD

In 1913 the Bureau of Social Hygiene, a euphemistic title for an antiprostitution group funded by John D. Rockefeller, Jr., engaged Raymond Fosdick to study police methods in Europe. In the following year he published his findings under the title *European Police Systems.*[2] Fosdick was generous in his praise of English and continental forces, though, he found the militaristic German spirit not to his liking. Only twenty-nine when he undertook his study, and not particularly well versed in Old World politics, in some instances he took European official statements at face value and measured them against American realities of which he had firsthand knowledge from his service in New York City government. Thus some critics have characterized him as an "innocent abroad."[3] However, his major finding was not in dispute. In Europe police administration was a professional career. The police commissioners in cities such as London, Paris, Berlin, and Vienna were appointed by the national government and kept in office for many years. They were independent of local politics, and their forces were as tightly disciplined as the military. The contrast with America, where the top administrators changed with every political breeze and the rank and file were undisciplined and corrupt, was fundamental.

The career of the London Metropolitan Police commissioner Sir Edward Henry was typical. In 1871 he had entered the elite Indian civil service. In 1891 he was seconded to the Indian police service, modeled after the RIC, as inspector general (chief of police) in the province of Bengal. In 1901 he was made assistant commissioner of the London Metropolitan force, and in 1903 he was appointed to the commissioner's post, which he held until 1918. He was instrumental in the development of the new science of fingerprinting, which had been pioneered in India as a form of legal identification, and by the end of his tenure, the "Henry system" was the standard fingerprinting technique utilized in Europe and America.

Henry's great rival in police science was Alphonse Bertillon, chief of the Criminal Identification Bureau of the Paris police. Prior to the introduction of fingerprinting, the "Bertillon system" of anthropometry (physical measurement), developed in the 1880s, had been the principal means of identification utilized by police throughout the world. Bertillon stubbornly resisted the Henry system and was embarrassed when his police failed to solve the theft of the Mona Lisa from the Louvre despite the fact that the thief left fingerprints at the scene. Though both the offender's prints and his measurements were in Bertillon's files, the prints had not been classified in a manner to permit identification and the measurements were useless, since, as the Paris press pointed out,

"Unfortunately this discourteous thief neglected to leave his measurements at the scene of the crime."[4] *

How refreshing to Americans were police conflicts which revolved around professional matters rather than graft or brutality. How different were Henry and Bertillon from Bill Devery, Clubber Williams, and Charlie Becker. Perhaps a more astute observer would have pointed out that European police administration, divorced from local politics, was a result of certain factors not present in the United States. In the first instance, the maintenance of order, particularly in the national capital, was a serious business to which all European cabinets attached prime importance. In 1848 they all had faced revolutionary mobs which in Paris and Vienna toppled the government and in Berlin, after initial success, were finally defeated by the army. Even in London the police had required the support of the military and nearly 150,000 special constables. Thus the administration of the police was as important as that of the armed forces.

In the sprawling United States, with no single center dominating every aspect of the national life, what happened in one city or a dozen would not seal the fate of the Republic. As late as 1898 the United States did not even have an army worthy of the name because one was not really required. In Europe an effective police service was guaranteed in the great cities by imposing strict controls over local citizens, although the degree of severity differed among London, Berlin or St. Petersburg. To create a similar system in the United States was, in the light of American political theory and reality, undemocratic and unnecessary.

More fundamentally, the police system of a country is a reflection of its general political and social arrangements. In Britain, authority was much more centralized than in the United States, and moral values more clearly defined. Power resided in a cabinet representing the leadership of the majority party in Parliament, and, within very broad limits, its will was supreme. Civil servants, including judges, were expected to carry out government policy as reflected in statutory law and administrative regulations and, in turn, were shielded by the doctrine of ministerial responsibility.

Though occasionally a police sergeant or inspector would be made a scapegoat, the higher officers were generally defended even when they were in the wrong. Sir Richard Mayne had been allowed to remain in

---

* Bertillon was also embarrassed when he identified (incorrectly) certain handwriting as belonging to the defendant in the famous case involving Captain Alfred Dreyfus. The death knell of Bertillon's system was sounded in 1903 when two American convicts in the same prison, Will and William West, were found to have identical measurements.[5]

office after the disaster of the Clerkenwell Prison explosion, and Mr. Gladstone's government had repeatedly stood by Howard Vincent despite his somewhat illiberal methods. Of course, there were limits. Between 1887 and 1890, the British government gently "sacked" three commissioners. Sir Edward Henderson was retired after eighteen years because of the Trafalgar riots, General Warren after less than two years because of his imperious behavior and quarrels with the Home Secretary, and his successor James Munro after equally short tenure because he took a different position from the government over police pensions.* Generally, though, police officials who stayed within clearly defined rules were safe from political reprisals.

In Britain, too, a change of government did not mean a major change of direction, since the ruling elites, drawn from the same backgrounds, molded in the same schools, and sharing the same social and professional contacts, were largely agreed on fundamentals. The Liberals might be more willing to permit demonstrations in Trafalgar Square than the Tories, but both supported the security of dwellings from invasion without warrant, and neither saw the police as a conduit for the collection of graft.

In the United States the situation was completely different. Power was widely diffused among local, state, and federal governments and the courts, legislature, and executive, as well as a number of informal sources such as party bosses, businessmen, and media lords. Nor was the law a particularly useful guide. In the United States it was manipulated by clever attorneys or appeals to public opinion to promote one set of interests at the expense of another. In no instance was it a body of rules governing the conduct of all. Changes in party or even individual office holders often meant dramatic shifts, and the police were seen as instruments to collect graft or to make dramatic raids for reformers. Thus an American police chief could not look to a constant policy or expect to be protected by his political masters. In essence, policing in Britain was a technical task with some political aspects; in the United States it was a political task with technical aspects.

American observers, however, frequently tended to overrate the British police. Many of the men at the top of Scotland Yard were little more than gentleman, dilettantes. Sir Melville MacNaghten, assistant chief and then chief of the detective branch (CID) from 1890 to 1913, devotes more space in his memoirs to cricket than he does to the Ripper murders. Moreover, while his descriptions of cricket matches are quite accurate and detailed, his accounts of major crimes are full of factual

---

* In 1890 Commissioner Munro had strongly supported an improved pension plan and resigned in protest when it was denied. This agitation was accompanied by a brief police strike.[6]

errors, such as the wrong date of the Ripper suspect's suicide. A successor, Sir Basil Thomson identified the prime Ripper suspect as a doctor, when in fact he was a lawyer.* [7] New York's Inspector Byrnes was clearly a more knowledgeable detective chief. The state of the CID at the beginning of the twentieth century may be gauged by the widespread popularity of Sherlock Holmes, who continually outsmarted Scotland Yard as portrayed in the characterization of the bumbling Inspector Lestrade.

The policing of London presented problems of lesser magnitude than American cities. Yet incidents that would be routine in New York or Chicago sometimes became major catastrophes in London, as illustrated by the famous "battle" of Sidney Street. In December 1910, a citizen reported a possible burglary in progress in a jewelry store in the Houndsditch section of the East End within the boundaries of the City of London. A detachment of City police that responded was attacked by an armed gang which shot five officers, killing three while making good their escape from the scene.

A combined investigation by City and Metropolitan detectives determined that the suspects were a so-called "anarchist" gang under the supposed leadership of one Peter the Painter. On January 2, 1911, members of the gang were traced to a rooming house at 100 Sidney Street, and a party of police armed with revolvers and rifles surrounded the house. They then proceeded to knock on the doors and, failing to obtain an answer, pitched stones at the windows! Not surprisingly they were met with a volley of shots which wounded two detectives. Reinforcements were summoned, and by the next morning the rooming house was besieged by 750 policemen and a platoon of the Scots Guards equipped with a machine gun. Also present were Sir Melville MacNaghten, Sir William Nott-Bower, commissioner of the City police, Detective Superintendent Pat Quinn of the Special Branch (who received a bullet through his coat), and the Home Secretary, Mr. Winston Churchill, complete with silk top hat. Within the house were exactly two gunmen, but they managed to hold their besiegers at bay until the afternoon of January the 3rd.

Incredibly, despite the presence of so many superior officers, there was considerable confusion and later dispute over who was in command. Churchill was criticized for attempting to take over, although most accounts exonerate him of the charge. At the height of the affair a battery of horse artillery galloped up, though no one could be found who summoned them. Finally the house caught fire and was allowed to burn down, killing the suspects. Even then the matter was not resolved. The mysterious Peter the Painter was never caught, and prosecution against

* Sir Basil was eventually forced to resign and later suffered the indignity of arrest and conviction for public indecency with a female companion in Hyde Park.[8]

several of the gang failed in court.*[9] Whatever their shortcomings, Byrnes, Williams, or Devery could not have done worse, since the capture of armed fugitives was a common occurrence in New York.

Fosdick, like most American observers, also failed to note certain other problems fostering within the Metropolitan Police, such as allegations that constables were compelled to make arrests so that inspectors could obtain charging fees, i.e., extra pay for booking prisoners, or the struggle between Catholic and Mason factions in the force, or, most serious of all, the smoldering union movement carried on clandestinely despite the bitter opposition of the commissioner and other senior officers.[11] Though the British police system contained many virtues, most notably a respect for law, much of its reputation rested on image rather than reality and clearly great weaknesses existed which would show up in incidents like the Ripper murders or Sidney Street.

Despite the fact that American perceptions of European police were incomplete, nevertheless, American reformers of the time were strong in urging the Europeanization of American forces, particularly in what they conceived to be the role of the police chief; and in the early years of the twentieth century, two American cities did in fact have police heads of long tenure who had been appointed by outside authorities. In Washington, D.C., Richard Sylvester, a former journalist, held the post of superintendent from 1898 to 1915. But while the Sylvester regime was well regarded by serious students of police administration,[12] the city was atypical, a sleepy southern town of 300,000 with neither industry nor large ethnic groups, save the relatively powerless blacks. It was hardly comparable to London, Paris, or New York. Thus it offered no real test of how a European administration would fare in the United States. Instead it was Boston, a major seaport with a heterogeneous population of 700,000, which for a time provided a replica of Old World policing.

THE ATHENS OF AMERICA

Boston had been one of the cradles of the American Revolution, and with the end of that struggle the middle-class merchants and professionals who had supported the rebel side were in a position to succeed to the wealth and social prestige of the beaten and departed Tories. Between the Revolution and the Civil War, Boston society was estab-

---

* It is possible the failure to convict was deliberate. The British secret service maintained a relationship with immigrant radicals as far back as the 1880s. While the police opposed the "anarchists," the intelligence agencies frequently used them.[10]

lished in a fixed pattern of dominance by those successful in trade and manufacturing. The puritanical New Englanders, however, did not content themselves with material success alone, and the so-called "Boston Brahmins" would continually seek to provide intellectual and moral leadership for the nation.[13]

One would assume that an elite of the best and the brightest would provide an example of justice. After all, as was proudly proclaimed, the puritans had come to America to be free to follow their own beliefs, and the patriots had fought for liberty. Their descendants, however, had no intention of sharing their power. As Lincoln Steffens described Boston in 1915, it had been

> ... founded by a lot of earnest Puritans from England who had the "truth" and wished to be free to practice it, who came to the new country to set up liberty and the Right. How can one believe in both liberty and the Right? The Puritans took liberty for themselves, but they could not grant it to others who were wrong. They believed in the Christian ideals, but they founded a system of economics—the only one they knew—which rewarded, nay, which requred, thrift, cunning, and possessions—the ownership of properties which would enable them to have without the necessity to do work, which they said they believed in and gradually learned to avoid. As they succeeded, some of them, and acquired wealth, they mistook their plutocracy for aristocracy and soothed their Christian ideals with a scholarly admixture of the ideals of Greek aristocracy. But they always kept their religion and their culture out of politics and business. They formed, as we all do, watertight compartments of the mind, learned from the start to think one way and do another. . . . Boston has carried the practice of hypocrisy to the nth degree of refinement, grace, and failure. New England is dying of hypocrisy.[14]

For a half century after independence political life in Boston went along smoothly, though by 1822, when the population reached 50,000, the old town meeting system became unworkable and had to be replaced by a regular city government. Local politics was dominated by the aristocrats, and among the early mayors were individuals such as Harvard President Josiah Quincy and General Harrison Gray Otis. Then, starting in the 1830s, the Irish-Catholics began to arrive in large numbers, facilitated by the promotional techniques of the Cunard Line, whose American terminus was in Boston. The puritans took to Roman Catholics no better in America than in Britain, and as early as 1834 Catholic convents were burned, and in 1837 a riot involving 15,000 people broke out when a Yankee fire company intersected a Catholic funeral procession.[15]

From the 1830s until the mid-twentieth century, Yankee-Irish rivalry would be the dominant feature of city and state politics. At first the

Yankees were too strong for the newcomers, but the ever-growing Irish could not be denied. They spread from neighborhood to neighborhood, and their young men came to dominate Boston Common, the great symbolic heart of the city, lying just below the solidly Brahmin Beacon Hill. In 1884 came the event Yankee Boston dreaded; a coalition of Democrats and Independents elected Catholic Hugh O'Brien mayor. His term was only for a year, and he was known to be an honorable man, but the Brahmins took no chances. The following year the Legislature, which they controlled and which also sat on Beacon Hill, transferred administrative control of the police to the state, leaving the city the right to pay the bills. Later, the Legislature would also transfer city finances, parks, sewers, and highways. From then on, Boston, in effect, would be run from Beacon Hill. Even in the occasional years when there was a Democratic governor, the Legislature, elected on a territorial and therefore predominantly rural basis, was safely Republican. If this were not enough, Massachusetts maintained an executive council chosen in similar fashion. This body, a survival from the days of royal governors, was required to approve various executive appointments as a further check on gubernatorial power. If Tammany Hall in both the literal and figurative sense sat astride the boundary between lower- and middle-class New York, Beacon Hill loomed over Boston, and the symbolism was not lost on those at the top or those at the bottom. To some, such dominance was natural and desirable. As Raymond Fosdick remarked, "Whether due to a large foreign population or some condition of civic inertia . . . the government elected by the city of Boston has generally been below the level of the government elected by the state of Massachusetts."[16]

The Yeomen of the Guard

The Boston police, prior to state control, did not differ greatly from comparable forces elsewhere, although Boston was never a wide-open town. Long before Inspector Byrnes, the city had a dynamic police chief in Marshal Francis Tukey, who headed the day police and night watch from 1846 to 1852. Tukey, a big, coarse man, was an early practitioner of the dramatic school of policing characterized by secret maneuvers, raids, and sensational charges. In 1848 his men drew a crowd by digging into the Boston Common and recovering a cache of allegedly stolen money. In 1851 he instituted public lineups of rogues, and in the same year he led a mass raid on vice which resulted in 150 arrests. But Tukey's style did not suit Boston, and in 1852 he was dismissed. He ran for alderman, attempting to turn the election into a referendum on his conduct, was overwhelmingly defeated, and left for California.[17] In 1854, a combined day and night police department was created.

A much more acceptable police chief was Edward Savage, who succeeded to the post in 1870 after a scandal involving the Detective Bureau. Savage, like many Boston cops of his time, was a northern New England farm boy. He came to Boston as a young man, and in 1851, at the age of thirty-nine, he joined the police force. As a beat officer, Savage displayed considerable sympathy for the unfortunate. Once he pursued a pimp to Portland, Maine, and arrested him for viciously beating a prostitute. In 1854 he was made a captain. As chief, Savage was influenced by the ideas of John Augustus, a Boston shoemaker, who in the 1840s began the practice of taking home convicted criminals in lieu of their being sent to prison, thus becoming the father of probation. When Savage retired in 1878, he requested appointment as the city's probation officer and functioned in that capacity until his death fifteen years later.[18] So advanced were his ideas that even men as prominent as Sir Howard Vincent came to study them.[19]

The chief virtue of the police department in the eyes of many was its nativist character. The first Irish-Catholic had been appointed in 1851 over Tukey's opposition. When he arrived for duty, crying out cheerfully, "I am Barney McGinniskin fresh from the bogs of Ireland" (although he had in fact been in the United States for twenty-two years), he was ostracized, and his career was short-lived.[20] Not until the 1870s, long after the New York force had become predominantly Irish, were the first Celts accepted. In time, though, they became the dominant element. The Brahmins, like the British aristocracy, found that the Irish, having taken the King's shilling, made very reliable soldiers and policemen. They had played a significant role as defenders of the empire from Africa to China. One facet of the Irish hatred of informers was their similar attitude toward men who broke their oath. Only when pushed to intolerable extremes would the Irishmen in uniform rebel.

Under state control, the department was administered by a board of three commissioners, but performance was unsatisfactory. Beacon Hill continued to complain that the police failed to enforce the liquor laws vigorously. In 1900 the underworld observer Josiah Flynt* found both vice and professional criminals operating in the city, as well as a certain amount of police corruption; however, he thought the situation was tame compared with New York or Chicago.[21] In 1906, the three-member board was replaced by a single commissioner and the police department was divested of the liquor licensing function.

The man chosen for the new post was unusual in many respects. Stephen James O'Meara was an Irish-Catholic immigrant—that alone

---

* Josiah Flynt Willard, well educated and a nephew of the temperance leader Frances Willard, took up the life of a tramp. See his *Tramping with Tramps* (1901), *The World of Graft* (1901), and *My Life* (1908). Willard, who used his first two names only, died of alcoholism while still under thirty.

should have disqualified him—but he had been born in Prince Edward Island, Canada, and was a Republican. He was also a former newspaper publisher and vice president of the Associated Press. O'Meara's family had moved to Boston in 1864, when he was ten, and he had grown up in the rugged, Irish Charlestown section. Like most of his peers, he went to work instead of college, starting as a cub reporter on the *Globe*. He then switched to the *Journal*, where he rose swiftly to reporter on the police and political beats, then city editor, managing editor, and finally, in 1895, owner and publisher. O'Meara's business acumen and Republican politics opened a number of doors normally denied an Irish-Catholic. He belonged to Boston's Union Club, served as a lecturer in government at Harvard, and was a personal friend of Senator Henry Cabot Lodge and Theodore Roosevelt. Of course, these were all second-table honors, since it was unthinkable that he would ever be put up for membership in the Somerset Club, where even firemen responding to an alarm had been made to use the service entrance. But being an honorary Yankee was the best he could hope for in Boston at that time. In 1902, O'Meara sold his paper and sought a public career. In 1904, he campaigned for the Republican nomination for Congress but lost to Eugene Foss.[22]

In the spring of 1906, Governor Curtis Guild appointed O'Meara police commissioner. In many respects, the appointment was ideal. O'Meara's varied affiliations gave him a unique understanding of both the Irish and the Yankee worlds, and his news experience provided a background in police affairs. The reorganizing legislation placed considerable power in the commissioner's hands. He was to be appointed for a five-year term by a governor who himself served only one year, and he would have the authority to hire, fire, and promote virtually at will, since the commissioner's decisions could not be reviewed by the courts or the civil service commission. And if 500 patrolmen achieved a passing score on the sergeants' exam, the commissioner did not have to appoint the man who stood first or one of the top three, but could reach down to number 500 if he chose.[23] In effect, O'Meara was given the standing and authority of a European police commissioner—he was appointed over, not by, the community, and the force would be under a quasi-military discipline.

It was not exactly a European administration, though. The governorship, which frequently changed hands, was much weaker than an English prime minister's post, and there was no cabinet officer or permanent civil service between the commissioner and the governor. Nor was there the stabilizing influence of a King over all of them. In many respects, therefore, O'Meara's power was greater than that of any of his European counterparts. Another difference was in the composition of the force. The cops were not outsiders, peasant lads sent in to police the urban proletariat; instead, they were drawn from the local Irish working class and so while administratively they may have been an army of occupation, socially they were not.

Being a Boston cop was an honorable post, since the job was non-political and difficult to obtain. To start with, the physical standards were high. In an age when the average citizen was 5'5", the minimum height for police appointment was 5'8", and Richard H. Dana remarked that "Boston policemen are physically finer than West Point cadets."[24] The mental tests, too, were considerably above the capacity of most blue-collar citizens.

The policeman's compensation, however, did not correspond to the difficulty of obtaining appointment. In 1913 the salary was set at $1,400 per year for an officer with six years service, slightly better than most blue-collar occupations, but the hours were long. A Boston cop on the day shift had to work a seventy-five-hour week and on nights eighty-seven hours, with but one day off in fifteen. Even a trip to nearby Revere Beach, just over the city limits, required permission from a captain. On the balance side, officers were permitted to accept off-duty paid details serving as guards at dances or in theaters, and some of their working hours were spent in reserve resting or sleeping in the station. But the paid details, which could increase a man's income as much as 50 percent, both helped and hurt morale, since they were parceled out to the stationhouse favorites, and added to the other frustrations over promotion and discipline by administrative discretion. Reserve duty in the station presented another problem. Many of the buildings were bedbug-ridden structures which exposed the officer (and his family) to disease.[25] The Boston climate also contributed to illness and death as tired men emerged from overheated stations to patrol the streets on long winter nights. In addition, there were the usual hazards of policing. In an era without antibiotics a gunshot wound in any vital portion of the upper torso was frequently fatal because infection would set in.

While Boston had a much lower murder rate than New York or Chicago, it was a rough, brawling city where the life of a young male in some neighborhoods was largely institutionalized brutality. In a time and place when common opinion held that Irishmen were the world's toughest people and even Italian and Jewish prizefighters had to take names like Kelly or Murphy to get bookings, blue-collar Boston Irishmen had to prove themselves constantly by fighting at the drop of a hat. Roxbury Crossing and Charlestown were particularly rough, but the premier area was South Boston, the toughest and most clannish Irish neighborhood in the city. "Southie" took a perverse pride in its fierce hostility to outsiders and any authority save its own. A popular local song, "F Street and Third," expressed the community's glory in

violent behavior particularly toward the outsider seeking even his legal
due:

> Over in Southie at F Street and Third
>   It's me home sweet home.
> We buy pianos for five dollars down
>   Then wait with a bat
> For the collector to come 'round.
>   Five flights of stairs is a hell of a fall,
> Especially with hard marble tile in the hall,
>   And after a while
> He don't come back at all,
>   Over at F Street and Third.[26]

During O'Meara's regime, the neighborhood was dominated by the
Gustins, a youth gang from the vicinity of St. Augustine's Church.

To police a dance or street fair in the Irish slums took courage, and
individual deeds became stationhouse legends—the night the reserves
from station 15 (Charlestown) fought their way through a crowd of a
thousand at Roughan's Dance Hall to rescue a comrade backed against
the wall and fighting off half a dozen attackers, or the way Patrolman
Florric O'Reagan of station 6 (South Boston) could knock a man out
with one punch.[27]

Despite various problems O'Meara's administration was generally
praised, and his police department was remarkably free from corruption
and restrained in the use of force in an era when payoffs and the third
degree were commonplace. On the other hand, the Boston police were
not pliant tools for the likes of a Parkhurst.

Prior to World War I, virtually every American city had a red-light
district, an area where houses of prostitution were concentrated and
officially tolerated. Despite the fact that state law made prostitution
illegal, it was argued that it was inevitable and best kept in a place
where it could be watched. New York Police Commissioner William
McAdoo (1904–1906), a former Congressman, described the Washington, D.C., red-light district* thus:

> It is so located as not to interfere with the citizens in general. . . . Any
> attempt to break up this quarter and scatter the vice throughout the city
> would be at once bitterly opposed by even the religious and moral ele-
> ments in the community. All that the police do is to see that peace and
> order prevail, that larcenies and robberies are prevented, and that the
> inhabitants are kept under careful espionage. A neighborhood like this

---

* The area was originally known as "Hooker's Division" because of the swarm
of prostitutes which clustered around General Joseph Hooker's troops during the
Civil War. Out of this came the term "hooker" as a synonym for prostitute.[29]

is often most useful to the police, because it is there that they hunt first for those dissolute and desperate men who are trying to evade contact with the law, and where much can be learned about the movements of criminals, either those who make their headquarters in the city or come from other parts.[28]

As a practical matter, such districts as San Francisco's Barbary Coast, Chicago's Levee, and New Orleans' Storyville became centers of crime and vice beyond simple prostitution. Nor was all such activity confined to the red-light district. In effect, the policy of tolerance was little more than a means of sanctioning organized crime. Of course, the counter-policy of total repression often produced even more corruption, as New York's periodic cycles of reform illustrated.

O'Meara's policy was different. He did not allow a red-light district but recognized that vice could not simply be eradicated. As he noted:

> I am not so simple as to suppose that any combination of effort by courts and police can ever drive vice . . . from a city . . . [but] Boston is almost the only city of its size or perhaps of half its size in the United States in which the police refuse to set apart prescribed localities where houses of ill fame may be carried on without penalty or interference; and Boston is right. All law breakers here are liable to the penalties of the law and the last who should be exempted are those who make a business of vice.[30]

Therefore, though Boston continued to have a vice district, centered around Scollay Square, where the Atlantic fleet socialized, it was not immune from enforcement action. On the other hand, police activity was not composed of raids and crusades which soon abated, but was kept at a steady level. Vice there would be, but not entrenched behind red lights.*

O'Meara's chief criticism did not come from vice lords, but from the professional moralists who wanted spectacular results. The powerful Watch and Ward Society (founded in 1878) included a membership of first families and in O'Meara's day was led by such towering figures as Episcopal Bishop William Lawrence and Endicott Peabody, headmaster of Groton.[31] While the commissioner's administrative tenure provided a certain security, he could also answer his critics with well-put arguments, which, since he was a former journalist, were his stock in trade.

* The sanctioned red-light districts would meet their demise in 1917, when, under provisions of the federal Draft Act, Raymond Fosdick, then an assistant to the Secretaries of War and Navy, closed 110 of them nationally. Despite the pleas of politicians such as the mayor of New Orleans, who argued for the "Godgiven right of men to be men," Fosdick persisted, even calling out troops to enforce the law.[32]

Each year the commissioner was required to submit an annual report to the governor. Such documents are usually terse, statistical summaries designed to obscure more than they reveal. Not so O'Meara's, which contained long philosophical discussions of various problems.

Concurrent with O'Meara's appointment there arose throughout the country great public concern over the problem of "white slavery," one of those issues which became a matter of dogmatic, conventional wisdom, intense moral indignation, and for a time vigorous federal law enforcement. Afterward it faded out, becoming something of a joke. According to the viewers with alarm who promoted this particular menace, virtually all brothel inmates were there involuntarily as a result of having been forced or tricked into sexual activities, after which, in shame, they entered houses of prostitution, where they were kept by strong-arm methods. As the legend continued, since prostitutes died within a few years from their wicked ways, new recruits were always needed. Thus a large traffic in white slavery was constantly carried on. At the height of concern, virtually any girl who disappeared was presumed to be a victim of white slavers, who were usually portrayed as swarthy Jews, Italians, or Frenchmen. No woman was safe and one's wife, sister, or daughter might be kidnapped and degraded.[33] William Travers Jerome had campaigned for district attorney of New York in 1901 displaying the brass checks used as tokens in houses of prostitution and violently denouncing white slavery.[34]

Like any myth, this one had some basis in fact. Some girls did enter prostitution as a result of trickery or force, although rarely were they total innocents who were kidnapped from their homes. More often they were what would be described as "loose" women on the edges of prostitution. The plain fact was that most prostitutes entered voluntarily, and most girls or women who disappeared simply ran away from parents or husband. Many women who could not or did not want to marry or remain married, or who had lost their husbands and could not find suitable means to support themselves, turned to prostitution as an alternative to starvation or drudgery. As New York's Mayor Gaynor told the Curran Committee:

> We have to deal with it . . . the best we can under the law and minimize it and put it into the hearts of people, of men, not to seduce women, and as to the merchants and storekeepers and manufacturers, to put it into their hearts to pay women wages that don't drive them on the town and into prostitution, and things like that we have got to do by slow degrees until the evil is done away with entirely. But for a man to pay a woman three dollars a week and then accuse me and say that there are too many prostitutes in the City of New York is infamous, and there are people here who are doing just that thing. (Loud applause by the spectators, and order rapped for by Chairman Curran.)[35]

The antivice study of which Fosdick's book *European Police Systems* was a part had come about from John D. Rockefeller, Jr.'s 1910 service as foreman of a New York grand jury investigating white slavery. While no doubt sincerely motivated, sponsorship of such a study permitted its backers to define the problem in terms of the failures of the police, not of the economic system.[36]

Most police chiefs had but two choices. If a chief presided over a wide-open town, he could defend red-light districts, citing such arguments as the necessity of appeasing man's biological urges; if he was a reform chief, he could crack down on white slavers, which meant locking up a few brothel keepers, preferably those with Jewish or Italian names. O'Meara chose neither. He not only dismissed the notion of a permitted red-light district but scorned the moral-betterment societies and their demands for spectacular results. Between 1909 and 1911, O'Meara painstakingly demolished the reform societies' arguments:

> Benevolent men and women in and about Boston have lately been shocked and imposed upon by means of a circular issued under the name of a chartered organization, soliciting subscriptions of money. The circular asserts that young girls are "sold" in Boston for immoral purposes, and "kept by heinous methods from their freedom;" and to this it adds: "We believe the annual traffic in human souls in this city amounts to hundreds." . . .
>
> There is no ground for even reasonable suspicion that in Boston women and girls are forced into an immoral life or compelled to remain in it under physical coercion or restraint. If such a case were known to the police, the victim would be released at once and her keepers arrested. A person who knew of such a case and failed to inform the police would be as black a criminal as the criminals themselves; and a person who pretended to such knowledge without possessing it might fairly be set down as an irresponsible gossip.[37]

On the methods of the societies and their private detectives, he wrote:

> An indignant citizen, who feels sure of the bad character of a house, demands that it be closed by the police. He forgets that we are not in an Asiatic despotism; that in this country every person is held to be innocent until his guilt has been proved; that the one thing which is of value to the police is the very thing which he cannot produce, or refuses to produce, and that is evidence that will convince or help to convince a court or jury. He protests that men and women drive up to the house and drive away late at night, that there are lights, music and merriment; and in his simplicity he does not know that if a policeman were to go before a judge asking for a warrant on such a state of facts he would be told that he did not know his business, that the appearances which he de-

scribed were to be found nightly in Commonwealth Avenue and Beacon Street as well as in the shady quarters of the city. He does not know that "spotter" evidence—the evidence of a man who for pay would enter these houses and join in their orgies—would not be worth the time it would take to present it to a scornful jury.[38]

The police . . . , stand at a disadvantage in so far as results are concerned, for they are compelled to keep within the bounds of both law and morals; they are allowed to enter suspected places as police officers with search warrants, or individually, under orders, to observe and report, but on no account to take part in immoral acts, or so to place themselves as to be open to the charge of immorality.

Any private organization, however, with no official responsibility and eager to make a case, is free to hire men and women by the day or the week who may go to any lengths for the sake of procuring evidence. They sometimes betray their employers, sometimes invent or exaggerate in order to earn their pay, and with juries have the standing which they deserve. But the police department cannot use its men in such ways, and would not if it could. The men of the police force are required to be manly and moral, and whatever they can do under their official obligation in a moral and manly way for the suppression of vice they will do— nothing more. They have not the gift of impersonating degenerates, and none among them would be allowed to spend his days and nights with degraded men and women for the sake of securing a conviction.[39]

The offended Watch and Ward Society clamored for O'Meara's ouster, but he gave not an inch. The law, not pressure from reformers, was the cornerstone of his policy:

I regard the strict observance of the laws as the most important lesson to be impressed upon the police of any city. Their authority is no more than that of a private citizen except in so far as such authority is conferred upon them specifically by the laws. Therefore, to the police in their official acts the laws should stand paramount to all other powers or influences. The temptation to break the laws or to go outside of them for the sake of securing what may appear at the time to be an advantage to the community should always be resisted. If the people of Boston were as well educated on this point as are their police, the police would have fewer calls to "clean out" this or to "suppress" that when neither can lawfully be done. No man without police experience can know the frequency with which citizens demand of policemen action which the laws do not permit them to take. The spirit of "lynch law" seems to be in all classes of citizens, and to manifest itself in individuals whenever their own profits or comforts are jeopardized.

[If] the police assume authority which the law does not give to them, and thus themselves become law breakers, the people of Boston will be the sufferers. Boston newspapers, as well as those of New York, are constantly praising Mayor Gaynor of that city for his attempts to bring its police back to the solid basis of law; and yet some of the same Boston newspapers, and doubtless many citizens, criticize at this time the Police Commissioner of Boston as narrow and technical because he has insisted steadily and still insists that the police for whom he is responsible shall follow the law at all times, not their own impulses.[40]

If houses of ill fame can be closed on a large scale, and immoral women can be driven from the streets by mere threats on the part of the police, the circumstance is in itself a reasonable indication that the business had previously been tolerated, and that when the spasm of reform has passed it will again be tolerated.[41]

In 1911, his old opponent, Eugene Foss, now a Democrat and governor of Massachusetts, reappointed him despite opposition from the reform societies, on the simple ground that no one had been able to show that there was a better man available.

As was true of Gaynor in New York, legality, not the quick public acclaim of the Parkhursts and Jeromes, was the basis of O'Meara's administration. But O'Meara had much stronger control over his police department than the New York mayor, and the Boston courts were more favorable to due process. During his time the third degree was standard American police practice, and the "lie detector" sometimes meant a rubber hose. Boston police did not employ these methods and were comparatively rigorous in adherence to legal requirements regarding search and arrest warrants. In 1931, long after O'Meara's death, a National Commission on Law Observance and Enforcement (Wickersham Commission) task force under Harvard civil libertarian Zacariah Chafée would uncover systematic police illegality. Of Boston it had this to say:

> The third degree and related types of police illegality are at a minimum in Boston. . . . The charges of brutality which have been received in Boston are relatively to other cities, not serious. . . . The tradition of the Boston police department against lawlessness is a most important factor. . . . The tradition was established by Stephen O'Meara.[42]

In 1916 O'Meara even banned the carrying of nightsticks, though concealed short billies were allowed.

Despite O'Meara's considerable accomplishments, there were some weaknesses beyond pay and working conditions. Cops had to be at least twenty-five, and the force tended to be old and a bit stodgy. Harvard's Leonard Harrison wrote in his 1934 study of the department:

> It [O'Meara's police department] maintained a high standard of integrity and self-respect, accompanied by sense of satisfaction that everything was all right as it stood. Tradition for the most part determined the

course to be followed. Imagination and experimentation were apparently not encouraged and a deep rut of conservatism was worn in this period.[43]

However, in 1915 Raymond Fosdick wrote that Boston probably had the best police force in the country.[44]

The Stage Irish

While the cops and their commissioner won the plaudits of most people, Boston's mayors cared little for them. City Hall was denied a share of the power and patronage and stuck with the cost, which because of the size of the force (2.3 officers per 1,000 population), was the highest per capita in the country.* [45]

During the O'Meara era, two men dominated the mayor's office, John F. "Honey Fitz" Fitzgerald (1905–1907 and 1909–1913) and James Michael Curley (1913–1917). Both were prime representatives of the brand of politics which prevailed in the city during the first half of this century. Given the exclusionary and discriminatory policies to which the Irish were subjected, they reacted in the expected fashion by drawing more closely together and expressing counterhostility toward their Yankee oppressors. To the Yankee image of the stage Irishman—by turns drunk, combative, and maudlin and not a trifle dishonest—the Irish could return the image of the Yankee Brahmin banker—haughty, arrogant, unfeeling, and at heart a master criminal.

It need not have been so. In the initial periods of Irish advance in the nineteenth century the leaders had been men who could build alliances beyond their own tribe. In this stage of political evolution the aspects of ethnic solidarity were downplayed in favor of more integrative approaches. At the turn of the century, the leading Boston Irish-Catholic was Patrick Collins, who had risen from coal miner to graduate from Harvard College and Harvard Law School, and despite his Fenian background was accepted as United States Consul General in London. Collins proclaimed:

> I . . . denounce any man or any body of men who seek to perpetuate divisions of races or religion in our midst. . . . I love the land of my birth but in American politics I know neither race, color or creed. . . .
>
> The moment the seal of the court was impressed upon our papers we ceased to be foreigners and became Americans. Americans we are and Americans we will remain.[46]

---

* Unrecognized even by Raymond Fosdick was the strength that large numbers provided. Without a comparatively high ratio of police to population, the beat system could not be effective. That is, the smaller the force, the larger the beat, thus lessening the extent of personal contact between the police and public.

In proof of his word he supported such political candidates as Charles Francis Adams. Collins was elected mayor in 1901 and reelected in 1903, serving until his death in 1905.

But while Yankee Bostonians could approve of men like Collins or O'Meara and even look fondly on Irish cops, they were not about to share power and prestige voluntarily. Nor were their exclusionary policies directed only at the Irish. In 1916 the Brahmin aristocracy, led by President A. Lawrence Lowell of Harvard, bitterly opposed the appointment of Louis Brandeis, a Jew, to the U.S. Supreme Court even though he was one of the most brilliant students Harvard Law School had produced and the ablest lawyer in Boston. As Brandeis himself said, those who opposed him were men "blinded by privilege, who have no evil purpose, and many of whom have distinct public spirit, but whose environment—or innate narrowness—has obscured all vision and sympathy with the masses."[47]

As the Irish population grew to a majority and could win the city's elections without allies, leaders developed who played to anti-Yankee hostility, and the stage Irishman became a reality. The Fitzgerald and Curley regimes were characterized by corruption, payroll padding, and silly charades. Candidates would outdo each other in bitter denunciation of their opponents and the Yankee bankers, while supporters would spread rumors that the rival Irish candidate ate T-bone steaks every Friday and was about to divorce his wife, marry a teenage girl, and become a Mason. Fitzgerald would frequently entertain the voters with his rendition of "Sweet Adeline" and pose with his photogenic family, thus emphasizing his cheerful nature and straightlaced behavior. So pure was the good mayor that he banned the turkey trot and tango as immoral.[48] Curley capitalized on a jail term he had served, explaining that the reason he had impersonated an applicant in a federal examination for letter carrier was to help a poor family man obtain employment. He would hurl bitter charges without foundation and occasionally engage in fisticuffs with various foes to show that he was truly a fighting Irishman.

Behind the scenes was the Boston equivalent of New York's "Big Tim" Sullivan—Martin Lomasney, "the Mahatma," boss of the West End. While Lomasney's unsavory reputation precluded his own occupancy of the mayor's office, he played the kingmaker role from the 1880s through the 1920s, switching with bewildering speed from candidate to candidate.[49]

In 1913 Curley drove Fitzgerald from office by threatening to discuss great lovers from Cleopatra to Toodles. While a rendition of the Queen of the Nile's doings would not have upset Honey Fitz, a very strong rumor linked him to a cigarette girl named Toodles, and he withdrew from the race.[50] Curley had posed the ultimate weapon in

Catholic Boston—a morals charge.* To an outsider the "Irish" politics of Boston was by turns amusing and a disgrace, a view shared by most Yankees. But as Edwin O'Connor wrote in *The Last Hurrah*, a thinly disguised fictional version of Curley's life, it rather suited the more astute Brahmins:

> Despite his dislike of the Irish, Cass [a Yankee banker] had not ignored them. He had studied them carefully, . . . in the interest of his own survival. The reported wit and charm of these strangers had completely eluded him, but he had found in them qualities he liked: sentimentality, intemperance, verbosity, and best of all, the lack of financial acumen.[52]

One Irishman who turned his back on the scene was Joseph P. Kennedy, the son of Patrick J., a powerful ward boss, and the son-in-law of Honey Fitz himself. Kennedy was also a Harvard graduate, and with such a background he would have certainly become mayor if he had been willing to play the role of a clown and accept the droppings of power from Beacon Hill. Instead, he chose business and a life largely spent away from Boston. In time, though, he and his sons would return and beat the Brahmins at their own game and with their own weapons; money, intellect, and moral force.

POLICE REBELS

While the mayors could not control the police, they could block pay raises and improvements in working conditions. Within the status hierarchy of working-class Boston, the cops were respected men. Their pay exceeded that of most blue-collar workers, and though construction workers made more per hour, they did not work as steadily or have a pension system. More importantly, the cops did not have to tip their hats to the politicians and local gang leaders. Though they came from the Irish blue-collar milieu, ties to Lomasney and his type were matters of friendship, not business. Neither the mayor or Senator Henry Cabot Lodge could get men appointed over O'Meara's refusal despite Fitzgerald's public tantrums and Lodge's gentlemanly old-boy pressures.[53]

World War I changed the patrolman's status. New England was a center of war production, and wages and prices rose accordingly. When America entered the war, there was considerable unpaid overtime duty

---

* Lomasney was more subtle. When he wished to shake up Honey Fitz, he would send a note with a P.S.: "that woman you were with was asking for you." The mayor would usually understand and grant the Mahatma's requests.[51]

for the police, and prices skyrocketed. Soon the cops were making less than streetcar men, who were traditionally recruited from those who failed to get on the police force.[54] In 1918 the police social club, an officially sanctioned body, met with the commissioner over pay and working conditions. O'Meara was sympathetic but counseled patience. Suddenly, in December, he died.

The new commissioner was a politician named Edwin U. Curtis, a stiff-necked, dignified middle-class Yankee who, as William Allen White said, looked like "one of those solemn, self-sufficient Bostonian heroes who apparently are waiting in the flesh to walk up the steps to a pedestal and be cast into immortal bronze."[55] In 1894, at thirty-three, he had been elected mayor, the youngest in the city's history, and his future appeared bright. The Legislature had been so confident of his re-election that it had provided for a two-year term for the mayor's office. But Martin Lomasney cleverly persuaded Josiah Quincy, descendant of two Yankee mayors, to run on the Democratic ticket, and Curtis was defeated. For the next twenty years, he held a number of minor appointive offices. When he accepted the commissionership, he was in poor health and in fact had but a few years to live, a condition of which he was apparently aware.[56]

In 1919 the police salary issue went to an arbitration panel, which recommended a $200 annual increase. The cops were dissatisfied, since this would buy very little in the postwar inflation. In August their association affiliated with the AFL. Commissioner Curtis warned that this was against the rules and threatened them with disciplinary action. Next, charges were brought against nineteen leaders of the union. The police stood firm and threatened to strike if their leaders were punished. For thirteen years Boston had benefited from a powerful commissioner and cops who were not patronage employees but men of respect: the faithful yeomen of the guard and their good gray colonel. But now the guardsmen, degraded and in many individual instances financially desperate, were mutinous. The conduct of their new colonel would demonstrate the dangers of giving unrestrained power to strong men.

Faced with an imminent strike, the political and business leadership of the city searched for a solution. The mayor of Boston was a Yankee Democrat, Andrew Peters, who had beaten Curley in a three-way race. Since Peters was a Protestant, Curley had not bothered to circulate the T-bone steak and teenage-mistress stories, although at the time Peters was in fact deeply involved with an eleven-year-old girl.[57] To the city's misfortune, 1919 saw all of Boston's strong men in temporary eclipse. Curley had antagonized many people in his term, one charge being that he failed to support the war effort by allowing peace meetings to take place. Lomasney had openly advocated a German victory over England as a help to Irish independence and broke with his hand-picked Congressman over the issue, electing Honey Fitz in his place. However, the former mayor had been unseated by the Congress because of vote fraud in his campaign.[58]

Given the weaknesses of city government, Mayor Peters appointed a committee headed by New England's wealthiest banker, James J. Storrow, a onetime captain of the Harvard crew, former president of General Motors, and unsuccessful candidate for mayor against Honey Fitz in 1909. During that hectic campaign, a South Boston mob had run him out of the community with snowballs and flaming torches. Storrow was Boston's man for all committees, since he was a principal in the city's most prestigious brokerage firm of Lee, Higginson and was himself successor in social prestige to old Major Henry Higginson, doyen of the Brahmins.[59]

Despite the rhetoric of Irish politicians, Storrow and his group were sympathetic to a compromise which would give the cops substantially what they wanted while saving face for Commissioner Curtis by requiring that the patrolmen's union not be affiliated with the AFL.[60] In radical theory and in accord with Boston Irish legend, this should have been entirely sufficient. Since the police commissioner was responsible to the state government and that government was solidly Yankee Republican, the bankers need but give the word to their puppets and the deed was done. The reality was a bit different.

Calvin Coolidge, governor of the Commonwealth since January, had not returned to Vermont after graduating from Amherst. Instead, he read law in Massachusetts, was admitted to the bar, and moved up through a series of minor political offices. Coolidge belonged to the western Massachusetts faction of the party, not to the Brahmin elite of the east led by Senator Lodge. While his fifth cousins, the Coolidges of Beacon Hill, held forth in society, he lived a humble life in a Northampton apartment with his wife and two children, and when attending the Legislature stayed in a $1.50 room in a downtown Boston hotel. As governor he paid an additional dollar for a second room, and this constituted his executive mansion.

While Coolidge has been portrayed as a stolid conservative, this is far from accurate. Quiet and cautious he was, but one of the bars to his social acceptance, besides lack of money and family standing, was his tendency to be friendly with ordinary people, to chat with streetcar conductors and drink a beer down at the local pub. As a state senator he voted in favor of such progressive measures as a state income tax, women's suffrage, direct election of U.S. senators, and the legalization of picketing. Later, as governor, he was in favor of the League of Nations.

In 1914, when the conservative Republican leader of the State Senate was upset by a combination of suffragettes and organized labor, the Republican machine put Coolidge in his stead, although not because of his progressivism. The Legislature was a serious place where the interest groups bought and sold various favors, and Coolidge could be depended upon to keep things running smoothly. However, despite the marketplace nature of his environment, Coolidge himself was completely honest. No man could bribe him because he did not want money or even power, nor did he want to gain social acceptance from the Brahmins, since he disapproved of their life style. Rather, in the words of William Allen White, he was a puritan set down amidst a twentieth-century urban society. Coolidge's family believed in the right of business to rule and the honor of government service. Such a man was amply qualified to preside over the government of Massachusetts. He could never be bribed or disgraced, nor would he create waves.[61]

In the beginning of the impasse between the cops and the commissioner, Coolidge was sympathetic to the bluecoats. He was by no means a law and order blusterer, and no threats emanated from the governor's office. If, for example, he had announced early that in the event of a strike he would use the state police and metropolitan park police as well as the National Guard, the strike might have never occurred. But Coolidge was not a right-wing zealot, and he did not wish to offend organized labor. On the other hand, he would not force the commissioner to compromise. In Coolidge's mind the man held an independent office, and in addition, the commissioner's view had influential support. Characteristically, Coolidge kept a low public profile, deciding, in effect, not to decide.

The year 1919 was a bad year for conducting a police strike. The antiwar activities of various groups had alarmed many Americans, and the Bolshevik Revolution threw up the menace of Communism. In February, a general strike had been attempted in Seattle but had been blocked by Mayor Ole Hansen. Bombs had been mailed to the homes of Attorney General A. Mitchell Palmer, Mayor Hansen, Supreme Court Justice Oliver Wendell Holmes, J. P. Morgan, John D. Rockefeller, and others. In July a race riot in Chicago had claimed thirty-eight lives.[62] In Boston itself, the telephone operators had struck in April and the elevated railroad employees in July. On May Day, 1919, when police clashed with parading radicals, two officers were shot and a captain died of a heart attack.[63]

As the strike loomed, the police department called for volunteers. One of the first was Harvard physics professor Edwin Hall, who wrote to the newspapers praising Curtis for his valiant stand and urged the youth of Harvard and other elite institutions to "come back from your vacations, young men, there is sport and diversion for you right here in Boston."[64] As it turned out, it was the spirit of the professor and not the bankers that prevailed. Neither they nor the politicians ran the police department, but a reactionary Yankee Republican supported by a large share of influential opinion which a cautious governor was afraid to offend.* There would be no compromise.

For their part the cops, though normally strong supporters of authority, were now militant. The union president, John McInnes, a traffic policeman and a resident of South Boston, had an outstanding career. As a teenager he had served in the famed Seventh Cavalry from 1888 to 1891, fought at Wounded Knee, and received combat injuries. He was also a veteran of the Spanish-American War, including San Juan Hill, and then was in the regular army, rising to the rank of first lieutenant. He joined the police department in 1906 and was detailed as a detective. A few years before the strike, he was suddenly transferred to traffic duty. During World War I he was a captain in military intelligence, working undercover among troops of foreign origin to check on their loyalty.[65] That such a man was about to lead a police strike was an indication of how desperate the cops had become.**

On Monday, September 8, the union leaders were suspended. The men immediately voted to strike the next day. At 5:45 P.M. on September 9, when the bell sounded for assembly in District 15, only one of the seventy-seven officers responded. Similar scenes occurred throughout the other division stations as 1,117 out of 1,544 patrolmen went on strike. In some stations there were tears and handshakes as comrades parted, in others anger. The oldest men usually stayed lest they lose their pensions, the rest went. At some locations disorderly or curious crowds waited outside to cheer, boo, or even hit the policemen. In Roxbury Crossing the urchins threw mud at the cops. In Southie the gangs began looking for ex-cops to settle scores. Officer Florrie O'Reagan, the department knockout champion, was fortunate to be on vacation, since the local toughs were especially anxious to meet him.[66] The number of strikers proved a surprise, since the commissioner had estimated seven to eight hundred patrolmen would remain loyal.[67]

Neither the volunteers nor the militia was summoned on the first night, and as darkness fell, trouble began. At 11:00 Tuesday night reports of riotous mobs began to pour into headquarters. At this juncture, the police department was under the actual command of Superintendent Mike Crowley, who had risen from the ranks, where his work as a detec-

---

* One Harvard faculty member who publicly supported the strike was visiting professor Harold Laski, but he was widely regarded as a Bolshevik.

** Why a man with his background was serving as a simple traffic patrolman rather than a detective inspector (lieutenant) has not been explained in any of the writings on the strike, although it might be of considerable interest in assessing McInnes's behavior. A possible explanation is that the regular hours and undemanding duties permitted him to work part time at his trade of bricklayer. This suggests both his need for money and the fact that a Boston detective's post provided no "fringe benefits."

tive sergeant caught headquarters attention.* Since Curtis knew nothing of police work, it was Crowley who mustered the small forces (mostly sergeants and detectives), sending them hither and yon in flying columns and taking personal leadership of one group himself. As mobs smashed windows and mugged pedestrians, the cops would appear and, firing into the air, charge into the fray. Crowley himself repeatedly dove into threatening crowds, singlehandedly scattering them.[69] It was rough going, however, and five people were shot and wounded in downtown Boston alone.

As expected, Southie was the worst. When Crowley arrived, he could not believe the condition of Broadway, the neighborhood's main thoroughfare. The mobs had looted the stores and thrown the contents into the street. Even the local priests could not control the crowds. One man who might have done something was James Michael Curley, now a private citizen. Southie had never been one of his strongholds, but he knew how to handle its people. While campaigning in 1913, he had stopped outside St. Augustine's to recite the Lord's Prayer. Out of the corner of his eye he noticed a local thug taking off with his expensive coat which had been left in the car. Without missing a beat, Curley implored the Lord to "give us this day our daily bread and forgive us our trespasses as we forgive those who trespass against us and get that son-of-a-bitch who is stealing my coat."[70] If humor failed, however, there was scorn. At one street-corner rally he addressed the howling men of Southie as follows:

> All you pick-pockets and crap shooters, I'm going to make myself heard if it takes me until six o'clock in the morning when you fellows are out at your occupation of stealing milk. I know these men. They are nothing but a pack of second story workers, milk bottle robbers and door mat thieves. [He loosened his tie and took off his coat.] . . . Here I am; does any one of you fellows want to step up here and make anything of it?[71]

Of course, Curley always traveled with a squad of burly supporters, frequently including the great John L. Sullivan.[72] Superintendent Crowley, a native of the district and in his youth a local boxer, also knew how to speak to a South Boston crowd. He and the detectives drew their revolvers and in repeated charges broke the mobs.

* Michael Crowley (1866–1933) was appointed to the Boston Police Department in 1888. In 1907 O'Meara rescued him from an outlying beat, to which politicians had condemned him for nineteen years, and made him a sergeant. The following year he discovered a dead body in a trunk and captured the murderer before he could jump out of the window. In 1910 he was made a lieutenant, and in 1913 he became, at forty-seven, the youngest captain on the force. In 1915 O'Meara jumped him over senior officers to superintendent, where he served until his death. Crowley was noted for his jovial good nature and propensity for singing Irish ballads. When radio came in, he occasionally sang on local stations.[68]

The next morning the volunteers began to arrive. A number of Harvard students, including the entire football team, journeyed eagerly from Cambridge to Boston to partake in the exciting events. Like other young Harvard men fifty years later who journeyed to Boston to participate in riots for quite different motives, they soon found that urban disorder was not exactly like football. The volunteers were sworn as special police, issued guns, nightsticks (the same ones which had been turned in in 1916), and billies and sent on patrol. At one corner, retired Admiral Francis Bowles exchanged greetings with General Francis Peabody, both walking beats. Among other volunteers were former Harvard football coach Percy Haughton, All-American halfback and baseball star Huntington "Tack" Hardwick, recently discharged from the army and now a young stockbroker, and Godfrey Lowell Cabot, a former U.S. Navy aviator.[73]

At this juncture, Mayor Peters urged Coolidge to call out the State Guard. The governor reminded him that mayors had the authority to mobilize units within their city, a fact that Peters, a Harvard Law School graduate, was unaware of. Mayor Peters then called out the Tenth Regiment, a mostly Irish unit commanded by Colonel Tom Sullivan, his public works commissioner who was a Southie resident, as well as some cavalry, for a total of 1,000 troops. He also issued orders taking control of the police department. With the volunteers and guardsmen, as well as the addition of various state and park officers, the number of men available exceeded the number on strike and the situation should have been brought under control. But the strike was a symbolic action which loosed the mob. Sixteen hundred cops were sufficient to police 700,000 people in normal times because only a few of them would be giving difficulty at any given moment. But when several thousand did so simultaneously, the police were inadequate. The strike was an invitation for a few thousand hoodlums to spring into action all at once.

In addition, despite their numbers, the guardsmen and volunteers were untrained in policing. Indeed, the guardsmen were not much as soldiers. General Peabody had never served a day on active duty, while Colonel Tom Sullivan had not seen service since the Spanish-American War. One young militia soldier shot a police captain while clumsily executing inspection arms.[74] Thus it might take ten guardsmen to accomplish the work of one policeman, and several thousand would be needed or else firepower would have to take the place of knowledge or numbers. As it turned out, the crowds on the first full day of the strike were nearly as violent as the previous night. Boston Common was completely taken over by crap shooters, and the volunteer cops were slugged and pummeled on downtown streets. In South Boston they were too frightened even to leave the station.

Coolidge had no choice but to follow the Mayor's lead and call out the remainder of the Guard. All through Wednesday afternoon alarm bells rang in the small towns throughout the state summoning the guardsmen to their armories as in the days of Lexington and Concord. In a number of instances, men who were not members joined up and were issued rifles. By nightfall units were en route to Boston, often passing cheering crowds of their Yankee neighbors.[75] Many were in a grim mood; the Eleventh Regiment from Lowell came off the train at North Station with fixed bayonets. At sundown the cavalry paraded through the aristocratic Back Bay section en route to downtown. Their arrival was not a moment too soon, as it turned out. Tack Hardwick and his special police teammates had been running back and forth sometimes faking an end run and other times charging into the opposing line, but by dusk they were out of plays and the mobs in tough Scollay Square had backed them against the wall. Just at the moment of apparent defeat, as if in a movie, they were rescued by a saber-swinging cavalry charge.[76]

In Southie the mob surrounded and stoned a militia detachment. Suddenly the guardsmen fired, killing two and wounding ten.[77] The Guard commander later denied giving an order to fire, and all of the casualties were, of course, "innocent bystanders." In Boston a hundred and fifty years earlier, soldiers behaving in like manner had been indicted and the victims became patriotic heroes. In 1919, the matter was brushed aside.

As the second night wore on and more reinforcements arrived, the trouble began to subside though one military unit virtually mutinied when they heard they were being assigned to South Boston. A striking policeman who overpowered and disarmed two volunteers was shot and killed, and his comrade, an officer who had been wounded by radicals on May Day, was arrested for robbery.[78]

One final task was left to bring the situation under control. Throughout the disorders, Boston Common was the scene of crap games. On the morning of Thursday the 11th, a Guard detachment was sent to suppress this symbolic nose thumbing and, after killing one doubting Thomas, accomplished the mission. The Guard also killed two boys in the Jamaica Plain district who had lifted a manhole cover.[79]

It was a glorious moment for Massachusetts Yankees. They had put down the revolt of both the rabble and the faithless cops. On every corner were bankers and ex-Harvard athletes with their revolvers, billies, and special police armbands, or Berkshire farm boys and North Shore fishermen in militia khaki with rifles and bayonets. The Yankees had recaptured their city. The *Boston Transcript*, favorite newspaper of the Beacon Hill tea-dance set, commented, "It's good to know many of of Boston's Bluecoats are true blue (bloods)."[80]

Thus did the strike of O'Meara's legalistic police culminate in an orgy of mob violence, shooting, and death. Opinion was now heavily against the cops, and organized labor was not sympathetic. Diamond Jim Timilty, the most powerful labor leader in the state and an old senate colleague of the governor, assured Coolidge that labor would not call a general strike. At this juncture the man of action was Mayor Peters, and by any fair judgment he should have been a hero. The cops did not work for him, but for the governor (a fact not well understood nationally), and he had tried for a compromise, but when that failed through no fault of his own, he had quickly summoned troops. All this was clear to Coolidge's political advisers, and forty-eight hours after the strike began, the governor restored Curtis to the control of the department and assumed the leading role for himself. To a telegram from AFL President Samuel Gompers asking for a compromise, Coolidge the resolute then replied with the famous line "There is no right to strike against the public safety anytime, anywhere." Here was a man to stem the Red tide and in November he was reelected governor by a smashing margin. In June, 1920 the Republican Convention nominated him for Vice President.

Interestingly, the London Metropolitan Police underwent not one but two strikes at approximately the same time as Boston, settling the second just a month before the Boston affair. It is regrettable that American police reformers did not pay as much attention to British police problems as they did to British police successes.

In 1914, shortly before the beginning of World War I, Commissioner Henry, who had been shot by a lunatic in 1912, petitioned for retirement, and the government apparently planned to replace him with General Nevil Macready, a dashing soldier with extensive police experience. Macready was the son of the famous Victorian actor William Macready, who was near seventy when Nevil was born in 1862. In the 1880s, as a young lieutenant in a Highland regiment on military police duty in Egypt, Macready had shocked his superiors by the frank way in which he handled the VD problem through licensing and inspection of prostitutes. Later, as a general, he commanded troops and police in putting down strikes in Wales. His tactics may be imagined by his observation that the strikers would have trouble sitting down for several days after his men's bayonets had reached the seat of the problem.[81] Unlike General Warren, though, Macready had considerable charm and not a little of his father's histrionic ability, so that even people he was mistreating often liked him. Such a man of action naturally became friendly with the powerful Winston Churchill, who had frequently utilized his services in riots, but the outbreak of World War I gave Macready other duties.*

* During the early years of the war, Macready was adjutant general of the British Expeditionary Force. As such, he caused the arrest of England's greatest

By the summer of 1918, the London bobbies were in the familiar squeeze between inflation and low pay, and in August 6,000 of the 19,000-man force struck, including a considerable number of Pat Quinn's Special Branch detectives, whose duty it had been to spy on the union. The war was still on, and the government might well have been justified in extreme action, particularly since the strikers invaded police stations and forced nonstriking officers to stop work. However, the Prime Minister, David Lloyd George, met with the strike leaders and seemed to give in to all their demands including postwar recognition for the union. He also sacked Commissioner Henry, who had been totally opposed to the union and had guessed wrong on the number of potential strikers.[83] Lloyd George was not about to see London turned into a battlefield and thousands of trained men lost to the service to salvage anyone's pride including his own. He was also not about to allow a union to lead the government around by the nose, but the clever Welsh politician knew how to manipulate a situation.

In September Macready was brought in as commissioner, and he set about to remedy various grievances while isolating the more intransigent officers. Thus he made concessions and spoke to mass meetings of the rank and file with fervor and compassion, usually ending with the crowd rising to sing "For He's a Jolly Good Fellow."[84] Most union leaders, of course, were not fooled, and they hated Macready and sought his ouster. In August 1919 they made the mistake of again striking, but only a thousand men followed them. All were dismissed, despite appeals to Lloyd George, and the police were again under firm control.[85] The astute Macready correctly calculated that policemen are simply not rebels at heart and that with adequate welfare and good leadership the agitators in the ranks could be overcome.*

The Boston police strike left a permanent legacy for the American police. It confirmed both their low status and their powerlessness. In the crunch both left and right had assailed or abandoned them, and despite years of faithful service the strikers were turned out in the street. For a half century no American police department would consider striking. During the period when their fellow blue-collar workers made dramatic gains in pay and working conditions, the cops lagged behind. Without the strike weapon they had no bargaining position. Denied the right to strike on the grounds that their task required special

---

barrister, Sir. F. E. Smith, M.P. when the latter, in military uniform, journeyed to the front without a pass to visit his friend Colonel Winston Churchill. Smith protested that he was a cabinet officer and thus immune, but Macready checked him by the argument "If you are a civilian, why are you here in uniform? If you're a soldier why don't you obey the regulations?" Smith was outraged, but Churchill roared with laughter.[82]

* After their dismissal some of the union leaders became members of the Communist party.[86]

dedication, they were denied high wages on the grounds that they were menials. Not surprisingly, many of them sought their job benefits under the table.

If, in fact, the Boston Police Department had been administered along British lines, Commissioner Curtis would have been removed and a more competent leader found. As it was, O'Meara's police force was destroyed but Boston politics continued in the familiar pattern. Mayor Peters passed into obscurity after one term. In 1922, Curley returned for the second of his four terms. Though the Brahmins detested him, he was actually their ideal, since he confirmed all they wanted to believe about Irishmen, and was in many respects their own creation. The real opposition to Curley came instead from another Irishman, His Eminence, William Cardinal O'Connell, Archbishop of Boston and powerful leader of American Catholicism. O'Connell was the vanguard of the new breed who held no brief for the stage-Irish role.

When O'Connell chose to exercise his political power, he was formidable. In the 1920s a messy sex scandal involving the blackmail of prominent men caused the removal of two district attorneys, one of whom committed suicide. The Cardinal then, in effect, appointed a district attorney to clean up the office.[87] For a long time his opposition to Curley, though known to insiders, was muted because of the American tradition of separation of church and state, but in the late 1930s a newspaper perpetrated a dirty trick worthy of Curley himself. On election morning it printed on the front page a statement of the Cardinal's, made years earlier, in a manner which would give the impression that His Eminence was endorsing Curley's opponent.[88] When Curley begged O'Connell to go on the radio with a repudiation, the Cardinal refused. It was the beginning of the end. After World War II, Curley would have one more term as Mayor, interrupted by a prison sentence* for alleged fraud while a Congressman, but Boston would then turn for its heroes to Honey Fitz's Kennedy grandsons.

After 1919 a new police force was slowly recruited from among war veterans, but it was never to be the same as in O'Meara's day. At the operating level the cops looked similar, although they no longer wore their London bobby helmets. The ordinary patrolman was still a strapping Boston Irishman, and the duties were still rough. One of the new recruits was William Clancy, who had been the first to carry the American colors into battle on the western front. Assigned to the Charlestown station, he was slain in Roughan's Dance Hall in 1920.[89]

In other ways it was different. The new force lacked the spirit of the old, and Prohibition was now the law of the land, with the result that corruption would be as prevalent in Boston as elsewhere. Given the

* Curley, a notorious sucker for investments in gold mines and schemes to convert base metals, despite rumors of his corruption was usually broke.

circumstances of their appointment, the new cops also had powerful claims on the beneficence of Beacon Hill, and as veterans and therefore twice-blessed heroes they would have a strong lobby in the Legislature. Gradually police commissioners lost their power over appointment, promotion, and dismissal, having to submit to civil service rules, trial board hearings, and court review.

Curtis died in 1922. His successor was fired as a result of a vice scandal in 1930, and in the next four years there were four commissioners. In 1934 Curley, then governor, managed to harass one of them with charges that he had spread manure from police stables to fertilize his lawn.[90] One doubts such tactics could have been used against O'Meara.

The discharged policemen campaigned for years to be taken back but to no avail. Despite their former service, in the eyes of many they were Bolsheviks. Some obtained police positions elsewhere, and for a few who became doctors or wealthy businessmen the strike was a boon. In 1936 Governor Curley appointed Diamond Jim Timilty's son Joe as commissioner with a request to restore some of the strikers, but Commissioner Timilty refused since they were now so long off the force that they would be useless.[91]

In a 1939 study sociologist William Whyte described the police–politics–organized-crime relationships of Boston in the same terms as were applied to any other city,[92] and in 1943 the roof fell in. In the aftermath of a December 1942 fire in the Coconut Grove nightclub which claimed nearly 500 lives, there were charges of laxity in the enforcement of safety regulations, and some of this spilled over to the police department with results including the suspension of a captain. Then a Yankee attorney general "with enormous capacity for righteous indignation,"[93] Robert Bushnell, brought charges leading to the indictment of Commissioner Timilty and a number of high-ranking officers on charges of protecting gambling.[94]

The worst blow, however, was the revelation that Irish gangs had been attacking Jews and vandalizing synagogues while the police department ignored the matter. These charges had double impact because they came in the midst of a war against Nazism and because the story had been broken by a New York paper, the Boston media refusing to touch it.[95] Prewar Boston had been a strong Coughlinite city, and it was later to back Joe McCarthy, but of course, when the war came, Irish youth rallied to the colors and their losses were heavy. While some young Irishmen were beating up Jews, their older brothers were dying from Nazi bullets. Boston was embarrassed, and recriminations flew back and forth.

At this juncture, leadership in resolving the situation came from an unexpected source. The governor of Massachusetts was Leverett Salton-

The Gordon Riots, London, 1780. The military restored order by killing more than 300 people. Afterward, the movement for a police force grew stronger. *Radio Times Hulton Picture Library.*

Sir Howard Vincent, Director of the CID (1878-1884), was accused of using "French" methods to fight crime. *Radio Times Hulton Picture Library.*

Detective Superintendent of the Special Branch (camera-shy man in the top hat) Sir Patrick Quinn, shown at the trial of Sir Roger Casement in London, 1916. The first policeman from the ranks to be knighted, Quinn knew the secrets of both revolutionaries and crowned heads. *Radio Times Hulton Picture Library.*

An actor's son, General Nevil Macready, London Metropolitan Police Commissioner (1918-1920), drew on his own histrionic ability to help smash a police strike. *Radio Times Hulton Picture Library.*

New York Police Commanders, circa 1890: Superintendent William Murray (seated in center), Detective Chief Inspector Thomas Byrnes (standing behind Murray); and Inspector Alex "Clubber" Williams (standing at far right). *Photograph by Jacob A. Riis, Jacob A. Riis Collection, Museum of the City of New York.*

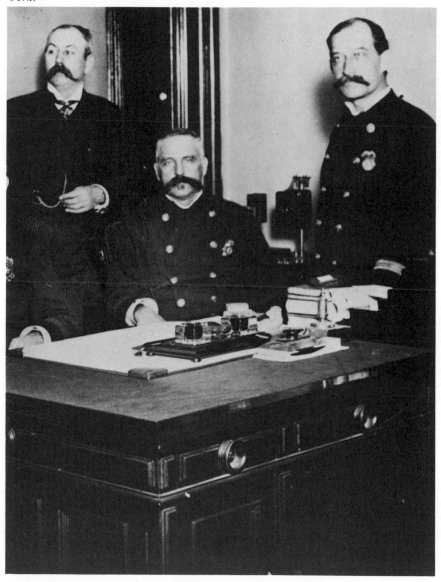

The Rogues' Gallery, 1886. This scene, staged by Inspector Byrnes for use in his book *Professional Criminals of America*, shows the method Byrnes used to obtain photos of criminals. Byrnes is standing at the left, looking on. *Photograph by Jacob A. Riis, Jacob A. Riis Collection, Museum of the City of New York.*

The Lexow Investigation, New York, 1894. A contemporary artist's rendering, showing Captain Max Schmittberger in the witness chair, with attorney John Goff standing and the Reverend Dr. Charles Parkhurst seated at far left. Schmittberger's confession to grafting was the high point of the drama. *Drawing by H.G. Dart, 1895. The Bettmann Archive, Inc.*

The Triumph of Tammany, 1898. Chief William Devery, on horseback, leads the first police parade after Tammany's return to power. *Museum of the City of New York.*

Richard Croker, 1899. Police and detectives clear the way for the Tammany boss as a news photographer records the progress of his stroll about his kingdom. Croker is in the center, wearing a derby hat. *Photograph by Byron, The Byron Collection, Museum of the City of New York.*

The assassination attempt on New York's Mayor William Gaynor, 1910, photographed a few seconds after Gaynor was shot. Although he recovered, many felt that the Mayor lost his grip on the city's affairs after the incident. *Museum of the City of New York.*

"Big Tim" Sullivan, circa 1909. In the early years of the twentieth century "the Big Feller" dominated the New York underworld by his power as he dominated any social gathering by his size. *Culver Pictures.*

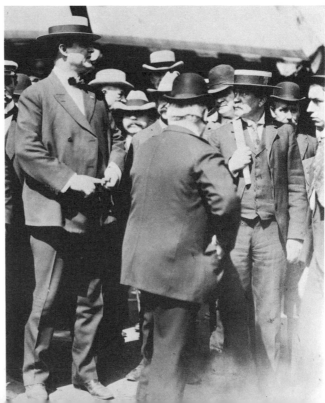

New York Police Lieutenant Charles Becker, whose 1912 conviction and subsequent execution for murder brought a reform administration to City Hall and the Albany State House. But some wondered if Charley Becker had been framed. *Museum of the City of New York.*

Stephen J. O'Meara, Boston Police Commissioner (1906-1918), created what was probably the best police force in America, but it vanished within a year after his death. *Courtesy, Massachusetts Historical Society, Boston, Massachusetts. Photographic reproduction by George M. Cushing.*

A nonstriking police sergeant talks with a militia trooper during the Boston Police Strike of 1919. The strike was crushed, but the city felt its costs for decades. *Culver Pictures.*

Pennsylvania State Troopers at the McKees Rocks Strike, 1909. Three troopers were killed and several were wounded at McKees Rocks, yet their reputation as America's most valiant (and controversial) police force grew. *Culver Pictures.*

stall, whose blood was probably the bluest in the state, since his family was one of two in Boston descended from the British aristocracy and therefore, unlike his inventive fellow Brahmins, actually entitled to a family coat of arms. The governor's father had been known as "the Squire" and had ridden a white horse about his estate where he threatened to shoot trespassers. Young "Salty" went to Harvard, of course, rowed in the crew, and rose in Republican politics.[96]

With such a background, Curley, his opponent in the 1938 gubenatorial race, had been entirely logical when he referred to Salty's homely but pleasant mug by stating "he may have a South Boston face, but he would not dare show it there." However, Curley was wrong about both Salty and Southie. The former immediately repaired to the latter, shaking hands, stopping in for a beer, and acting like a regular fellow. Soon an Irish ancestor was discovered, making him eligible for membership in an exclusive Celtic association with rules about family origins copied from the Brahmins. Salty became a favorite in Southie and with the Irish voters in general.[97] Therefore, while his Yankee attorney general was thundering moral indignation and working to supplant the governor,[98] Salty quietly replaced Commissioner Timilty with Colonel Tom Sullivan, whose regiment had been a bit rough on Southie in 1919 but who was himself a good Irishman. Salty then firmly but compassionately called the community to its senses with a reminder of the war in which he, like many others, had lost his son. This put an end to the trouble without the necessity of massive repression, which would have left a bitter taste for a generation. In the following year, he was elected to the U.S. Senate and remained there for twenty-two years until he retired at seventy-four, while the attorney general quickly disappeared from public life.*

Five factors characterized the O'Meara police force, perhaps the most successful community police department in the history of the United States. These were:

1. A relatively high ratio of police to population, which permitted full utilization of the beat system.
2. The employment of officers from the local community, which avoided connotations of an army of occupation.
3. A high standard of integrity.
4. A strong hand for the top administrator.
5. A strict adherence to legality.

* Attorney General Bushnell was a graduate of Harvard College and Harvard Law School and at the time of the police department investigation was forty-six years of age. With excellent local and national publicity, he was thought to have a brilliant political future. But he failed even to win reelection as attorney general. The following year he moved to New York, where, five years later, while conducting the defense of a Pentagon general convicted of war frauds, he died at fifty-three.[99]

In O'Meara's time only the first two were common in American police departments. After 1919 numbers 3 and 4 became less apparent in the Boston police department. In the post-World War II era, Colonel Tom Sullivan served fourteen years as commissioner. In general he was able to restore integrity, but, though he superficially resembled O'Meara, he lacked the power of the old days, and the following words from Leonard Harrison's description of O'Meara's time are perhaps a more apt description of the Boston Police Department under Sullivan:

> Tradition for the most part determined the course to be followed. Imagination and experimentation were apparently not encouraged and a deep rut of conservatism was worn in this period.[100]

Pennsylvania and New Jersey: The American Constabulary (1905–1940)

On the cold rainy morning of Friday, April 20, 1917, Secretary of War Newton D. Baker, accompanied by the Army Chief of Staff, arrived at the United States Military Academy at West Point. Though it was not the traditional June week, he was there to graduate the class of 1917. Two weeks earlier America had entered the World War and officers were needed immediately. An aura of excitement, not felt since 1861, hung in the air and as each of the 139 seniors walked across the gymnasium stage, the cheers of the underclassmen shook the building.[1] The following year some would die, others would win promotion and honors. In time, a few would become generals including three who would reach the highest ranks of the army. Perhaps the most unusual career lay before a young New Jerseyan, Herbert Schwartzkopf. He would fight and win promotion in France and in later years become a general; but the last would be achieved on his reputation as a policeman, not as a soldier. Schwartzkopf was to become America's most famous constabulary chief.

THE HAUNTING SPECTER

Though rural Britain adopted a London-type police system within a generation of its introduction in the capital, as late as 1905 no similar development had taken place in the United States. Until the Civil War, the traditional system of sheriffs and constables proved sufficient for the rural areas. After the war, the extensive development of railways and the improvement of roads enabled large numbers of criminals, economically dispossessed people, and adventurers to "tramp" their way across country, often sustaining themselves by preying on isolated settlements. While the railroads themselves quickly created police departments for their own protection, the rural areas did not. Nineteenth-century burglars such as Langdon Moore found their most lucrative targets in the small-town banks of the Northeast where industrial development provided well-filled vaults but local governments failed to provide police protection.[2] As in Britain, though, crime was but one of the problems exacerbated by social change.

In the aftermath of the Civil War, America found itself a major industrial nation, and with the new status came serious clashes between management and labor. Unfortunately, at the very beginning of this era there occurred an incident which deeply shocked the upper classes of the western world and colored their reaction to labor protests from then on. This was the Paris Commune. In 1871, after the city's fall to the Germans, radicals seized a section of Paris and proclaimed a revolutionary society. The French Army, many of its members released from German prison camps, crushed the rebellion, killing and imprisoning thousands. Confused and ineffective though it was—the revolutionaries were not clear as to what they really sought, and Karl Marx for one complained because they had shot the Archbishop of Paris instead of dynamiting the Bank of France—it provided a vision of what might happen should radicals lead the proletariat against the upper classes.[3] Henceforth, to paraphrase Marx, the American elite would be haunted by the specter of the Commune. The New York draft riots had demonstrated the ease with which a single city could be sacked, and the new industrialism would soon provide an example of how the entire nation could be convulsed and in the process illustrate certain weaknesses in the security forces.

In the late nineteenth century when the control of civil disorders required assistance beyond the local policing arrangements, forces of special deputies or constables were frequently employed. Since the job of a "special" on riot duty was likely to be hazardous and short-lived (sometimes in the literal sense), the recruits were drawn from the pool of floating labor, from drunks and drifters who needed the money, or from toughs looking to throw their weight around and commit thefts from the property they were supposedly protecting. Sometimes an agency such as the Pinkertons or a lesser entrepeneur would, in addition to furnishing guards, provide strikebreakers.

The alternative to specials and private guards was the state militia.

Like the rural police system, this body was the result of English history, most notably the fear of a standing army, although in Britain the failure of the militia when assigned to riot duty had been manifest and a prime reason for the creation of the new police. Whatever its short-comings, the militia was the cornerstone of American military strength. On the eve of the Civil war the regular army numbered only 16,000 men, while, if official state records are accurate, the militia comprised approximately 3 million, with the state of Pennsylvania alone providing 350,000.[4] But although militia rosters constituted a form of draft regis-tration, signifying the number of men potentially available, they did not indicate the number ready for duty. Only a few thousand were orga-nized in units, and the level of training and equipment varied consider-ably. Relatively effective forces like New York's Seventh Regiment were rare. After the Civil War the regular army was increased by only 10,000 and the militia system continued intact, but when tested in American industrial strife, it proved as ineffective as in Britain.

In 1877 several railroads announced pay cuts for their employees, sparking serious disorders in a number of states. The drama began in July with a wildcat strike by B & O employees in Martinsburg, West Virginia. When the local sheriff failed in an attempt to disperse mobs blocking trains, the militia was summoned and after some minor blood-shed it too gave up. The railroads then prevailed upon President Ruther-ford B. Hayes to dispatch U.S. regulars. He did and the disorders faded away.

As West Virginia calmed down, trouble broke out in Baltimore, and here too the militia was mobilized. But Baltimore was a rough city used to manhandling troops.* When the alarm bells rang to assemble the militiamen, the city's toughs also gathered and attacked a regiment at-tempting to march to the railroad station, the general assembly point. The troops fired, and the riot which followed claimed at least ten lives. Most of the militiamen simply fled the scene, discarding their uniforms as they ran. Another regiment managed to reach the depot unmolested but cowered inside until rescued by the city's tough police department. Finally, regulars and Marines were summoned, and the Baltimore situa-tion was brought under control.[5]

This was only the beginning, however. Pittsburgh was next to rise. Here the city's police department (recently reduced by half due to a budget cut) sympathized with the mobs, as did the Pittsburgh regiments of the National Guard. Therefore, the state dispatched a brigade from Philadelphia. When they arrived, they made a colorful sight in their operetta-style uniforms; one regiment even favored black plumed hats.

---

* Among the more famous incidents was the pitched battle between Baltimore mobs and the Sixth Massachusetts Infantry when the regiment marched through the city in 1861.

But the Pittsburgh crowds were not impressed and in a bitter battle drove the militia out of town at a cost of at least twenty-five dead including five guardsmen. The mob then celebrated its victory by burning millions of dollars worth of railroad property.[6] In other parts of the state the militia was equally unsuccessful, its men frequently surrendering their weapons. At Altoona, 500 troops gave up their rifles without a shot and marched away led by a vocal quartet from a Negro company, singing in "excellent harmony."[7] Only after regulars entered the state were the authorities able to restore order.

In cities with reliable police departments it was a different story. In Buffalo charges with the nightsticks dispersed the mobs, and at the opposite end of the state, the New York cops, not long after their triumphs in the strike of '72 and Murray's charge of '74, needed only to appear at meetings to ensure order. In Chicago the police were eager for combat, and when it came, they and the militia killed some twenty members of the mob, so that when the regulars arrived there was little for them to do except sit down and listen to a concert by the Chicago Symphony Orchestra.[8]

The strike of '77 was to be a blueprint for future disorders. Where a strong police force existed, order was maintained. When regular troops were employed, they too were effective even though their numbers were few. In 1877 the army had but 3,000 men available east of the Mississippi, but the presence of small detachments of the regulars was usually sufficient to restore order. In Pittsburgh, fifty U.S. soldiers marched unchallenged through the burned streets after the National Guard had been driven out. The army also operated a very effective intelligence service through signal corps sergeants stationed in every major city as weather observers. Their reports telegraphed to Washington enabled the government to accurately assess various local situations and move its forces with maximum effect.[9]

Given the amateur nature of the militia, its repeated failure was predictable. Even when the guardsmen managed to muddle through, it was usually the occasion for sighs of relief. Young Louis Brandeis, mobilized with the Kentucky Guard to combat strikers in Louisville, recorded the joy of his parents as well as the community when he and his mates came through unharmed. A Louisville paper had characterized them as "striplings who know no more the use of a gun than a Chinaman of an English spelling book."[10]

The task of dispersing mobs without shooting them is one of the most difficult of operations, requiring a high degree of training, discipline, and confidence between officers and men. It is not something which can be learned by an occasional drill session. In a thousand incidents from Pittsburgh in '77 through Boston in 1919 to Kent State in 1970, the militia would frequently fail to perform adequately in situations of civil disorder. Incidents of indiscriminate shooting, often without orders, would be legion, while on other occasions militia troops would melt away before hostile mobs or fraternize with them, the latter being a common phenomenon in the face of white rioters during racial conflict.[11]

In contrast, the regular army, while sometimes accused of excessive force, would never be charged with lack of discipline. The difference between regulars and militia was illustrated by two incidents which took place in Pennsylvania during the troubles of 1877. In Pittsburgh a group of workers inquired of a regular army sentry, "If there was another row, you wouldn't shoot us, would you?" "Not shoot!" said the regular. "Why, damn ye, I'm paid to shoot." At Wilkes-Barre some Irish miners asked an Irish soldier if he would fire on his countrymen. "That" he replied, "would depend upon the captain's orders."[12]

The Keystone State

The incursion of industrialism into rural America, besides bringing in crime and disorder, created more ethnic ghettos, so that many mining or mill areas had Italian, Irish, and Negro districts in the same fashion as the cities, with the usual communal or nativist versus immigrant conflicts, and in no area of the United States were the problems of rural crime, industrial disorder, and ethnic conflict more apparent than in Pennsylvania. With the discovery of coal and iron deposits in the state in the 1850s, there came Irish, English, and Welsh miners to work the fields. By the Civil War whole settlements of foreigners existed in Pennsylvania, and the Irish especially had a reputation for violence. Sometimes the disorder took on a political cast. An Irish secret society known as the Molly Maguires was alleged to have been responsible for a number of murders of mine officials from the 1860s onward. Finally, in 1877, they were arrested on the basis of the testimony of a Pinkerton undercover agent name James McParland, and twenty of them were subsequently hanged.*[13] Disorders continued as Slavs and Italians flocked to the fields in the '80s and '90s. Nor was industrial disorder confined to the mines. In 1892, the workers at the Carnegie steel plant in Homestead, Pennsylvania, struck, and while Andrew Carnegie vacationed in Scotland, his manager, Henry Frick, brought in a force of 300 Pinkerton detectives to protect the plant. On the 5th of July, as barges towed the detectives up the Monongahela River, the strikers opened fire, and after a pitched battle during which several detectives and strikers were killed, the Pinkertons surrendered. Afterward, many of them were

---

* A further noteworthy circumstance was the fact that one of the state prosecutors in the case was the man who hired the Pinkertons, Franklin B. Gowen, president of the Reading Railroad and Coal and Iron Company.

brutally beaten and mutilated. This so alarmed the authorities that the entire 10,000-man Pennsylvania militia was sent to Homestead and the strikers were tried for treason against the state, though, despite a personal charge to the jury from the chief justice of Pennsylvania, they refused to convict.*

The Homestead strike attracted worldwide attention, and a young Russian-born anarchist, Alexander Berkman, who shared a *ménage à trois* with Emma Goldman and Johann Most, journeyed from New York and shot Frick. Though badly wounded, he survived, and Berkman spent the next fourteen years in a Pennsylvania prison, emerging as a leader of American radicals.[14] The usually ferocious Most repudiated the shooting, and an angry Emma Goldman horsewhipped him at a public meeting.[15]

Pennsylvania's troubles continued into the twentieth century. In 1902 a general strike in the anthracite coal fields paralyzed the state's economy; there was widespread violence, and again the militia was called out. Finally, in what was then an unprecedented step, President Theodore Roosevelt intervened and brought about a settlement.

To some the reign of violence was symptomatic of deeper problems. In October 1901 the *Atlantic Monthly* published an article called "The Ills of Pennsylvania," in which the anonymous author declared that the state was the most corrupt in the union.[16] While articles attacking the corruption of political machines were common fare in the respectable journals of the time, they were usually aimed at Democratic machines with Irish bosses, a description which did not apply to Pennsylvania. From the Civil War on the state was overwhelmingly Republican because, the state's being a manufacturing area, both labor and management supported the high-tariff policies which were then a staple of the GOP. Pennsylvania was in fact the strongest machine state in the country, since there was no rural-urban, Republican-Democratic division. Philadelphia, the leading city, turned out four-to-one Republican majorities. It was as though Tammany were an adjunct to the machine of Boss Platt. As in New York the Republican party was run by a United States Senator, the boss of bosses, Matt Quay, and upon his death by Boies Penrose. Political lesser lights like Ed Vare, boss of Philadelphia, sat in the State Senate where the deals were made, and satraps like Vare's brother, William, were sent to the less important U.S. House of Representatives.

Given its great power, enhanced by ties to the dominant national Republican party, the Pennsylvania machine could hardly fail to be

---

* In the history of the United States there have been but two successful prosecutions for treason against a state. These involved, respectively, Thomas Dorr, who led Dorr's Rebellion in Rhode Island in 1842, and John Brown, for the raid on Harper's Ferry, Virginia, in 1859.

corrupt. Yet somehow a Republican machine, bossed by native Americans, never seemed to arouse reformers to the level of concern which immigrant-dominated Democratic machines inspired. In fact, as the *Atlantic Monthly* article pointed out, the machine served well the real power of Pennsylvania, its business corporations such as the Pennsylvania Railroad, whose president ruled over 150,000 employees, 200 of whom earned higher salaries than the governor of the state. The anonymous author claimed that the Pennsylvania elite, particularly the Quakers, so decent in their personal life, had forfeited their civic responsibility in exchange for profit.

When the article appeared, there was fury in the clubs and mansions of Rittenhouse Square. The writer's identity was soon uncovered. He was young Mark Sullivan, a Pennsylvania native, then a student at Harvard Law School and on the threshold of a brilliant career in journalism as editor of *Colliers* and social chronicler of *Our Times*. Leading the counterattack on him was a distinguished Philadelphia judge, historian, and trustee of the University of Pennsylvania, Samuel Pennypacker. Boss Quay decided that so staunch a defender of the state's honor should be its governor, and in 1902, in the last significant act of the dying Quay's life, the machine installed Pennypacker as chief executive.*

Despite his sponsorship Pennypacker was not a hack, and in his own fashion he faced up to the problem of crime and disorder in the industrial areas. As a first step he dismissed the fat businessman who served as commanding general of the militia; an individual who had never seen active service but was a connoisseur of wines, a racing devotee, big spender, and lover of gaudy uniforms, replacing him with an experienced soldier.[18] However, the governor realized that reforming the militia was not the real solution. Prior to Pennypacker's regime the state granted police commissions to organizations of private guards as a so-called "coal and iron police," but so blatant a use of state authority by private organizations raised the obvious charge that the de facto state police were simply tools of management. In the Philippines after

---

* Mark Sullivan celebrated the governor's devotion to Senator Quay with a poem:

> Then sadly Pennypacker comes
>   Forth to the graveyard gray,
> And lays a grateful wreath of plums
>   Upon the tomb of Quay. . . .

> "O Master," 'twixt his sobs he saith,
>   "When all cartoonists die,
> When editors, all gagged to death,
>   'Neath broken presses lie,
> Four noble statues I'll erect
>   With public funds to pay;
> The Gilded Hog, the Yellow Dog,
>   Myself and Matthew Quay."[17]

the Spanish-American War, a constabulary force had been formed with native enlisted men and American officers. Such a force resembled the Royal Irish Constabulary and similar bodies utilized to deal with rebellious populations, and it was to this model that Pennypacker turned.

The Jungle Patrol

The creation of the Philippine Constabulary was not a result of a long evolution or deliberate plan, but was improvised out of practical necessity. After seizing the island from Spain in 1898, with hardly a fight, in the next year the United States was confronted with a native insurrection which fully occupied 70,000 American soldiers, or three times as many men as had been in the entire U.S. Army a year earlier.

In the familiar pattern, the western troops easily defeated the insurgent field army but were perplexed by guerrilla tactics. Sentries had their throats cut, and whole companies were overrun by foes who appeared without warning and vanished back into the jungle. Against such opponents the troops and their commanders discarded the rules of war. One general organized search-and-destroy missions with instructions to kill all able-bodied men. Another general ordered Samar Island turned into a desert and every male over ten killed.[19]

At first, the American public knew nothing of all this. The army imposed a tight censorship to suppress news until after the reelection of President McKinley in 1900. But correspondents managed to get word out, and accounts began to appear in the American press.[20] As the nature of the Philippines campaign became clear, some Americans objected to the treatment of the natives, more worried about American casualties. The army's reaction was to court-martial junior officers on war crimes charges. However, this backfired on the brass. For example, when Marine Major Tony Waller was tried for wiping out a village on Samar, he admitted to the charge but pleaded that he had obeyed orders from Army General Jacob Smith. Eventually, the general himself was brought to trial and forced to retire.[21]

Clearly, U.S. soldiers could not be used as the primary counterinsurgency forces. The casualties and hardships they sustained destroyed morale and evoked criticism at home, while the massacres continued despite the official line propagated by Governor General William Howard Taft that the Americans were there to protect their "little brown brothers." As the army sang,

> I'm only a common soldier man in the blasted Philippines
> They say I've got brown brothers here but I don't know what it means,
> I like the word fraternity, but still I draw the line—
> He may be a brother to William Howard Taft, but he ain't no brother
>   of mine.[22]

At this juncture the Americans fell back on the British expedient of utilizing native troops, or in later phraseology, "Asian boys to fight Asian boys," under the leadership of American officers. Thus, in 1901, the Philippine Constabulary was created. It quickly rose to a strength of 7,000 enlisted men and 250 officers. Under the new plan American troops remained in the settled areas while the constabulary and Philippine scout detachments of the army moved into the jungles.

While a few regular army officers accepted constabulary posts— Captain Henry T. Allen of the Sixth Cavalry became commandant with the rank of brigadier general—most did not, and the officers had to be recruited from American adventurers. Not surprisingly, these were a wild bunch. Winfield Scott "Winnie" Grove, a former militia sergeant, got into an argument with the native governor of Laguna Province at an official reception, took him outside, and beat him up. This was too much for the Governor General. "A goddamn scandal," Taft declared, and Grove was ordered court-martialed. But the native governor gallantly declined to press charges and Taft ended up making Grove chief of detectives in Manila where he could keep an eye on him.[23]

Grove was tame compared with Constabulary Major Jesse Garwood, a big, blond, mustachioed, western gunfighter type who became a legend as a lover and a policeman. Garwood's tactics were to threaten governors with guns. On one occasion he told a recalcitrant province chief to face a mirror, then executed a quick draw and blasted the mirror image in the heart. In order to keep in practice for such escapades, he shot apples off the head of his Filipino houseboy in William Tell fashion. But Garwood showed to best advantage with native officials' wives. As he moved through his district, each local headman would tender a reception, which Garwood reportedly would climax by seducing the official's wife. His opening gambit was said to be invariably to whisper in Spanish, "Señora, if you will pardon a personal question, I should like to know why a beautiful and cultured lady like yourself should throw herself away on a shriveled-up, wrinkled little cuss like your husband?"

Garwood's police methods were equally unorthodox. Once when a native wanted to join his force, he told him to bring the head of a local bandit named Jose Tinto. Since the man did not know Tinto by sight, he had to bring two heads before he got the right one, but Garwood was satisfied and the jungle patrol had a new recruit. Though Garwood achieved spectacular results in his police work, his personal conduct eventually forced his resignation.[24]

Whatever embarrassing incidents occurred, the constabulary was a success. When the force was organized in 1901, there were still 50,000 United States soldiers in the islands. By 1904, the troops had been reduced to 12,000. In two years of counterinsurgency operations prior to the establishment of the constabulary, 752 U.S. soldiers were killed.

In the first five years of constabulary operation, the army had but 239 killed while, by comparison, the constabulary itself lost over 1,000. Between 1907 and 1913, the number of army deaths fell to a total of 23, and from then on not a single American soldier was killed by insurgents in the Philippines. Finally, whatever happened in the back country did not involve American personnel, save a few soldiers of fortune,* and therefore did not make news in the states.

The Black Hussars

It was a modified version of the Philippine Constabulary which was to be the solution in Pennsylvania. America was to establish its first militarized police force, although in Pennypacker's disarming version the decision appears to have been some sort of humorous afterthought. As he later wrote:

> When I assumed the office of Chief Executive of the State, I found myself thereby invested with supreme executive authority. I found that no power existed to interfere with me and my duty to enforce the laws of the state, and that, by the same token, no conditions could release me from my duty to do so. I then looked about to see what instruments I possessed wherewithal to accomplish this bounden obligation—what instruments on whose loyalty and obedience I could truly rely. I perceived three such instruments: my private secretary, a very small man; my woman stenographer; and the janitor, a Negro. So, I made the State Police.[25]

Despite the governor's bland assertions, the force was meant to crush disorders, whether industrial or otherwise, which arose in the foreigner-filled districts of the state. The organization and management of the Pennsylvania State Police was in fact that of a military body frankly modeled after the RIC and the Philippine Constabulary. Its first commandant was Captain John B. Groome, a Philadelphia sportsman and Spanish-American War veteran, who had commanded an elite Pennsylvania National Guard troop with considerable experience in policing strikes. The 220 officers and men were virtually all drawn from the armed forces, including a number from the Philippine Constabulary. Members were required to be unmarried and to reside in barracks. Troopers were mounted and armed with carbines, pistols, and riot batons. While supposedly statewide, the force was actually deployed in four troops to cover the mining districts.

The mission of the state police was clear—to beat down the foreigners. In the words of their greatest admirer, Katherine Mayo,

* After 1913 most American officers were weeded out by a policy of Filippinization.

In the beginning the major part of the mine laborers came from Ireland
... [from which] sprang that unspeakable society of murderers, the
"Molly Maguires." ... Then came the Slavs and the Italians, who practically filled the field at the period in hand.

Peoples totally unused in their countries of origin to any form of
self-government, but accustomed on the contrary to see the sword of the
King always bared before their eyes, Slavs and Italians alike here looked
in vain for outward evidence of authority and law.... Liberty that they
knew not how to use, money that they knew neither how to spend nor
save, meant license, greed, drunkenness—and through drunkenness all
brutalities let loose.[26]

Thus virtually all troopers were native Americans and their motto
was "One American can lick a hundred foreigners."[27] Miss Mayo, a successful writer of her day, was not a bleeding-heart liberal or sob sister,
but a vigorous exponent of red-blooded, two-fisted, 100 percent Amer-
icanism to whom the world was full of danger from foreigners, Negroes,
and labor agitators. Her description of the arrest of a Negro in a rape
case provides some of the flavor of her views and the type of language
appropriate for heroes in the time of Teddy Roosevelt:

Groping along the eerie bulk, the Sergeant found the door and knocked.
No reply. Again, and louder. "Who's there?"

"The State Police. Open your door!"

Then came a snarl like the snarl of a wild beast hideous out of that
shapeless night.

"Open, or we break the door in!"

A howl of imprecations, obscenities, and defiance, ending in a shriek:
"The first man in I'll kill!"

"Why, now men, we *have to get in*," observed the Sergeant to his
troopers, very quietly.... As the door flew off its hinges, the Sergeant
stood in the threshold, revolver raised. His glance, searching the black
blank within, saw something forming upon it, two eyes—the outline of
a face.

"Hands up!," snapped the Sergeant. And with that lunging at the
muzzle of the revolver, the Negro seized it in his teeth. Snarling, froth-
ing, he tore at the cold steel, grinding it between his great jaws.

Shoving the gun back into its holster, the Sergeant gripped the mad-
man by the shoulders and sat him down.[28]

Unfortunately, the suspect turned out to be the wrong man.

In 1905 the state police commenced their duty and quickly rode into
a storm. The troopers, known as the Black Hussars, or by their enemies
as the Cossacks, were wont to gallop into the foreign settlements and
conduct sweeps or even search-and-destroy missions. A typical incident
occurred in April 1906 at the town of Boston Patch. A crowd of Italians

had allegedly fired on some other workers at the local colliery, and the foreman called for assistance from Troop B. A small detachment, under Sergeant Jesse Garwood, late of the Philippine Constabulary, responded and forcibly entered and searched the miners' homes, removing weapons and other contraband. This was Pennsylvania, however, not the Philippines, and the mine workers' union pressed charges of criminal trespass against Garwood and his men, but nothing came of them.[29]

Even the local cops were likely to be hostile. One constable in Wilkes-Barre township posted the following notice:

NOTICE TO POLICE

April 13, 1906

To any member of the State Police Force under the Act of May 2, 1905:

Please take notice that according to the above Act, Section 5, your duty is wherever possible to cooperate with the local authorities in detecting crime, etc. I am the duly elected Constable and Peace Officer of Wilkes-Barre Township, Luzerne County, Pa., and without consulting or co-operating with me you have since yesterday arrested people without warrants when you have not witnessed them commit any crimes. You are roaming around the streets in my bailiwick like Russian Cossacks and inciting the peaceable residents of said township. You are doing this for the last twenty-four hours. Therefore, you are hereby notified that I can control the situation myself and I have not been notified of any disturbance and if I am notified I will call upon you.

Respectfully yours,

JOHN SUNDAY
Constable and Peace Officer[30]

At the end of April 1906, the troopers shot twenty strikers in Mount Carmel, Pennsylvania. Though the lieutenant in command was arrested for assault and battery, the state exonerated him and his men of all charges; in the words of Governor Pennypacker, the troopers "established a reputation which has gone all over the Country . . . with the result that the labor difficulties in the Anthracite coal region entirely disappeared."[31] Clearly, the state police met the same needs as the Philippine Constabulary. A small body of hardy professionals tougher than their opponents, they not only brought law and order but obviated the need for civilian militia boys to do the rough work. Even the unfriendly local cops came to rely on them for the dangerous tasks, since nothing daunted the troopers. In August 1909, during a bloody steelworkers' strike at McKee's Rocks, a crowd clashed with the state police. In the ensuing battle three troopers were shot, two of them fatally, and two others were almost beaten to death before their comrades could ride to the rescue.[32] Far from being disheartened, the force was proud. Jesse Garwood said, "A [state] policeman can arrest anybody, anytime," as he went alone into a saloon after a man surrounded by armed bodyguards.[33]

In February 1910, Philadelphia experienced a violent streetcar strike in which its police department cut a poor figure. A militia detachment sent to help were relieved of their uniforms and rifles, and their commanding officer of his sword, after which they fled behind the shelter of the city's mounted police. The mayor then asked for the state's entire 10,000-man National Guard to reinforce his 4,000 police. Instead the governor sent in 185 troopers. The contrast between the municipals and comic-opera militiamen and the soldierly troopers was the same as between the militia and the regular army in Pittsburgh in '77. Again the crowds were awed into submission, although the troopers were somewhat helped by advance newspaper stories which added to their fearsome image:

> The state mounted police from the coal regions, hated and dreaded, known as the Black Hussars, are to encamp at dawn this morning in the City Hall. They fire to kill, and carry automatic guns.
>
> They are cool, but when they get started, they move like a shot; and when it is necessary to shoot, they do it without the slightest hesitation.[34]

For a decade after the birth of the State Police, the United Mine Workers pressed for the abolition of this "Cossack" force, and this became a plank in the state Democratic platform. During World War I, however, the union was embarrassed by having to ask for state police protection against the more radical International Workers of the World (IWW). A typical incident took place in September 1916 at Old Forge, Pennsylvania. There the local sheriff had forbidden the radicals to meet, and when they defied his orders, the state police raided the meeting hall and arrested all 262 people present. After the release of some undercover informants, the rest were sentenced to thirty days. In this particular case the United Mine Workers were quite satisfied with the "Cossacks."[35]

Within a generation the primary reason for the creation of the Pennsylvania State Police largely eroded. From 1914 on, massive immigration to the United States ceased and the mining population became more Americanized. Political protest grew less violent with increasing acceptance of the union movement. Thus Pennsylvania's industrial belt was no longer a land of cultural deviance and incipient rebellion, but just another rural slum. Though occasionally active against strikers, the state police began to concentrate on rural crime and traffic rather than civil disorder, and under Governor Gifford Pinchot in the 1920s were more concerned with enforcing Prohibition laws than riot control.[36] Jesse Garwood, now a lieutenant, grew bored, resigned his commission and wandered off to the West. Ironically, the force became increasingly composed of the descendants of the foreign stock which it was created to suppress.

A DISCIPLINED POLICE

While the original reason for the existence of state police gradually faded, the model did not because it offered certain advantages over alternative systems of policing. The troopers provided a professional force in place of the small-town constables and rural sheriffs. Also, the image of a disciplined, efficient, and relatively incorruptible police appealed to those who were appalled at the state of big-city policing. This was particularly true of nativist elements, whose strength was greatest in state government.

In the twentieth century, the automobile increased the necessity for state police by providing a means for city criminals to prey upon rural areas which still relied on the policing arrangements of fourteenth-century England. In New Jersey, one of the states most affected, as late as 1916 a survey indicated that sixteen of twenty-one sheriffs did nothing to combat crime; instead they concentrated on running the county jails and serving as court officers.[37] A typical incident of the time occurred in Burlington County when Mr. A. D. Rider, a wealthy cranberry farmer, was returning from town after picking up his payroll, accompanied by his daughter, his brother, and a hired man. En route they were ambushed by ten men who began shooting. Rider's brother was killed and he and his daughter were wounded, but the assailants were driven off by the hired man, who was armed and fired back at them. After treatment, the Rider group returned to the scene where they found the sheriff, the coroner, and the county detective, Ellis Parker, but no pursuit was being organized. In fact, Detective Parker left the scene to go to the Mount Holly fair, explaining that there were "a lot of fakirs" there and he had to watch them. Through Mr. Rider's own efforts the bandits were eventually tracked down and arrested in cooperation with the Philadelphia police.[38] Clearly, a better system was needed and a strong woman would lead the fight to achieve it.

If Governor Pennypacker was the father of America's state police, Katherine Mayo was surely their mother. In 1913, while Miss Mayo was visiting a friend in Bedford Hills, New York, a young construction foreman was killed nearby, defending a payroll from bandits. She was upset because no efficient rural police existed to investigate the crime, particularly since the victim was a "good American," the killers were Italian, and the local authorities were too frightened to act. The angry Miss Mayo had heard of an organization of Pennsylvania troopers who handled such incidents, and she determined to investigate the matter. Much taken with the Pennsylvania State Police, she produced three books about them and agitated for a similar body in New York State. Theodore Roosevelt sent a copy of the first book, *Justice to All,* to every member of the New York legislature when it was considering a bill to created a state police, and in 1917 Miss Mayo was rewarded by the establishment of such a force.[39] Other states such as Michigan organized similar bodies as replacements for the departed National Guard in that same wartime year and after the war made their state police bodies permanent.

As in Pennsylvania, men of social standing and military experience were favored for the command positions. New York appointed Colonel George Chandler, M.D., as superintendent, and when he stepped down in 1923, he was succeeded by Major John Warner, a National Guard cavalry officer and Harvard graduate who had studied music in Europe. In 1926, Warner gained further prestige by marrying Governor Alfred E. Smith's daughter Emily. In all, approximately a dozen states created state police bodies on the military constabulary model,* the remainder settling for state highway patrols—organizations with relatively limited jurisdictional scope. That is, while the state police undertook responsibility for traffic *and* crime control in rural areas and small towns, highway patrols were confined to traffic enforcement on state roads.

Despite the size and significance of state police forces in Pennsylvania, New York, and Michigan, the most important state police command and the most famous constabulary commander were to emerge in New Jersey. Various factors militated for a state police in the Garden State. Between 1910 and 1915 twenty-two persons were killed there in industrial disorders, a 1915 IWW strike at Patterson being the most spectacular incident.[40] A second factor was that the mobility which the auto afforded criminals was particularly troublesome in New Jersey, since the state bordered two major metropolitan areas, Philadelphia and New York, with large criminal populations. The proximity of big-city crime and indigenous industrial disorder caused many rural legislators to favor a state police over a highway patrol, while organized labor and city politicians were opposed. Most prominent among the latter was the boss of Jersey City, Frank Hague, head of one of the most powerful political machines in the country. Like any city boss, Hague was not

* All but West Virginia and Oregon were states east of the Mississippi and north of the Mason-Dixon line. Though the Texas Rangers somewhat resembled a state police force, they numbered less than fifty men and a much larger highway patrol was also maintained.

eager to see a state law enforcement agency created, since it might interfere with the corruption which provided the lifeblood of his machine. Hague could also speak from the perspective of a successful police administrator, since he had been the "reform" commissioner of public safety in Jersey City.

The Captive City

In 1891 Augustine Costello, undaunted by the ingratitude of certain New York policemen who, despite his flattering description of them, had beaten his head in, produced a similar book about Jersey City police and in one stirring passage described how the local cops broke up the Red Tiger gang of the city's "horseshoe" slum district:

> Captain C. P. Smith was assigned to command this precinct in 1887, and was given a few more men. He assumed the offensive against this mob of Red Tigers, and after a few months had them all in jail and the mob broken up. Amongst the worst of this mob were, William Thomas, William Konoski alias Billy Dutch, John Hague alias Big Pete, Michael Tully alias Sap, John Tully alias Monk, Thomas Turley, John Lane, John Gallagher alias Red, John Sullivan alias Tiger, and Hugh Hague. A proper detail now patrols that part of the city. The Red Tigers are entirely broken up, and the streets are safe to travel at all hours of the day and night.[41]

Not all of "the mob" went to jail. John and Hugh Hague, for example, went straight, the latter becoming a city fireman. Their equally tough younger brother, Frank, went through the same gang experience, became a cop, and then, in a manner of speaking, became a supercop. During his thirty years as mayor of Jersey City, Democratic leader of Hudson County, and the most important politician in the state, Frank Hague was not a boss like Croker, Sullivan, Quay, or Lomasney, but a dictator like Huey Long or even Trujillo or Mussolini. His regime illustrated some of the realities of New Jersey policing.

In 1897, at twenty-one, Hague became a constable, and a few years later he became a deputy sheriff. In that capacity he journeyed to Boston in 1904 and committed perjury in the criminal trial of a burglar friend. Though he was indicted by the state of Massachusetts, New Jersey refused to extradite him. By 1910 he was a power in Jersey politics, and to head him off the boss of Newark brought forth Princeton President Woodrow Wilson as a gubernatorial candidate. In a spirited election featuring slugging and widespread fraud, the scholar was elected. Once in office, Wilson disowned his supporters in favor of Hague, then switched back again, thus outsmarting both bosses. Hague retaliated by ordering State Treasurer Edward "Teddy" Edwards, a

Jersey City bank president, to dock Wilson's pay every time the governor left the state to campaign for President.[42]

In 1913 the various reform elements of Hudson County forced adoption of a widely urged panacea—the commission form of government. As a result, Frank Hague was named public safety commissioner. Thus the reformers inadvertently accomplished what a boss would not dare to do—install a voracious politician as chief of police.

Hague immediately began to cry that crime and vice were rampant, the cops lazy, corrupt "swaggering bullies," and demanded the right to hire and fire them and to outlaw the police union. Through a legal trick he obtained the authority sought, and the frightened cops voluntarily gave up their union. Hague now had the same powers as his contemporary, Commissioner O'Meara of Boston, and he quickly used it to dismiss his enemies, putting 125 men on trial before him in one day. He also created a 100-man spy squad for surveillance over cops and citizens alike.

Throughout the next thirty-four years Hague would bulldoze the police. A favorite technique to increase efficiency was to put in false calls for assistance and woe betide cops whose arrival was slow. If they were lucky, they might only get a tonguelashing from Hague, sometimes accompanied by kicks and blows. In a fit of anger he might bring them up on charges and fire or fine them, although in a puckish mood he might turn over the fines to the officers' wives. As a lesson in obedience Hague ensured that the former head of the Police Benevolent Association was passed over for promotion ten times. Other policemen were used as hostages. For example, when the state's chief justice rendered an opinion Hage disliked, the man's policeman relatives were shifted from their soft jobs to walking beats.[43]

His publicity as a reform police chief helped him to be elected mayor in 1917, over an opposition which included the rival bosses of New Jersey, and President Woodrow Wilson. He then began his rule of the city and county in earnest.* The key to Hague's control was the police department, which despite the harsh discipline was one of the largest and best paid in the nation.** Because of his absolute power over the

---

* At the outset, though, he suffered one defeat. Hague's support of the war was not as enthusiastic as President Wilson would have liked, and the Commander-in-Chief feared for the new military port at Hoboken, in Hague territory. He therefore ordered the army to seize the city and the Secret Service to lock up any possible war resisters, so that for the duration Hague's territory was annexed by a stronger ruler.[44]

** In 1940, for example, Jersey City paid its patrolmen $3,000 per year and its chief $9,000. The department employed 916 officers and the Hudson County and Hudson Boulevard Police 67 and 105, respectively. Since the county was totally composed of incorporated towns, these forces operated largely within Jersey City. In terms of officers per population and salary levels, Jersey City ranked highest in the nation among cities of comparable size.[45]

cops, he was able to suppress all dissent. Anyone wishing to speak or distribute literature was required to obtain a permit, and Hague's opponents were of course refused. If they persisted, they were slugged by the cops and frequently deported out of the state.

While some people objected, most did not. Hague provided jobs, building projects, and excellent free medical care for his constituents. During a fuel shortage he solved the problem by simply ordering the police to confiscate carloads of coal passing through on the way to New York. When the owners inquired under what law he had acted, he replied, "the law of the nightstick"; it was enough.[46] His strong anti-Red and antivice pronouncements made him popular with the American Legion and the Catholic Church. Prostitution was not permitted (except in roadhouses outside of town), though the city contained major bookmaking operations, particularly after Mayor La Guardia ran some big gamblers out of New York City.

If any Hudson County citizens protested to other bodies, they were wasting their time. In 1919 Teddy Edwards was elected governor, and in 1922 he went to the U.S. Senate. Virtually every governor and Senator thereafter was either a servant or an ally of Hague's. Appeal to the courts was also futile, since most judges owed their appointment to him, including his own son, who, despite flunking out of college and two law schools, managed to pass the state bar exam, which two-thirds of the other candidates failed. After one year as a law clerk the young man was appointed to New Jersey's highest court.[47]

Hague also took care to maintain close relationships with the powerful New York governor, Al Smith, serving as his floor manager at the 1932 Democratic Convention. Afterward, though, he quickly switched to FDR and obtained control of federal patronage and various welfare programs. The Department of Justice was also somewhat restrained against Hague. Even though he had to hand over $60,000 in payments for tax "irregularities," no criminal indictment was sought.[48] By the 1930s the press generally referred to the boss as Frank "I am the law" Hague, though this statement was taken out of context and the situation in which Hague made it had been a creditable one for the mayor. In trying to get a state official to issue working papers for two truant boys rather than send them to reform school, he had countered the official's protest that the law forbad it by saying, "I am the law, do it."[49]

At the same time Hague rose to power, New Jersey was becoming prosperous. In 1914, the completion of the Hudson River Tubes had enhanced the state's position as the railroad link to the South and Midwest. The war added to the rail traffic and ocean shipping. New Jersey also benefited from the industrial and housing spillover from New York and Philadelphia. Its strategic position as a center of production and a transportation hub was noted by German spies, who on several occasions blew up munitions, including the setting off of a 1916 blast at Black Tom Island, on Hague's doorstep, which killed four people in the most spectacular act of foreign sabotage in American history. Hague fastened on the economic growth by significantly increasing the taxes on railroad and other industrial property in Hudson County. Much of the revenue was spent on health services for the voters, but some doubtless went into various pockets. In the 1920s the development of the highway system further added to New Jersey's strategic position.

The Spirit of West Point

In 1921, the New Jersey Legislature passed a bill creating a state police, but Governor Edwards promptly vetoed it, and when it passed over his veto was expected to name a Hague man, Lieutenant Thomas Broadhurst of the Hudson County Boulevard Police, as superintendent. Since the superintendent would be appointed for a five-year term and would appoint all other members of the force, this would ensure that the state police, if it did not become another adjunct to the Hague empire, would at least not pose any threat. However, Edwards surprised everyone when he chose a twenty-five-year-old West Pointer, Captain H. Norman Schwartzkopf.

Herbert Norman Schwartzkopf was born in 1895 in Newark, where his father, a second-generation German-American, was in the jewelry business. In 1913 he was appointed to the U.S. Military Academy, where he developed a reputation as more of an athlete than a scholar (graduating 88th in a class of 139) and, in the fashion of the social set he was entering, dropped his first name for the more distinguished H. Norman. He entered the war-expanded army as a second lieutenant of cavalry, but horses were not needed in France so he transferred to the artillery. By the summer of 1918 he was a captain and battery commander in the Third Division fighting on the Marne, where he was gassed.

At the end of the war, Schwartzkopf was assigned to the army of occupation as a provost marshal. In 1919, he returned to the U.S. and was posted to the Seventh Cavalry (of Custer fame), at that time on the Mexican border at El Paso, where once again he was engaged in military police duties. In July of the following year his father became disabled, and Schwartzkopf resigned and returned to Newark to run the family business.[50] Whether his departure was totally a result of his father's illness is not certain. Many young officers were resigning after finding the humdrum existence and dim future prospects of the peacetime army disappointing. Among those who stayed were his classmates

Mark Clark, Matt Ridgway, and Joe Collins.* All three men became distinguished four-star generals. Had Schwartzkopf stayed on, his West Point background and combat experience (which contemporaries like Ridgway, Dwight Eisenhower, and Omar Bradley lacked), along with his obvious drive and energy, might well have led him to the top commands.

When Schwartzkopf learned of the state police job, he was interested and was advised to apply for it by a wartime comrade, Captain Irving Edwards, son of the governor. Apparently, His Excellency preferred his son's advice to Frank Hague's, and he appointed Schwartzkopf as superintendent on July 1, 1921.

Schwartzkopf lost no time in stamping the military mold on the state police. He began by styling himself "Colonel," though given the strength of his command (120), "Captain" might have been more appropriate. The senior officers of the force were required to have two years of commissioned military service, and in fact the first four appointed were all ex-cavalrymen. The entrance test for recruits was straight out of the spirit of West Point and Teddy Roosevelt. It required the applicant to define "hero," "coward," and "mollycoddle." Recruits were obliged to enlist for two years, and it was a misdemeanor crime to resign without permission. Troopers were also forbidden to marry during their first tour of duty.[51]

The first contingent of 116 troopers trained at the state National Guard camp from September to December 1921 under their own officers as well as instructors from the Pennsylvania State Police and the Royal Canadian Mounted Police. Eighty-one survived the course and in December were issued pistols and rifles and assigned to barracks. Those in the northern part of the state were provided with motorcycles, while in the less developed southern area horses were the patrol vehicle. As south Jersey acquired highways, the horses were abandoned, but the motorcycles would remain for over thirty years, killing fifteen men as against five murdered in the line of duty in the same period.

While some areas of the state welcomed the troopers, others did not. Two rural slums, the Pineys in south Jersey and the Sourland Mountains in the middle of the state, were the most difficult. In the first seven years of operation three troopers were murdered, a rather high figure for so small a body. In 1926, in an incident reminiscent of Pennsylvania in the early days, there occurred the so-called "Battle of Jutland." It began when troopers were called upon to assist the Society for the Prevention of Cruelty to Animals in the service of a minor warrant at a Sourlands farmhouse near Jutland in Hunterdon County. The occupants

---

* Collins, the upwardly mobile son of an Irish regular army sergeant, was another who chose to use a more formal name, J. Lawton; Ridgway and Clark, officers' sons, did not feel a similar need.

resisted with firearms, and in the ensuing gun battle a woman was killed. As a result, the local authorities prosecuted fourteen troopers and convicted three of them, including a lieutenant, of manslaughter and assault. All received several years in prison.[52]

Also in the early years came a foreshadowing of the event which was to traumatize the force and cost Schwartzkopf his post. In 1922, the bodies of a man and woman shot to death were found in a lovers' lane near New Brunswick, New Jersey. The man was the socially prominent Reverend Edward Hall, and the woman, Eleanor Mills, was a choir singer in his church; both were married but not to each other. The resultant investigation made the Hall-Mills murder case one of the crimes of the century. The state police were assigned to assist local authorities, (though Governor Edwards ordered Schwartzkopf personally to catch the killer). The primary investigation was carried on by Jersey City and Newark detectives. After a period of time, the case was closed with no arrests. In 1926 Hearst's *New York Journal* pressured New Jersey authorities to accept the account of the so-called "pig woman," Jane Gibson, a local farmer who claimed to have witnessed the murder.

A new investigation was begun with a Hague political lackey as special prosecutor. Implicated by the pig woman, Reverend Hall's wife and her two brothers were arrested and charged with the crime. Despite dramatic testimony by the pig woman, who was brought in on her "death bed" (she actually lived four more years), the defendants were acquitted. The state police suffered embarrassment when a former trooper testified that he had been bribed to leave the state because he had information linking Mrs. Hall to the murder. Since he was also a deserter from the army and the navy, for which he was then in Alcatraz, his story lacked credibility.[53]

Though there were some complaints against the state police, in general their public relations were good. In contrast to other states, organized labor was friendly, since Schwartzkopf kept his force out of strikebreaking.[54] Another satisfied party was Boss Hague, since the troopers stayed clear of municipal affairs. Indeed, relations with the Jersey City police were cordial, and Inspector Harry Walsh, a Hague favorite and later chief of police, was the first man awarded the State Police Distinguished Service Medal.[55]

Pride of the Marines

New Jersey apparently had as good a man in Captain Schwartzkopf as the Pennsylvanaia State Police had had in Captain Groome a generation earlier. In 1926 and again in 1931, Schwartzkopf was reappointed. The success of men like Groome and Schwartzkopf and the prestige of the military stemming from World War I led to a revival of the trend to appoint soldiers as police chiefs. In 1923 Philadelphia mayoral candidate W. Frederick Kneeland campaigned on a pledge to appoint a general to head the police.

The fact that the law required the city's safety director to be a Pennsylvania resident was no obstacle, for America's greatest military hero was both a general and a Pennsylvanian. Marine Brigadier General Smedley Darlington Butler was a living legend. He was born in Chester County, Pennsylvania, in 1881, the year of birth of another great military hero, Douglas MacArthur. And again like his contemporary, whose father, Lieutenant General Arthur MacArthur, was Commanding General of the United States Army, Butler had a father who was a powerful figure. Thomas Butler, a leading Quaker lawyer and descendant of a family which had accompanied William Penn to Philadelphia, served in Congress from 1897 to 1928 and was a prominent member of the House Naval Affairs Committee, becoming chairman during the years of Republican control of the House. Young Smedley had a typical Quaker upbringing, but in 1898, when he was sixteen, he made the unusual decision for a Quaker to leave school and fight in the Spanish-American War. Though he was legally too young, the Marine Corps was happy to commission a sixteen-year-old lieutenant whose father sat on the Naval Affairs Committee, the major controller of Marine Corps appropriations. At the time no one apparently thought to question the wisdom of permitting a young schoolboy to lead a platoon. Douglas MacArthur had thought of running away to join the army, and Franklin Delano Roosevelt considered joining the navy at sixteen, but unlike the headstrong Quaker, MacArthur and FDR were both persuaded that they were too young.

Butler was too late for any real action in Cuba, but he obtained a regular commission and was sent off to the Philippine insurrection and to the Boxer Rebellion, where he was wounded and recommended for the Congressional Medal of Honor. However, officers were not eligible at that time. In 1901, while still a minor, he was promoted to captain of Marines and in 1908 to major and battalion commander in Nicaragua at a time when Douglas MacArthur (West Point 1903) was still a lowly lieutenant. Indeed, Butler was to be a general before his great contemporary reached major. This despite the fact that Butler had not completed high school and never in his career attended any type of miltary staff college.[56]

Butler the Quaker was clearly a fighter, in or out of warfare. He was frequently at odds with his superiors and in various forms of hot water. The Marine Corps of his day was part of America's colonial police force, battling what would later be called national liberation movements via counterinsurgency warfare. This was somewhat less gentlemanly than regular combat, as the Philippine court-martial of Butler's friend and patron, Major Tony Waller, had demonstrated. In 1912 Butler rigged the Nicaraguan elections at gunpoint,[57] but nothing serious happened to him, since he could always rely on his powerful father.

In 1914, Butler won his first Congressional Medal of Honor when American forces under Colonel Tony Waller stormed Veracruz. The following year he was in Haiti, where he led the attack on the last remnants of resistance at Fort Riviere, receiving his second Congressional Medal of Honor from Assistant Secretary of the Navy Franklin D. Roosevelt. With the occupation of the island Waller, now a brigadier general, became a virtual czar over the puppet native government.* In addition to the Marine occupation force, there was created a 2,700-man Haitian gendarmerie with native enlisted men and Marine officers. To head the force with the rank of major general, Waller and Roosevelt chose Butler, then thirty-four and a lieutenant colonel. As second in command, Butler in turn selected Marine Major Alexander Williams, son and namesake of the famous Inspector "Clubber" Williams of the New York City Police Department.

FDR attempted to preserve the fiction that the Haitians were running their own affairs but the truculent Butler had no time for such nonsense. When President Dartiguenave attempted to enter an official limousine ahead of Roosevelt, Butler seized him by the collar and yanked him back. Given such realities, the Marines showed little mercy to the *caco* "bandits," in Butler's words, "hunting them like pigs,"[59] and reports of atrocites were frequent. With the approval of Franklin Roosevelt, Butler also forcibly conscripted native labor on various construction projects, and later there were complaints that Marine officers were getting rich on graft.[60] Any objections were met by force. When in 1916 the Haitian Assembly sought to impeach the President for looting the national treasury and to fire Major General Butler, the latter disbanded the Assembly at gunpoint.[61] Later, the NAACP was to file a formal complaint resulting in a U.S. Senate investigation, but Butler emerged unscathed.

When America entered World War I, Butler turned command over to Williams and persuaded Roosevelt to assign him to France as a Marine brigadier general. Given his previous record, one would have expected him to take Berlin singlehandedly and crown himself Kaiser after hanging Wilhelm II. But a new cast of favorites was in power, and old heroes were forgotten. Theodore Roosevelt was refused a commission; Butler was given command at the Port of Brest, where he distinguished himself by organizing a system of duck boards to bridge the mud. This

* Littleton Tazwell "Tony" Waller was born in 1856 and commissioned a second lieutenant of Marines in 1880. In 1882 he led a landing party in conjunction with British forces at Alexandria, Egypt. In 1916 he was promoted to brigadier general. Passed over for Commandant, he retired as a major general and died in 1926.[58]

time the glory went to John J. Pershing and Douglas MacArthur, who jumped from captain to brigadier general. In the postwar era, Butler had to content himself with organizing football teams at the bases he commanded. Many suspected that his horizons in the 17,000-man Marine Corps were limited, and that any new conquests would have to be political. Thus the 1924 summons to the city adjacent to his father's congressional district was a welcome one, and Butler took a year's leave from the Marines.

Philadelphia's history was akin to those of Boston and New York. Before the Civil War, the city had its anti-Negro and anti-Catholic riots. After the war, though, Philadelphia assimilated immigrants better than most other cities. Its manufacturing provided more skilled jobs, and it had a large supply of single-family homes and land for expansion.[62] The local Republican machine won every mayoral election from 1884 on, and with the state also a GOP bastion, Irish or Italians who wished to advance had to become Republicans. In 1903, Lincoln Steffens described Philadelphia as "corrupt and contented."[63]

The political alliance of police and organized crime was probably worse in Philadelphia than in other places. In 1917, Philadelphia had been even more obstinate about shutting down its Tenderloin red-light district than such open "sin" cities as New Orleans, and Raymond Fosdick had to call out the Marines to accomplish the closing.[64] In 1915, the chief of detectives had blithely informed Fosdick that no crime records were necessary because he kept the details of all cases in his head.[65] Between 1887 and 1920 the city had thirteen safety directors.

When Butler took office, there were reputed to be 80,000 speakeasies and 1,500 brothels operating with impunity, drawing criticism from the maverick Republican governor, Gifford Pinchot.[66] The police department maintained forty-six district stations, while New York City with four times the manpower had eighty-four. Each station and its magistrate's court were under the domination of the local ward leader and thus part of the machine of Boss William Vare, who had succeeded to his brother Edwin's mantle when the latter died in 1922. As expected, William had quit Congress for a State Senate seat. Vare, who had put Mayor Kneeland in office, was in the process of becoming state boss and in 1926 would complete his efforts with election to the United States Senate, though campaign financing irregularities caused that body to refuse to seat him.[67]

Boss Vare welcomed Butler by recommending for police superintendent a certain lieutenant who he described as "an honest man." Butler refused, and later he demoted the officer as a crook.[68] The general was determined to be supreme commander in the colorful style of his Marine days, and his opening moves were dramatic. Though in a civilian position, Butler appeared in a specially designed uniform with a hol-stered .45 caliber pistol and let the cops know he meant business, Marine style. He described the officers he had seen as "fat, lazy fellows, swinging their clubs while dives ran wide open," ordered the abolition of police and fire unions, and demanded a clean-up within forty-eight hours. As might be expected, some cops, tied by a lifetime to the ma-chine, hesitated, and Butler demoted them. Others, particularly the Tenderloin district commanders, old hands at giving the illusion of a clean-up, got busy and won his temporary praise. In the first week, 973 speakeasies were raided though of course, as Lieutenant Becker had shown, vice raids were easily effected in a corrupt city and meant little.

Butler's bombastic tactics were good for headlines, and other cities even posted guards to turn back the expected wave of Philadelphia hoodlums fleeing Butler's shoot-to-kill orders. The general enjoyed the attention and happily promised to make Mayor Kneeland President. However, he was not up against Haitian rebels, but Philadelphia Re-publicans, and the courts took a dim view of raids on private premises, or with John Doe warrants. Butler also learned that police officers were not bound by the military code of honor and he later said that at least half of his station commanders had double-crossed him. In return, he reduced the number of stations to thirty-three, cutting off some relation-ships with ward bosses.

At the end of his year's leave, Butler could point to 4,000 speak-easies and 1,000 stills raided and praise from drys such as Governor Pinchot. His leave was extended another year; however, the opposition grew stronger. Hotel operators complained that strict enforcement of the Prohibtion law was hurting business. Soon Butler was publicly blast-ing the mayor, while his health seemed to crack and his behavior became more erratic. He charged, then failed to prove, bribe offers and accused an audience of civic leaders of carrying him to his death. The situation drew to a head when Butler's men raided a formal ball at the plush Ritz Carlton Hotel and he demanded that it and another major hotel be padlocked. Business interests, which looked forward to 1926 and the 150th anniversary celebration of the Declaration of Independence, en-couraged editorial opposition to Butler.

At the end of the second year, President Coolidge was persuaded not to renew the general's leave, although the mayor implored him publicly to do so. The naive Butler then resigned from the Marine Corps, but the mayor had a quick change of heart and on Christmas Day, 1925, fired his controversial safety director just in time to start the sesquicentennial year. Instead of marching in at gunpoint to save his job, Butler blasted the mayor's treachery and uttered a profound com-ment on American police administration to the effect that "Sherman was right about war, but leading the Philadelphia police department was worse."[69] His experience was a clear demonstration that constabulary methods were unworkable in the face of urban political reality.

The Philadelphia police soon returned to normal but General Butler did not. He became a fanatic teetotaler and even more erratic. He was permitted to withdraw his resignation from the Marines and was assigned to command the base at San Diego. It should have been a happy reunion with his old comrades, and Colonel Alexander Williams, now a regimental commander, threw a large welcoming party at his own home. However, Butler became upset because he was offered a drink, and an argument followed which led the general to bring court-martial proceedings against Williams on a charge of insubordination. This breach of social and military camaraderie brought a storm of criticism on Butler, which was not helped when Williams was found guilty, relieved of his command, and transferred. A few months later Williams died when his car plunged into San Francisco Bay.[70]

Butler's subsequent career was even more confusing. In 1931 he became the first American general to be placed under arrest since the Civil War when by order of President Hoover he was court-martialed for slandering Mussolini in a public speech. After he apologized, the court-martial was dropped, though Franklin Roosevelt had offered to testify in his behalf. Passed over for Marine Commandant, he retired and became a candidate for U.S. Senator from Pennsylvania but was badly beaten. At this stage of his career his views also changed drastically on various subjects. He became an anti-imperialist and a pacifist and denounced American policy in a number of speeches. In 1934 he was again in the headlines claiming that Wall Street financiers had offered him large sums to lead a fascist coup against the New Deal. People at that time did not seem to take this claim seriously, although for his various statements Butler became a hero to pacifist and anti-imperialist elements. In the light of Vietnam and Watergate, there has been a modest revival of interest in him. Whether Butler's views represented a genuine change of mind or simply bitterness at the failure of his career is not certain. Franklin Roosevelt, whose Presidency he claimed to have saved by blocking a facist coup, never gave him any reward or recognition, perhaps because as late as the summer of 1940 (a few days before his death at 58), when France was falling, Butler was an isolationist denouncing war as a racket.[71]

Had he been spared a few more years, there might have been a place for him in World War II. It is possible that if Butler had not been embittered by his police experiences, he (and Colonel Williams) might have yet rendered service in an arena where their talents would have been useful.

Crime of the Century

After a decade of existence, the New Jersey State Police was a strong and stable organization. Then came another so-called "crime of the century" more notorious than the Hall-Mills murders. This time state police had a predominant role, and this time the alleged offender was caught by the police (not the press), convicted, and executed, as a result of which the state police were nearly destroyed.

In 1927, Charles Lindbergh had become America's number one national hero by flying alone from New York to Paris. With further adventures and marriage to an heiress, Lindbergh's fame increased. In 1932, he and his family were living on an isolated estate near Hopewell, New Jersey, in Hunterdon County, where on the evening of March 1 his twenty-month-old son was kidnapped. Since Hopewell had only a two-man police department, the New Jersey State Police took charge of the case, although from the outset their efforts were supported by the assignment of detectives from Newark and Jersey City to work under state police direction.

The case itself has been the subject of considerable analysis and to recap its details would require a separate book.[72] The essential facts are these: A ransom note in English with a German idiom was found at the scene along with a ladder. In April, $50,000 in gold certificates was paid on behalf of the family to an unknown man in a Bronx cemetery by Dr. John Condon, a retired educator who had signified his willingness to become involved by an advertisement in a Bronx community paper. Several days later, the baby's body was found buried in a shallow grave a mile from the mansion. Thereafter, a full-scale investigation was conducted by a task force composed of the state police, the New York City police (because of the Bronx angle), and the FBI, which in 1933 would acquire jurisdiction over future crimes of this nature by passage of a federal "Lindbergh" antikidnapping law.

For two years the investigation continued. There was the usual problem of conflicting jurisdiction. The police were also hampered by various other problems such as Lindbergh's decision to retain New York gangsters as go-betweens during the ransom payment phase, false confessions and plots put forth by confidence men, and publicity seekers whose activities were often supported by various distinguished personages. In one instance millionairess Evelyn Walsh McLean, owner of the *Washington Post*, was bilked out of $104,000 by a former G-man and ex-convict, Gaston Means who claimed to be in contact with the kidnappers. In another incident Special Assistant Secretary of Labor Murray Garson (later jailed as a wartime Washington influence peddler) injected himself into the case with the claim that he would solve the crime within forty-eight hours. His chief contribution was to turn the Lindbergh mansion upside down and then accuse Colonel Lindbergh himself of the kidnapping.[73] The antics of various freebooters were reminiscent of the Hall-Mills case. Given the opportunity both crimes presented to gain wealth and glory, this was perhaps inevitable. Such cases are in fact political events of the first magnitude, and if Schwartz-kopf had been shrewd, he might well have turned the investigation over to another agency such as the FBI. But, of course, this would have been the act of a coward or a mollycoddle.

In September 1934, the police task force arrested a suspect in the Bronx area. The case against Bruno Richard Hauptman, an immigrant from Germany, where he had served time for burglary, was based on several factors. One, he was identified as the passer of some of the ransom money and was found in possession of several thousand dollars worth. Two, the German expressions in the ransom note fit Hauptman's own phraseology, and experts declared his handwriting the same. Three, the wood in the ladder found at the scene supposedly matched some wood that was missing from Hauptman's attic. Four, he was identified by Condon as the receiver of the ransom and by others as being in the vicinity of Hopewell on the night of the crime, though such identifications were somewhat tenuous.

From the state police standpoint, however, the case had many em-barrassments. In the first instance, although a search of the vicinity was conducted at the time of the kidnapping, it had failed to uncover the shallow grave. One would have expected a rural constabulary to perform more effectively in the woods. Second, the state police had admittedly bungled the search for fingerprints and the examination of footprints at the scene and failed to safeguard the vital ladder to ensure that the chain of evidence was unbroken. A third charge was that in the course of the investigation an English maid employed by Lindbergh's in-laws had been questioned so strenuously that she committed suicide. More general complaints were that the state police lacked the skills to solve the case, having given more emphasis to spit-and-polish uniforms than crime detection. An arrest was made because the suspect, Hauptman, passed and continued to pass gold certificates in the Bronx and with the abandonment of the gold standard in 1934 such bills became un-usual. Thus a gas station attendant noted Hauptman's license, and this led to his capture. Finally, it was alleged that the state police had refused to cooperate with other police organizations, particularly in the early stages of the case.

To the charges of incompetence the state police could reply that the New York City Police Department and the FBI did not have any greater success and each had as many investigators as any American force at the time, although their investigations were primitive compared to those of continental detectives. Further, it was the NYPD which conducted the interrogation of Hauptman and failed to obtain a confession, though, in the opinion of some, his every action in the case was an attempt to dramatize himself. The charge of noncooperation was, of course, answered with a denial, pointing out that Jersey City and Newark detectives, led by Inspector Harry Walsh, had been intimately involved, though a more realistic answer might have been that no agency ever cooperated with another one in a matter that was so sensitive.

If the state police were shaken by the investigation, they might have been salvaged at the trial, but instead Schwartzkopf was fatally damaged by what, in retrospect, would appear to be unfair tactics. Unless a defendant is willing to plead guilty because the case against him is overwhelming, a criminal trial is a contest in which at least two groups compete and the spectators take sides. The Hauptman trial, which opened in Flemington, New Jersey, in 1935, was to become a battle royal. While the evidence against Hauptman was strong, he had not been caught in the act and there was no confession. In these circumstances some people were willing to support his defense, though they may not have personally believed in it. A reporter who finds the rival paper has better access to the prosecutor naturally gravitates toward the defendant, and the Hauptman defense was actually financed in part by Hearst's *New York Evening Journal* in exchange for exclusive stories. A particular group may feel threatened by the trial, as were German-Americans (despite the role of Colonel Schwartzkopf), who held various fund-raising events for the defendant. A rival politician may wish the district attorney to fall on his face. Others may simply wish to root for the underdog or the more handsome lawyer. Columnists Walter Winchell and Alexander Wolcott were proprosecution, while special correspondents Clarence Darrow and Ford Madox Ford were partisans for the defense. Ford expressed his view that since Hauptman had been a combat soldier in the war, leaders in that conflict were responsible for his behavior.

One advantage to the state was its superior resources. With an army of investigators available, every defense witness could be checked out. In any prominent case many people come forward to be a part of the action. Though such individuals may seem respectable, inquiry may reveal that they are in fact criminals, psychopaths, or professional witnesses. One pleasant gentleman who testified for the defense admitted to having been declared legally insane and five times incarcerated in mental institutions. In contrast, unless large sums can be raised because of the accused's wealth or political background, no similar resources are available to the defense. In March 1935 the jury found Hauptman guilty and he was sentenced to die. Pending execution, he was taken to the state prison.

Even after his conviction Hauptman had many supporters. Prominent writers such as H. L. Mencken and André Maurois made favorable comments, the latter suggesting that since the execution had been delayed (due to the defendant's appeals), it was unfair to carry it out. Hauptman's most prominent supporter, however, was Harold Hoffman, the governor of New Jersey, a Republican who had been elected in 1934 after service as motor vehicle commissioner, a post in which he had not seen eye to eye with Schwartzkopf. Since 1934 was an early New Deal year when very few Republicans were doing well at the polls, the victory was a noteworthy one. At thirty-eight, Hoffman was the youngest governor in the country.

Hoffman's success and the fact that he governed an industrial state adjacent to the media capital of America made him a natural for consideration as a presidential nominee in 1936. In that era governors, not senators, were the source of presidential candidates, and four of the seven United States Presidents in the twentieth century up until that time had been northeastern governors, including Wilson of New Jersey twenty years earlier. In fact, the Republican Convention of 1936 did turn to a governor who had managed to buck the Democratic tide, Alfred Landon of Kansas. Thus it was natural for Hoffman to cast an eye toward Washington, but to get there he needed national recognition. Theodore Roosevelt had won attention as New York police commissioner; Calvin Coolidge received even greater publicity from the Boston police strike. Hoffman himself was not unaware of the possibilities present in the great trial which opened just a year before the presidential primaries would start.

The warden of the state prison, Mark Kimberling, had been Schwartzkopf's second in command when the state police were formed. In 1929, since Schwartzkopf showed no signs of leaving, he resigned and took the prison post. In October 1935, in violation of the law and unknown to Schwartzkopf but with Kimberling's approval, Hoffman made secret visits to the prison to interview Hauptman. In January 1936 Hoffman ordered the state police to reinvestigate the case.

Another who was dissatisfied was Burlington County Detective Ellis Parker. Parker had held his post since 1893 and had not looked with favor on the creation of the state police. Within his domain he ruled as something of a feudal baron, claiming success in over 20,000 investigations, and managing to attract national attention.* Hoffman and Parker now began to consult together on their theories of the case.

Hoffman's visits to the prison were revealed, and created a sensa-

* A book on Parker stated that his record was "better than Scotland Yard or the Sûreté," and Parker was "the best detective in America if not the world."[74] The criteria used to compare a two-man office in rural New Jersey to the national detective forces of two world powers were not specified.

tion. In March 1936, shortly before Hauptman's scheduled execution, Ellis Parker added to the confusion by providing a suspect who he claimed had confessed to the Lindbergh kidnapping. The individual, a mental patient whom Parker's agents had seized in New York and forcibly removed to New Jersey, was quickly exonerated, and Hauptman was executed in April. Forty years later the case remains controversial, though no legal proceedings have cast any new light on events. The strength of the prosecution's case was demonstrated when Hauptman's new attorney, Samuel Leibowitz, then one of the foremost criminal lawyers in America, after examining the evidence attempted to persuade Hauptman that his only chance for life was to confess his guilt and name any accomplices.*[75]

In the aftermath the Republican Convention which convened in June did not consider Governor Hoffman. In fact, he was elected a delegate only because Hague ordered Democrats to go into the Republican primary and vote for him. But the chief executive did have the pleasure of notifying Colonel Schwartzkopf that with the expiration of his third five-year term on June 30, his services would be no longer required. Warden Kimberling was appointed superintendent in his place. Hoffman also demoted one of the key detectives in the case. Ellis Parker was not considered for superintendent, since he had been indicted by a Brooklyn grand jury for kidnapping in the episode of the mental patient. Even Governor Hoffman's refusal to extradite him did not save "America's greatest detective," as a federal grand jury indicted him under the Lindbergh law and Parker was convicted and sent to a federal penitentiary, where he died in 1940.

The fired Schwartzkopf, who was now famous, became the host of "Gang Busters," a popular radio program of the day. When World War II broke out, he returned to the service as a brigadier general, heading the 20,000-man Iranian national gendarmerie. Later, in the 1950s when anti-American Premier Mossadegh nationalized the Iranian oil fields, Schwartzkopf's contacts in Iran permitted him to play a major role in the coup which ousted the Premier and returned power to the Shah.[76]

In an interesting sidelight, in 1954, Schwartzkopf was again in New Jersey state service as administrative assistant to the attorney general overseeing the state police, motor vehicle department, and alcoholic beverage control board, although in reality his power was only a shadow of its former substance. In this capacity he was called on to investigate the state director of employment security for alleged irregularities in the running of his office, including telephone conversations with organized-crime bosses. The director was former Governor Harold Hoffman, who loudly protested his innocence, but in June he was found dead of a

* Leibowitz had been retained by Evelyn Walsh McLean, still anxious to play a role in the case even though she had been swindled in her earlier effort.

heart attack in a New York hotel room and with him was a letter in which he admitted embezzling $300,000 over a period of years from a bank where he was an officer, a fact which might have explained his obeisance to Hague, a man whose spies knew many things.[77]

In retrospect, Schwartzkopf built a constabulary organization which by the tenets of police reform was a model operation. There was no systematic corruption or overt political influence in the New Jersey State Police, yet the Democratic Hague machine and the Atlantic City vice empire of Republican Nucky Johnson raged unchecked.*

New Jersey would continue to be the premier state police command in America. Its jurisdiction, astride the heart of the northeast corridor and rail and highway routes from New York to the Midwest, encompassed the most important transportation network in the country. Also, its size, relative to other police departments in the state, gave it an eminence beyond that of any other state constabulary force. Even today state police of Pennsylvania and New York are overshadowed by the much larger Philadelphia and New York City forces, while New Jersey's troopers are the largest police department in the state.

By World War II America's state police were less elite and innovative than they had been a generation earlier. The top posts no longer went to young military officers, but as in the cities were reserved for those who started at the bottom. The state police, however, continued to maintain a better appearance and a tighter discipline than the locals.

After winning her struggle to institutionalize the state police, Katherine Mayo turned to larger fields, investigating American rule in the Philippines and approving of it, so that her writings were considered a significant factor in delaying the grant of independence. In 1927 she became the center of worldwide controversy with the publication of her book *Mother India*. In it she had denounced various Hindu customs such as child marriage and strongly supported British imperial rule, causing herself to be denounced by Indian leaders from Gandhi down.[78]

In October 1940 she died in Bedford Hills while working on a book about the menace of the international drug traffic. No doubt, it would have been in the same spirited style of her earlier works. Despite the controversial nature of her views, common enough in the time of Teddy Roosevelt but a bit extreme during the administration of Franklin D., she had exerted an influence on police administration and other affairs afforded to few women of her time. In fitting recognition of her work, the New York State Police provided pallbearers and an escort for her funeral. But an even higher tribute was rendered by the British empire. Though its very survival was at stake and its forces were spread thin

---

* As a Republican lawbreaker in the time of FDR, Johnson finally succumbed to a federal prosecution and resultant imprisonment for income tax evasion.

in that grim autumn of 1940, a British naval detachment arrived at the gravesite to share with the troopers the guard of honor over the body of the lady who had served both of them so well.[79]

In some respects, state police forces are illogical in organization and mission. Since they are primarily rural forces, there is no reason why taxpayers in an entire state should furnish police services for one portion of it. The real justification for organizations such as the New Jersey State Police lay in their tasks of protecting strategic transportation networks and as a force beyond local politics. While the Jersey troopers proved an efficient rural police force and highway patrol, the task of combating organized crime and official corruption was politically impossible. The Lindbergh case showed what could happen to even the strongest members of such a force should they displease a political master. Its lesson was heeded, and the potential of the nation's state troopers is as yet unrealized.[80]

New York: The Finest and the Fall of the Hall (1914–1945)

May 9, 1931, was a bright and sunny day ideal for a parade up Broadway, the greatest street in the greatest city in America if not the world. But perhaps it was not the ideal year. The Depression had made many New Yorkers fearful, and the daily revelations of municipal scandals made them angry. Protests by the unemployed led to clashes between police and citizens, and today it was the police who were on parade. It was in fact to be the last of the great New York police parades. Normally, the city's dapper mayor, James J. Walker, would lead the bluecoats, but fearing hostile crowds he had cancelled out. At the last minute, however, he told Commissioner Ed Mulrooney, himself a thirty-five-year police veteran, that he would walk along for a few blocks. As the mayor stepped off with the police band blaring Irish and patriotic tunes, there were a few boos but they were drowned out by the cheers. The familiar scene seemed to bring forth some deep emotion from the sidewalks of New York, and the mayor decided to continue on, eventually going the whole route.[1] It was a historic moment. The old Tammany police department of Byrnes, Williams, Devery, and other colorful characters was marching into history.

ADMINISTRATION OF THE FINEST

On January 1, 1914, John Purroy Mitchell took his oath as mayor of New York City. For the third time in twenty years, police scandals had given the city a reform administration. At thirty-four, Mitchell was the youngest chief executive in the city's history.

For Mitchell, as for many other people, the future was bright. America was at the height of what would be known as the Progressive Era. In Washington Woodrow Wilson's New Freedom administration was completing its first year. At Chicago in 1912 Teddy Roosevelt had accepted the nomination of a diverse group of "Progressives" with a ringing declaration that "we stand at Armageddon fighting for the Lord" while Jane Addams led the crowd in singing "Onward Christian Soldiers."[2]

The world war which began in 1914 was to usher in vast changes in America and the world, the dimensions of which are yet to be determined. One major result was to split the progressive movement: Roosevelt urged intervention while Jane Addams championed pacifism. Mayor Mitchell was to be just one of the millions whose hopes were crushed in the catastrophe about to engulf the world, but thoughts of war were not what occupied his mind in January 1914.

Given the circumstances of his election, reform of the police, an objective which had eluded his predecessors, was a high priority of the new mayor. As the century progressed, there was a realization that the achievement of large results required more than a Victorian faith in moral exhortations and the leadership of men of high character. Industrial managers were finding that old-fashioned techniques, whether of the paternalistic or sweatshop variety, were insufficient to manage modern factories, and political reformers were perceiving that there was more to government than "turning the rascals out." Thus the twentieth century saw the emergence of a number of administrative doctrines.

One of the most popular for a time was scientific management, also called "Taylorism" after its founder, Frederick Winslow Taylor. As an industrial foreman, Taylor developed time and motion studies to determine the most efficient methods of work and thereby increase productivity. To organized labor such ideas were an attempt to make men into machines, and the labor movement resisted. Surprisingly, so did many employers, and Taylor was dismissed from several management jobs. His strongest support came from intellectuals such as Felix Frankfurter and Louis Brandeis.

In 1913 the introduction of Taylorism into the Boston Navy Yard prompted Congressman James Michael Curley to demand of Assistant Secretary of the Navy Franklin D. Roosevelt that such methods be forbidden. Caught between the demands of Curley and organized labor on one side and those of various Harvard professors on the other, Roosevelt vacillated until Congress, by statute, forbade the use of scientific management techniques in government agencies.[3]

Contemporaneous with Taylorism there developed another type of administrative science emphasizing management principles, such as span of control and unity of command, which were soon to be applied to government via the new "public administration" movement. The movement's center was in New York, where the first government budget was adopted in 1910, preceding by eleven years a similar step in the federal government. That same year Rockefeller money had helped to found the Bureau of Municipal Research under the leadership of a former social worker, Henry Bruere. Within a short time the Bureau became virtually a branch of New York City government. Its essential premise was that administrative science could be separated from political "values" and that government performance could be improved by applying scientific methods in a manner akin to civil engineering. A favorite device was the survey. As Luther Gulick, one of the leading proponents of the new public administration, observed:

> Surveys conveyed the idea of the inclusive, objective, and scientific approach which the Bureau applied to its work. It went at the city government much 'as an engineer goes at a tract of land before laying out the streets, sewers and water pipes.[4]

Police administration too was to produce its scholars of the new science beginning with the publication in 1910 of Leonhard Fuld's Columbia doctoral dissertation, *Police Administration*. Where previous writers on the police had described scandal, crime, and the individual exploits of officers, the new breed viewed crime and police as variables which could be manipulated through administrative tools. As Raymond Fosdick noted in the aftermath of the Becker scandal, it was "due entirely to the lack of adequate administrative control ... but the tools are at hand for the correction of such abuses." The Curran Committee, assisted by Bruere's Bureau of Municipal Research, reached a similar conclusion that the scandal was the fault of "bad administration."[5] As Professor Felix Frankfurter of the Harvard Law School wrote regarding one survey of municipal criminal justice:

> The problem is more comprehensive and its elements more manifold than the good-man–bad-man explanation of political phenomenon assumes. . . .
> A personal victim for a complex community failure satisfies the sense of the dramatic, at the same time that it affords the luxury of vicarious punishment. But where the whole system of criminal justice has broken down under the weight imposed upon it by industrial urban life, the trail of authentic and thorough diagnosis must not be diverted from essential causes to occasional officials who exploit those causes. . . .To resist effectively the local demand for "head-hunting" requires disinterested, scientific direction . . . in the hands of men whose professional interest is the scientific administration of justice.[6]

Clearly, this was very different from Reverend Parkhurst's notion that blame for police failures rested with "rum-soaked devils."

By 1914 Raymond Fosdick, though just past thirty, was the leading scholar of police administration. His experience in New York government, his studies of European and American police, and his editorship of the *Journal of Criminal Justice* afforded him the premier position in a not too crowded field. In his book *American Police Systems* Fosdick presented the major trends then current among the new-style police reformers. It began with the traditional view which fixed responsibility for crime and vice on the foreign-born and their children as well as the Negro population—in the latter instance a recognition of the growing number of blacks in northern cities. Continuing in the same fashion, Fosdick perceived a relationship between crime and the various human indulgences, pointing out the dangers from the drug addicts, whose numbers in New York City alone he estimated at 300,000, a figure that would have included nearly 10 percent of the adult population of the city.[7] To Fosdick as to Parkhurst the failure of the police was manifest; however, he rejected the Parkhurst type of moral crusade, observing:

> It suits the judgment of some and the temper of others to convert into crime, practices which they deemed mischievous or unethical. . . . Meanwhile, our police are caught in an embarrassing dilemma and there is little hope of a sound and healthy basis of police work until our lawmaking bodies face the fact that men cannot be made good by force. . . . Permanent advance in human society will not be brought about by nightsticks and patrol wagons.[8]

To Fosdick the main objection to vice was not in its immorality, but in its corruption of government, particularly the police. To remedy the situation, he fell back on his European experience, urging that America adopt the system of long-term professional police administration by experts responsible to public authority outside the local political process. Thus proponents of administrative science like Fosdick both agreed with and diverged from the more traditional reformers. Both located the roots of crime and disorder and the failures of the police in the unrestrained lower classes, but where the Parkhurst type believed that moral integrity of leaders was sufficient to produce administrative efficiency, Fosdick's group believed that efficient administration by experts would produce integrity. As the organ of Progressivism, *The Outlook*, observed, "The way to make the police less arbitrary and tyrannical is to make them more efficient."[9]

To Fosdick, Boston's Commissioner O'Meara and the autonomous authority he possessed provided the best current model, but O'Meara himself was primarily a man of common sense rather than an "expert," whereas the new reformers thought police administration had to be based on system and method, not just individual capacity.

So great was Fosdick's prestige that despite his youth and lack of direct police experience he was seriously considered for appointment as Mitchell's police commissioner. However, the Mayor was too astute a politician to put in another police head like Waldo whom the cartoonists could portray as a Boy Scout or, in Fosdick's case, a schoolboy. So he turned to the more traditional choice of a senior military man, offering the post to Colonel George Washington Goethals, a West Point–educated army engineer who had just finished building the Panama Canal. Goethals would accept only on the condition that, like O'Meara, he would have the right to dismiss officers without subsequent court review and to promote without regard to civil service rules pertaining to time in grade. Mitchell had the so-called Goethals bill introduced in the Legislature, but that body did not act favorably on the court review section, and Goethals declined the commissionership.[10]

Mitchell's next choice was his secretary, Theodore Roosevelt's protegé Arthur Woods, whose career as deputy commissioner had ended in the furor of the George Duffy case. After leaving the department, Woods, now forty-four, had become a businessman and socialite and was soon to marry a granddaughter of banker J. P. Morgan. In April 1914 he was appointed police commissioner. In age, experience, and social background he was an ideal choice. Though not exactly an administrative expert, he had made the ritual study of European police and moved in circles where the new science was being developed. If anyone could bring administrative principles to the police, Woods was the most likely person.

In 1914 New York was "the big town" in every sphere, and since it was the national media capital its happenings were carried to the world. Its cops, long known as "the Finest," were frequently tarnished by scandal, and experts considered Boston and Washington to have better departments, but the 10,000-man New York City police force was by the very fact of its size and location the natural leader of the field. Cops all over the country consciously or unconsciously followed New York's lead in everything from mundane things like discarding their London bobby helmets to major structural changes such as the adoption of a single-commissioner form of executive control. If the ideas of the Bureau of Municipal Research took hold in New York, they would spread throughout the country.

When Woods took office, his 10,000 subordinates, from patrolmen to inspector, had to decide the degree to which they would cooperate with his regime. Despite the semimilitary nature of the organization, the cops were not soldiers. Instead, in the British tradition, they were civilians who held legally independent public office. As civilians, from the 1890s on, they maintained benevolent associations or quasi-unions, although the very idea of police unions was not entirely appropriate since the police could not truly be compared to ordinary blue-collar workers. In their capacity as public officials they had discretionary powers over individual life and liberty which on occasion were as great as those of doctors and lawyers, and, given the random and episodic nature of police work, it was often the lowly beat cop rather than the captain or inspector who made the decision to shoot, club, arrest, or release a suspect. In other respects, though, such as discipline, promotion, or assignment, the cops were at the mercy of their superiors and the politicians.

To what values, then, was an individual officer or the collectivity of the department to respond? At least four different images of policing were available. An officer could accept the job as a patronage post useful for loafing, grafting, or indulging his personal passions for liquor, sex, or brutality—in effect the Tim Sullivan model of policing as practiced by Bill Devery. A somewhat different version of the political nature of policing was the perspective of the police as a mediating force between various factions and clashing ideologies. This was the basis of the Dick Croker–Boss Murphy–Inspector Thomas Byrnes policy of restraint. In this version the cops regulated vice activities, keeping them at an acceptable level, were tough on crime, were respectful toward various elites, and, if they took graft, accepted only "clean" money from people like the Canfield crowd.

A third approach was what might be termed "legality," wherein the officer saw himself as a servant not of politics but of the law, itself an inviolate force which regulated everyone including the elites. This was the notion of policing which Mayor Gaynor had espoused during his service as a judge. A fourth approach was that of the emerging administrative science. Like legality, it viewed the police as "nonpolitical" servants, but of rational public policy rather than the tortuous processes of law. Of course, sophisticated analysts might scoff at the notion that administrative science was nonpolitical. To the Bureau of Municipal Research claim that politics and administration were separate, they would respond that administrative science was itself a brand of politics which by placing the conduct of government in the hands of an educated elite would produce decisions favoring the upper class. In fact administrative science might be characterized in New York terms as uptown politics in opposition to the downtown variety of the Sullivans.*

* Perhaps the best illustration of the difference between the two is found in methods of judicial selection. Downtown politics usually favors the direct elections of judges, which in practice means that neighborhood lawyers with degrees from night school reach the bench after years of faithful party service and/or large

In reality there was probably a greater division between administrative science and legality than between the former and political policing of the Croker-Murphy variety. As legal scholar Herbert L. Packer noted in discussing the crime control and due process models of criminal justice:

> The due process model views the criminal process as conforming to the rule of law. It is a model stressing the possibilities of human error, especially the frailty of authority under pressure. Above all, it is a model emphasizing *legal* guilt over *factual* guilt. Thus, an accused is to be held guilty if, and only if, the factual determinations made against him have been presented in a procedurally regular fashion by lawfully constituted authorities acting within duly allocated competences.
>
> The crime control model, by contrast, emphasizes *factual* guilt. Its principle is efficiency through rational administration or "the system's capacity to apprehend, try, convict, and dispose of a high proportion of criminal offenders whose offenses become known." This model stresses social control over individual justice. Its operative norms are those of a productive enterprise; its success is gauged by a high rate of apprehension and conviction in the context of mass administration of criminal law.[11]

While administrators like Commissioner Woods might support civil liberties in the abstract, when the "public interest" clashed with legality, the latter would inevitably give way. By and large, the crime control model was preferred by even the legal profession. In the year Woods took office, the U.S. Supreme Court announced the so-called "exclusionary rule" whereby evidence unlawfully seized could not be admitted at a federal criminal trial.[12] That is, if a police officer spotted one of the Eastman or Kelly gangsters, frisked him, and found a concealed weapon, the search was illegal because the officer had no legitimate basis for conducting it, mere suspicion being insufficient. However, in the absence of an exclusionary rule, the weapon could be introduced in evidence and the offender convicted and sent to prison under the Sullivan law. Despite the federal decision most states, including New York, did not adopt a similar rule, and police work continued in the old style. Under prevailing state law proper redress for the person who was unlawfully searched was to sue the officer as an individual. This was a dubious remedy, since a jury was unlikely to find in favor of a gangster, nor was suing police officers a wise policy for citizens in general. There-

"contributions" of money. Uptown politics usually favors gubernatorial appointment of the judiciary, with the result that judges are more apt to be drawn from graduates of prestige law schools who are partners in leading firms. While much virtue is claimed for the latter method, it is not clear that members of the Union League Club make better judges than members of the Fourth Ward Marching and Chowder Society.

fore, the remedy was a dead letter, save for high-status citizens who were victims of gross misconduct, which usually arose as a result of a mistake.

From ordinary cops up to administrative reformers like Woods, the importance of disarming gangs was greater than some legal mumbo jumbo, and in practice the application of legality by proponents like Gaynor appeared ludicrous. Cops were reprimanded for using their clubs on the likes of Owney "the Killer" Madden, or for briefly detaining a street-corner tough like George Duffy. So bad had things gotten under Gaynor, the cops argued, that he had to call in Charlie Becker to restore order. Nor were the cops impressed by the respect for law shown in the upper world. District attorneys such as Jerome or Whitman and judges like Goff, not to mention the Wall Street crowd, viewed the law as a sword to attack their enemies or a shield for themselves, but never as a fixed set of rules which might restrain them. Thus legality had little to commend itself to the police or anyone else, and in this respect reform was no different from Tammany.

As with any New York police chief, Commissioner Woods's first priority was the vice problem. While he rejected the moral-crusade posture, he was still obliged to take vigorous repressive measures. Given the widespread nature and the entrenched position of gambling, prostitution, and saloons, not to mention drugs (whose addicts Woods placed at 200,000),[13] this was no mean feat. New York had more dives in one police precinct than existed in all of Boston. For Woods to accomplish his goals meant persuading the cops to take enforcement action, or more bluntly to refrain from accepting payoffs. To the bulk of the department, a vigorous antivice policy was unrealistic and even dangerous. Reform was not seen by many police as a good long-term prospect. Reformers tended to disappear rapidly, and cops who cooperated with them ended up in disfavor, the loss of parade privileges being the mildest form of discipline. Nor were the bureaucratic aspects of administrative science particularly appealing to the rank and file, since administrative science tended to view the cops in a military manner, stressing strict obedience and tight discipline.

Commissioner Woods, a genial and gentlemanly person, strove mightily to win the confidence of his bluecoats. With some, particularly specialists, he succeeded by innovations which enhanced the various technical skills. For example, he created a homicide clinic along with a psychopathic laboratory to study murder and sex crimes. For cops like Captain Arthur Carey, who was placed in charge of homicide, the Woods administration was the highest point of their career.

For the mass of police Woods introduced increased training and made inspirational speeches, always careful to praise the heroism and devotion of his men. For example, he declared:

> The bravery of policemen is so genuine and splendid, and their support of each other, no matter how menacing the physical danger, so inspiring, that one cannot but feel that these perversions of the spirit [grafting] are unnatural, forced growths, which must inevitably be sloughed off as intolerable and inconsistent, leaving a body of men, brave as lions, true to each other, and true to the highest standards of honor.[14]

Ultimately, though, the values of most cops would be dictated by their social background. When Robert Peel decided that Anglo-Saxon policemen, even of comparatively high rank, would not be gentlemen, policing became a working-class stronghold. In consequence the social milieu and world view of New York cops was the same as that of the Tammany bosses. They would never go to Harvard, be received in the White House, or marry J. P. Morgan's granddaughter. In their hearts virtually all big-city cops were Tammany men, even those from Chicago or San Francisco who had never seen the lights of 14th Street or heard of Big Tim. The spirit of Tammany, i.e., the practical politics of the who-gets-what variety and the cultural maxims of ethnic and blue-collar America, would rule urban policing even when the local machine was out of power, since its values were those of the cops. Thus the very fact of his being a reformer placed the commissioner in an antagonistic position to his force, and ultimately it was necessary to fall back on the "shoefly" spy system to maintain control.

In the nineteenth century the precinct roundsmen (later called sergeants) were expected to keep strict watch on patrolmen, but this made them unpopular and many opted for a buddy relationship with their men. Later special headquarters roundsmen were used to make confidential inspections on a citywide basis. Such officers were also used to investigate corruption. Thus there developed a "shoefly" or headquarters investigator who checked up on cops and was utilized to raid protected vice resorts.*

One such cop was "Honest" Dan Costigan, who had made his reputation as a detective sergeant on the Chinatown beat, where he ignored the various temptations in order to enforce the law. As a lieutenant in charge of one of Commissioner Waldo's strong-arm squads, Costigan had publicly criticized Charley Becker for attempting to protect gambling.

Under Woods Costigan was promoted to inspector and placed in charge of a confidential squad. Duty as a shoefly was not calculated to win the esteem of one's peers, and given the fact that no reform was likely to be permanent, the shoefly might later pay for being too zealous. Still, such assignments provided an entrée to the high command and

---

* So called because on spotting these headquarters men, cops would make their shoes fly away. Alternatively, such men were known as shooflies.

eventual promotion. One of the most aggressive of Costigan's men was Sergeant Floyd Horton, a rather atypical cop in that he was a Republican, Protestant, Mason, and teetotaler of English descent, in the opinion of the mostly Irish force just the type to be a shoefly. But Horton's partner and close friend, Sergeant Lewis Valentine of Alsatian-Irish descent, was a Democrat, Catholic, and member of the Knights of Columbus with no objection to an occasional drink.[15]

Valentine had joined the force in 1903 at twenty-one. For ten years he remained an obscure uniformed cop in Brooklyn, finally winning promotion to sergeant. As a shoefly he would be a detective sergeant and three years later a lieutenant. But it was a tough and lonely job, and Valentine and Horton were a much-hated pair. When Costigan suspected a precinct commander was on the take, he would send the shoeflies in to make raids on the protected joints and embarrass the commanding officer. If a cop was believed to be crooked, Costigan's men would attempt to trap him. In 1916 Costigan heard that a Brooklyn patrolman had offered to fix a case against a sailor arrested in a fatal brawl. Valentine, disguised as a sailor, arranged a payoff with marked money, then overpowered the cop and booked him at his own stationhouse. The officer, another Brooklyn Irishman, turned out to be a friend of Valentine's brother, and family connections were brought to bear, but to no avail. The cop was convicted at a criminal trial, but Valentine was not the most popular man in his social set thereafter.[16]

The clever Costigan also liked to pick rookies right out of the police academy for assignment to his squad, particularly if they did not look like cops. One such was Johnny Cordes, whose boyish appearance and 145 pounds on a 5' 10" frame, made him very uncoplike. The "Dutchman," as he was called, had been raised among the drug-using Hudson-Duster gang of Greenwich Village and then moved to Harlem. In both places he acquired street savvy and soon was making his living as a six-day bike rider and general hustler. In 1915, at age twenty-five, on a bet, he took the police exam, passed, and was snatched out of the academy by Costigan. As a cop, Cordes continued his unorthodox ways, donning various disguises and operating as a lone wolf. Despite his size, the Dutchman was tough and usually preferred his fists to a gun. Cordes received some of the hostility directed at shoeflies, but it rolled off his carefree personality.

Commissioner Woods moved on a loftier plane than his shoeflies, but he too was to feel the weight of rank and file resentment. It was ironic that the reformers' demands for civil service protection for the police had now made the latter more resistant to reform. In the nineteenth century a member of the force who spoke out against a Tammany commissioner would have been fired, but by 1914 the police were speaking out against the commissioner with impunity, particularly through their own associations, and it was these organizations which defeated the Goethals bill.

Foremost among the police spokesmen was Lieutenant Richard Enright, president of the Lieutenants' Benevolent Association, a member of the force since 1896, and a protegé of Bill Devery. In 1914 Enright, then an acting captain in headquarters, was number one on the civil service list for promotion to permanent rank. But in February, at the outset of the new administration, he threw down the gauntlet. At a banquet of the Lieutenants' Association attended by Enright's friend former President William Howard Taft, the lieutenant held forth on the problems of the New York City Police Department:

> During the last thirteen years, nine Commissioners have come and gone, with an average service of a little more than one year. With them have come and gone some thirty-three Deputy Commissioners, and all the fads and fancies mixed with ideas, good and bad, that mortal man has ever dreamed of. Everything has been tried upon the police dog.
>
> Some have been lawyers, some have been Judges, some have been railway men, some have been schoolmasters, some have been bookkeepers, some have been bartenders, some have been plumbers, some have been milliners, and some have had no visible means of support. We have had everything but a clamdigger and an undertaker.
>
> . . . For twenty years, and year by year, the police force of this city has been reformed. At the beginning of each crusade we are persuaded that this time the right men and the right methods will prevail. In a short time the job is pronounced a success, but if any one should ever succeed in making this job a success it will be a sad day for the scribes and Pharisees of this town, who will then be out of a job.[17]

Former Deputy Commissioner Woods was not amused, and he passed over Enright three times, which in accordance with civil service law sent him to the bottom of the captain's list. From then on, Enright was even more outspokenly bitter against the reform administration, making common cause with Frank Prial, president of a civil service employees' association, who had been dismissed from his city job when the Mitchell regime took office. Prial, who became a state official, organized a new group known as the Civil Service Forum and with Enright obtained support from a public employee newspaper, The Chief.[18] Enright, a fine orator, was a frequent banquet speaker and missed no opportunity to attack the Woods regime. Naturally, the administration fought back, and Costigan had Valentine and Horton make a thorough investigation of Enright and his association, provoking more bitterness.

In effect, despite his own desires, Woods became increasingly the boss, not the leader, of the cops, supported by a few like Carey, Costigan, Valentine, and Horton and opposed by the many under the leadership, but not the command, of Enright. The police department would not strike unless driven to desperation as in Boston, and the relatively well-paid New York cops were not in financial straits, but they would not cooperate, and their negative attitudes were communicated to the public in thousands of daily encounters.

The Fall of Mitchell

The Mitchell regime also had other problems, mostly of its own making. The guiding light of the administration was the Bureau of Municipal Research, with Bruere as Mitchell's mentor.[19] As proponents of administrative efficiency they tried to reduce the welfare rolls, and their efforts led them into a clash with the Catholic Church, whose charity operations were conducted with city funds. The church favored liberal policies toward the poor, many of whom were Catholics. Angered at the opposition Mayor Mitchell had Woods's police department tap the phones of clergymen. In 1916 this practice was disclosed before a state investigating commission with the inevitable Frank Moss as counsel, and the Catholic mayor lost favor with many of his coreligionists.[20]

The wiretapping investigation revealed how the crime control model was at the essence of police administrative science. When challenged by the state commission, Woods defended his methods, noting that

> ... the same method which would be utterly unjustifiable if used with reference to law abiding citizens is in my best judgment and firm conviction not merely justifiable but a duty when it is used to protect law-abiding citizens against crooks.

However, under cross-examination, Woods had to admit tapping the phones of Catholic priests, Protestant ministers, lawyers conferring with their clients, and a Wall Street law firm engaged in a controversy with J. P. Morgan and Company.* When asked how differentiation was made between criminals and respectable citizens, Woods replied he made such judgments personally, causing Frank Moss to observe, "That makes you a czar." Woods then lost his temper, declaring,

> You know that you cannot do detective work in a high hat and kid gloves. We have got to use the methods of the crook and speak the language. There is too much snappy talk about the rights of the crook. He is an outlaw and defies the authorities. Where do his rights come in? If people spent less time talking about the dear criminals and more time helping the police to run them down we would have fewer criminals.

* The firm was alleged to have falsely represented itself as Morgan's agent, but given Woods's relationship with Morgan, his action was probably ill advised.

During the course of the investigation Woods had to appear before a grand jury and indictment loomed, but the matter was dropped and the following month he received an honorary degree from Harvard and married J. P. Morgan's granddaughter.[21]

The mayor, who had instituted the eavesdropping, was also hauled before a grand jury but was not indicted. Mitchell, "humorless and self-righteous" in public affairs,[22] was a playboy in his personal life, another fact which disturbed many of the electorate. He much preferred the company of the Park Avenue, Newport smart set and the dance floors of the classy Broadway night spots to the Holy Name Society benefit in the parish basement. The response to such conduct was aggravated by the widespread belief that Mitchell was totally under the influence of his new associates. His tough stance on welfare was but one example; another was his vigorous internationalism, which was then a common sentiment of the eastern establishment. As mayor he plumped hard for aid to the Allies and military preparedness—positions which did not endear him to the city's German and Irish populations or the sizable socialist element.

In the summer of 1915 Mitchell and Woods both went off to the new Reserve Officers Training School at Plattsburg, New York. There they paraded before Theodore Roosevelt and General Leonard Wood and listened to fight talks from the former which brought a rebuke from the pacifist in the White House, who at the time thought a country could be too proud to fight.[23]

One of the most effective anti-Mitchell ploys was a cartoon portraying him alongside William K. Vanderbilt with Mitchell saying, "He called me Jack." Like Whitman and the other upwardly mobile politicians, Mitchell was thrilled by such attention, but the city masses were not.[24]

The era saw a growth in radical sentiment, particularly in the crowded slums of the East Side. The toll of 146 lives, mostly young Jewish and Italian girls, in the 1911 fire at the Triangle Shirtwaist factory, a modern, "fireproof" building was exacerbated by locked exits designed to keep out union organizers.[25] District Attorney Whitman failed to obtain convictions against the owners, and more significantly, despite the formation of a blue-ribbon investigating commission of Morgan bankers and other elite, the East Side ignored them in favor of its own indigenous leaders, whose ideas of reform were not those of the Citizen's Union. As young Rosa Schneiderman of the garment workers said at a public meeting:

> I would be a traitor to those poor burned bodies . . . if I were to come here to talk good fellowship. . . .

We have tried you, citizens! We are trying you now and you have a couple of dollars for the sorrowing mothers and brothers and sisters by way of a charity gift. But every time the workers come out in the only way they know to protest against conditions which are unbearable, the strong hand of the law is allowed to press down heavily upon us.

Public officials have only words of warning for us—warning that we must be intensely orderly and must be intensely peaceable, and they have the workhouse just back of all their warnings. The strong hand of the law beats us back when we rise—back into the conditions that make life unbearable.

I can't talk fellowship to you who are gathered here. Too much blood has been spilled. I know from experience it is up to the working people to save themselves. And the only way is through a strong working-class movement.[26]

The city government had no idea of how to deal with the city's poor. Though Commissioner Woods did establish employment and juvenile units as a type of social service in the police department, throughout the Mitchell administration cops repeatedly clashed with strikers and radicals; and while Woods declared that he had ended the free use of police clubs, the same claim was made by all reform administrations, before and after. Irish cops sent to spy on Catholic priests could hardly be expected to display restraint against Jewish radicals.

In the mayoral election of 1917, the liberal reform community worked feverishly for the handsome, dashing mayor, and 2 million dollars was spent on his behalf, the largest sum in a mayoral election up until that time. If Tammany had put up such an amount, it would have been accused of buying the election, but as a political editor of the *New York Times* remarked, "Reformers are allowed to do things which would land regulars in the hoosegow."[27] The Democrats put up John F. "Red Mike" Hylan, a Brooklyn politician and Hearst favorite whom Tammany reluctantly had to support. The Socialists brought forth their own candidate, Morris Hillquit. Hearst had opposed America's entry into the war, and many of Hylan's votes and virtually all of Hillquit's were antiwar.

The pacifistic, liberal Princetonian Raymond Fosdick knew where a right-thinking American would stand. In April 1917 he ran into Jane Addams in the Washington railroad station as she was returning from leading an antiwar delegation to the White House. Recognizing him, she sobbed, "Oh, Raymond, this is terrible," but he pushed her aside. He was off to the army and his own war against the red-light districts.[28]

In addition to the hostility from antiwar, radical, and welfare groups, Mitchell was opposed by the city employees, particularly the police. In the face of so much opposition he was overwhelmingly defeated. Both

Woods and Mitchell joined the army, and the mayor was killed a few months later when he fell from a plane while training as a pilot.* Woods returned safely, lectured at Yale and Princeton, and received a number of accolades. As with Teddy Roosevelt, his accomplishments were more a matter of tone and aspirations than realizations, though he had been allowed to remain for many years—a political impossibility—he doubtless would have accomplished much as he was an able man.

In the postwar era, all of the key figures in the Mitchell administration secured lucrative private posts. Bruere, the former social worker, became a bank president. Fosdick and Woods settled into service under the Rockefeller banner. The former, always an astute trend spotter, became president of the Rockefeller Foundation, where he would continue to seek an answer to the disorder of the world in administrative systems, being a leading proponent of the League of Nations.** Woods became president of Rockefeller Center and under President Hoover headed a commission to help the unemployed.

Lieutenant Enright Speaking

Red Mike, a very simple man, had begun his career as an elevated motorman but was fired for reckless driving when he nearly ran over his superintendent. Later as a politician he carried on a perpetual war against the transit interests. As mayor, one of his chief functions was to provide the police band to serenade Mr. and Mrs. Hearst. He also appeared regularly at opening nights of movies made by Mr. Hearst's companion, Marion Davies (Douras), and urged everyone to see them.[31]

The fall of the reformers naturally affected the fortunes of many policemen. Mayor Hylan appointed as commissioner one of Woods's civilian deputies, Frederick Burgher. It was not a happy choice. Commissioner Burgher was a Prussian sort, one who clicked his heels and saluted in the presence of the mayor. Twenty-three days into the new

* Mitchell's death was the subject of considerable speculation, since he had failed to fasten his safety belt. Some wondered if he wanted to die, since he was very depressed. But he had overcome various obstacles to get into the service and was eager for combat; thus his friends felt that if he sought death, it was likely that he would have preferred it at the front. An alternative explanation is that the tight safety belt aggravated his chronic headaches which were a product of his having been poisoned by an enemy during a stormy period in his early life when he worked in South America.[29]

** Fosdick was one of the first to recognize that long-term power lay in the back rooms of foundation work rather than the spotlight of temporary public office. In 1912 he turned down an appointment to assist Whitman in the Becker prosecution because it "led nowhere," and despite his reputation as an expert in police administration and a prostitution fighter he correctly discerned that such interests were the wrong side of the intellectual tracks. As president of the Rockefeller Foundation he largely ignored criminal justice in favor of international peace and medical research.[30]

administration Hylan informed his secretary, Grover Whalen, that he had had a dream which told him to fire Burgher. Whether the dream was influenced by the mayor's detective brother-in-law, who had been rebuffed when he offered a few suggestions to the new commissioner, is not known. At any rate, the commissioner was summoned to the Mayor's presence. Entering, he clicked his heels, saluted, and reported. Hylan yelled, "You're fired." The commissioner, dumbfounded, clicked his heels, saluted, and wordlessly withdrew.

Red Mike now had another inspiration. The ideal replacement would be Lieutenant Richard Enright. Whalen reached him on desk duty at a Brooklyn precinct and ordered him to headquarters, where he was given his appointment and ushered into the commissioner's office still unable to comprehend what had befallen him. When a telephone rang, the commissioner leaped to answer, "Lieutenant Enright speaking," in the manner of a desk officer, and Whalen had to remind him of his changed circumstances.[32] The mayor had bypassed scores of captains, inspectors, and deputy chiefs for a lowly lieutenant. In the past many men had become chiefs or commissioners via their political connections in the community, but Enright was the first of a new breed which would not flourish until fifty years later, a man whose constituency was the police themselves. The union steward had been made president of the company. But this was on the condition that he serve well those who owned it, in this case Messrs. Hylan and Hearst.

Enright was to remain as commissioner for eight years, the longest time of any man in the department up until then and the second longest to date. Despite his background and allegiances he was not without administrative talent. At the outset, however, he settled scores in the usual fashion of a Tammany brave on a scalping expedition. The shoefly squad was abolished and its members suitably chastized. Costigan was demoted to captain and Valentine and Horton, now lieutenants, were sent to precincts. Valentine was eventually passed over three times for captain and went to the bottom of the list, but Horton was to be the most abused. He became the first man ever denied membership in the Lieutenants' Association. Then, in December 1920, while on the way home from his precinct, he surprised some burglars. In the ensuing gunfight he was fatally wounded, though he managed to write down the license of the bandits' car, and as a result they were captured. The circumstances of his death brought Horton the police Medal of Honor and entitled him to posthumous membership in an organization of decorated cops known as the Honor Legion. But even in death membership was denied.[33]

If the new regime punished its enemies, it was generous to its friends. A deputy police commissioner's post was given to Judge Goff's son, and the mayor appointed Marion Davies's father a criminal court magistrate. The Hylan regime also restored Frank Prial to the city payroll as a deputy comptroller. From this post he retained his presidency of the Civil Service Forum, became publisher of *The Chief*, and with Enright established a close relationship with the Delahanty Institute, a civil service cram school. From then on a smart cop looked to *The Chief* for inside news and Delahanty's to prepare him for promotions.

In many ways Enright resembled Devery, but he lacked his mentor's touch of humor. An irascible and combative man, he was constantly embroiled in some feud, and his annual reports, in contrast to the usual terse statistical summaries, ran to 300 pages and were filled with long tirades against his enemies, and statements such as "there is only one expert on crime in New York"—himself.* [34] On one occasion he instituted prosecution for criminal libel against a judge and a state legislator because they referred to the police department as "Enright and his grafters."[35] On a more positive note, he became an important international spokesman for police, and under his leadership an international association of chiefs of police undertook to develop a national system of criminal identification records which in 1930 was transferred to the FBI as a nucleus of its identification section.

The Man in the Doorway

The Enright regime encompassed the first years of Prohibition, during which New York police, like their comrades everywhere, were to become part of a vast morality play which would dominate national politics for a generation.

While Prohibition is now generally condemned as a foolish experiment responsible for the corruption of government and the growth of organized crime, this is somewhat of an exaggeration. Organized crime and corruption were well entrenched long before the Volstead Act established Prohibition. The Becker case had propelled Arnold Rothstein forward as a key figure in the police–politics–gangster combine, although he was more a prime minister than a czar, the top man in a coalition rather than supreme ruler. First and foremost he was a gambler, operating and playing in high-stakes card and dice games, along with the other midtown gamblers of the Canfield tradition. Though such men portrayed themselves as gentlemen, some were not above using crooked dice and marked cards. It was also a practice to allow losers to cancel their debts by steering other suckers.[36] Thus to the cops who

* The reports also include news stories and cartoons, many of them critical of Enright. In some instances an Enright tirade runs for pages, is dropped, and ten pages later is resumed with increased fury. Like O'Meara, Enright was one of the few police chiefs ever to produce annual reports of any real help in determining his department's policies.

knew them well the appellation of gentlemen applied to their success and influential contacts rather than to their code of behavior.

But gambling was only one aspect of Rothstein's life. He was also a bondsman putting up bail for accused criminals. In this capacity, he had direct relationships with cops, lawyers, and judges. Then, as his power grew, he became banker for a drug syndicate, labor racketeers, and peddlers of stolen goods. His own lawyer characterized him as "a man who dwells in doorways. A grey rat waiting for his cheese."[37] He was in fact a twentieth-century Jonathan Wild. With his glamour and Broadway celebrity status, he was the ideal bridge between respectable people and the underworld. Having a civilian like Rothstein occupy this position avoided the risk of direct underworld involvement by high-level policemen or politicians, who would of course, continue to receive payoffs. But while the new system shielded the top police and political figures, it also ultimately lessened their power vis-à-vis the gangsters.

To some extent the growth of organized crime paralleled the similar centralizing tendencies in business and government represented by the new administrative science. Prohibition simply accelerated the process.

When Big Tim died in 1913, leadership of the Sullivan faction passed to Tom Foley, also a bondsman, who operated out of his saloon in lower Manhattan near the criminal court building. Like Rothstein, whose allegiance was to Boss Murphy and the Tenderloin gentlemanly gambling faction, Foley managed to bridge downtown and uptown. The presence of Woods as head of the police department was somewhat inconvenient, but the bulk of the force, dominated by the spirit of Tammany, its former and future master, was not at all inaccessible to Foley or Rothstein. The resurgence of Tammany under Hylan set the seal on the dominance of organized crime, and if the cops had any doubts, an incident early in Enright's regime convinced them.

It began under the Woods administration when in May 1917 a Rothstein dice game was held up. Such occurrences were common in his career, since there was always some gun-crazy thug trying to stage a large score regardless of the victim's power. Though all of Broadway knew of the affair, it might have passed without wider public notice. But the gossipy Herbert Bayard Swope, ever one to relish trouble for others, sought Commissioner Woods's opinion on the matter. Woods observed that Rothstein was "too yellow" to report the crime and prosecute the robbers. When Swope dangled this before Rothstein, the gambler was forced to respond by fingering the hoods to the cops. They were convicted and sent to prison. Then one of them, a drug addict murderer, escaped with the announced intention of killing Rothstein. Under the code of conduct for Broadway big shots, Rothstein could not show fear lest he lose his power and position. For some months he appeared openly in his usual haunts, expecting a bullet at any minute.

Finally the bandit was shot to death in a Detroit robbery, but the memory haunted Rothstein.[38]

In January 1919, detectives under the orders of Inspector Dominick Henry broke into a Rothstein gambling game on West 57th Street. The nervous Rothstein, mistaking this for another holdup, opened fire, slightly wounding two of the raiders. When the mistake was realized, everyone, including the cops, was embarrassed. Rothstein, found hiding on a fire escape, drove the wounded officers to the hospital in his own limousine, all the while making profuse apologies. Whether other amends were made was subject to later dispute. After some delay Rothstein was booked for assault to murder, but the cops were quite disposed to forget the matter and the charges were eventually dismissed. But William Randolph Hearst alleged that Swope, now executive editor of the rival *New York World*, had paid $32,000 to fix the case.* Since Hearst was de facto mayor, the charges had to be taken seriously, and an investigation was started by the police department and the district attorney. The whole affair was a struggle between Hearst and Hylan, on one side, and Swope, Boss Murphy, Tom Foley (who controlled the district attorney and the courts), and Arnold Rothstein, on the other, over who was to be the senior partner in governing New York.

As is usual in such affairs, when elephants fight, the grass gets trampled. Inspector Henry and an assistant district attorney named Smith had been feuding, Henry accusing the latter of making illegal slacker raids during the late war and of trying to persuade him to form an alliance to drive Jewish gamblers out of the Tenderloin and leave the Christian ones operating. Soon attention focused on the argument between the police and the DA, and Rothstein, Swope, and the other major figures were forgotten. Eventually Inspector Henry was indicted for perjury, convicted, sentenced to five years in Sing Sing, and fired from the force. After two years he won a reversal and then had to sue to be returned to duty. Though eventually he got back his rank, he had gone through a harrowing period. The lessons to the police department were clear: stay out of the affairs of Arnold Rothstein and the Broadway crowd of political and newspaper figures who surround him.[39] Even the suspicion of fixing the 1919 World Series did not harm Rothstein. Though he denied involvement, his name appeared prominently in every account, and his lieutenants Abe Attell and Rachel Brown were indicted with the eight White Sox players.

So ineffective were Enright's cops that wanted men could walk past them with impunity. In 1920, Rothstein's lieutenant Nicky Arnstein

* In fairness to Swope, he had been in Paris at the Versailles Peace Conference through the entire period.

was the subject of a manhunt in connection with the theft of 5 million dollars in bonds. The case involved the murder of young bank and brokerage messengers, including one whose face had been mutilated with twenty-seven knife cuts to prevent identification, since the boy was so young that his fingerprints were not on file.[40] But Arnstein's glamour and upperworld connections caused many to treat the matter as a funny caper. In May, when Nicky finally arranged to surrender, he and Fanny Brice, accompanied by Bill Fallon, premier criminal lawyer of Broadway, drove down to the criminal court building in the Arnstein family's open Cadillac. For a portion of the trip they traveled down Fifth Avenue as part of the police department's annual parade but were unmolested. Parking the car, Fanny and Fallon waited with a reporter in Tom Foley's saloon while Nicky went into the criminal court building, where Arnold Rothstein had arranged bond. Within a few minutes the car was stolen. While Fanny wailed with more fervor than she ever did on the stage for Ziegfeld, her companions invoked the sacred name of Rothstein. A local thug went to the phone and shortly afterward Monk Eastman drove up in the car with apologies, stating he did not know the vehicle's ownership.[41]

In the 1890s Inspector Byrnes and Clubber Williams were the only ones who could have produced such fear in the underworld. After their time this power belonged to Big Tim. Now it was possessed by a man who though publicly accused of fixing the national pastime, went scot free. Beautiful people in tune with the times can do no wrong, and Rothstein was very much in tune with the popular urge to get rich and have a daring glamorous life. He even appears as a character in the symbolic novel of the period when Jay Gatsby points out Meyer Wolfsheim:

"Who is he, anyhow, an actor?"

"No."

"A dentist?"

"Meyer Wolfsheim? No, he's a gambler." Gatsby hesitated, then added coolly: "He's the man who fixed the World's Series back in 1919."

"Fixed the World's Series?" I repeated.

The idea staggered me. I remembered, of course, that the World Series had been fixed in 1919, but if I had thought of it at all I would have thought of it as a thing that merely happened, the end of some inevitable chain. It never occurred to me that one man could start to play with the faith of fifty million people—with the single-mindedness of a burglar blowing a safe.

"How did he happen to do that?" I asked after a minute.

"He just saw the opportunity."

"Why isn't he in jail?"

"They can't get him, old sport. He's a smart man."[42]

The theft of U.S. government bonds and various Wall Street bucket shop frauds brought a federal investigation aimed at Murphy, Foley, and Rothstein. Nicky Arnstein, convicted in the bond case, was offered a chance to avoid prison by squealing on the supposed higher-ups. But good guy Nicky refused and went to Leavenworth Penitentiary.

A by-product of the various probes was the indictment of super-mouthpiece William Fallon for jury bribing. Though he was acquitted, his career was shattered.* Fallon had been considered a brilliant attorney, but he was actually an actor who was able to put on dramatic shows before Tammany judges. When transported to the federal courts and real judges, the Fallon blarney failed totally; Judge Learned Hand characterized his arguments as "preposterous."[43] Fallon soon collapsed into alcoholism and an early death.

POLICE REFORM, TAMMANY STYLE

In 1924 Boss Murphy died, and shortly afterward Tom Foley followed. Prior to Foley's death a worthy successor had arisen in the person of a Harlem district leader, Jimmy Hines. The ex-blacksmith fit well the brawling, tough-guy image of a Sullivan type. When in 1921 he displeased Boss Murphy, the latter sent thugs to beat up Hines's workers, whereupon Jimmy and his boys shot up Murphy's district headquarters.[44]

While Hines succeeded to the headship of the Sullivan types, leadership of respectable Tammany now passed to its favorite son, Governor Al Smith, himself one of the great legends of American politics. His career, intrinsically bound up as it was with Tammany and Prohibition, illustrates much of the reality and illusion about the rulers over the New York City Police Department.

The public image of Smith, both at the height of his power and in later legend, was that of an Irish-Catholic of intelligence and dedication to liberal ideals, a product of Tammany who rose beyond it. In truth, though he was a devout Catholic, the rest was mostly invention. To begin with, he was but one part Irish and three quarters other stock.**

While honest in the sense of not accepting payoffs from vice, he did

---

* Fallon's defense was to claim his indictment was a plot by William Randolph Hearst, and throughout the trial he gave the impression that he possessed proof that Hearst had fathered an illegitimate child with Marion Davies. As it turned out, Hearst had nothing to do with the case and Fallon had no proof of any kind. Such was the nature of criminal trials in New York City at the time that such irrelevancies could decide guilt or innocence.

** Indeed, since his paternal grandfather was an Italian immigrant from Genoa, by the style of his time and place he was an Italian.[45]

serve as sheriff of New York County (1915–1917), a fee office which paid $60,000 annually, and as governor he was wined, dined, and entertained by wealthy men who did government business. Upon leaving office in 1921 and again in 1929, he was installed as the president of a large business enterprise where his chief task was to petition government bodies for various favors. As a presidential candidate he allowed questionable financial transactions to be made in raising campaign funds.[46]

In terms of intellect, though he was knowledgeable in the practical aspects of government, Smith's formal education ended at fourteen, and he admitted to never afterward reading a book. Nor can one stand in awe of a presidential candidate who upon arriving in Butte, Montana, confessed he had never heard of the place.[47] More importantly, Smith, who began as Tom Foley's errand boy, continued as a faithful Tammany lieutenant, and as late as 1913, while speaker of the Assembly, he led the successful drive to impeach Governor William Sulzer for the twin sins of refusing to obey Boss Murphy and attempting to increase regulation of Wall Street. Indeed, Smith was a great admirer of Wall Street, to the point of having an executive of Dupont as his 1928 campaign manager. After leaving office, he became an ardent conservative spokesman endorsing both Alfred Landon and Wendell Willkie for President. However, as governor of New York from 1919 to 1928 (minus two years), he was a relative liberal in utilizing the power of the state to promote social welfare on a modest scale—although the most solid accomplishments were construction projects undertaken by Secretary of State Robert Moses, whom Smith made a virtual czar. Compared with the Harding-Coolidge national administration, though, he *appeared* to be almost radical, an image heightened by his avowed wetness, which infuriated the Prohibitionists.

Prohibition was in fact a godsend to Tammany-type political machines. Not only did it swell the payoffs to the bosses, but it provided a safe issue on which to mobilize the electorate and to discredit all reformers of the good-government variety. Even in the early '30s at the height of the Depression, Smith would assert that Prohibition was the key national problem and rebuke FDR for discussing economics.

Thus Smith was the logical successor in the line of Tammany leaders who opposed dirty graft, disliked reformers, and never forgot to protect Wall Street. Characteristically, as Murphy had done upon ascension to the leadership in 1902, Smith's first concern as boss was to clean up the New York City Police Department, which was giving the party a bad name. In practice this meant getting rid of Enright by eliminating Hylan as mayor—a feat which also would harm Smith's bitter enemy William Randolph Hearst.[48]

Several able men, such as Robert Wagner, refused the job, since to be mayor of New York and boss of its police department led nowhere. Wagner chose to wait until the following year and ran successfully for the U.S. Senate. Smith's choice then fell on James J. Walker, the son of a Tammany brave, who as a young man had preferred writing music in Tin Pan Alley over working for the wigwam on 14th Street. As a state senator his chief accomplishments had been bills permitting prize-fights and Sunday baseball. Like Mitchell, he loved the Broadway night-life* and was little troubled by the dictates of St. Patrick's Cathedral, known as the "powerhouse" because of its enormous influence on local politics.

Smith extracted from Walker a pledge to give up his mistresses and to appoint a Smith designee as police commissioner, the governor's choice being George McLaughlin, the state superintendent of banking. In Smith's view what the police department needed was a good sound business administration, not the fancy ideas of theorists. Indeed, he had publicly ridiculed the idea that cops should go to college.[50] Walker crushed Hylan in the primary and his Republican opponent in the general election and celebrated the latter occasion in the arms of his mistress. "Beau James," as one admiring biographer called him, became one of the best-loved men in the bright, happy time and place over which he reigned, but beyond appointing McLaughlin he would no more honor his commitment regarding the police then he would those concerning his extramarital affairs.[51]

The police department which McLaughlin prepared to clean up faced the perennial problem of controlling the gangs, now more powerful than ever. As in the past one solution was the strong-arm squad, and the 1920s produced some of the toughest cops. One was Captain Cornelius Willemse, a rugged Dutch immigrant. After he retired in 1924, he wrote two books in which he freely admitted using the rubber hose and blackjack as casually as others employed the knife and fork. So accepted were such tactics that the introduction of his second book was written by the world-famous historian Henrik Willem Van Loon.[52]

Another strong-arm was Bobby McAllister, called the "flying cop" because of his fame as a track man. McAllister was also a boxer and in 1923 was tapped for the "gangster" squad. As the squad's commanding officer explained to him:

Now lemme tell ya what we're gonna do. We're going after the shake-down mugs, the tough guys, the muscle guys. But we're not gonna col-

---

* Indeed, for a time Walker and Mayor Mitchell, both married, shared the affections of a Broadway performer. When the young lady was fired for repeatedly being late, she had the show's midnight license revoked, and it was not restored until she was hired back at twice the salary.[49]

lect any evidence against them, we're not even gonna arrest them—we're gonna give 'em some of their own medicine—we're gonna work 'em over. We're gonna search this town from one end to the other and wherever we find 'em, we're gonna beat 'em up. This isn't according to the book, but we're gonna forget the book. When we get through with them, they're either gonna be too scared to shake down the storekeepers, or they're gonna be in the hospital.[53]

McAllister made the headlines with indictments and jailing for incidents of alleged bribery, perjury, and murder, all of which he overcame. Fired as a cop, he became a cabaret singer and member of the United States Olympic Team; eventually he got back on the police force, where he served until he retired as an inspector in the 1950s.*

Even more famous as strong-arms were Johnny Cordes and Johnny Broderick, who between the two world wars were probably the best-known cops on the force. As a Costigan shoefly Cordes had felt the wrath of the Enright regime, but after a short spell on a Harlem beat he made his peace with headquarters and was restored to detective work. As a boy Cordes worked for a blacksmith named Jimmy Hines, and it is possible that his old employer assisted in resolving the problem. In any event, Cordes was still a controversial lone wolf. In 1922, he arrested for larceny an ex-convict named McKenna, who had been a Whitman stool pigeon in the Becker case; as a reward, when Whitman had become governor, he had pardoned the man. McKenna took a dislike to Cordes, and the latter hit him over the head with a tire iron. Whitman, now in private practice, defended McKenna on the new charges, but Cordes prevailed.

In 1923, Cordes walked unarmed into a drugstore robbery. When it was over, two Hudson-Duster addicts were in custody and Cordes had five gunshot wounds, including two from an off-duty cop who mistook him for one of the holdup men. For this he received the department Medal of Honor. While recuperating, Whitman's friend McKenna came to call, announced to Cordes that it was God's will that he die, and proceeded to strangle him until the weak Cordes beat him off. In 1927, Cordes was again shot and became the only member of the force to win a second Medal of Honor.[54]

Johnny Broderick, "the Boff," came from the Gashouse district and joined the force in 1923 after service as a labor slugger and bodyguard to Samuel Gompers and, briefly, a city fireman. His early career was on the gangster squad with McAllister, and then the industrial squad, ostensibly fighting labor racketeers. In 1928, Broderick was involved in

---

* His autobiography, *The Kind of Guy I Am*, is an interesting if not entirely detached account of the leading police, politicians, and gangsters of the 1920s.

a curious controversy. Communists were extensively involved in organized labor, and it was alleged that they had gotten clearance from Rothstein who lent them 1.75 million dollars for bribes, $110,000 of which went to Broderick. Nothing came of the charge, although it was revived in later years, but clearly Rothstein did have dealings with the Reds, who seemed to think, for a while at least, that the cops were with them.[55]

In the more traditional sphere, in 1926 Broderick mowed down three Tombs prisoners attempting to escape after killing the warden and a guard. In 1931, with Cordes accompanying him, he captured cop killer "Two-gun Crowley," a baby-faced Irish boy who made appealing copy for the newspapers. The Boff was also a bitter enemy of certain of the more flamboyant hoods. One of his favorite tactics was to wrap a lead pipe in a newspaper and, upon sighting a gangster of the Eastman variety, whack him over the head; to a bystander it looked like a friendly tap. Another Broderick ploy was to beat up gangsters such as Legs Diamond and leave them upside down in a garbage can. In one instance Broderick went to the funeral of a Hudson-Duster and spit in the dead man's eye. Heavyweight champ Jack Dempsey declared that Broderick was the only man he was afraid to meet outside the ring, although, in fact, the Boff was badly beaten up on several occasions and many cops thought he was part bluff. He also occasionally slugged total innocents. In one such incident of this at Madison Square Garden his career was saved only by the press, which strongly defended him. In fact, his image rested to a great extent on the fact that Broadway show business figures relied on him for informal protection, and rave accounts of Broderick's career were written by, among others, Ed Sullivan, Gene Fowler, and Toots Shor.[56]

The real strength of the dynamic duo of the Dutchman and the Boff lay in the fact that they had what the gangster did not, the legal right to use deadly force and the practical power to slug hoods on sight. Attempts to combat them via lawsuits or formal brutality complaints were futile. Given their public relations image and powerful respectable connections, a criminal could make no headway, for to complain would open him to unfavorable media exposure.

If strong-arm squads were the answer to the toughs, confidential squads were the traditional remedies for police corruption, and McLaughlin brought Lew Valentine to headquarters as a captain and eventually deputy chief to play the Costigan role. Once again, the battering ram was used against gambling joints, including some conducted in the presumed sanctity of Tammany clubhouses. Valentine also continued to add to his ferocious image. In one instance, when a search failed to turn up marked money on a cop suspected of corruption, Valentine fed the man an emetic, though in department legend the story was twisted to a stomach pump.*

Commissioner McLaughlin gradually realized that Walker had no intention of respecting the advice of Smith or St. Patrick's Cathedral, and he soon resigned. To everyone's surprise his successor, Joseph Warren, a close associate of the mayor, continued the shoefly system. Despite headline-making raids, however, little real impact was made on organized crime. Then in 1928 Arnold Rothstein was murdered in the Park Central Hotel, and the coat of George McManus was found at the scene. McManus, a well-connected gambler with a brother in the church, another in the police department, and protection from Jimmy Hines, was angry at Rothstein for welching on some gambling debts run up in a McManus game. According to legend, he drew a pistol to frighten Rothstein and it accidentally discharged. Again, the cops stalled and fumbled trying to avoid involvement, and no real attempt was made to secure the crime scene or obtain a death-bed statement from the victim.[58] The press fanned public indignation, and Walker, casting about for a new police commissioner, chose the prominent man about town Grover Whalen, manager of the John P. Wanamaker department store.

Whalen was an Irish-American born in New York in 1886. In 1918 he was made secretary to Mayor Hylan, whom he described as another Abe Lincoln.[59] Later he was the city's official greeter, in which capacity he perfected the tickertape parade for visiting celebrities which was such a feature of New York in the 1920s. As Frederick Lewis Allen remarked, "Whalen learned that if one timed the VIP parade for the noon hour, a ready made crowd could be found celebrating lunch."[60] In appearance Whalen was tall, handsome, and well tailored, with his trademark, a flower bought fresh daily, in his lapel. Indeed, he resembled the model department store floorwalker, and in 1925 he was made manager of Wanamaker's.

Before accepting the commissioner's post, Whalen went through a highly publicized agony of indecision useful to Wanamaker's public relations. Since downtown merchants were traditionally a powerful pressure group for increased police protection, the opportunity to place one of their own at the head of the police department was of such symbolic and practical importance that it was eagerly grasped. Also, since Whalen was a front man, his loss to the business would not be catastrophic. In December he ended the suspense by bowing to the call of duty. To ease

---

* Another legend was that Valentine had pushed a cop into the river knowing that he could not swim. In fact, when a cop claimed to have rescued a drowning victim, the suspicious Valentine had him change into trunks and dive into a swimming pool. The man floundered about and Valentine, fully dressed, jumped in to the rescue.

the pain, it was agreed that his full Wanamaker salary would continue while he served as police commissioner.[61]

Whalen's first act was to shake up the force by dropping the chief inspector and the commander of detectives. He then moved downward. Johnny Cordes had captured George McManus, but it had not been one of his more difficult feats. No dogged pursuit down dark alleys, followed by a blazing gun battle; rather, McManus had called Cordes and arranged a meeting at a hotel. When Cordes arrived, McManus requested that he be allowed to get a haircut (since his picture would be on the front page), and Cordes, who had pulverized individuals for not promptly submitting to arrest, consented to read the paper while McManus became tonsorially elegant.[62] When these facts became known, the press excoriated its hero Cordes, and he was promptly suspended. However, both McManus and Cordes beat their respective raps and were soon back on their beats.

On another level, the new commissioner also took steps to eliminate the shoefly squads, dropping Valentine from deputy chief to captain and exile. Shoeflys hurt morale and upset the chain of command, said Whalen, and besides, Valentine had been up to the old trick of wiretapping. Whalen also broke up the homicide squad and retired its long-time commander, Inspector Arthur Carey.

In 1929 the economy crashed, and Whalen's police department faced a city where widespread protest became the order of the day. The commissioner, himself a Red fighter in the great tradition of Murray and Byrnes, publicly warned of the dangers of Communism and refused permits for the Communists to hold meetings. He assigned fifty undercover cops to infiltrate the party. At the funeral of one Red killed by the police four of the sixteen-man guard of honor were detectives. In 1930 the Communists sponsored a rally in Union Square, and when it dispersed, the participants ran through the shopping district and, in a tribute to the commissioner, broke the windows of Wanamaker's department store. The Reds were no longer under the delusion that the cops were on their side.[63]

Whalen recalled Woods in his looks and suave manner, but where Woods was a serious administrator, Whalen was essentially a public relations poseur. He liked to make dramatic gestures such as flying to Chicago to confer with the local cops during a so-called "gang war" between Al Capone and New York rivals.[64] To prepare for the Red revolt which was just around the corner according to Whalen, he organized police air squadrons under young Deputy Commissioner Rodman Wanamaker, an Olympic polo player and son of his former boss, and armed cops with .38 caliber revolvers in place of their .32s. His long-run misfortune is that he lived in an era before the 6 o'clock TV news. His short-run problem was the onset of the Depression. The city no longer laughed at the Walker regime and its police department, but demanded a clean-up, the dimensions of which were clearly beyond Whalen. In 1930 he resigned and returned to Wanamaker's, but unfortunately for him, the Depression also destroyed the department store.

With Al Smith's defeat for President in 1928, the Sullivan-type leaders took control of Tammany Hall. Coincidentally, in that same year the old wigwam on 14th Street was torn down, and Smith chose not to return to his native East Side, but moved into millionaires' row on Fifth Avenue. Both events were symbolic. In 1929, Walker was re-elected by a large margin over Congressman Fiorello H. La Guardia, who scored Tammany scandals to no avail. The Depression was not yet apparent, and the public was not quite ready for a change. The next year, though, would be right for a new avenging angel to smite the tiger.

The new avenger, Judge Samuel Seabury, was a worthy successor to Parkhurst, Jerome, and Whitman, with far better social credentials. Born in 1873, he was a direct descendant of John and Priscilla Alden, and the ancestor for whom he was named had been the first Episcopal bishop of America (though as a Tory he fled after the Revolution). Seabury's own father was an Episcopal minister who was rich in prestige but poor in cash. Young Sam began his career as a strong supporter of Henry George and public ownership. Elected a magistrate in 1901 as a Democrat and a State Supreme Court justice in 1906, he had presided over the second Becker trial and as a result was elected to the Court of Appeals (the highest court in the state) the same year Whitman became governor.

Seabury's judicial duties did not inhibit his political activities, and he spent a good deal of time romancing William Randolph Hearst in an effort to obtain higher office. In 1916 he opposed Whitman for governor but was knifed by Hearst and lost. Back in private life "the judge," as he liked to be known, made a fortune in private law practice, including a million dollars from the Gould estate. As late as the 1940s, he would defend his corporate insurance clients' right to maintain racially segregated housing. This was the man who would now put on another morality play against the backdrop of the Great Depression.[65]

The Seabury investigation, as it was called, began as a probe of the New York Magistrates' Court after some of the judges had been linked with Arnold Rothstein and other racketeers. Seabury, appointed by Governor Franklin Roosevelt, thundered at the political nature of the judiciary, though his own career was hardly exemplary in that respect.

The investigation was provided with drama when a Tammany man who was slated to testify, Supreme Court Justice William Crater, disappeared, never to be seen again, providing periodic Sunday supplement stories for a generation. Irony was the theme when Magistrate Jean Norris, the first woman on the bench and assigned to prostitutes' court to deal with her fallen sisters, was found to be corrupt and oppressive of defendants. Nor was her acceptance of fees for posing in judicial robes in an advertisement for Fleischmann's Yeast deemed a proper practice. Magistrate Norris was removed from the bench. When a paid police informer, one Chile Acuna—whom the press quickly named "the human spitoona"—testified to setting up women for shakedowns, the police were dragged into the probe, and then there was some embarrassment when several vice officers could not explain their large bank accounts.* [66] The Seabury investigation was also helped by the backstage advice of retired Inspector Costigan and the testimony of Captain Valentine.

Seabury was quick to realize that he had a formidable vehicle to carry him back into the political arena. As with previous investigations, all witnesses were examined, that is, rehearsed in advance so as to provide maximum effect. As new revelations developed, the investigations broadened to include the Manhattan district attorney, a sixty-eight-year-old Tammany wheelhorse, and New York City government in general. Comedy was provided when a Tammany sheriff testified that his huge bank account came from a "magnificient tin box." The DA, however, presented Seabury with a dilemma. The incumbent was no immigrant politician, but a fellow Episcopal vestryman, so here, of course, a high standard of proof was required and Seabury concluded that while gross irregularities had occurred, the DA himself was blameless.[68]

As the investigation progressed, Seabury zeroed in on really big game—in the first instance Mayor Walker, who had received "loans" from persons doing business with the city. But ultimately Seabury's target was the man who had appointed him, Governor Franklin D. Roosevelt. By maneuvering FDR into a position where he would have to take action against the mayor, Seabury would present him with a dilemma. To be nominated and elected to the Presidency, it was desirable to have support in New York. FDR was already in dispute with Al Smith and Tammany, and to remove Walker might kill the prospect of support. However, failure to remove the mayor would damage Roosevelt's prestige nationally. If FDR stumbled, a possible alternative candidate was Seabury himself, and the judge authorized preparation of a campaign biography and arranged for out-of-town speaking engagements.[69]

Jimmy Walker solved the problem by what he thought was a clever move. As the storm clouds grew, the mayor's popularity declined, but

---

* Though the Tammany district attorney was unmoved by a vice detective who banked $80,000 in three years on a salary of $2,500, the federal attorneys were not. Young Assistant U.S. Attorney Thomas Dewey prosecuted his first criminal case, and the detective received three years in Atlanta Penitentiary.[67]

he still held a place in the hearts of many, as shown by the 1931 police parade. In August 1932 he resigned, secretly planning to run for mayor to fill his own vacancy, relying on public sympathy to win back his job. At this juncture, however, St. Patrick's Cathedral let it be known that the mayor's morals made him unfit, and Tammany got the message.[70] Walker sailed for Europe and FDR became President (though Tammany and Seabury both voted against him at the Chicago convention). Seabury did, however, have a measure of satisfaction promoting the successful fusion candidacy of Fiorello La Guardia for mayor in 1933. As in 1894, 1901, and 1913, Tammany went down in the wake of scandal, although, this time, the police were far less responsible than the wigwam itself.

THE FALL OF THE HALL: VALENTINE AND THE LITTLE FLOWER

The new mayor, perhaps more than Smith, was the true personification of the honest, intelligent, dedicated, and patriotic ethnic. La Guardia had spent part of his youth at a western army post, where his immigrant father was a bandmaster, and then served abroad in the United States consular service. Returning to New York, he became a lawyer, champion of labor, and bitter enemy of Tammany. But his intense patriotism would not let him join the Socialists so he became a Republican, eventually serving in Congress. Like his fellow party members of patrician stock, he was an all-out interventionist in World War I. When war was declared, he became a pilot, flew in combat, and was decorated. In the 1920s he was president of the City Council, Congressman from East Harlem, and unsuccessful candidate for mayor.[71]

In the 1932 Democratic landslide La Guardia lost his Congressional seat, but the following year Seabury, the doyen of reform like Parkhurst forty years earlier, forced La Guardia's nomination on the Republicans. If Walker, the Broadway prince, was the right man for the '20s, "the little flower," symbol of the discontented common man, was the ideal mayor for the Depression.

The previous waves of reform had brought men such as Theodore Roosevelt and Arthur Woods to the commissioner's post. No similar results would occur under La Guardia. His first commissioner was Major General John F. O'Ryan, who had commanded a New York National Guard division in World War I, and the new chief inspector was Valentine, the shoefly. One of the prerogatives of the chief inspector was membership in the Honor Legion, but when the delegation arrived at Valentine's office for the presentation, he angrily refused to accept it, citing the Legion's treatment of Horton fourteen years earlier. With this gesture, Valentine signaled the force that he was not going to forgive or forget.[72]

Commissioner O'Ryan wanted to take a hard line against strikers and demonstrators who swarmed through the Depression-ridden city, but La Guardia, an ally of organized labor, could not permit this, and in a few months the commissioner departed and Valentine replaced him. The tightened discipline instituted by the shoefly was too much for a police force acclimated to Prohibition; in the first five years of the new regime eighty-three cops, ranging from patrolman to inspector, committed suicide.[73]

Valentine, a practical-minded career cop, was not an adherent of administrative science. Keeping the lid on corruption and other scandals was his main task. Although La Guardia was thoroughly honest, not even benefiting from legal fees or sinecure business appointments, his posture toward corruption had certain realistic ambivalencies and his attitude regarding excessive force was extremely equivocal. He did claim the usual credit for ending the practice of beating up pickets and labor demonstrators, although the growing strength and respectability of organized labor under the New Deal accomplished this in other places too. But his man Valentine constantly advocated ferocity against gangsters, demanding that they "tip their hats" to cops,[74] and in one instance, while personally conducting a lineup, berated officers who had brought in a murderer without "mussing him up." Civil libertarians who were strong supporters of La Guardia complained to the mayor. His response was not only supportive of police violence against gangsters and murderers but even more extreme than Valentine's.*[75]

There was serious question, though, whether La Guardia hated all gangsters. East Harlem's rackets were untouchable, since the district leader, Vito Marcantonio, was the mayor's protegé. Brooklyn racketeer Joe Adonis was equally untouchable in La Guardia's first term, but when in 1937 he switched his support to the mayor's opponent, the police descended with such fury that Adonis had to transfer operations to Frank Hague's New Jersey until the end of La Guardia's term in 1945.[77] Nor, despite Valentine's efforts, were Jimmy Hines's contacts with the police department closed. The spirit of Tammany continued to reign in the force, though as in any reform administration it was somewhat subdued.**

* On taking office La Guardia had announced that Inspector Byrnes's old "deadline" for crooks was no longer Fulton Street, but the city limits.[76]

** Hines boasted of controlling the Sixth Police Division in Harlem. Even Tom Dewey as district attorney found opposition from lower-level cops. For example, in one major citywide vice raid on eighty houses of prostitutions, half were tipped off. Later a cop assigned to guard witnesses in an important case testified for the defense.[78]

Given the sophistication of the racketeers, the police department was hardly equipped to go after the top leaders, and during Valentine's regime most of the headlines against organized crime were made by district attorneys. Brooklyn DA William O'Dwyer sent a number of gangsters involved in the so-called "Murder Inc." to the electric chair, although he too was selective and later his tenure as mayor (1945–1950) was marred by various charges including some relating to his district attorney days. However, the champion racket buster was Special Prosecutor Thomas E. Dewey, later New York County district attorney, who was to repeat the Whitman-Becker episode, though this time Big Tim himself was in the box in the person of Jimmy Hines, and the gangsters convicted were not a few penny-ante thugs but big shots like Dutch Schultz, Waxey Gordon, and Lucky Luciano. Again, there would be doubts about prosecutorial ethics. Dewey, like all his illustrious predecessors, "prepared" witnesses, maintained good public relations by judicious leaks, and benefited from the backdrop of a grim public opinion. Dutch Schultz actually planned to have Dewey assassinated, as though Becker had put out a contract on Whitman instead of Rosenthal (if indeed he did put out a contract). However, cooler mob heads prevailed, realizing that Dewey's murder would only make things worse. Later Dutch Schultz himself was murdered.[79] Like Whitman, Dewey was to ride into the governorship but not the White House.

The fall of Jimmy Hines and Murder Inc. was to bring about a new Rothstein in the person of Frank Costello, a smooth, modest coordinator of organized crime. In the 1930s the old Tammany Hall died and never really revived. One of the reasons advanced for its collapse centers on organized crime. According to this version the reformers so weakened Tammany that the gangsters took over; in effect, Parkhurst, Whitman, and Seabury in their blind zeal took New York away from Croker, Sullivan, and Walker and gave it to the Mafia. This provides delightful irony for those who see the reformers as bigoted fools.

Certainly there is a surface reality to the assertion. Eastman and Kelly were clearly beneath Big Tim, and even Rothstein could not tell Boss Murphy what to do, but Lucky Luciano was de facto district leader south of 14th Street in the '30s, and Costello was the real boss of Tammany in the '40s. In 1931 Luciano's gunmen forced out Harry Perry, a Sullivan by marriage, from his district leadership in Little Italy and replaced him with an Italian (though given the ethnic composition of the district, this was no more than fair). In 1933 gunmen formed a blockade in the area south of 14th Street to assure election of a Tammany district attorney. But in general, the gangsters did not attempt to take over the Hall. Instead, the wigwam's own collapse provided a vacuum into which Costello was able to move.[80]

From 1933 on, Tammany was shut out from federal, state, and city patronage by the antagonism of FDR, Governor Herbert Lehman and Mayor La Guardia, and after 1937 the district attorney's office was lost to Dewey. During the 1930's and 1940's leader followed leader, but the organization could not recover from various mistakes it had made, such as opposing Roosevelt. Thus another explanation is that Tammany fell because of poor leadership. In the past, however, smart leaders had come to the fore after disasters. Perhaps the basic problem was neither opponents nor leaders, but that Tammany no longer had its traditional role to play.

With the beginning of World War I in Europe immigration was curtailed, and in the postwar period Congress imposed severe quotas. Thus as one group moved out of lower Manhattan, it was not automatically replaced by another. Between 1920 and 1930 alone, the population south of 14th Street declined by 400,000. Manhattan's relative importance also declined. In 1920 the borough had 40 percent of the city's population. By 1940 it had only 25 percent.

Another blow to Tammany was the establishment of the welfare state by the New Deal. Whereas the typical New Yorker of 1900 was an immigrant or the child of immigrants living in a Manhattan tenement, the New Yorker of 1940 was a native-born American living in an apartment or bungalow outside Manhattan. The turn-of-the-century lower-class citizen looked to the local boss for welfare, jobs, and justice. To the New Yorker of 1940 the boss was FDR, welfare was provided by the WPA and jobs by the AFL and CIO, and justice of the police court variety was much less likely to be required by the nonslum resident.

In 1900, the saloon was the center of social life and prostitution a practical necessity in an age when a rigid code of morality ruled relations between young males and "nice" girls. In 1940, the saloon was only one of many forms of recreation, and casual sex was much more likely to be carried on by nonprofessionals. Thus by 1940 the organized-crime situation of New York was considerably altered. To a large extent prostitution and nightlife were run for out-of-towners. Drugs were not a problem to working- or middle-class America, and liquor was legal including Sundays. In effect there was no public demand for organized-crime activities with the exception of gambling in some areas of the city.

The World War II era also produced a period of harmony between various classes and interests as labor was given a share of power and the country united to fight fascism. Thus the mediating function of Tammany was rendered obsolete. In postwar New York State, a Rockefeller would be elected governor four times with strong labor support.

The '30s and '40s called for a period of stability in police administration. There was no need for wide-open vice of the Tenderloin or

Prohibition variety. Vice continued and remained a lure to some, and lucrative for those who ran it and those who regulated it. Cops and vice operators, unlike the more successful politicians, could not get the honest graft of contracts and legal fees, so they tried to make do. But things were carried on in a quiet way. The modest call flat and horse-betting wireroom replaced the red-lighted bordello and gambling mansion. Not until the sixties brought a change of national mood would vice and gambling operate openly, the latter even being run by the state.

The perennial political struggle between regular and reformer continued in New York, but the police department became less openly committed to one side or the other than in the past. Indeed, some thought the police were impervious to the politics of reform or spoils. Cops who wanted to participate in corruption could do so without political approval, and in Brooklyn, beginning in the 1940s, a number of police officers undertook to organize their own bookmaking empire setting up a manager of their choice. The result was a massive scandal which shook the department and the city in 1949.

Cops who chose to concentrate on career concerns burrowed deeper within the bureaucracy, resenting "civilian" interference. Starting with Enright, and especially from Valentine's day onward, it became the fashion for the police commissioner and many of the deputy commissioners to be selected from the career ranks; in only five of the forty-two years following Valentine's ascendancy was the force presided over by a civilian commissioner. When a young man aspired to a police career, he signed up at Delahanty's to prepare for the entrance exam. The same pattern followed for promotion until he reached captain. From then on he looked for favor to the top brass, who were themselves career cops. Thus the New York City Police Department became increasingly attached to internal bureaucratic concerns and remained in the backwater of innovation in police administration. While the department achieved a kind of stability and relative independence from politics, many felt it was gained at the price of stagnation. After the fall of Commissioner Woods, the field of police administration began to look elsewhere for national leadership.

Chicago: The Town They Could Not Shut Down (1857–1945)

The cops sat listlessly about Chicago's Des Plaines Street police station. A few hours earlier when they had assembled from all over the city the mood had been tense. Radicals were holding a meeting to protest police brutality against strikers. Though the meeting was still going on less than a block away, the crowd, which at first had numbered over a thousand, had dwindled to three or four hundred. A bit earlier a sudden cold wind had blown up and a dark cloud had passed overhead. Now it was raining lightly—typical changeable Chicago weather. With the diminution of the crowd the mayor and police superintendent had gone home, and the cops expected to be dismissed shortly.

Suddenly the order was given to fall in. The meeting was going to be dispersed. One hundred and seventy-nine police officers in three columns advanced toward a wagon from which a speaker was addressing the crowd. Captain William Ward, the district commander, stepped forward to utter the familiar words of the riot act— copied from the English statute of 1714, with the substitution of the people for the King. "In the name of the people of Illinois I command you to peaceably disperse," he proclaimed, and then, pointing to nearby members of the crowd, said, "And I command you and you and you to assist." The last was a legal stratagem, not a real request for help. Anyone refusing to assist an officer in the exercise of his duties was liable to a criminal charge. The speaker began to climb down saying, "But captain we are peaceable." Suddenly a whizzing noise was heard overhead and a bomb exploded in the midst of the police. The cops charged, guns blazing, as the alarm bell in the police station rang wildly in the night. Eight policemen and two citizens died as a result of the night's happenings, while seventy police and uncounted citizens were wounded.[1]

May 4, 1886, would be a date to remember. The first anarchist bomb had gone off in America. For a generation people would argue over the event and its aftermath. That such an incident involved the Chicago Police Department was not a surprise to many observers, and indeed, the department was shaped by a long line of violent events.

THE SURVEYOR GENERAL

In retrospect, the period after World War I was a major turning point in the development of American police administration. Among the more significant events were the onset of Prohibition, the collapse of O'Meara's Boston Police Department, and the fall of the Mitchell-Woods administration in New York followed by its loss of interest in the doctrines of administrative science. With the departure of Fosdick and Woods for greener pastures, leadership in the field fell to others. For a time it came from a pinnacle of the American establishment, the Harvard Law School. There Dean Roscoe Pound, Professor Felix Frankfurter, and other faculty undertook surveys of police and crime in such cities as Cleveland and Boston. But by the early 1930s interest faded as the focus of Frankfurter's attention shifted to the more rewarding tasks offered by the New Deal.[2]

Given the stagnancy of the New York City police, the cause of administrative science would have to be advanced in some other community. Ironically, this task would fall in large part upon a native New Yorker, operating out of the Institute of Public Administration, the renamed Bureau of Municipal Research which in its heyday under Bruere had been virtually a branch of city government. Between 1923 and 1955 over fifty cities and states would request Bruce Smith to survey their police departments. Not until 1952 would he receive a call from New York City; police administrative reform became a road show which could never make it in the big time of Broadway. But then, in fact, as Smith's career would illustrate, it would never play a very long run in any city.

Clarence Bruce Smith was a Yankee patrician from Brooklyn. Born in 1892, the son of a real estate broker, he grew up in comfortable circumstances. Smith did not fit in well at Wesleyan College, being expelled for discharging shotguns and rolling cannon balls down the street. Though he was to spend his life trying to reform the police,

Smith himself, tall, broad-shouldered, and rugged, admired the lusty, brawling spirit of the American frontier. As he wrote:

> Men lived violently and died by violence in great numbers ... on the Great Plains, throughout the vast empire that is Texas, among the river towns of the Mississippi, and in the mining settlements of the far West. . . .
>
> [T]heir final passing will be regretted by many law-abiding Americans who consider violent outbreaks to be an evil but necessary feature of a vigorous race.[3]

Wesleyan refused to give Smith a recommendation for transfer to Columbia until an uncle who was a wealthy donor put on the pressure.[4] Later, Smith was to be a critic of political influence on the police:

> The private citizen who seeks to avoid the effect of police restrictions naturally turns to local party representatives for aid. No matter how meritorious his complaint may be, his motives in doing so are nearly always selfish. He wants something "fixed"—so it is fixed, and by a politician who distrusts abstract justice even more than does the private citizen. Justice under the law proves to be too impersonal, too little concerned with individuals, too preoccupied with major social results, to lend itself to the multitude of petty adjustments which seem so necessary to our polyglot citizenship.[5]

Difficult as it might be to see the influence of a wealthy donor on a college and a Tammany boss on a judge as similar matters, of course it was as important to an immigrant that his son kept out of jail as it was to a patrician that his got into a good school.

In 1916, Columbia professor Charles Beard, then director of the Bureau of Municipal Research, hired Smith, a recent graduate of Columbia Law School, to assist Clement Driscoll, a former New York deputy commissioner of police, in a survey of the police department of Harrisburg, Pennsylvania. Driscoll briefed Smith and then left him on his own. Though the young man knew little of police administration, he was able to produce a report. The following year he went off to France as an army pilot. When he returned to the Bureau, it no longer had a close relationship with New York and had become smaller and less exciting, but it was to be his professional home until his death in 1955.

During the '20s, Smith surveyed several police departments and wrote a book on the state police. Like many of his fellow police reformers, he felt the greatest affinity for the constabularies maintained by states such as Pennsylvania and New York, and occasionally accompanied those of New York on raids. These strictly disciplined bodies of hand-picked men, living in barracks in rural areas remote from the centers of urban politics, had much to commend them to him. In 1928–1930 he headed a committee of the International Association of Chiefs of Police, which set up the FBI uniform crime reporting system. Though modern writers have found much to criticize in the UCR, it was a major improvement over the haphazard police records which had existed up to that time.

While Smith busied himself with administrative science, an event occurred in Chicago which passed into international folklore. On February 14, 1929, seven men connected with the Bugs Moran gang were machine-gunned to death in a garage by men generally believed to be rival gangsters working for Al Capone. Gang murders were common in Chicago: between 1927 and 1930 alone, 227 were recorded.[6] In this case, however, the circumstances were unusual, not only in the numbers killed but in the fact that the killers were dressed in police uniforms and carried out the deed in broad daylight in a highly congested area. The so-called "Valentine Massacre" created a sensation, and demands for reform were heard on all sides. The result was the appointment of a citizens' committee to study the police department. As its director the committee engaged Bruce Smith. The survey which ensued was to be his most dramatic, and its fate was to symbolize that of most of his work.

CITY OF THE BIG SHOULDERS

Since the demise of the Woods and O'Meara police departments, there were no major city police forces which reformers could look to as models. Smith's assignment in Chicago offered an opportunity to install administrative science in the nation's second city. However, reform of the Chicago Police Department was not perceived by anyone as a simple task. The Valentine Massacre was but one of many similar events and associated phenomena which even before the twentieth century had given the city a worldwide reputation as a capital of crime, licentiousness, and corruption of the most daring kind. Even Chancellor Bismarck lamented his inability to visit America and see "that Chicago."[7]

From its inception, the city experienced the same struggles over moral virtue that characterized New York, but the reformers never won. On three occasions in the first half of the twentieth century (1901, '13, and '33) the fusion elements of New York were able to elect a mayor; no similar event occurred in Chicago. In New York and Boston the reformers were bolstered by an old-money elite. In Chicago the leading citizens of the nineteenth and early twentieth centuries were individuals such as Marshall Field, Potter Palmer, Gustavus Swift, and Philip Armour who made their own fortunes and continued to preside over their business affairs. Nor were their businesses—retail merchandising, hotels, and hog butchering—as aristocratic as the banking or brokerage of the Morgans and Storrows. Even though the leader of Chicago society, Mrs. Potter Palmer (whose husband among other things owned the Palmer House Hotel), was accepted by some European royalty, when the Infanta of Spain arrived in the City for the Columbian Exposition of 1893, she declined to meet "the wife of an innkeeper."[8]

Throughout the nineteenth century Chicago was "the West," and its ethos resembled a frontier town. In such an environment lack of breeding or involvement in scandal meant nothing; if an individual had money, all doors were open. Chicago epitomized the new industrial society in its admiration for success over morality. For example, Charles Yerkes, who as czar of the street transit companies practically owned the city in the 1890s, had come to Chicago after a jail term for fraud in his native Philadelphia. Skinny Madden, the city's pioneer labor boss, declared, "Show me an honest man, and I'll show you a damn fool."[9] As might be expected, politicians were not models of civic respectability. In eastern cities elements of both the Republican and Democratic parties were often spearheads of reform. In Chicago, the various party factions were generally equally rapacious, and the replacement of one by the other was likely to mean more corruption as the hungry outs sought to make up for lost time. As Will Rogers said about the city's "better element," "the trouble with Chicago is there ain't much better element."[10]

Public struggles over morality fueled the city's politics and provided entertainment, but they tended to mask the more serious problems of widespread violence; and long before 1929 the imagery of moral crusades and the reality of the ever-present violence shaped the Chicago Police Department which Bruce Smith now prepared to reform. In times of national crisis, from the 1870s onward, the city could always be depended upon for a major riot, often with extensive casualties. Labor slugging was developed into a business, and race riots were virtually institutionalized. Bombing and machine gunning became art forms which Chicago taught to the nation.

Yet it was a great city in more than size. Here was real life of the kind that inspired Dreiser and Sandburg. As the latter wrote:

> Hog Butcher for the World,
> Tool Maker, Stacker of Wheat,
> Player with Railroads and the Nation's Freight Handler;
> Stormy, husky brawling,
> City of the Big Shoulders:[11]

And there was honest work of the railroads and open hearths. Many found the social climate bracing:

I loved Chicago and still do. It's a big sprawly town—dirty, dingy, alive, real, no hypocrisy or false frills there; teeming with life much closer to the heart of America than any Eastern city.[12]

While these sound like the words of some midwestern Babbitt, they were actually uttered by Elizabeth Gurley Flynn, a New York Communist leader.

Down on the Levee

Chicago's first prominent mayor was 6' 6" "Long John" Wentworth, who was elected in 1857. Wentworth, like his contemporary Fernando Wood in New York, organized the city's first real political machine. In 1861, when the Legislature put his police department under state control, the angry Wentworth fired the entire force, leaving the city without protection until the state force could be organized.[13]

In the pre–Civil War era the Sands, a collection of shanties along the lake front, was the city's equivalent of New York's Five Points as a center of crime and vice. It was an eyesore, but instead of waiting for a half century to obtain slum clearance, the powers did the deed in Chicago style. In 1857, while the male residents were lured away to a horse race, police and vigilantes led by Mayor Wentworth descended on the settlement and set it ablaze. The fire department refused to respond, and the Sands burned to the ground.[14]

The center of prostitution, gambling, and wild saloons then moved to an area just south of the downtown business district known as the Levee. Among its denizens was a bartender named Mickey Finn who invented a world-famous drink. At the turn of the century, this district would migrate a mile south to the so-called "new Levee." New or old, the Levee would be encompassed politically within the First Ward, whose Democratic party organization would become the Chicago equivalent of the Sullivan faction of Tammany Hall. In addition to the Levee there were two Tenderloin districts, on the west and north sides of the city, each with its own political organization.

After the fire of '71, the political boss of Chicago was a gambler named Mike McDonald who ruled the Democratic party until the 1890s. In addition to his primary interest, he also operated a newspaper and the Lake Street elevated line. Like many Chicago politicians and gangsters, McDonald despised the police despite his business relations with them. When approached for $10 to bury a policeman, he reportedly replied, "Here, take $50 and bury five of them." His vivacious young wife surpassed this. During one of the occasional raids on his headquarters known as "the store," a cop poked into the living quarters and was shot by Mrs. McDonald. Naturally, she was acquitted. A spirited couple were the McDonalds. When his wife ran off to Europe with the family priest, the angry Mike married a Jewish girl, converted to Judaism, and went about wearing a skull cap.[15]

As McDonald faded, Chicago looked for a new boss and found him in Mont Tennes, whose power rested on ownership of the racing wire services at the time when gambling was changing from faro and roulette to bookmaking. Tennes's associate was Big Jim O'Leary, whose mother's cow, according to legend, kicked over the lantern which started the Chicago Fire. In his old age he gave the press a famous statement regarding his relations with the police, claiming that he never paid a dollar for protection:

> I could have had all kinds of it, but let me tell you something. Protection that you purchase ain't worth nothing to you. A man who will sell himself ain't worth an honest man's dime. The police is for sale but I don't want none of them.[16]

This, of course, was romantic nonsense on a par with the legend of his mother's cow. Big Jim was another crook who recognized the value of image and sought to project himself as "straight" and thereby escape responsibility for the corrupt conditions he had helped create. In similar vein, Tennes would regularly announce, over a period of twenty years, that he had retired from the gambling business.

In Chicago as in New York, the relative status of cops, gangsters, and politicians varied over time, but in general the cops occupied the lowest rung, and the police department never developed as an autonomous power center. The politicians fared differently. Their influence on organized crime ebbed and flowed with various tides. In the '90's, the First Ward came under control of two Irish-Americans who were to rule it for a half century as "lords of the Levee." The brains was Michael "Hinkey Dink" Kenna, a saloonkeeper, and the voice was "Bathhouse" John Coughlin, a former bathhouse rubber. These two served coterminously as alderman. In personality and appearance they were almost total opposites. Kenna, 5'1" (thus the name Hinkey Dink), spoke seldom and shunned the spotlight, while Coughlin, a burly 6-footer, dressed like a peacock, favoring green suits with silk hats, red vests, and similar paraphernalia. Coughlin also eagerly sought publicity with attention-getting quotations delivered in the kind of garbled grammar Chicagoans loved. He also brought out (ghost-written) poems, such as "Dear Midnight of Love" and "Ode to a Bathtub."[17] "Dear Midnight of Love" was actually sung in a special program at the Chicago Opera House, although the only singer who could be obtained was the thirteen-year-old daughter of a detective on the Levee beat.*

---

* Despite this somewhat unusual debut, the young singer, May de Sousa, went on to a successful career on the European stage.

Where Kenna was a shrewd behind-the-scenes strategist of such note that Dick Croker brought him to New York to assist in the 1897 mayoral election, "the Bath" had a human touch which offset the grafting charges of the reformers. In this respect, he was Chicago's version of George Washington Plunkitt or Jimmy Walker, though not as sophisticated as the latter. It was this quality which prevented serious attempts to jail him and would later restrain Capone from shooting him. Chicago would not have approved in either case.

The brains, charm, and power of Hink and Bath, however, did not forestall criticism. Indeed, so infuriating were the First Ward bosses that the conservative *Chicago Tribune* once endorsed their Socialist opponent for alderman.[18] The source of voting power in the ward was the flophouses where floaters could be quartered, while the sources of payoffs were the saloons, gambling joints, and houses of prostitution in the Levee. In the first decade of the twentieth century, the most famous landmark in the city was the bordello known as the Everleigh Club, operated by two young sisters on Dearborn Street.* The club was opened in 1900 by these two southern belles, Ada and Minna Lester, then twenty-two and twenty-four respectively. Its furnishings, decor, and cuisine, as well as the beauty and skill of its inmates, were said to be unmatched in the city. Only wealthy gentlemen known or properly recommended to the madams were admitted.

While the Everleigh Club was the most famous, there were scores of other houses within a few blocks, ranging from imitations of the Everleigh to 50-cent cribs. The social center of the district was Freiberg's Café, run by Ike Bloom (born Gittleson). In addition to having houses of prostitution, Bloom served as collector of graft and was so popular with the cops that his picture hung in a place of honor in the 22nd Street police station.[20]

In the early years of the century the rising man of the Levee was "Big Jim" Colisimo, an Italian immigrant who arrived in Chicago in 1880 at the age of ten. By age thirty-two he had married a brothel madam and organized a group of his fellow Italians, two facts which won his appointment as an underboss in the First Ward. In 1910 he opened Colisimo's Restaurant, which soon became a popular dining place for the city's elite. Big Jim's ethnic, political, vice and upperworld connections were to make him the most important leader of organized crime in Chicago.

Despite Colisimo's power, he, like other Italians, was constantly preyed upon by the so-called "Black Handers," bandits who lived by extorting money from other Italians by means of death threats. On some

---

* The club's name was allegedly adapted from the sisters' grandmother's practice of signing her letters "Everly Yours."

occasions Colisimo would pay off; on others he or his lieutenant, a transplanted New Yorker named Johnny Torrio, killed the extortionists. Thus Colisimo was not the boss, or "Don," of the Mafia.* He was an Italian, but his power rested on his connections with the politicians and gangsters of various ethnic groups, men like Coughlin and Ike Bloom.

The highlight of the Levee social season was the annual First Ward ball run by Hinkey Dink and Bathhouse. As the *Chicago Tribune* wrote:

> If a great disaster had befallen the Coliseum last night there would not have been a second story worker, a dip or plug ugly porch climber, dope fiend or scarlet woman remaining in Chicago.[21]

At midnight Kenna and Coughlin, arm in arm with the Everleigh sisters, as the Lester sisters came to be called, would lead the grand march. They were followed by contingents of whores with their own police escort to club the drunks who attempted to tear their gowns off.

Such affairs made Big Tim's shindigs, then gracing New York, look like church socials, but their very fame and daring were the cause of their undoing. Though Chicago was untroubled with reform mayors, as in New York the twentieth century brought a trend toward restraint. Like many things in Chicago, restraint was a relative quality; Chicago's restraint was another town's wide-open, and Chicago's wide-open was like nothing else anywhere (save possibly San Francisco or New Orleans). From 1879 to 1887, and again in 1893, the mayor was Carter H. Harrison, who frankly admitted that he allowed wide-open vice. He owned a considerable section of real estate in the old Levee. "Our Carter" suited Chicago just fine, but in 1893 his career was terminated by a deranged assassin. After his demise City Hall was less tolerant of vice; then, in 1897, the Bath and Hinkey Dink brought forth the ideal mayor in Carter Harrison "the younger," who served in office for twelve years between his first election and 1915. But while he began by espousing the same views as his father, the younger had traveled widely, studied at German universities, and entertained presidential ambitions, and in time, like Croker and Murphy, he would come to the conclusion that wide-open town policies were passé, since they damaged his image.

Despite their political weaknesses, the Chicago reformers could always put on a good show and attract attention. One of the earliest was the noted evangelist Billy Sunday, whose failure was immortalized in the city's theme song, "Chicago, Chicago, the Town That Billy Sunday

---

* Nor were the Black Handers a highly organized conspiracy. The extortionists usually shared an Italian heritage but operated individually or in small groups. Despite various police actions the Black Hand flourished until approximately 1916, when a number of people involved were indicted by the federal government and tried before Judge Kenesaw Mountain Landis (later commissioner of baseball), who sent them to prison for using the mails to extort.

Could Not Shut Down." In 1893 the "better" element formed a civic federation under banker Lyman Gage (later McKinley's Secretary of the Treasury) and invited the English journalist William Stead to visit the city. As editor of the *Review of Reviews*, Stead considered himself the pope of journalism (his telegraphic address was Vatican, London). He threw himself into a host of causes with a sure sense of his own righteousness and a confusing inconsistency. He was for world peace and naval expansion. A devotee of freedom, he admired Czar Nicholas II. One of Stead's favorite causes was the abolition of prostitution, and once, to dramatize how young girls were sold into white slavery, he had openly purchased a juvenile prostitute, leading to his arrest for abduction. Stead was a strong believer in the duty of what he modestly called "God's Englishman" to right all wrongs and lead all people toward betterment.[22] Stead eagerly accepted the invitation to help reform Chicago, and the following year he published his findings under the title *If Christ Came to Chicago.* The book reported the exact locations, with diagrams, of the bordellos, gambling joints, and opium dens and indicted the system of payoffs.

It was a great success, but the Levee went on. Indeed, howling reformers were part of the Levee scene. The Everleighs allowed them the privileges of the mansion in the afternoon; Lucy Page Gaston, the anti-cigarette crusader, was a special favorite there. More ostentatious reformers would organize demonstrations, but they too could be accommodated. Ike Bloom always allowed them to pray in the middle of the dance floor at Freiberg's. His honky-tonk band was trained to play hymns in the proper tempo, and Ike himself would go down on his knees to join in the prayers. Immediately afterward the whores would resume dancing.[23]

In 1901 the celebrated English evangelist "Gypsy" Smith arrived.* On the night of October 18, Smith led a crowd of 20,000 persons, many of them wearing long black gowns and carrying torches, on a march into the Levee. As one account described it:

> As the evangelist stepped into 22nd Street he raised both hands above his head and began to sing while the torches flared into flame and the band struck up "Where He Leads Me I Will Follow." Slowly, almost at half step to the accompaniment of hymns played in the tempo of a funeral march, the crusaders shuffled back and forth through the district traversing every street, passing and repassing every brothel and every dive. In front of the Everleigh Club, the House of all Nations and other notorious resorts, the evangelist and his congregation knelt in the street entoning the Lord's Prayer, reciting the 23rd Psalm and singing "Where's My

---

* Rodney Smith was born of Gypsy parents in Epping Forest, England. His father was later converted to Christianity.

Wandering Boy Tonight?" ... The Levee received this strange visitation in almost utter quiet. The brothels, saloons, and dives were closed and darkened and the streets were deserted save for a few prostitutes and pimps who huddled in the doorways. ... ten minutes after the departure of the crusaders, the Levee had swung to life. Red lights gleamed, doors swung open, corks popped, music blared from pianos and banjos, and from their hiding places swarmed the pimps, streetwalkers and thieves. While Smith prayed in the Alhambra Theatre, the Levee enjoyed the biggest night in its history; hundreds of boys and young men whose previous knowledge of vice had been gained by hearsay, now learned of it through firsthand experience.[24]

But though at first it was laughed off, the publicity was to take its toll. In the first decade of the century, when myths of white slavery were at their height, the Levee was a frequent target, and in 1905 the federal government brought charges against some of the operators for bringing prostitutes into the country in violation of the immigration laws. In December 1908, the usual protests against the First Ward ball were heightened by the *Tribune*'s threat to print the names of any persons in attendance, so that many respectables did not show up or kept their masks on for the entire night.[25] The following year a Republican mayor, though no reformer, refused to issue a liquor permit and the ball was a flop, so that the affair passed into history.

The next casualty was the Everleigh Club. In 1911 the sisters had the bad taste to distribute a booklet describing their brothel. This was too much for Mayor Harrison, and he ordered the place shut down, over the protest of Bathhouse John. The famous brothel closed forever with Minna Lester providing a noble statement:

> You get everything in a lifetime. Of course, if the Mayor says we must close, that settles it. What the Mayor says goes, as far as I am concerned. I'm not going to be sore about it, either. I never was a knocker, and nothing the police of this town can do will change my disposition. I'll close up the shop and walk out with a smile on my face.[26]

Actually, the Everleighs had screamed bloody murder and threatened to squeal on the entire system of politics and police, but threats from Colisimo's gunmen had restrained them. Later, out of Chicago, they did in fact provide a detailed account of the payoffs.

At the time the Everleighs closed, the reform movement was at its height in Chicago. It was funded by Julius Rosenwald, Chicago's version of New York's Jay Schifflein, and led by professor Charles E. Merriam of the Rockefeller-funded University of Chicago. Despite attacks on Merriam's status as a professor at "the Rockefeller university," he almost defeated Harrison for mayor in 1911. About the same time the

Mann Act, named for a Chicago Republican Congressman, made it a federal crime to transport women in interstate commerce, for immoral purposes, providing new weapons against vice. On the West Side, Colisimo's opposite number, the notorious pimp Mike "de Pike" Heitler, was receiving unfavorable publicity and Jane Addams and her Hull House associates put up a reform candidate against the machine. Faced with these threats, Harrison now determined that the segregated red light district had to go and in 1912 the police were instructed to take action.

As Honest as Coppers Go

The police department to which Mayor Harrison issued his orders was hardly an effective instrument. In the previous half century, no chief had ever served more than four years in the post. Cops were expected to be as political as Bathhouse John's vote hustlers, and in 1898 Harrison had dismissed 400 of them because they were affiliated with the opposite political party.[27] The police department was a very valuable political property, particularly useful at election time. In 1894 Bathhouse had been threatened with some serious opposition and the police of the First Ward gave an indication of what they could do for a friend. As one account reported:

> That night at the Harrison Street police station, lieutenant Charles Holden summoned a group of stalwarts slated for election detail in the First Ward.
> "Listen boys," said the lieutenant, "I don't want you taking any part in this election but the man who always looks out for the First Ward police over there in City Hall [Bathhouse] needs our help!"
> The squads went to work that very night. Men wearing Skakel [Bathhouse's opponent] buttons were heaved into cells. Saloonkeepers who displayed Skakel campaign pictures were forced to close promptly at midnight. Equipment in gaming houses owned by pro-Skakel gamblers was confiscated and destroyed. . . .
> [H]oodlums led by Johnny Dee, a professional slugger, were directed to serve as a roving squad for the protection of Coughlin voters. The police, Dee was informed, would be looking the other way should self defense entail the applications of billys, blackjacks or brass knuckles on bellicose Skakelists.[28]

In 1905 Hearst's agents sought vainly for control of the police department so as to assure the election of his delegates to the 1908 presidential nominating convention.[29] In 1903 the City Club had retained Captain Alexander Piper, late of the United States Army, who as deputy police commissioner in New York had led the Canfield Club raid, to conduct a secret investigation of the Chicago police. Utilizing a squad of private detectives, he produced a report that declared that as a whole the force was inefficient and undermanned. There was practically no discipline, and according to Piper many members loafed and drank while on duty and were in collusion with saloonkeepers.*[30]

In 1910 the police response to complaints against the Levee was to promulgate rules for the district such as these:

> Messengers and delivery boys or any persons over the age of three or under the age of eighteen years shall not be permitted either in the district or any of the premises.
>
> Short skirts, transparent gowns or other improper attire shall not be permitted in the parlours or public rooms [of the bordellos].[31]

Since prostitution was illegal under Illinois law, the rules, in effect, modified or negated state statutes. Given the subservience of the police to organized crime, they were somewhat unreliable as vice law enforcers. Harrison himself expressed the common-sense view that he expected the police chief to be "as honest as coppers generally considered honest go," i.e., relatively honest. When he had ordered the Everleigh Club shut, Inspector John Wheeler had refused and had to be replaced by another officer to effect the closing.[32] The captain of the 22nd Street station, Michael "White Alley" Ryan, was a First Ward man and completely ignored headquarters directions to clean up the Levee.

However, Chicago, like New York had its faithful police captain of the Max Schmittberger type. In fact, it had two of them. One, Herman Schuettler, a 300-pound giant, served as deputy chief off and on from 1901 to 1917. Whenever a crackdown was required, Schuettler was put in charge, and his raiding squads would chop up Tennes's gambling joints or Mike de Pike's brothels. As a young detective Schuettler had been involved in a number of gun battles and while off duty in a bar, when taunted by an ex-convict, had killed the man with a single blow of his fist. His raids made good copy and he was a press favorite, but somehow the rackets went on.**

Though there was some doubt whether the mob leaders really disliked Schuettler, there was no mistaking their hatred for the 280-pound Captain Max Nootbar. Born in Germany, he attended Heidelberg University and served in the German Army as well as the U.S. Cavalry. In the latter most of his comrades were Irishmen, and it was necessary to whip them before gaining acceptance. In 1896 he became a Chicago

---

* Though nothing lasting came of the report, the term "piperizer" became the Chicago version of "shoofly" for the next forty years.

** Herman Schuetller (1861–1918) was appointed to the CPD in 1883 and rose quickly as a detective to become head of the homicide squad. In 1891 he was made a captain and in 1901 deputy chief. He was appointed chief of police in 1917 and served as chief until his death.[33]

cop.* Assigned to the Levee district during a period when it was flourishing, he quickly applied for transfer. When it was refused, he went down the line personally raiding joints and throwing the inhabitants into the street, and when he returned to the station, his transfer order was waiting.[34]

Though Nootbar was the ideal man for a real clean-up of the Levee, Harrison dared not assign him to the 22nd Street station as a replacement for White Alley Ryan lest he provoke an open breach with Kenna and the Bath. Instead, action came from the outgoing Republican state's attorney, who in 1912 began a drive on the Levee, after which he promptly committed suicide. His Democratic successor widened the effort to the West Side. As a result, Mike de Pike and a police inspector were jailed and other officers were dismissed or quit. The unpopular Heitler fell victim to the Mann Act and was sent to a federal prison.**[35] Harrison then appointed a special morals squad within the police department to enforce the vice laws. As head of the unit he selected Major Metullus Funkhouser of the Illinois National Guard and put under him as inspector, W. C. Dannenberg, a redheaded firebrand who as a federal agent had been involved in the various white-slave raids in the Levee.

White Alley Ryan, left in command at the 22nd Street station, denounced outside interference and Dannenberg's use of stool pigeons, and Levee detectives busily circulated pictures of Dannenberg and his men to various dive operators. In April 1914 a famous Levee character called Duffy the Goat killed one of the informers. Colisimo, Bloom, and company then sent an emissary to Dannenberg himself with an offer of $2,200 per month for protection, but as they probably expected, their man was arrested. They then took a stronger line.

In New York the Becker case was raging, and Chicago was to have its own version. Johnny Torrio imported his cousin Roxy Vanilla (Vanille), a New York gunman and alleged pal of Gyp the Blood (one of the murderers of Herman Rosenthal), to assassinate Dannenberg. On the night of July 16 the inspector and his squad raided a Levee resort and afterward were followed into the street by a hostile crowd. Simultaneously, they were trailed by Vanilla and a carload of hoodlums. Two of the raiders became separated from their colleagues and when surrounded drew their guns. At that moment two headquarters detectives

---

* Max Nootbar rose rapidly as a protegé of superintendent Francis O'Neill (1901–1905) and in 1910 was made a captain in charge of the training division. A tough lawman, Nootbar was also a man of high culture. Injuries from an auto accident forced his retirement in 1922.

** In contrast to Colisimo or Bathhouse Coughlin, Heitler did not consort with the upper world or spout poetry. Instead he dressed in the gaudy pimp's costume of the day, displayed crude mannerisms, and openly acknowledged his involvement in prostitution. Heitler's insensitivity and bad press image made him a favorite target of various reformers, and, unlike most vice lords, he received several jail sentences. Eventually he was murdered, allegedly by the Capone gang.

came by and seeing the strange gunmen intervened. This led to a general shooting in which a headquarters sergeant was killed and his partner and the two Dannenberg men were wounded, as well as several bystanders and Roxy Vanilla. Apparently, when the detectives shot at each other by mistake, the gangsters, seeing their opportunity, joined in.

Even in Chicago this was too much, and into the Levee went Captain Max Nootbar on Harrison's personal order. Down went Ike Bloom's picture from the squad-room wall at the hands of Nootbar, and down the stairs of the stationhouse went Ike Bloom himself, propelled by the boot of "Big Max" after uttering a few remarks. Thanks to the state's attorney, the mayor, the Dannenberg squad, Captain Nootbar, the press, the reformers, and the changing times, the Levee was dead.[36]

Big Bill

This seeming victory for good government did not quite have that effect. In the Becker case the problems in the police and political organizations were to enhance the power of organized crime under Rothstein as prime minister. In Chicago, this role was to go initially to Colisimo. With the temporary revocation of his license, Big Jim perceived that the old segregated Levee was dead and began to branch out into the South Side black belt and even to the suburbs. The black ghetto with its famous "black and tan," racially mixed cabarets was to replace the Levee.

In the 1915 mayoral election, Harrison was denied his party's nomination. Colisimo backed the Republican "Big Bill" Thompson, who was victorious. The new mayor was just the sort of showman Chicago loved. The scion of a wealthy Boston family, he had been brought to Chicago as an infant. As a boy of fourteen he had gotten into a brawl with the cops and had been jailed. His millionaire father demanded that Police Lieutenant Mike Schaack of the East Chicago Avenue station be fired but accepted an apology from the mayor. It was clear, however, that master Billy was too rough for Yale as originally planned, and he was shipped to a western ranch, were he lived off and on for a decade and acquired a taste for cowboy life. As mayor he would wear a cowboy hat and pose as a two-fisted westerner. Big and rugged, he was a notable football player, and though a patron of Levee bordellos, as a young man he had been elected alderman with the endorsement of the Municipal Reform League.[37]

The advent of the Republicans did not mean reform. The previous Republican mayor, Fred Busse (1907–1911), had been a crude barroom brawler and general low-life type. As soon as he had been elected his pal, Barney Bertsche, had strapped on two guns and begun collecting from the joints in the First Ward. In quick succession he fought two gun battles with the police, killing a detective and wounding two patrol-men.[38] The Thompson regime was worse. In effect, it was as though Big Tim Sullivan had been elected mayor of New York after the Becker case.

The election of Thompson simply meant the end of Kenna and the Bath as the fix for organized crime. Under Thompson's regime the South Side mob led by Colisimo would deal directly with City Hall. The First Ward Democrats did continue to exercise their aldermanic prerogatives in regard to permits for business activities in the downtown area,* and Colisimo remained on good terms with them, forbearing to take advantage of the reversal of position. They were even allowed a cut of the vice pie and to name their own man as boss of South Side prostitution. Later, Colisimo's successors, Torrio and Capone, would continue the arrangement but without the personal friendship which had existed between the lords of the Levee and Big Jim. This was more harmonious than on the West Side, where an Italian-American who challenged the Irish boss was eventually assassinated. Nevertheless, after 1915 the Levee was gone and the Bath and Hink were no longer lords over the gangsters. The Bath himself became increasingly a figure of fun, but Kenna remained high in the party councils.

His generosity to the First Ward only added to the view of many that a true gentleman was Jim Colisimo. Increasingly, he left his more sordid affairs to Torrio while he mingled with the nice people. Torrio, in turn, brought in another New York gunman named Al Capone to assist him. By 1920 Colisimo had fallen in love with a beautiful and respectable singer, Dale Winter, who, stranded temporarily in Chicago when her show closed, had gone to work in Colisimo's club. In April he divorced his wife and married Miss Winter. In May he was assassinated. Though the Archbishop of Chicago, Cardinal Mundelien, refused permission for a Catholic service (because of the divorce), 20,000 people attended the funeral including a *Who's Who* of city leaders, and Bathhouse, a faithful churchman himself, led the mourners in the Catholic prayer for the dead. It was widely believed that the chief mourner, Johnny Torrio, had ordered the execution either out of rivalry for power or because Colisimo was neglecting business for love. Neither Dale Winter nor Colisimo's ex-wife claimed any of his estate, which, while substantial, was missing a goodly portion of cash.[39]

Under Thompson, the police department declined from its temporary improvement. Captain Nootbar was removed from his command, Dannenberg was fired, and the morals squad was abolished. In 1917 the state's attorney indicted the police chief, William Healy, along with

---

* In 1923, when the number of aldermen per ward was reduced to one, Kenna stepped aside for the unpaid but powerful post of ward committeeman.

several other police officials and political figures and the bondsman and fixer William "Billy" Skidmore. Though not convicted, the chief resigned, and Herman Schuettler was put in his place.

Dismissals of ranking officers on the death of a mob leader meant little in the general climate of corruption, yet prosecutions of individuals were always good publicity. As sociologist Walter Reckless wrote, "the usual pattern in Chicago was to indict *individuals* as responsible for *conditions*."[40] In this way critics could be appeased while the system went on. In a city with a very weak basis of support for reform the choice was not between the machine and the reformers, but between the machine and the gangsters. The substitution of Thompson for Harrison and the Torrio-Capone gang for Bathhouse and Hinkey Dink was clearly not a step forward.

In the early '20s Torrio's group was the most powerful in the city, but there were others almost as strong. On the North Side was Dion O'Bannion, who operated out of his floral shop opposite Holy Name Cathedral, headquarters of the Catholic Archdiocese. O'Bannion supplied not only flowers for funerals but in a number of cases the corpses, since he was one of the city's most proficient murderers. The O'Bannions eventually clashed with the Torrio-Capones, leading to the resignation of Torrio, the death of O'Bannion as well as numerous others, and finally the Valentine Massacre. The two gangs were fundamentally different. The Torrio-Capone group were businessmen rising out of the commercial enterprises of the Levee district, while the O'Bannions were classic neighborhood tough guys grown up to adult gangsters, like the Eastmans and Kellys in New York.

O'Bannion, a product of a North Side Irish slum, had been an altar boy and choir singer at Holy Name Cathedral and for a profitable sideline frequented the tough saloons of the area singing sentimental Irish ballads. His sweet voice and crippled leg caught the sympathy of Adam Geary, a professional killer and gang boss who eventually ended up in a state penitentiary for the criminally insane. Soon, the tough altar boy was cracking safes and committing murders on his own. In time, he grouped with other Irish, German, and Jewish toughs into a gang of election sluggers and petty crooks dominating the near North Side. All of them had careers similar to O'Bannion's. For example, Nails Morton organized a Jewish defense group to protect his coreligionists from attacks. He was indicted but not convicted for the murder of two detectives in a saloon altercation. In World I he was a much-decorated hero. When a horse threw Nails to his death after he returned from the war, his gang buddies expressed their grief by kidnapping and killing the horse. Prohibition made the O'Bannions an important group, but the skills it required were far beyond their capabilities.[41]

Torrio, on the other hand, claimed never to carry a gun and preferred to talk rather than fight. At the beginning of Prohibition, terms were agreed to with the approval of the Thompson administration, and the Torrios and the O'Bannions peacefully coexisted. However, the difference between the two groups was illustrated by an incident of the early '20's. One night police wiretappers heard a gangster call O'Bannion to inform him that one of his beer trucks had been captured by two detectives and was being held on a West Side street for a $300 ransom. O'Bannion, furious, refused to authorize payment, saying it was cheaper to have the cops killed, and advised the caller to contact gunmen to carry out the task. The wiretappers immediately dispatched a squad of riflemen to support their endangered comrades. In the meantime the gangster, pondering O'Bannion's advice, called Torrio to obtain a second opinion, and Johnny authorized payment, stating he did not want any trouble.[42] Nor did Torrio see any need for killing the opposition. He was in so solidly with the city authorities that if a rival set up in business, it was much easier to have the cops raid the place.

The election of William Dever as mayor in 1923 changed the situation. Dever was an honest and upright individual, but he was the candidate of the Cook County Democratic machine run by Boss George Brennan, Hinkey Dink, and Tony Cermak, a West Side politician who also headed the Saloonkeepers' Association. The police chief Dever chose, or was given, was Morgan Collins, a former medical student who had joined the police department and while still young had risen to the rank of captain. While some critics portrayed the Dever regime as one of reform, in fact its policies were more those of restraint, à la Croker, Murphy, or Harrison. As early as 1919 the Chicago Crime Commission had received confidential information that Collins had accepted payoffs while a district commander, and in 1916 he had been exposed as a member of the Sportsmen's Club, which included Mayor Thompson as well as a number of professional gamblers.[43] Collins's administration was to be characterized by a number of spectacular raids, but as the Illinois Crime Survey of 1929 indicated, the Schuettler and Collins regimes were best seen "as a time when payoffs were taken away from the politicians and given to the police."[44]

The Dever-Collins upset to the equilibrium which had been established by the Thompson regime was to plunge the city into massive gang wars. Under Collins, some gangsters were allowed to operate, and others were not. The Torrio group, as the closest allies of Thompson, were hard hit. O'Bannion, in contrast, seemed in favor. The chief of detectives even attended a testimonial for the gangster.[45] In a neat trick O'Bannion sold a brewery to Torrio, and as the latter took possession the police, led by Chief Collins in person, raided the place, arrested Torrio, and turned him over to federal prosecutors. Collins heightened the drama by personally tearing off the insignias of some local district officers who were supposed to be on duty to prevent the brewery from operating. As a result of the raid, Torrio and some others, including two of the cops, were given jail terms of several months duration.[46] Shortly afterward, O'Bannion was assassinated and a gang war began which forced a wounded Torrio to flee to Brooklyn, leaving Capone in charge. During the Dever regime he largely operated out of the suburb of Cicero, whose name he made notorious.

In 1927 Thompson returned to office promising a wide-open town. His brand of showmanship still delighted Chicagoans. The mayor held a public meeting where he displayed a cage of rats and carried on a mock debate with the rodents, which he identified by the names of his leading opponents. Big Bill also decried British influence in the school system and threatened to punch King George V in the snoot should His Majesty come to Chicago.[47] Thompson had opposed American participation in World War I and his isolationist and anti-British sentiments appealed to many ethnic voters. Even the anglophobic *Chicago Tribune* was attacked by Thompson for being pro-British. Englishmen like W. T. Stead and Gypsy Smith, as well as various lesser lights who had visited the city,* left a latent anti-British hostility even among many of Anglo-Saxon background.

With the return of Thompson, Capone became the top gangster, although the conflicts continued and Scarface Al never dominated more than half the city. His effective reign was also relatively short. Though it was well publicized, in part because of the introduction of the machine gun into gang warfare in 1926, the period of the Capone ascendancy actually lasted only two years. The real period of rule by the Capone gang came after the boss's own departure, and the Valentine Massacre of the remnants of the O'Bannion gang, now under Bugs Moran, brought forth such pressure that Capone was soon in jail in Philadelphia on a concealed weapons charge. In 1931 he was convicted in Chicago Federal Court for tax violations and sentenced to prison.

Reform, Chicago Style

When Smith arrived in Chicago in 1929, many leaders recognized the impossibility of a reform on moralistic lines and saw the new administrative science as a more viable possibility. This was a view that accorded with the Institute of Public Administration's notion that there was a definite dichotomy between politics and administration. In its view, politics dealt with values, while administration dealt with facts.

---

* For example, in 1902, John Frazier Foster of the *Yorkshire Post* had visited the city and attacked its vice conditions—and Thompson, then an alderman, had clashed with him.[48]

According to the IPA, it was necessary to reform administration first, then values would follow.

Smith's committee agreed not to investigate corruption, but instead to concentrate on administration, and its report was largely in this vein, although the first chapter was a bit of a shocker. Noting the general impression that the police department was "rotten to the core," it modestly recommended that the city discharge the entire force of 6,700 officers.*[49] Passing quickly from this, it came to Smith's main proposals, which were to bring the department into accord with standard organizational and administrative principles—shorter spans of control, fixed responsibility for particular tasks, etc.

Commissioner William Russell, who'd been a career police officer, cooperated with the committee, which seemed to bode well for implementation of its recommendations. But unfortunately, at the time the report was released a major scandal engulfed the city administration. In June 1930 the *Chicago Tribune*'s ace organized crime reporter, Jake Lingle, was murdered in a crowded downtown railroad station.** At first the press thundered vengeance, but investigation disclosed that the $65-a-week journalist had lived like a millionaire and had indeed been involved in financial transactions with gangsters. Worse, from the standpoint of the reformers, Lingle's closest friend and business partner was none other than Commissioner Russell, the two men having become friends in the Levee area twenty years earlier. The word began to circulate that Lingle had run the police department through Russell.[50] The commissioner was dismissed and his successor broke off relations with the committee. But reform was saved by the 1931 mayoral election. As in New York, the Depression had soured voters on their colorful mayor, and they elected a budget cutter, "Saving Tony" Cermak of the Saloon Keepers' Association, who, Thompson claimed, had saved a $2-million-dollar personal fortune on a $15,000-a-year salary as president of the Board of County Commissioners.[51]

Since reform was a relative thing in Chicago, the committee sought to work with the new regime and Smith returned to Chicago for an additional year. The new commissioner was James P. Allman, a thirty-year veteran who had caught Smith's fancy. Allman had been a captain in the Englewood district, the city's most important commercial center outside of the Loop, and his alliance with its powerful business groups

* Some doubt exists of the seriousness of this proposal. Certainly the press, public, and politicians of the time assumed it was serious, and a generation later Smith would remember it that way; however, others thought it was simply tactical.

** Eventually a man was convicted of the crime on the word of an ex-convict informer but was given the relatively light sentence of fourteen years. The informer received $25,000 for his services, and the state prosecutor was elected to the United States Senate. In the intervening years no evidence has been presented to refute the verdict.

made him impervious to organizational pressures. However, Tony Cermak had no intention of reforming Chicago. Allman would provide a respectable front and a measure of discipline for the force, but his appointment was conditional on acceptance of political control over the police. City Hall would make certain allotments of power and the ward bosses would control the district police stations[52]—in effect, a nineteenth-century type of police administration.

The Chicago (Cook County) Democratic machine was a different type of organization from the Thompson group. The latter's machine was largely personal, while the Democrats were a true organization dependent upon grass-roots strength rather than one man's personality. Thompson was a political boss of the Curley-Fitzgerald Boston variety, while the Cook County Democracy was Tammany Hall, and at the time its New York counterpart was falling into decline the Chicago machine was setting out on a reign which is as yet unended.

Cermak began parceling out various fiefdoms to organized crime, and when the Capone forces objected, a squad of detectives, working under the mayor's personal orders, shot and wounded Capone's successor, Frank Nitti, though the gangster had offered no resistance.[53] A few months later the mayor was assassinated. The death of Cermak at the side of President-elect Roosevelt was apparently the work of Giuseppe Zangara, a deranged individual shooting at the Chief of State, but many Chicagoans wondered at the happy timing for the mob. Secretary of the Interior Harold Ickes, himself a veteran Chicago reformer, flatly disbelieved that the bullets had been meant for FDR.[54] Nor did the men of the police department mourn "Saving Tony," since he had reduced their wages and dared them to quit; in 1932, as the mayor pointed out, he could get all the cops he needed for $15 a week.

Commissioner Allman was to hold office for fourteen years, and this combined with the end of Prohibition brought a measure of stability into Chicago police administration. Even the death of Cermak had no effect, since another machine man, Ed Kelly, replaced him. Kelly and his partner, Boss Pat Nash, were rather typical Chicago politicians. Soon after their acension to power, both had to pay substantial sums to the federal government for income tax violations. During the Kelly regime the Capone mob, under Nitti, suffered no inconvenience, nor did any other substantial organized-crime figures. A major scandal engulfed the police vice squad in 1941, and in 1943 seven captains were fired (but later reinstated) for failure to suppress gambling. Thus the Allman tenure, while stable, was hardly a period of reform.

When conditions in the city were decried, one could always point to the suburban areas as worse. A chief of the county police resigned the day after being photographed in a cozy rendezvous with bondsman and fixer William Skidmore.[55] From 1932 to 1950, the Cook County state's attorney's detectives were presided over by Chicago Police Captain Dan "Tubbo" Gilbert, a former labor union "organizer," bodyguard for Boss Brennan, and intimate of Jake Lingle. Gilbert had a meteoric rise to captain after his appointment to the force in 1917.

Of all the Chicago policemen from the founding of the force to World War II, Gilbert was the most powerful, and the closest in type to a Byrnes or Devery. In 1950, he was labeled America's richest policeman after testifying before the Kefauver Commission, which found his ties with organized crime to be exceedingly close. As a result, the Democratic machine asked him to step down—to head its county ticket in the race for sheriff. Again the voters temporarily were not amused and the party suffered a disaster, one of a series which paved the way for the rise of a new leader named Richard J. Daley.[56]

Throughout Chicago's history, the only effective efforts against organized crime were carried on by the federal government. Over the years, the federal bag ranged from small fry, such as the Black Handers sent up for extortion, to middle-size figures like Mike de Pike, for Mann Act violations, on to big shots like Torrio and Capone, for bootlegging or income tax convictions. During the Allman regime, the pattern would continue with the convictions of William Skidmore for tax evasion and the top leadership of the old Capone gang for extortion, a case including as a by-product the suicide of Frank Nitti.

THE CULTURE OF VIOLENCE

If Pennsylvania was the state in which conflicts of industrial America were fought out, Chicago was the city. After the draft riots and the events of the 1870s, New York was never again the scene of citywide disorder, whereas Chicago became progressively worse. If there was to be an American Commune, Chicago seemed the likely city in which it would occur.

As sociologist Allan Grimshaw has written:

In only one northern city is evidence available which indicates that social violence, of greater or lesser intensity, is an almost continuous phenomenon. This is Chicago.[57]

The fear of revolutionary violence merged with the general disorder of a wide-open town. Even the physical environment contributed to the problem. Large portions of the city contained industrial areas interspersed with residential neighborhoods. Railroad tracks and yards were everywhere, while slag heaps, open hearths, and the stockyards, with their distinctive odors, dominated whole districts. The worker at home could not escape the sights, sounds, and smells of industry. Truly it was a dehumanizing environment, and a University of Chicago sociologist, Frederick Thrasher, sought to explain the high rate of juvenile delinquency in certain neighborhoods by the degree to which industrialism intruded into residential enclaves.[58] General Nelson Miles, Civil War hero and indian fighter, commented that Chicago had "more men engaged in cruel occupations and living in scenes of blood and slaughter than any other."[59] In such an evironment violence was not a last resort, but frequently the first. In most years the Chicago murder rate was twice as high as that of New York City.[60]

Even the city's newspapers had hired guns. When Hearst decided to enter Chicago, he chose the Annenberg brothers, Max and Moe, to lead his circulation drive.* The *Tribune* and the *Daily News* fought back, and in one three-year period, between 1907 and 1910, twenty-seven newsboys and sluggers were killed. Later some analysts concluded that the newspaper wars were the start of organized-crime violence. Certainly, a number of gunmen who made headlines in the twenties came into prominence during this time.

Policemen too were shot and killed by politicians or mob bosses on a scale virtually unknown elsewhere. Though Mayor Busse's aide Barney Bertsche personally shot three cops and one of them fatally as noted earlier, he remained an influential figure, as did Nails Morton after similar escapades. In New York no gang leader could have remained in power after such an incident. Even Rothstein's shooting of two policemen by mistake had led to a major outcry. Nor could any Tammany mayor have associated with thugs as openly as did Chicago mayors Busse and Thompson. In 1922 union gunmen murdered two cops during an attack on employers' property. In 1928 the homes of a police captain and a former police chief were bombed. In 1925 two Capone gangsters named Scalisi and Anselmi murdered two detectives who attempted to question them. The Illinois Supreme Court overturned their murder convictions, ruling as a matter of law that it could not be murder if a policeman was killed while attempting to make an arrest without legal grounds. Whatever the legalities of the case, taught as first principle to every police recruit, it appeared to affirm the low status of the force.[62]

Nor was public office a guarantee against violence. Indeed, the opposite was true; public officials were assaulted and murdered and had their homes bombed. Even the most powerful feared violence. In the 1920s Mayor Thompson and Colonel Robert McCormick, publisher of the *Tribune*, each suspected the other of plotting his assassination, and

---

* Max Annenberg later went to work for the *Tribune*, and in the 1920s Moe, who left Chicago after 1907, bought out Mont Tennes's wire service.[61]

both moved about protected by machine gunners, and in McCormick's case an armored car.[63] Like Captain Gilbert, many policemen who reached high rank in the department began their careers as bodyguards for the powerful.

Not surprisingly, the police were rather quick on the trigger. In the 1880s the burglar Langdon Moore accused detectives of deliberately killing one of his accomplices.[64] In the 1920s a gang leader was shot to death in the back seat of a police car taking him to a court hearing after exchanging words with the arresting officer. Where Broderick and Cordes used their fists on New York gangsters, who dared not pull guns, Chicago cops, who were often shot without warning by hoodlums and politicians, relied on their guns more than any major-city force in America. In the typical years 1926 and 1927, 20 police were killed, and the police in turn killed 89 citizens.[65]

If the city's elite had to use hired guns to fight each other and police traded shots with hoodlums on a routine basis, they could hardly be expected to show restraint toward radicals. As early as 1875 the *Chicago Tribune*, the leading newspaper in the West, had run an editorial entitled "Warnings to Communists":

> If the Communists in this country are counting upon the looseness of our police system and the tendency to proceed against criminals by due process of law, and hope on that account, to receive more leniency than in Europe, they have ignored some of the most significant episodes in American history. There is no people so prone as the American to take the law into their own hands when the sanctity of human life is threatened and the rights of property invaded in a manner that cannot be adequately reached and punished by the tortuous course of the law. Judge Lynch is an American by birth and character.... Every lamppost in Chicago will be decorated with a communist carcass if necessary to prevent wholesale incendiarism or prevent any attempt at it.[66]

In 1878, the fashionable Citizens Club presented the city with a Gatling gun in the same beneficent way that chambers of commerce buy ambulances or fire engines. In 1886, a man who was later national leader of the American Red Cross proposed to form a vigilante group to hang radicals.[67]

In the railroad strike of 1877, the police raced about in Marshall Field's wagons (they did not yet have their own) chasing mobs, and at the legendary "battle of the roundhouse" officers killed seven men. Before the disorders ended, thirteen more died. During the course of the rioting, wealthy merchant Levi Leiter asked the *Daily News* to cease publication because by its support of the strikers it was inflaming the situation.[68] Allan Pinkerton, head of the detective agency, blamed the riot on the socialist agitator Albert Parsons, though Parsons had cut a very unheroic figure. At the height of the trouble he was hauled off to the mayor's office and informed that the Board of Trade men were ready to lynch him. He was then thrown into the street, where he wandered about dazed. Other radical leaders were also brought in and given the same lamppost speech.[69] In the aftermath the police busied themselves with military drills and practiced with their Gatling gun, while their superintendent styled himself colonel.[70]

As the police developed their skills, so too did the radicals. Parsons, a former Confederate soldier, had been a federal carpetbagger in Texas after the war, where he married a Mexican girl. Coming to Chicago, he and his wife Lucy, whom the *Tribune* referred to as "citizeness Parsons,"[71] became prominent in the city's radical circles. But the heart of the movement was provided by the German socialists such as August Spies, a friend of Johann Most. In 1883 Most, Parsons, and Spies played leading roles at a socialist convention held in Pittsburgh.

The rhetoric of the Chicago radicals was in the spirit of the Commune, with cries for bombs and murder. Willis Abbot, later editor of the *Christian Science Monitor*, recollected

> ... turning away from one of the stands with a sense that what was being preached was not precisely a doctrine of general good will. The speaker, after pointing out the necessity for doing away with the capitalists, ... went on to assure his hearers that it was particularly necessary that the children likewise be slain, since the curse of capitalism was in their blood.[72]

On one occasion some radicals gave a *Daily News* reporter a bomb and told him to take it to his editor and show him what they were up to.[73] Truly they loved the notoriety of their position and like later radicals expressed great surprise when people tended to believe their threats.

In the spring of 1886 Chicago was in the throes of a strike for the eight-hour day, and on May 3 trouble developed at the McCormick Reaper works when union men attacked some nonstrikers. The police opened fire, killing two and wounding several others.[74] In reaction, Spies and his group, though not connected with the union, called a protest meeting for the night of May 4, to be held at Haymarket Square on the near West Side. Among the handbills distributed were some calling for the crowd to come armed, and a thousand people gathered. A half block away at the Desplaines Street police station, a detail of policemen under Superintendent Frederick Ebersold and Mayor Harrison were also assembled. At 8 o'clock, after a chill wind suddenly blew up, followed by rain, the crowd began to drift away. Mayor Harrison thought the meeting peaceful, and he and Superintendent Ebersold departed, leaving Inspector "Black Jack" Bonfield in charge. The inspector was in the

Alexander Williams mold, having gained a considerable reputation for clubbing people, especially during a streetcar strike the previous year.[75] Shortly after the departure of his superiors Bonfield ordered his men to form into columns and led them toward the crowd. Immediately after Captain William Ward uttered the words of the riot act, a bomb landed in the midst of the police, who began to fire their revolvers.[76]

The city, appalled by the police casualties of eight dead and seventy wounded, demanded action, but the police brass were split. Bonfield argued for an all-out assault on the radicals, while Superintendent Ebersold and the detective chiefs wanted to proceed with caution, believing that the rash Bonfield was partly responsible for the disaster. Bonfield's position was supported by Captain Mike Schaack, now in command of the North Side. His area included the German section of the city, and he had available a squad of mostly German detectives which he used for surveillance of anarchists. While Bonfield raided the West Side cracking radical skulls, Schaack's men hunted down anarchist leaders. Their most notable capture was Louis Linge, a young German immigrant who was a bomb maker. He did not come easy though, and Linge and young Detective Herman Schuettler engaged in a life and death struggle for Schuettler's gun until another detective knocked Linge unconscious.[77] Before long the jails were full of anarchists. Finally, it was decided to try eight men on the grounds that their speeches and writings had caused the bombing. This was a new departure; the more traditional course would have been to prove that the defendants conspired with the actual bomber, but he was not known.

Large sections of the American bar, including such luminaries as Lyman Gage and former Senator Lyman Trumbull, as well as General Ben Butler of Massachusetts (who carried the appeal to the Supreme Court), denounced the trial, but the defendants were convicted and sentenced to death. Attempts to save their lives were based on a mixture of humane concern, fear for the legal precedent, and eccentricity. The wife of a defense counsel, Mrs. William Black, in a letter to the *Daily News* wrote:

> Anarchy is simply a human effort to bring about the millennium. Why do we want to hang men for that, when every pulpit thundered that the time was near at hand?[78]

A rich Vassar girl insisted on marrying August Spies, whom she did not know, and when permission was denied had the ceremony performed by proxy.[79]

The Haymarket affair would be another of the great controversies in American history. Certainly, Bonfield's actions seemed precipitous, especially since Mayor Harrison had found the meeting so unexciting that he left. However, the anarchists had continually called for violence, and at least one of them, Louis Linge, had made bombs. Finally, unless one accepts the agent-provocateur theory, somebody (the bomber) came to the meeting contemplating rather serious trouble.

The governor commuted three sentences to life, and Linge blew himself up in jail with a small explosive cap. The crucial decision not to commute the other sentences eventually was made by Marshall Field at a meeting of civic leaders. Afterward Field and other members of the business community donated land north of the city to the government on the condition that a regular army regiment would be stationed at Fort Sheridan so as to be available in Chicago.[80] In November 1887 Spies, Parsons, and two others were hanged.*

In 1889 a new mayor fired both Bonfield and Schaack, the latter for trying to cover up a murder committed by one of his detectives.** When Schaack, in a book, attacked Superintendent Ebersold, he in turn charged that Schaack had attempted to continue anarchist groups in existence by the use of undercover agents so as to keep the pot boiling.[82]

While the debate over the Haymarket raged, in 1892 the Democrats managed to elect their first Illinois governor since before the Civil War. John Peter Altgeld was born in Germany in 1849, grew up in Ohio, and came to Chicago in 1875 from Missouri, where he had been a prosecuting attorney. In many ways he resembled his contemporary New York's Mayor Gaynor, a rural boy who made his fortune in the big city, became a judge, and was frequently critical of the police, for Altgeld was another strong civil libertarian. Here was a rare find, a Chicago politician who could provide moral leadership to the community, particularly the working-class citizens who supported the Democratic party. However, he was also intensely ambitious for both wealth and power. Before he was forty, Altgeld had made a million dollars in real estate, but his business dealings consistently interfered with his duties as a public official. While a judge, he was fined for contempt of court in a civil suit involving a damage claim he made against the city. As governor he took a private loan of public funds from the state treasurer and then violated the law by hurriedly replacing the money after the official suddenly

---

* The citizens of Chicago erected a monument to honor the slain officers, a statue of a policeman with the inscription "In the name of the People of Illinois I command peace." Its history has been checkered. Legend has it that on November 11, 1927, on the fortieth anniversary of the executions of the Haymarket defendants, it was knocked from its pedestal by a derailed streetcar. In 1969 and again in 1970 it was bombed by radicals. The model for the statue was Officer Thomas Birmingham, the "handsomest and most perfect specimen of the Chicago Police Department," who had been in the riot of 1886. Birmingham eventually became an alcoholic, was dismissed from the force, and died a pauper.[81] The statue now reposes in the Chicago Police Academy.

** On the murder of Dr. Patrick Cronin, see Chapter 8, page 273.

died, and his accounts were required to be sealed. Later, a bank he was involved with failed, losing a great deal of state money. As a politician he was a protégé of the gambling boss Mike MacDonald, who liked Altgeld's ability to pay his own campaign expenses. Thus his relatively short public career was a mixture of liberal ideals and political and business deals.[83]

Within a few months of taking office, Altgeld responded to the pleas of his close friend Clarence Darrow and others and freed the three remaining anarchists. He did this not on the expected grounds of mercy, but rather on the grounds that they were innocent and their trial had been a frame-up. Nor did he stop there; he went on to blame the bombing on Inspector Bonfield, hypothesizing that the bomber was a previous victim of police brutality looking for revenge.[84] Such a proposition was highly questionable, since a number of more direct means of revenge were open, and the governor offered no proof beyond speculation. In an attempt to correct a trial outcome which was contrary to commonly accepted rules of evidence, the governor had discarded those same rules in behalf of his cause. If Altgeld expected praise, he was mistaken. The *New York Times* editorialized:

> Governor Altgeld has done everything in his power . . . to encourage again the spirit of lawless resistance and of wanton assault upon the agents of authority . . . exactly in tone with the wildest Anarchist leaders.[85]

Even Darrow and Jane Addams felt he was mistaken in criticizing the trial judge. Practically the only praise was from Johann Most—not exactly a helpful source.[86]

But for Altgeld the storm was just beginning. In 1894, the workers of the Pullman Sleeping Car works in the "model" village of Pullman, on the far South Side of Chicago struck because of wage reductions brought about by the panic of 1893. Despite pressure for arbitration, Pullman and his largest stockholder, Marshall Field, refused to compromise. At this juncture, the workers approached the newly formed American Railway Union, whose president was Eugene Debs.

Debs, then thirty-nine, had been secretary-treasurer of the Brotherhood of Railway Firemen and a minor public official in his home town of Terre Haute, Indiana. Disgusted by the internal conflicts and elitism of the various railroad brotherhoods, in 1893 he had organized an umbrella group of mostly unskilled laborers which quickly grew to 150,000 against the brotherhood's 90,000. All of his life Debs was to be a generous idealist, for which he would pay dearly. A strike by the infant union against the railroads with the opposition of the old-line brotherhoods was ill conceived, but the pleas of the Pullman workers were compelling. The

Debs union decided to refuse to handle trains with Pullman cars. In a short time railroads in many states were paralyzed by lack of switchmen.

In Chicago, the center of strike activity, both the city police and the militia were dispatched to various trouble spots, but conditions were relatively peaceful. Though the police worked twenty hours a day, their behavior was generally restrained. In contrast to 1877 and 1886, the police appeared to sympathize with the strikers, who were led by ordinary workers rather than radical agitators. The railroad managers, however, were not disposed to compromise. It was necessary to break the strike if the trains were to be moved, and neither Altgeld's militia nor the Chicago police were willing to do that. Thus the railroad lawyers looked to Washington and United States Attorney General Richard Olney.

Olney had made his way to the top of the Boston Bar without any connections on Beacon Hill, by skill as a lawyer for various railroads, though in Washington he became associated with the Henry Adams set. Olney was a strange character. As a young man it was his practice to physically assault individuals who disagreed with him. Later, he would kick dogs out of his way and shoot cows which trod on his property. He refused to speak to his daughter for the remaining thirty years of his life over a minor misunderstanding. More importantly, he was not at all embarrassed by the fact that as Attorney General of the United States he continued to receive substantial retainers from various railroads. Indeed, he appointed another railroad lawyer as Special U.S. Attorney to represent the government in dealing with the strike. Since, in Olney's opinion, stoppage of rail traffic was an obstruction of interstate commerce.[87]

Acting on Olney's authorization, the U.S. Marshal in Chicago swore in 5,000 deputies from the skid rows of the city to guard railroad property. Their contribution was largely to steal from the stalled railroad cars, so that many had to be arrested by the city police. Next, on the pretext that the strike was preventing the delivery of U.S. mail, the Justice Department secured injunctions against the union, and President Cleveland ordered the army to protect the railroads.

Marshall Field's gift now paid rich dividends as early on the morning of July 4, in a neat symbolism, the entire garrison of Fort Sheridan entrained for Chicago, the vanguard of troops en route from army bases all over the United States. It appeared that at last the Commune was upon the nation, in the city where its appearance had long been forecast, and as in Paris the army would shoot down the workers.

Until the arrival of the regulars no deaths had occurred. Those who opposed the federal intervention would argue that disorder was intensified by the introduction of the army, while those who favored it would claim that the troops arrived just in the nick of time. At any rate, in the next few days thirteen people were killed in Chicago, though none of them by federal troops.* Debs was arrested and was given six months for contempt of court in ignoring the injunction. The strike of both the railroad and Pullman workers was broken, and many were soon in dire straits, though the "better elements" of Chicago organized a relief program.[88]

When the federal intervention became known, Altgeld fired off a telegram protesting dispatch of U.S. troops without a request from the state, an argument used by southern governors two generations later. President Cleveland, in essence, told him to mind his own business. Again he was seen as Altgeld the Communist, anarchist, friend of murderers, and inciter of riots. His legal position was attacked by scholars as diverse as the conservative Thomas Cooley, president of the American Bar Association, chief justice of Michigan, and author of *Constitutional Limitations*, and the liberal Woodrow Wilson.[89] At the next election, New York Police Commissioner Theodore Roosevelt made a special trip to Chicago to denounce the Communist Altgeld. Said Roosevelt:

> He would connive at wholesale murder and would justify it by elaborate and cunning sophistry for reasons known only to his own soul. For America to put men like this in control of its destiny would be such a dishonor as it is scarcely bearable to think of.[90]

Altgeld's previous statements in pardoning the anarchists had made it easier for opponents to overcome his arguments in the Pullman case by pointing out that he was a radical himself. It was possible that had he not been so zealous in excusing three admitted advocates of murder, he might have been better able to defend the hundreds of thousands of ordinary workers whose pleas for bread for their families elicited even the support of the police and militia.

In 1896 Altgeld was defeated for reelection as governor. The few remaining years of his life were unhappy. A grand jury looked into his various conflicts of interests, and he narrowly missed indictment.[91] His business failed, and he lost all his property. In 1899 he ran for mayor of Chicago and finished third. In 1902, aged fifty-four, he fell dead while addressing a meeting to support the Boer cause in the South African war, and the following year the Legislature had to appropriate $5,000 so his wife would not lose her home. Richard Olney was promoted to Secretary of State as a reward for his services, and Eugene Debs became a socialist. He would tangle again with the federal government, lose, and be sent to the penitentiary.

---

* Five were killed by militia, the rest by marshals or unknown persons. The regulars did kill a man in nearby Hammond, Indiana.

The mantle of leadership for civil libertarians now passed to Altgeld's law partner, Clarence Darrow, and Jane Addams. Darrow has come down to us as a great liberal crusader, though in his lifetime his commitment was seriously questioned. His clients included railroads, banks, the Hearst newspapers, gambling boss Tennes, cops and politicians charged with grafting, and the traction interests. He even defended the latter when they were charged with jury bribing. His services to labor unions usually required the payment of a large fee. As Darrow himself admitted when asked by one of Jane Addams's associates why he had agreed to represent the streetcar company:

> I did it for the money they paid me.... Judged by the higher law, in which we both believe, I am practically a thief. I am taking money that I did not earn, which comes to me from men who did not earn it, but who gave it because they have a chance to get it.[92]

Even his famous criminal defenses such as the Loeb-Leopold and Massie cases* were undertaken on behalf of rich clients. Of course, Darrow could always claim "sociological" reasons to accept cases, though such an explanation wore thin when he was retained to help draw up the property settlement for Edith Rockefeller McCormick's divorce.

Darrow was an especially important symbol to the Chicago Police Department, since the city was his home base and he frequently appeared in its criminal courts. He was also tied very closely to the city's politics. His first important recognition came with appointment to the lucrative post of Chicago corporation counsel by the city machine in 1893. In 1903, he was ambitious to run for mayor on the Labor party ticket; when he failed to receive the nomination, he supported Mayor Harrison, who managed to narrowly defeat a genuine reformer, John Marshall Harlan.[93] The police, like the labor organizers, found it difficult to reconcile Darrow's pursuit of wealth with his socialist views and his reform ideas with his alliances with machine politicians and grafters. To his explanation that he was simply stealing from an evil system they could retort that they did the same.

Jane Addams, in contrast, did not pursue wealth. Instead, Hull House became a major center for reformers, particularly females, while providing a watchdog operation over the police. Though, like that of all reformers, its impact was minimal.

The class struggle was to continue in Chicago, and as late as 1937, on Memorial Day, police would kill ten strikers who were attempting to

---

* On Loeb–Leopold and Bobby Franks, see page 222 below. In the Massie case the defendant was a socially prominent naval officer stationed in Hawaii, charged with the murder of an Oriental who had allegedly raped his wife.

sit in at the Republic Steel plant.[94] This notwithstanding the fact that organized labor was a powerful element in the local political machine.

BLACK AND WHITE

The black community of Chicago was always more important politically than in New York or most other cities. A Chicago black was elected to the State Legislature as early as 1872, and by 1894 there were twenty-three blacks in the police department,[95] preceding by many years the appointment of the first Negro on the New York force. In 1928, the city would send the first black man to Congress since Reconstruction, again a quarter of a century before New York. But unfortunately, friction between the races was also more pronounced than in most northern cities.

In 1882 a black man named Bill Allen (also known as Joe Dehlmar) killed a police officer who attempted to arrest him for shooting two other Negroes, one of them fatally. He then hid out in the basement of a West Side brothel, where a prostitute betrayed him. As police closed in, he wounded an officer and fled into the nearby neighborhood. Three hours later he was killed in an exchange of shots with Sergeant John Wheeler, later a famous inspector. None of the foregoing was particularly unusual; rather, it was the aftermath that was the harbinger of relations between the races. Allen's dead body was removed to the Desplaines police station, where a white mob, believing he was still alive, stormed the building in an attempt to lynch him. Only the revolvers of "Black Jack" Bonfield and his men held them at bay. Finally, the police chief arrived and arranged for the body to be exhibited. In the words of a contemporary writer:

> A line was quickly formed, reaching up the alley and across to Desplaines Street. The crowd passed in eager procession and was satisfied by a simple glance at the dull, cold face. The scene from the steps of the station was a most remarkable one. All the afternoon that line moved steadily along, and the officers were busily occupied in keeping it in order. The crowd increased rather than diminished and until darkness settled down they were still gazing at the dead murderer . . . for forty-eight hours his body was on exhibition and was viewed by thousands.[96]

Conflict between the races in Chicago was exacerbated by the practice of employing Negroes as strikebreakers. In the stockyard strikes of 1894 and 1904 and the steel strike of 1901, Negroes were brought in from the South with the promise of high wages. Often they were ignorant of the fact that a strike was in progress, and when it was over they would be discharged and sent home on special trains. In 1905, during a citywide teamster strike, Montgomery Ward's and Marshal Field's brought in southern Negroes to drive for them. Mobs roamed the streets, throwing rocks and pulling blacks off wagons and beating them senseless. Police muscle was active against the mobs, and by the end of the strike 18 men had been killed, 400 injured, and 900 arrested.[97]

During World War I more Negroes came up from the South. As a result, the black population doubled to 100,000 and began to spread to the heretofore all-white neighborhoods. A feature of Chicago always was the presence of rigid and well-known boundary lines between various groups, especially, but not exclusively, black and white. Thus youngsters grew up acutely aware of occasionally being on the wrong side of a racial line or the Irish-Polish or Italian-Jewish boundaries. In the World War I era, the chief point of friction was along Wentworth Avenue, which separated the black belt from the white stockyards district. A high school boy named Langston Hughes was just one of many beaten when he wandered across the boundary.[98] The black residential invasion was also resisted by the widespread use of bombs; between 1917 and 1919, twenty-four were exploded, but no arrests resulted.[99]

The stockyards district was dominated by the Ragen Colts, a gang consisting of some 2,000 mostly Irish boys and young men.* Though best known for athletics, the Colts were also election sluggers, and as one member said, "When we drop into the polls, others drop out."[100]

The increasing black population meant more political power for Negroes. In 1915 they elected an alderman, the city's first, and their great friend Big Bill Thompson was elected mayor. In Thompson's first term, 1915–1919, the percentage of blacks on the police force doubled to 2 percent of the 3,500-man department, and complaints of misconduct or bad treatment by white cops were at least investigated. Thompson also saved the Second Ward ghetto police station from closing. On the negative side, he opened up the black belt to the white vice operators such as Colisimo, and in 1916 the black alderman was one of those indicted, along with police chief Healy and several police captains.[101]

In the aftermath of the vice scandal and the growing racial tensions, Captain Max Nootbar was sent into the ghetto. There he clashed with a black vice operator, "Emperor" Jones, and flattened him as he had Ike Bloom. Jones retained Clarence Darrow to sue Nootbar for $50,000, but the captain defended his own case and won. Later he disarmed a gunman about to assassinate the Emperor, and Jones decided that Big Max was not such a bad fellow after all.

* James Ragen, brother of the gang's founder, became a major figure in the Annenberg wire services and was assassinated in 1946—a case that developed into a major scandal. One result was the dismissal of two police captains who had arrested the alleged murderers. Later one captain was murdered.

In the summer of 1919 came a classic race riot. In other cities racial clashes had occurred after an incident such as an alleged rape of or assault upon a white person. In New York City, for example, in August 1900, when a Negro stabbed a white detective to death in a West Side street near the black ghetto known as San Juan Hill, white citizens sought vengeance against all blacks. Later, the police department was criticized for its bias in making arrests by a Citizens' Investigative Commission with Frank Moss as counsel.[102] The partiality of the Chicago Republican regime to blacks rankled whites, particularly when Thompson praised heavyweight boxing champion Jack Johnson, who they thought was a despoiler of white women, but the Chicago riot was a direct clash over living space. On Sunday, July 27, stone-throwing incidents took place between whites and blacks at the 29th Street beach. A frightened black youngster drowned, and other blacks assumed (falsely) that he had been stoned to death. They demanded that a police officer present arrest some whites, but instead he attempted to arrest them and was mauled. In the ensuing disorder a Negro police officer shot and killed an armed black man. Within a few hours the rioting spread to nearby areas of the South Side as members of one race caught in a neighborhood predominantly occupied by another were beaten and in some cases killed. For the next four days mobs of toughs from both sides roamed about, and the whites, led by the Ragen Colts, invaded the black belt inflicting punishment.

The Chicago Police Department was largely drawn from the white working class, and this doubtless affected many of the department's attitudes. Of the 38 people killed in the riot, 7, all black, were killed by the police, while 16 whites and 15 blacks were killed by members of the opposing group. Early on it was clear that the militia was required, but Mayor Thompson and Governor Frank Lowden both hesitated, and the troops were not employed until the evening of the fourth day. In the interim many officials did not act responsibly. One white alderman announced to his constitutents that they should arm themselves because police captains had informed him that they could "no longer hold them."

The official investigation of the riot was critical of the police department, though some individual officers played a heroic role in the streets. Captain Nootbar stood in the middle of the rioting mobs shooting at each other and managed to calm them by words alone. Detective Sergeant Thomas Middleton, a black officer, toured the streets standing in an open car amid sniper fire urging peace. Later he was wounded while trying to halt a clash. The investigating commission generally praised the militia—one of the few instances in which such forces performed well.[103]

The formal end of the riot did not mark the end of racial hostility, and it became a fixture of city life from then on. On several occasions in

the 1920s police and black nationalists clashed with fatal results.* As
the city's upper classes saw a threat from the white ethnic working class,
so the latter saw a threat from blacks, and vice versa. More positively,
from World War I on the Chicago Police Department was one of the
few with any significant representation of blacks on the force, and several members of the race were appointed as captains.** Such gains arose
not from civil rights concepts, but from the strategic position blacks occupied at first in the Thompson machine and later in the dominant
Democratic organization. Again, those who might have provided moral
leadership for the city failed by omission or commission to work for
racial justice and harmony.

The legacy of violence affected the police department as much as
that of politics and corruption. Chicago invariably led major cities in the
relative numbers of police killed by citizens and citizens by police. Nor
could the violence be confined to the streets. While third-degree tactics
were common in many cities, as the Wickersham Commission reported,
inevitably the commission found Chicago one of the worst cities. In two
of the most notorious murder cases in the city's history, the murders of
Bobby Franks (1924) and Susan Degnan (1946), the police department
was embarrassed by having announced prior to the capture of the actual
murderers (in both cases brilliant University of Chicago students) that
confessions had been obtained from other suspects. In both instances,
the confessors turned out to be innocent citizens who alleged they had
been beaten.[106]

As in New York and elsewhere, notions of legality had no real influence on affairs. Darrow, the stereotypical rich, radical lawyer, had no
more faith in the law than Inspector Bonfield. As he explained:

> A trial is not won or lost in court, it is won or lost in the community.
> Judges and juries are moved by the currents of opinion that seep into
> the courtroom from the newspapers and the streets and the market place.
> A person accused of a crime is instantly convicted in the headlines, and
> he must win his acquittal in the headlines.[107]

Many policemen and prosecutors entirely concurred.

In Chicago, unlike New York, the political choice was not between
reform and the political machine, but between the machine and or-

---

* For example, in June 1920 a black nationalist group burned an American flag,
killed two whites, and wounded a black policeman. The leader of the group was
hanged.[104]

** In 1930 blacks constituted about 5 percent of the city population and 2 percent of the police force,[105] a comparative ratio more favorable to blacks than
exists in many cities today.

ganized crime. Thus in reality the policy debate in police administration was not strict enforcement versus a certain degree of tolerance of vice, but between tolerance and wide-open. Given such a political environment, neither the city administration nor its police force could ever hope to come to grips with its real challenge, the culture of violence. In the twentieth century Chicago remained a brawling, wide-open nineteenth-century city. For some this constituted its charm, for others its shame

7

California: The New Breed (1901–1942)

In April 1903, a man being held for robbery and murder escaped from the county jail in Bakersfield, California, and fled to the city's red-light district, where, with a companion, he barricaded himself in a gambling joint. A posse led by Deputy Sheriff Will Tibbett stormed the house, killed the escapee, and captured the other man. But Tibbett and his brother-in-law, the town marshal, were both killed. Tibbett left behind four children, including a son, Lawrence, who grew up to become a world-famous opera singer. Among the large crowd, watching this drama of the fast-disappearing Old West, was a twelve-year-old friend of the Tibbett children. That boy's father would also become a murder victim, but that was years in the future, and by then the boy would be the state's leading law enforcement officer. His name was Earl Warren.[1]

THE PARIS OF AMERICA

Historically, California has comprised two distinctive sections, north and south, with the former dominant until the 1920s. It was in the north that gold was discovered, water was plentiful, and the West's most important city, San Francisco, emerged. The south was comparatively barren of resources, particularly water, and its principal city, Los Angeles, was for a long time a sleepy village on the edge of the desert.

Beginning with the gold rush days, San Francisco was a dynamic city with a mixture of ethnic groups, "attracting the blood of all lands and the law of none."[2] The city's first political boss, Senator David Broderick, an alumnus of Tammany, was killed in a duel with State Supreme Court Justice David Terry. Years later, such bad blood developed between Terry and fellow Californian, U.S. Supreme Court Justice Steven Field, that the latter had to be assigned a federal bodyguard. One night the two jurists met in a restaurant, and the bodyguard killed the unarmed Terry. When the guard was indicted for murder, the U.S. Supreme Court took jurisdiction away from the state courts and exonerated him.[3]

California was also as stringent in its treatment of minorities as any southern state. The Mexicans, who had been the dominant element before the gold rush, were quickly reduced to peonage, and the Chinese who arrived afterward were periodically massacred. At the turn of the century the Japanese became the leading menace, and in 1900 Mayor James Phelan of San Francisco ordered them to be segregated in schools and housing.[4]

Given its relatively short history and frontier conditions, California had no native elite (save for the Spanish landowners who were shoved aside), and power belonged to those who controlled the most money. At the beginning of the twentieth century, the state was virtually a fiefdom of the Southern Pacific Railroad. Office holders from the governor on down were its servants, the dominant Republican party its vehicle for control.

In the cities the usual political machines flourished in alliance with local vice operators. San Francisco in particular became world-famous as a sin city, and its Barbary Coast waterfront dives were as well known as New York's Tenderloin or Chicago's Levee. The more discriminating customers, though, did their sinning in the uptown Tenderloin off Market Street in the city's principal business district. A third vice area was centered in Chinatown, which provided underground passages, opium dens, and tong warriors to thrill the white tourists, obtain their money, and confirm their prejudices about Orientals.

San Francisco's first cops had been the vigilantes of mining camp days and their tradition lived on into the twentieth century though in 1856 a regular police department had been formed. The youth gangs of the city were notably violent, and the term "hoodlums" was coined to describe them.* Given the violence of the city and its widespread vice, the police force was both rough and corrupt. The Barbary Coast was a particularly tough beat. A persistent legend relates that in the 1890s six policemen were overpowered one by one and shanghaied in the dive of one Calico Jim, who then left town. Upon return from their voyage, it is

* The origin of the name is uncertain. It may have stemmed from an individual name such as Hodlum or a gang rallying cry, "Huddle 'em."[5]

said, the police drew straws and the winner tracked Calico to Peru and killed him with six bullets, one for each man.* Officers patrolling the Coast, in addition to their usual guns and clubs, took a cue from the sailors and carried large knives useful for close-quarters fighting. In one incident Sergeant Thomas Langford, attacked by several men whom he found burglarizing a store on Pacific Street, drew his knife and cut off the head of one of the thieves.[7]

Chinatown was a more pleasant area to work, since the local gamblers paid off handsomely and never complained. In 1904 a San Francisco newspaper estimated the Chinatown gambling payoffs at $8,000 to $9,000 per month.[8] Some other districts were equally profitable, and San Franciscans accepted police corruption as a normal feature of life. As Jake Ehrlich, dean of the city's criminal lawyers, has explained:

> Always a robust-minded town, San Francisco had convinced itself that vice was a necessary evil. There were many, as a matter of fact, who weren't nearly as convinced that it was as evil as they were that it was necessary. All were aware, however, that the police were not exactly overpaid, but most assumed that they were able to pick up enough extra money here and there to subsidize the deficit between what they received and what it took to support them and their families.[9]

Police violence, too, drew few complaints until 1901. In that year the cops were utilized to break a major strike. The labor organizers, noting the reason for their failure and the fact that the president of the Board of Police Commissioners was also the president of the Chamber of Commerce,** decided that they must neutralize the police. Consequently, they formed a political party, and in the November elections captured the mayor's office. Within a short time, San Francisco became the strongest union town in the country, with the closed shop and high wages the rule.

The genius behind this success was neither an old-style boss nor a radical reformer, but a brilliant young lawyer. Abe Ruef was born in San Francisco in 1864, two years after his French-Jewish parents came to the city. At eighteen he received his Bachelor of Arts in classics from the University of California at Berkeley, and by twenty-one had graduated from law school and been admitted to practice. The young man had a flair for politics and organized and briefly ran a reform club with his friends John H. Wigmore, later dean of Northwestern University Law School and one of the most prominent legal scholars of his time, and

---

* Though this story is repeated in the official history of the San Francisco Police Department,[6] its authenticity is dubious. Nevertheless, the police believed it and acted accordingly.

** Like many eastern cities, San Francisco and Los Angeles maintained a board of civilian police commissioners.

Franklin K. Lane, who became Woodrow Wilson's Secretary of the Interior.[10]

Ruef was one of those dynamic individuals bound to succeed in any field he chose. As it happened, he drifted into the local Republican machine and then, in 1901, became the unofficial leader of the Union-Labor party. He installed as mayor a popular orchestra leader, Eugene Schmitz, who was president of the Musicians' Union. Schmitz knew little of politics but was handsome, debonair, and made a useful front.

The advent of the labor government meant that cops could no longer crack workers' heads, but its effect on vice was less restricting. The previous mayor, Jim Phelan, whose personal honesty was apparently beyond doubt, had favored restraint as opposed to a wide-open town, but, as in Chicago, San Francisco's restraint looked like other places' wide-open, and even after Phelan left office his appointees continued to dominate the four-man Board of Police Commissioners, being replaced by laborites at the rate of one per year. Meanwhile, in 1901 one Jerome Bassity (also known as Jere McGlane) became the city's vice lord, à la Colisimo in Chicago. Bassity, an opium user, was a bad choice who attracted much unfavorable publicity by shooting up Tenderloin joints and wore expensive diamonds on his fingers and toes. A reporter described him as "possessing a moral intelligence scarcely higher than that of a trained Chimpanzee ... [with] low, cunning lights in the small, rapacious, vulture like eyes ... [and a] low, dull, uncomprehending brow."[11]

In 1905, Union-Labor was re-elected for a third term and took complete control of the city, including the Board of Police Commissioners, which promptly elevated a labor man, Detective Sergeant Jerry Dinan, to the chief's post. While Ruef approved, he also worried. He recognized that the very scope of labor's power might lead to public scandal, and his own conduct was hardly exemplary. His law practice boomed as many individuals sought his counsel. One group of clients was the owners of French restaurants. The Paris of America was a great dining-out town and the restaurants provided excellent Gallic cuisine—on their ground floors. On the upper floors other aspects of French culture were available, which inspired police raids. The labor-dominated police commission sought to revoke the licenses of some of the restaurants, but after the owners secured Ruef as counsel, their licenses were saved.

The election had brought to power a new Board of Supervisors (City Council), simple men who had long heard that such a post was a road to riches. Ruef attempted to disabuse them of this notion, explaining that it was illegal for public officials to take bribes. When they pointed out that he was not doing badly himself, he made the distinction that it was no crime to retain him as a lawyer, since he did not hold office. Finally, he agreed to pay each supervisor $2,000 a year out of his own money if they would stay honest.[12] Thus San Francisco headed into the fateful year 1906 as a riproaring wide-open town where everybody—worker, prostitute, cop, vice operator, and politician—made money, though not exactly from each according to his ability or to each according to his need.

Even in a workers' paradise, however, there were some who were unhappy. First, there were the antivice crusaders such as Donaldine Cameron, a woman who ran a Presbyterian mission in Chinatown and frequently led the police in raids against the houses of prostitution. The leading foe of the Barbary Coast was Father Terence Caraher, pastor of St. Francis Church. "Terrible Terry," as the Pacific Street dive operators called him, established picket lines around their places, hauled them into court, and led police raids to chop up their premises. Father Caraher was a man of very strong views who disapproved of many things. He railed against public dancing and movie houses as vicious and immoral and condemned San Francisco's trolley cars as "dance halls on wheels . . . full of lewd women and beastly men."[13] So ferocious was he that police chiefs generally preferred to cooperate rather than risk the wrath of Terrible Terry. Another unhappy group was the Chamber of Commerce crowd, who had to pay union wages and no longer ran the city. The most important antilabor group, however, was the Progressives.

A Jew Under Torture

In the midst of the labor-management struggles of California there arose a political force which eventually overshadowed both groups. Progressivism came out of educated WASPs under the age of forty who sought individual realization beyond the corporate lockstep or the equally unappealing socialist doctrines. It was a type of middle-class revolt against bigness and impersonal power. As one of the Progressives wrote, "Nearly all the problems which vex society have their sources above or below the middle-class man. From above came the problems of predatory wealth. . . . From below came the problems of poverty and pig headed brutish criminality."[14] As an example of the emergence of the Progressives, while men like Congressman Grove Johnson of Sacramento were content to serve as spokesman for the Southern Pacific, accepting the financial rewards and political plums, his sons Hiram and Albert were not. The two young lawyers became leaders of the antivice fight which toppled the Sacramento political machine and, as city attorney, Hiram continued his attacks on prostitution and gambling. An angry Grove Johnson, in a public speech, described his sons as "one [Hiram] full of egotism and the other [Albert] full of booze."[15] The brothers moved to San Francisco and, true to their father's characterizations,

Albert died of alcoholism and Hiram got rich, famous, powerful, and so egotistical that he may have cost both Charles Evans Hughes and himself the Presidency.

The most important San Francisco reformer was Fremont Older, editor of the *Bulletin*. Older was in the great tradition of crusading journalists, and the Union-Labor party with its corruption affronted him. He suspected that the Chinatown gambling payoffs were going to Ruef and Mayor Schmitz. To obtain evidence, he put the sergeant who headed the Chinatown squad on the *Bulletin* payroll at $125 per month. The sergeant then admitted to receiving bribes but had no evidence against the higher-ups. To obtain this information, it was necessary to persuade the boss gambler, Chan Cheung, to talk. Therefore Older arranged to have him kidnapped, held incommunicado, and threatened with a murder indictment in order to scare a confession out of him. But the aged Chinese refused to talk, and the plan fell through.[16]

After the 1905 election mobs of laborites danced under Older's window and hooted him and his wife as they walked along the street.[17] On the verge of a nervous breakdown, he left San Francisco for Washington, where he attempted to persuade President Theodore Roosevelt to assist in smashing the labor government.* Specifically, Older wanted Roosevelt to assign United States Special Prosecutor Francis Heney and Secret Service Agent William Burns to San Francisco. At the time the two were in the midst of prosecuting a U.S. senator and congressmen in connection with land frauds in Oregon. After some reluctance it was agreed that the government would release them for private hire. The three men, Older, Heney, and Burns, were to lead one of the most dramatic graft probes in American history because their target was not simply a few dishonest officials, but the corporate structure behind. In effect, they would adopt Lincoln Steffens's view that capitalism was the root of corruption.

Francis Heney was the archetypal crusading prosecutor. As a small boy he had moved to San Francisco with his family and grew up in the tough "south of the slot" (south of Market Street) section. Though he weighed only 125 pounds, Heney developed a reputation for fighting and was later expelled from the University of California at Berkeley after he challenged another student to a gunfight. Eventually he received a law degree and settled in Arizona. In 1891 he shot and killed a local doctor. The incident was to be a subject of controversy in Heney's later career,

---

* Older might not have been permitted to go ahead with his plan, since his publisher, R. A. Crothers, was lukewarm. But in 1904 the publisher himself was slugged from behind and an investigating detective declared that "it was a case of too many scotch highballs." Crothers demanded that the officer be broken, but Ruef instead had him made a sergeant.[18]

with his enemies claiming cold-blooded murder and his friends self-defense. The agreed-upon facts are that Heney was handling a divorce for the man's wife, and the doctor and the lawyer tangled. The lawyer had a gun and the doctor did not, and Heney killed the man.[19] Later, he returned to California. In the eyes of Theodore Roosevelt this was an ideal man to uphold the rule of law, and in 1904 he appointed Heney as special federal prosecutor. William Burns was an Ohioan who had joined the Secret Service in 1891 and made a great reputation as a detective, including sending a high official of the San Francisco mint to jail for theft. In 1911 Justice Department investigators accused Burns and Heney of rigging the Oregon prosecution to pack the jury with political enemies of the defendants.[20] (See page 268.)

At the outset Heney realized that the investigation would be expensive, and Older obtained financial support from former Mayor Phelan and Rudy Spreckels, a local millionaire who put up $200,000. Older also obtained Heney's appointment as a special district attorney, while Burns worked without official position in charge of a small army of private detectives. In April 1906, before the investigation could get under way, an earthquake leveled large portions of the city, an event which put the public in a serious mood.

The investigation and prosecution which followed extended over four years and involved so many complexities that a full explanation would require a separate book.[21] At the outset Ruef, in a bold move, attempted to have himself appointed district attorney to stop the investigation. This was blocked by the courts, helped by the presence of a mob which as Heney said "put the fear of God into that Judge."[22] The crowd had been assembled by stories in Older's paper; later, a lynch mob attacked Ruef, who was only saved by the combined forces of Chief Dinan's police and a crowd of Tenderloin gunmen.[23]

Next, Burns had Ruef arrested for bribery in the French restaurant cases, and the judge, bitterly hostile to Ruef, turned him over to the custody of a specially appointed elisor (one who acts in the place of the sheriff or coroner), William Biggy, a former police commissioner. Biggy held Ruef in a private home, and Burns was allowed to interrogate him at will, seeking a confession. Later, Burns and Biggy moved Ruef to Mayor Schmitz's former home, where Ruef slept in a bed under which was a strongbox which Burns called the mayor's "treasure chest," though Schmitz claimed it was to store his violin. When Ruef asked for reading material, Burns and Biggy supplied books such as *Half a Rogue* and *The Malefactor*.[24]

It was an unusual situation to say the least, in that a defendant was given over to the custody of his prosecutors, who put him under various psychological pressures. One popular magazine of the time described the Ruef interrogation as "A Jew under Torture."[25] A confession was needed, since other evidence was not forthcoming. However, the resourceful Burns and Older also capitalized on the machinations of Terrible Terry. Skating rinks had become popular in San Francisco, but Father Caraher denounced them as places where young girls were seduced. Burns planned to have the Board of Supervisors introduce an ordinance forbidding children under eighteen to patronize the rinks unless accompanied by their parents. Such a rule would destroy business, and to defeat it the rink owners would have to pay off the supervisors. Burns had discovered that one supervisor who also owned a rink was a fugitive embezzler from Oklahoma. To win the man's cooperation, Older made up a dummy newspaper with headlines exposing him. Shown the paper, he agreed to cooperate and arranged the bribe.[26] Several supervisors were arrested, and some of them began to talk. Ruef, promised immunity by Burns, also confessed to grafting, and as result Schmitz and Chief Dinan were indicted.

At this point the San Francisco business community was deliriously happy at the disgrace of the labor government, but its joy was shortlived. Ruef further confessed to receiving bribes from the United Railroads (URR) traction company, and its chief officers were indicted, including the president, Pat Calhoun; his assistant, Thornwell Mullally; and Tirey Ford, URR general counsel and former attorney general of California. Immediately the whole conflict changed, and the business community began to fight the prosecution bitterly.

Pat Calhoun, grandson of the great John C., was a worthy opponent of Heney, having fought a duel in Georgia while representing the interests of J. P. Morgan and Company. Calhoun flooded San Francisco with private detectives under Luther Brown of Los Angeles, and with Brown came the state's foremost criminal lawyer, Earl Rogers. The city became a virtual battleground as private detectives trailed one another, investigated jurors, and shot it out in the city streets while bombs exploded in witnesses' homes. Luther Brown kidnapped Fremont Older and allegedly was taking him to be murdered when the editor was rescued by a posse led by Franklin K. Lane. In turn, Burns's detectives raided Calhoun's headquarters at gunpoint. In the midst of this a new nonlabor mayor was elected, and William Biggy was appointed chief of police.

The fighting in the courtroom was as venomous as in the streets. Heney and Rogers traded insults; Rogers spoke of Heney's having shot a man in the back, and Heney recited a tale of various drunken exploits by Rogers. The press was equally hysterical. Hearst's *Examiner* printed cartoons of Heney with an X marking the spot on his neck where a bullet might enter. On Friday, November 13, 1908, a man shot Heney in open court, the bullet going in where the X had indicated. Older held Heney in his arms while spectators knelt to pray, but Rogers whooped that Heney "got what was coming to him, but is too mean to die."[27] President

Roosevelt telegraphed a message of fire and brimstone, and lynching was in the air.

The assailant, an ex-convict who had been thrown off a jury by Heney, was taken to jail, where he blew his brains out with a Derringer. Burns, who had personally searched him, swore that it was murder. Chief Biggy denied it, claiming that the gun was concealed in a boot. Burns, having made Biggy chief, had fallen out with him when Biggy resisted Burns's attempts to run the police department. The prosecution forces now demanded that the chief be sacked. Biggy then fell off a police launch traversing San Francisco Bay and drowned. The only witness, the engineer of the launch, went insane.

With Heney near death, Hiram Johnson took over the prosecution of Ruef. The immunity Burns had offered for his confession was not honored on the grounds that Burns had been acting as a private citizen. In summing up the case against Ruef, Johnson told the jury that a not-guilty verdict would be proof that they were bribed.[28] With incipient lynch mobs roaming the streets, the members of the jury were careful not to put themselves under that suspicion, and Ruef was convicted and sent to prison.

He was the only one. The others were acquitted or the juries could not agree. Heney recovered, but the tide quickly turned. He ran for district attorney in 1909 but was defeated by a Stanford football hero, Charles Fickert. In the same contest, Patrick Henry "Pinhead" McCarthy, president of the Building Trades Union, was elected mayor. Upon taking office, DA Fickert dropped all charges, while McCarthy declared for a wide-open San Francisco, saying he would make it "the Paris of America." The prosecution's tactics had backfired. Spreckels and Phelan, who bankrolled the investigation, were revealed as owners of a rival traction group to the URR, the coercion and entrapment tactics utilized became generally known, and *The Nation* spoke for most opinion when it said:

> Even a reformer cannot turn despot and run the machinery of government himself without provoking an immediate reaction. The best kind of reform is that which comes from the people themselves by regular democratic means, and not that which emanates from a handful of men financed from the well-filled purse of a business rival of some of the men accused of wrong.[29]

In 1910, Hiram Johnson was elected governor, bringing in a Progressive administration which broke the power of the Southern Pacific Railroad. Heney failed of election to the U.S. Senate in 1914, losing to Jim Phelan, and in 1918 lost the governorship. Due to his unpopularity in San Francisco, he moved to Los Angeles and eked out a living at law. In

1931, he was appointed a superior court judge for Los Angeles County. Spreckels and Calhoun both went bankrupt a few years after the trial.*

Shortly after the prosecution ended, Fremont Older repented his role in the case, believing that Ruef had been railroaded. He therefore took the lead in attempts to free him but was unsuccessful. In 1914 the California Supreme Court did order his release, but on a technicality the order was overturned.**

"Sunny Jim" Rolph was elected mayor in 1911, and served for twenty years, only leaving to become governor. The wave of antivice activity which was sweeping the nation had its effect in San Francisco. In 1912, a Chicago police captain toured the Barbary Coast and declared it worse than the Levee.[30] In 1916 vice chieftain Jerome Bassity was run out of town. Finally, in 1917, the Coast, along with other red-light districts across the country, was shut down as a war measure. After that, San Francisco vice had to be discreet; i.e., it could not advertise in the newspapers.

MURDEROUS TIMES AND THE BLAST

Given the prosperity of northern California, labor was a valuable commodity there. In the barren south, many of whose residents were sickly and had immigrated in the hope that the desert air would benefit their health, a supply of cheap labor was readily available. In contrast to the cultural diversity of the north, most of the residents in the south were from midwestern states and of middle American culture—in the 1920s, for example, the annual Iowa Day picnic in Los Angeles would bring out 150,000 former Hawkeyes[31]—and Angelenos therefore tended to be conservative. Thus, if San Francisco was the best labor town in America, Los Angeles was probably the worst.

Under the leadership of General Harrison Gray Otis, publisher of the *Los Angeles Times*, the city followed a strong open-shop, antiunion policy. Otis, a Civil War veteran and native of Ohio, had come to California in 1876, and in addition to having his newspaper interests had made a fortune in real estate. During the Spanish-American War and

* Calhoun, however, recouped part of his fortune. In 1931 Lincoln Steffens published his autobiography, and with his usual inaccuracy described Calhoun as dead and made a number of allegations against him. The very much alive Calhoun threatened to sue, and the publishers had to withdraw the early copies of the book. Calhoun was killed in 1943, at the age of eighty-seven, when he was struck by a car while returning from an all-night party.

** Justice Frederick Henshaw, who had voted to release Ruef, had signed the papers even though he had not actually been present at the hearing. Later the justice was revealed to have taken a $400,000 bribe in an unrelated case. The incident led to California adopting a provision for the recall of judges.

Philippine insurrection he had served as a major general. Many opponents attributed the antiunion policy to General Otis's cussedness, but in reality he simply acted in accordance with economic determinism. The south could not compete with the north unless production costs could be maintained at significantly lower levels to offset the relative lack of resources. In effect, southern California was in the position of an underdeveloped nation which could achieve economic growth only by increasing the productivity of its work force. In 1910 the cost of doing business in Los Angeles was about 40 percent lower than in San Francisco owing to the differential wage policy. If unions could succeed in establishing themselves in the south, the differences would disappear.[32] Thus the law enforcement agencies of Los Angeles, assisted by various private police, were utilized to combat union operations.

Beginning in 1907, the forces of organized labor undertook a major effort to unionize Los Angeles. Among the leaders of the drive was P. H. McCarthy, soon to be mayor of San Francisco. Behind the scenes they were supported by San Francisco business interests anxious to eliminate the Los Angeles differential. The struggle attracted national attention and the big people of the American left, such as Eugene Debs, Bill Haywood, and Emma Goldman, journeyed to Los Angeles to fight the *Times*. Similarly, business organizations throughout the country contributed funds to back General Otis.

The clashes between union and management were bloody. In 1910 the city passed the toughest antipicketing law in the country. Otis himself played the role of general, racing around town from one trouble spot to another with a cannon mounted on the hood of his car.[33] His home, known as the Bivouac, became a fortress. On October 1, 1910, the *Los Angeles Times* building blew up and twenty-one persons were killed.

The union men insisted that leaking gas had caused the explosion. The city police department was not sufficiently skilled to conduct the investigation, and William Burns was retained to assist it. General Otis, who had publicly attacked Burns in the San Francisco graft prosecution, was outraged by the choice. As special counsel the authorities appointed Earl Rogers. Rogers and Burns were not exactly on friendly terms after their war in San Francisco, and in theory it *was* a terrible choice, but it worked.

After San Francisco, Burns had organized a private detective agency. The big businessmen whose lives he had made miserable were realists; they held no grudges and quickly put Burns on retainer. One of his first clients was the American Bankers Association, which dropped its previous relationship with the Pinkerton Agency. At the time of the Los Angeles case, Burns was already investigating a series of bombings of construction projects throughout the United States. Among the suspects were Ortie McManigal and Joseph B. MacNamara, the latter a brother of James J. MacNamara, secretary-treasurer of the International Association of Bridge and Structural Iron Workers, a prominent leader in the AFL and personal friend of its president, Samuel Gompers. Burns immediately suspected J. B. MacNamara and McManigal of complicity in the Los Angeles case. In 1911 the two men were arrested in Detroit by Burns' men accompanied by a special detail of Chicago police detectives. They were then secretly removed to Chicago and held for two weeks in the home of one of the Chicago officers, as Burns wrote, to avoid the "technicality" of a writ of habeas corpus.[34] There Burns used psychological ploys to persuade McManigal to confess. It was the Ruef case all over again. McManigal gave in, implicating the MacNamara brothers in the bombing of the *Times* as well as a number of other explosions. J. J. MacNamara was seized in Indianapolis and taken to California. Eventually kidnapping charges were brought against Burns, but nothing came of them, since he was always careful to have local officers with him so that technically he was not the one making the arrest.

When the MacNamaras were brought to Los Angeles, the general view outside business circles was that they were innocent. Organized labor from Gompers down rallied behind the accused and raised a huge defense fund to retain Clarence Darrow. Simultaneous with the bombing prosecution, the city was in the midst of a mayoral campaign between the Otis forces and the Socialist candidate, lawyer Job Harriman. Harriman's victory appeared likely, and the arrests only added to his momentum because most people saw them as a frame-up by the antiunion law enforcement authorities.

The Otis forces were obviously desperate, since loss of the election would mean loss of the police as an antilabor tool, and the incumbency of a Socialist mayor would make it impossible to sell the 17 million dollars in bonds required to finance various improvement schemes in which the city fathers had heavy investments. Harriman himself agreed to defend the prisoners in conjunction with Darrow.

As in the San Francisco trials, armies of detectives moved back and forth to shadow jurors and each other. A Darrow investigator was caught bribing a juror, and Darrow himself was accused of complicity. The arrest badly shook the great defense attorney, whose activities in the case had definitely skirted the law. For example, his brother-in-law had paid a prosecution witness to disappear, and Darrow was aware that the prosecution had bugged his office, learning a number of embarrassing facts. Worse, Darrow realized that the MacNamaras were guilty.[35]

At this moment, Lincoln Steffens decided to resolve the situation. According to his account he persuaded the MacNamaras to confess. In return, General Otis allegedly agreed to support nominal sentences and to drop the charges against other bombers still at large.[36] Lincoln Steffens was a credulous man all his life, but that he would really believe that the ferocious General Otis would agree to such an arrangement strains the imagination. The confessions of the MacNamaras in open court was a bombshell. Samuel Gompers wept, in the country at large a number of supporters went insane, and at least three killed themselves.[37] Job Harriman, who had not been told of the deal, was overwhelmingly beaten at the election.

J. B. MacNamara was sentenced to life imprisonment and his brother to fifteen years. The other bombers were eventually pursued and captured. Darrow himself was tried twice for jury bribing, with Rogers as his defense attorney, though the two hated each other. After a jury failed to reach a verdict, Darrow signed an agreement never to practice law in California and left the state to the jeers of organized labor and radicals, an opprobrium he shared with Lincoln Steffens. Theodore Roosevelt said Steffens "acted like an utter fool."[38] Darrow did have the satisfaction of beating Rogers out of his defense attorney's fee, just as Rogers persuaded the authorities not to pay Burns the promised rewards for solving the Times bombing.

The failure in Los Angeles doomed the labor movement in southern California for two generations and strengthened the antiradical posture in the state including San Francisco, where McCarthy was ousted as mayor. From then on, crews of strikebreakers merrily broke heads while the police either stood by or joined them. In 1919, after World War I and trouble with the IWW, the State Legislature passed a criminal syndicalism law, and by 1924, 128 men had been sentenced to San Quentin under it for terms of from one to fourteen years.[39]

Nationally, thirty-eight leaders of the Iron Workers were convicted at federal conspiracy trials held in Indianapolis after the Los Angeles case, and all were given prison sentences. The Los Angeles case would be a landmark in American history, giving the lie to the belief that social movements could not be stopped by applying law enforcement techniques. If the Times bombers had been acquitted or even convicted after a hard-fought trial, most people would probably have believed the case a frame-up. As a result of the confession, the public identified organized labor and socialists with murderous violence, and consequently many people were ready to believe the worst about both groups.

In 1916 San Francisco was again the scene of a great dock strike. Sunny Jim Rolph was mayor, and, though supported by labor, he was a vigorous law and order western cowboy type. Later, as governor, he would refuse to send the National Guard to stop a lynching in San Jose and afterward would congratulate the mob on their work.[40] Thus he allowed the police and private guards to support the employers. As one shipping executive said, "The way to keep the peace was to send several ambulance loads of union men to the hospital."[41] World War I was on at the time, and a number of other troubles swirled about the city. Within an eight-month period two policemen were shot dead in gun battles with anarchists. As a result, the police chief bought an armored car and issued rifles to his men.[42] The German consul and several of his agents were arrested for bombing British ships, and the militia was on the Mexican border fighting Pancho Villa.

The Chamber of Commerce, like other business elites, was pro-Allies and anxious for intervention. In July it scheduled a preparedness parade in imitation of a similar event that had been held in New York under the leadership of General Leonard Wood. In the circumstances of class conflict, organized labor refused to participate, and to some the parade seemed like a flexing of business muscles. As a center of class warfare, the city had attracted radical leaders including Emma Goldman and Alexander Berkman. In January Berkman had started a paper prophetically titled *The Blast*. Another local radical was a tough young Irishman from the East named Tom Mooney. In July, Mooney attempted to organize the United Railroads. The company resisted, and with police help Mooney and his supporters were beaten off. Mooney was well known to the police, having been a friend of the MacNamara brothers, and during various struggles against the Pacific Gas and Electric Company (PG&E) had himself been arrested with explosives, although he was acquitted at a trial.* Mooney's friend Warren Billings was not as fortunate, having been sent to Folsom Prison on similar charges. At the time of the parade Mooney was under periodic surveillance by PG&E detectives led by a former Pinkerton agent named Martin Swanson.

In the supercharged environment, warnings of violence against the parade were sent to the newspapers. However, the police chief chose to play golf on that day, leaving command of the protective forces to Captain Duncan Matheson, a Nova Scotia–born Scotsman noted for his stern morality and competence.

At 1:30 P.M. on Saturday July 22 Matheson blew his whistle to start the parade down Market Street. In the lead were Thornwall Mullally of the Chamber of Commerce and Mayor Rolph in his usual cowboy regalia. At 2:06, as a contingent of war vets passed Stuert Street near Market, a bomb exploded on the sidewalk, killing outright or fatally injuring ten persons and wounding forty. Captain Matheson quickly moved to the scene. Realizing the potential for mass panic, he coolly ordered the parade to continue, and the vets, many dripping blood, drew themselves to attention and marched onward. Even hostile writers agreed his action prevented worse casualties from panic.[44] As Matheson

---

* Mooney's friends claimed the explosives were planted in his boat. At the time of his arrest Mooney gave a false name but was identified by the Berkeley police chief, August Vollmer.[43]

dealt with the crowd, Lieutenant Steve Bunner, a former Abe Ruef bodyguard, surveyed the bloody scene and decided to wash it down with
firehoses, thus removing a considerable portion of the physical evidence.

In a hurried conference between the mayor and the police chief,
Captain Matheson was put in charge of a special "bomb" squad which
included Lieutenant Bunner, Sergeant Charley Goff, a former Jim Cor-
bett sparring partner who had once been Heney's bodyguard, and a
brash rookie named Draper Hand. Naturally radicals were suspect, and
even Fremont Older told people "it must be Mooney."[45] The police,
however, were not on good terms with District Attorney Charles Fickert,
since many of them were allied to other political factions. Sergeant
Goff, for example, despised the DA. In the circumstances Fickert frequently conducted his own investigations, further angering the cops.[46]
Since the PG&E detectives had been investigating Mooney for some
time, detective Swanson consulted with Fickert and entered into a secret
arrangement to assist in the case. Within a short period Mooney and
Billings were arrested and charged with the bombing. They were given
strong support by various left-wing and Irish groups, the latter providing as Mooney's defense attorney a Tammany wheelhorse, Bourke Cochran, formerly Charley Becker's lawyer. Nevertheless, the defendants
were convicted and sentenced to life in prison.*

The Mooney-Billings case was to become another great controversy
and a litmus test of ideology. According to Ernest Jerome Hopkins, a
strong partisan of Mooney's innocence:

> [I]n California today, if you express the belief that the real bomber
> escaped, that brands you as a revolutionary and, it may be *particeps
> criminis;* whereas if you say in a New York liberal group that Billings and
> Mooney set off the bomb, you are thereby and therefore a slave of a
> capital and a rotten log in the path of progress.[47]

In the initial stages, however, many people remembered the *Los Angeles
Times* case and were hesitant to go out on the limb for Mooney. Later,
there was strong evidence that key prosecution witnesses had committed perjury, and Fremont Older took the lead in the fight to save the
prisoners.

As with the graft trials or the *Times* case, partisans of both camps
broke every law in the book to "serve justice." Detectives working for
the defense trailed jurors and broke into Martin Swanson's office.[48] A
prominent Mooney supporter who was a Communist attempted to take
over the defense team for the party, but when he failed he switched
and became a spy for right-wing groups and was eventually convicted

---

* Mooney was actually sentenced to death; his sentence was then commuted
to life.

for burglary.[49] The prosecution forces battled among themselves. Captain Matheson arrested a state witness for perjury against the wishes of District Attorney Fickert. Detective Goff, now a lieutenant, went further and, working with federal agents and the Solicitor for the United States Department of Labor, John Densmore, bugged Fickert's office. Little of interest was heard regarding the Mooney case, but much came out about the operations of the district attorney's office. The McDonough brothers' bail bonding firm appeared to have a great deal of influence with the D.A. as well as the police department. Solicitor Densmore prepared a transcript of the conversation interspersed with is own comments on the Mooney case, and Goff leaked it to Fremont Older, who promptly published it.[50]

Fickert fought back, denouncing Older:

> Once before Older succeeded in dominating absolutely the District Attorney's office of this City and County. The base use which he made of it, he has confessed with groans of repentance. I shall save him from a second shame. Neither he nor anyone else shall control that office while I am its head.
>
> Whatever may be said of his motives, it may be argued they were for the purification of the city and for the punishment of crime. Here and now he is to the forefront, seeking the acquittal of red-handed murderers, the blood of whose innocent victims calls aloud not for vengeance, but for the just retribution of the law. With him, in this malign work are arrayed all the forces of evil in the city, all the anarchists of the United States, and the time has come, my fellow citizens, for you to know these things and knowing them to aid in upholding justice and seeing to it that San Francisco is not made the home and refuge of anarchism under Older and his criminal crew of Berkmans, Emma Goldmans, and Mooneys.[51]

For a topping the burly Fickert then slugged the elderly Older when next they met and had to be restrained from kicking the editor's prostrate body. During the incident an Older assistant ran to his paper's composing room yelling that Fickert had killed the editor, whereupon the night shift grabbed wrenches and raced to the scene, just missing the departing Fickert.[52]

Older continued to play his usual games. As an admirer described him, he would "bribe or do anything for justice."[53] When he learned of the bribe given to Supreme Court Justice Henshaw many years earlier, he offered to hold the story if Henshaw would order a new trial for Mooney. In 1920, to block Captain Matheson's appointment as chief of police, he persuaded Detective Draper Hand to go to Mayor Rolph and charge that Matheson had framed evidence against Mooney and Billings. The charge was not proved, though Rolph did pass over Matheson in favor of another man. After Matheson switched to support of a new trial, Mooney's defense lawyers withdrew their charges against Matheson, and in time Detective Hand was fired and later convicted of larceny.[54]

During the course of Older's various crusades he had feuded with the Hearst press, which on one occasion had urged vigilante action against him. Later Older characterized Hearst's efforts to backtrack from support for Fickert as those of "a rat deserting a sinking ship." But when the owners of the *Bulletin* rebuked Older for his preoccupation with Mooney, he grew alarmed at the prospect of losing his job and yielded to the urgings of his socialite wife that he accept a lucrative offer from Hearst. Older then became editor of the *San Francisco Call*, disappointing many of his liberal friends.*

The Mooney defense became a vehicle for various publicity stunts and fund-raising ventures ranging from grape boycotts to proposed national strikes. In 1931 Jimmy Walker, in the midst of his trouble as mayor of New York, journeyed to San Francisco to represent Mooney as attorney. Fickert had long since left office and fallen on hard times. Walker got Fickert drunk and wrung from him a statement supporting a new trial.[56] But it was to no avail for either Mooney or Walker, since Judge Seabury continued on Jimmy's trail and the California courts refused to grant Mooney a new trial. In the '30s the Communists moved in, and Mooney in jail became a useful propaganda and fund-raising device, with the Reds keeping the money.

Despite numerous appeals for a new trial or executive clemency, neither the California nor the federal courts, including the U.S. Supreme Court, afforded relief. Five consecutive California governors also refused to pardon. In essence, the courts and governors found the testimony of key prosecution witnesses credible despite periodic recantations followed by recantations of the recantations. For example, Older persuaded a prostitute to deny her eyewitness identification of Billings as the bomber, but she later accused Older of browbeating her.

The Mooney case was to drag on for twenty-three years with periodic rehearings including a habeas corpus petition which went on for thirteen months and permitted Mooney, though a prisoner, to be discreetly at large in San Francisco. It is likely that the tactics of the defense caused judges and governors to distrust their veracity as much as the defense distrusted the prosecution.

Mooney himself noted, however, that the same high-pressure tactics had been successful for the celebrated Charlotte Anita Whitney. Miss Whitney, a niece of United States Supreme Court Justice Steven Field and a Wellesley graduate, had been convicted of criminal syndicalism in 1919 on the grounds of her membership in the Communist Labor

* Though Older lived until 1935, neither of his autobiographies deals with his career after 1920. In the '30s, as editor of the San Francisco *Call-Bulletin*, Older was the nominal head of one of the most virulent antiradical papers in America.[55]

party. Her conviction was upheld by various courts, including the United States Supreme Court. However, in 1927, Governor Clement C. Young had pardoned her even without an application from the defendant, because she was "a lady of culture and refinement." Mooney's comment was that she had a "Rolls-Royce protest," while he had only a "Ford."[57]

The Mooney forces participated actively in California politics, sometimes with bizarre results. In 1922 they supported for governor the ultraconservative Friend Richardson, darling of the *Los Angeles Times*, who during his term did not pardon a single prisoner. Finally, in 1938 the Democratic candidate for governor, Culbert Olson, accepted financial support from the Mooney camp, signing a secret written agreement that if elected he would grant a pardon.[58] He was successful, and Mooney went free, but Billings, because of his previous conviction, had to wait. In granting the pardon, Governor Olson, in Altgeldian style, declared that the whole case had been a frame-up, and, like Altgeld, Olson too returned to obscurity after one term.

Mooney's first act as a free man was to ask his faithful wife for a divorce. He was not a lovable individual and is now largely forgotten. As the leading account of the case noted:

> Mooney often called for a Zola, but no Zola ever came. The case was too complex, the human qualities too mottled to stir the artist's spirit.... Mooney was vain and repelled many of his own friends.... He was a small man of mixed clay. Moreover, there was no execution to heighten the tragedy. The injustice simply dragged to its tardy, untidy end, which came in political acts of justice, slightly soiled by the circumstances of politics.[59]

Given the ambiguities of the case a new trial would have seemed in order, but the political leadership of the state, whether on the bench, in the legislative halls, or in the governor's mansion, failed, including the state's most popular and powerful politician, Hiram Johnson. The wounding of Heney had thrust Johnson into the limelight, and he had no intention of leaving it. While Johnson opposed the power of others, he strove mightily to build his own. State employee salaries were tapped for his campaign expenses, and in 1914 as governor he made a deal with the San Francisco vice interests, thus easily winning reelection, while the uncompromising "extremist" Heney was beaten for the Senate and eliminated as a rival. In 1912 Johnson was Theodore Roosevelt's vice presidential candidate on the national Progressive ticket, but he broke with TR over World War I and because he could not bear being number two. In 1916 California, a strong Republican state, went into the Democratic column, defeating Charles Evans Hughes for the Presidency. Many attributed it to Johnson's hostility after Hughes allegedly snubbed him, though the Hughes campaign in California had been badly conducted.

Governor Johnson himself was elected to the Senate, and for a time he tried to hold both offices, hating to give the governorship over to anyone else. He remained in the Senate until his death in 1944, making peace with the conservative factions, and because of his isolationist views became a favorite of William Randolph Hearst. In 1920 he turned aside proposals for the vice presidential nomination because as always, being number two had no appeal. The nomination went to Calvin Coolidge.[60]

In its restlessness and shifts, Johnson's career was typical of California politics. Given the dynamic growth of the state, most residents were rootless newcomers, particularly in the south. Only San Francisco had anything resembling an eastern population and politics. In Los Angeles between 1920 and 1930, a decade when the city population doubled, surpassing San Francisco, only 20 to 25 percent of the residents were native Californians, and half had been residents for less than five years. Adding to the unsettled atmosphere was the vast number of people who were old, sick, or failures, looking for panaceas, from religious revivals to various brands of socialism.

Political volatility was further enhanced by Progressive legislation which permitted cross filing, whereby candidates could run in Democratic, Republican, and Progressive primaries at the same time. Thus party labels meant little, and consistency and regularity were not necessary virtues. The key to success in California was not old family, a Tammany-style machine, or even money per se, but the ability to gain publicity. In this respect, the press, under publishers or editors like Otis and his son-in-law Harry Chandler, in LA, Fremont Older in San Francisco, Joseph Knowland in Oakland, Friend Richardson in Berkeley, and William Randolph Hearst everywhere, possessed enormous power. In southern California, a second force was organized religion, with its preachers and entrepreneurs made even more powerful by the introduction of radio, so that Los Angeles constantly struggled between the fundamentalist views of many citizens and Hollywood-style freethinking. Thus it was to press and pulpit that the rootless and discontented Californians turned for guidance between the two world wars.

PROFESSIONALISM

The Chiefs

The political climate which produced aggressive individualists independent of ties to party, class, or ethnicity was to have a similar effect in policing. In 1905 the sleepy college town of Berkeley, California, elected a popular local mailman, Gus Vollmer, as town marshal in charge of a six-man force. It was in this community of 20,000 that the precepts of police administrative science would be enthroned. With his election as marshal, Vollmer began a career which would make him the most prominent police chief in America and, despite the fact that his education ended with grade school, a university professor.

August Vollmer was born in New Orleans in 1876. When he was eight his father died, and his mother took the children to her family home in Germany for two years, then returned to New Orleans. Disturbed by the violence in that city, in 1890 she decided to move to California. In 1898 Vollmer, then living in Berkeley, enlisted in the army for the Spanish-American War and served in the Philippines. At twenty-nine, he was still happily delivering mail and playing at volunteer fireman when the publisher of the *Berkeley Gazette*, Friend Richardson, later state governor (1923–1926), and others persuaded him to run for marshal on an antivice ticket. The incumbent was accused of permitting gambling in Chinatown and of not enforcing the law forbidding the sale of liquor within one mile of the University of California campus.

In 1906 the Berkeley population doubled after the San Francisco quake, and in 1909 the marshal post was redesignated as chief of police. Vollmer instituted a number of innovations, including the distribution of the force based on better calculations of workload, the use of automobiles, the institution of formal training, and the adoption of scientific detection methods such as the polygraph. Vollmer was able to devote a good deal of time to systematic study, since unlike big-city chiefs, he did not have a heavy workload or intense political pressures to keep him occupied. The department also established close liaison with the university.[61] Thus Vollmer had a laboratory atmosphere impossible to create elsewhere, and gradually he developed a concept of police service which went beyond previous notions of administrative science.

While Vollmer shared the reformers' sentiments regarding both moral and administrative improvements, he also developed the idea of patrolmen as something more than efficient menials. He saw them as social workers dealing with a range of societal problems which manifested themselves in crime and disorder. In his view, policemen should become college-educated professionals akin to doctors or lawyers. While the distinction is a matter of emphasis rather than a rigid doctrine, reformers like Arthur Woods, Raymond Fosdick, and Bruce Smith could be seen as proponents of a bureaucratized police with some emphasis on social service, while Vollmer favored a socially sensitive police with some emphasis on bureaucratic efficiency. And while all of them urged what has been loosely labeled "professionalism," in Vollmer's case the meaning was more in accord with the definition of a profession: a dedicated body of educated persons comprising a distinctive corporate entity with a prescribed code of behavior. This was somewhat different from the good civil servants envisioned by earlier reformers, whose version of professionalism was in the more common usage of one who does a job well—for instance, a "professional" bus driver.

Carried to its logical conclusion, a bureaucratic police force would not require college-educated cops except at the top, while Vollmer's professional force would need them at all levels. In fact, the Berkeley Police Department began to obtain a steady flow of recruits from the university, so that in the early 1920s it included such men as William F. Dean, later major general in the United States Army, who was captured while commanding the 24th Division in the Korean War, and O. W. Wilson, Vollmer's protégé, who became dean of the University of California School of Criminology and superintendent of police of the city of Chicago (1960–1967). In one instance a black student athlete named Walter Gordon came to Vollmer threatening to break the windows of a restaurant which refused him service. By the time the interview ended Gordon had become a Berkeley cop. Later he rose to be governor of the Virgin Islands and then judge of the United States Court of Appeals.[62]

Vollmer was a new breed, one of the first great police reformers to arise from the service itself. Men like Woods, Fosdick, and Smith had come from solid upper-middle-class backgrounds, received Ivy League educations, and rubbed elbows with the Roosevelts, Wilsons, Rockefellers, and Morgans. In a nonpejorative sense they looked down at police from the heights of social prestige and never themselves thought of serving in a position below that equivalent to deputy police commissioner of a great city. Thus it was natural that they saw policemen as efficient servants. Vollmer and later police leaders like him, such as O. W. Wilson and William H. Parker of Los Angeles, looked upward from the lower strata of American society, and it was natural that they would want to convert policing into a profession akin to law or medicine, opting for the social worker, efficiency engineer, or scientific investigator role as it suited their taste or the public's. In similar fashion, Vollmer would embrace higher education for cops and the "scientific" fads and fancies of the moment, arguing strongly for IQ tests, the polygraph, or the latest theory of criminal behavior. Unfortunately, this would lead him to attach his name to many dubious writings which he would later regret. The well-educated easterners were always more scholarly and cautious.

Vollmer was also intensely ambitious and politically astute, a true California Progressive. He consistently promoted himself by public relations, claiming a first for everything, even though such innovations as police training were in effect before Vollmer's time. His friend, coauthor, and biographer Alfred E. Parker, basketball coach at Berkeley High

School, would go even further with embarrassing and grossly incorrect assertions, such as crediting Vollmer with the creation of the FBI.[63]

Naturally Vollmer took the lead in various cooperative associations such as the California Police Chiefs and the International Association of Chiefs of Police (IACP), but like Johnson and other California politicians he was also careful to brook no rivals. When the governor and Legislature finally agreed to create a State Bureau of Identification, largely through the efforts of Vollmer's friend Max Fischer, superintendent of identification in the Sacramento Police Department, Vollmer, as chairman of the advisory board, arranged for the directorship of the agency to go to a Berkeley officer, embittering Fischer.[64] In a letter to O. W. Wilson, then chief of Wichita, Kansas, Vollmer gave advice worthy of a Tammany boss. Vollmer told Wilson to

> ... prepare a tremendous, concentrated offense plan. ... Your friend [his political opponent] will be blasted out of the community before he realizes what has happened ... see that the entire town is covered so that no person escapes. ... Have the delivery boys of the opposition paper tailed so that you know their subscribers, and during your campaign, arrange to have the [sympathetic] *Wichita Eagle* placed in their hands.[65]

During World War I, Vollmer attempted to use political influence to obtain an appointment as a U.S. intelligence officer, but his application was turned down by the military.[66]

Although the police department and its chief received many accolades, its methods had little influence even in the Bay Area. Both the San Francisco and Oakland departments were quite traditional forces, and their commanders regarded Vollmer and his college boys as fine for the campus area but doubted their capacity to do "real police work." Captain Matheson, as chief of San Francisco detectives, declared:

> Give me the practical detective with actual experience in handling criminal cases and with ten such men I will do more work than any college professor or so-called expert can do with one hundred of his trained "nuts."[67]

Matheson's successor Charley Dullea (later chief of police)* clashed with Vollmer when the latter called the San Francisco cops "morons." Such was Dullea's revulsion that he would order his chauffeur to detour

---

* Charles Dullea, born in San Francisco in 1888, joined the force in 1914 after service in the United States Marines. By 1929 he was captain of inspectors (chief of detectives). In 1940 he was appointed chief of police; he served until the end of 1947. He was one of the best-known and most influential police officers in the U.S. and in 1947–48 was president of the IACP. He served later as member of the California Adult Authority (parole board).

around Berkeley.[68] Other observers, though sympathetic to Vollmer's ideas, felt he operated in an atypical environment and his methods would never work in a major city. Therefore, in 1923, when he accepted appointment as chief of police in Los Angeles, there was skepticism over his prospects.

Los Angeles had not had a distinguished police history. Scandals were common, and Vollmer was the sixteenth chief in twenty years. One of the most colorful of his predecessors was Charles Sebastian, a handsome Missourian who was named chief in 1911. In 1915 he resigned to run for mayor but was accused of illicit relations with young ladies. Defended by Earl Rogers, he beat the charge and was elected. The next year, however, the accusations were proved, and to them were added new charges of extortion. Sebastian countered by staging a phony attempt on his life, but the plot was revealed and he resigned.[69]

The real power in the department lay outside, in men like Reverend "Fighting Bob" Shuler, an antivice crusader whose radio preaching made him one of the most influential men in the city. Fighting Bob was president of the Ministerial Association and a stern moralist; he even dropped his support of a woman school board member because she smoked a cigarette.[70] Shuler had been instrumental in bringing Vollmer to Los Angeles, giving approval after a personal visit to Berkeley. Another influential conservative was Harry Haldeman, president of the far right Better America Foundation. A less ideological power broker was Guy McAfee, a former detective who served as one of the city's gambling bosses. The city's law enforcement officials generally tended toward the conservative side, and in 1922 the police chief, county sheriff, and United States Attorney were all revealed to be members of the Ku Klux Klan.[71] The city also had one of the most aggressive Red squads in the country under the famous Captain Red Hines.* In general the members of the city elite, led by the *Los Angeles Times* and the Better America Association, were hostile to attacks on the police department since it was their defender against the radicals and labor organizers. But the persistent criticism led them to give Vollmer a try.

When he arrived in August, he arranged to meet with emissaries of the underworld, who warned him that he must achieve a *modus vivendi* or face all-out opposition. Many police chiefs, even honest ones, assumed that gambling interests must be tolerated because of their power and the belief that organized criminals were helpful in keeping common

---

* William "Red" Hines (1897–1952) joined the LAPD in 1921 after long army service. He was assigned to duty as an undercover operator and penetrated the IWW. He then was made an acting captain in charge of the Red squad, a position he held for some fifteen years. In 1938 a reform administration broke him to patrolman and sent him to walk a beat in the sticks. In 1943 he retired from the LAPD and worked as a private security consultant.

Smedley Butler, here shown in his specially designed and tailor-made uniform as Safety Director of Philadelphia, 1924, was one of America's greatest military heroes. But Philadelphia's policemen were not Marines, and the citizens were not native insurgents. *Culver Pictures.*

Arthur Woods (right), New York City Police Commissioner (1914-1917), and his successor (below), Lieutenant Richard Enright (1918-1925). The victory of Enright, the career cop, over the Harvard patrician determined the direction of the New York City Police Department for half a century. (Woods) *Courtesy of the New-York Historical Society. Photograph by Pach Brothers.* (Enright) *Courtesy, Alfred J. Young Collection, N.Y.C.*

The Strongarms: New York City
Detectives John Broderick (above)
and John Cordes (right) in the 1930s.
Whether they were being shot at,
decorated, or disciplined, this dynamic
duo made more headlines than any
other cops on the force. (Broderick)
The News, *New York's Picture Newspaper.* (Cordes) The News, *New
York's Picture Newspaper.*

Three of America's leading policemen in 1936: Colonel H. Norman Schwartzkopf of the New Jersey State Police (far left), New York City Police Commissioner Lewis J. Valentine (far right), and FBI Director J. Edgar Hoover (next to Valentine) meet with prosecutors to discuss the Lindbergh kidnapping. The case caused relations among the lawmen to become somewhat strained. *Wide World Photos.*

The Haymarket Riot, Chicago, 1886. The first radical bombing in America killed eight policemen, and the arrests, trial, and executions which followed divided the country. From a contemporary artist's rendering. *Culver Pictures.*

A contemporary artist's impression of the U.S. Army encampment during the Pullman strike, Chicago, 1894. The Pullman strike was only one of many violent incidents in Chicago's history. The police were sympathetic to the strikers, so federal troops had to perform police duty. *Culver Pictures.*

Key figures in the San Francisco Graft Probe, 1909. Seated at left is prosecutor Francis Heney; standing left, Detective William J. Burns; standing right, editor Fremont Older; seated right, financial backer Rudy Spreckels. *Courtesy, The Bancroft Library.*

Cops grill Tom Mooney (seated center) in the San Francisco bombing, 1916. At left is Lieutenant Steven Bunner. Standing behind Mooney is Captain Duncan Matheson; to his left is Police Chief David White. Facing Mooney is District Attorney Charles Fickert. The case became the political trial of the century. *Courtesy, The Bancroft Library.*

Berkeley Police Chief August Vollmer (above) and Alameda County District Attorney Earl Warren (below), 1920s. The professionalization of California police resulted from the propaganda of Vollmer and the political power of Warren. (Vollmer) *Courtesy, The Bancroft Library.* (Warren) *Wide World Photos.*

Allan Pinkerton and his agents with the Union Army, 1862. The young
immigrant laid the foundations for detective and secret-service work in America.
The Bettman Archive, Inc.

FBI agent-in-charge Melvin Purvis (right) and Treasury Detective Chief Elmer Irey (below). The dapper Purvis raced about the country shooting down the likes of Dillinger and Pretty Boy Floyd before he quit for Hollywood. The mild-mannered Irey brought down Al Capone and the Huey Long and Pendergast machines with a pencil. (Purvis) *Wide World Photos.* (Irey) *Wide World Photos.*

crooks such as burglars and con men out of town. Vollmer himself favored red-light districts,[72] but he did not go along with the gamblers, and his attacks on vice were strongly supported by the press. Vollmer also stepped up the drive against ordinary criminals, warning that "many will die," and in fact several were gunned down by police.[73]

In these circumstances, the familiar underworld response is to discredit the individual opponent. Vollmer's appointment as chief of police was challenged as illegal, since he had not taken a civil service exam. He was required to do so, and he passed easily. However, he was not to escape humiliation. A woman accused him of breach of promise and allegedly attempted suicide over him. Vollmer, who was divorced at the time, was tall, goodlooking, and not unattractive to women. Though he denied the charges and filed a countersuit, the case received considerable publicity.* Eventually the charges were dropped, but by that time Vollmer had returned to Berkeley and was married to another woman.

Vollmer's approach in Los Angeles was a bit pedantic. He ordered IQ tests and advanced bright officers over the heads of slower counterparts—"low grade mental defectives," according to Vollmer—and presented the city with a complete plan for revamping the department. The document looked like an academic symposium featuring a series of articles by a diverse collection of individuals ranging from Ph.D.s with their pet theories of crime causation to radicals such as an IWW lawyer who indicted capitalism and the Red squad, on to ordinary police commanding officers who complained about the threats from movies and the Chinese or Negroes. When Vollmer had arrived, he had formed a "crime crusher" squad; in the planning document the lieutenant in command of it explained its function was "to knock their ears back."[75] It must have seemed a weird document to the city fathers. In the summer of 1924, with his first year in office coming to a close, the Los Angeles press predicted accurately that the first of September would see "the end of August," and Vollmer returned to Berkeley.

Vollmer was to continue as Berkeley police chief until 1932. He headed the police task force of the Wickersham Commission set up in 1929 to survey the effects of Prohibition on law enforcement. Vollmer's 1931 report stressed the familiar themes of the need for strengthening the authority of police chiefs, though like New York's Commissioner Enright he preferred career men to "outsiders." There was also the

---

* Sex charges were not a rare practice in Los Angeles in that era. A few years later a crusading city councilman was enticed to a pretty widow's house, seized by the vice squad, and taken downtown minus his trousers. A detective writing of the incident tended to support the councilman's claim that the trousers had been removed by the police in order to embarrass him. Later, a member of the police commission was the victim of a similar plot but foiled it.[74]

usual call for educated police recruits. The report had little effect on the police profession, since there were no institutionalized mechanisms to implement it. Professor Chafee's report on third-degree tactics was much more influential because the Supreme Court began to look at police practices in this area.[76]

Vollmer's influence was more apparent in the careers of the young men like O. W. Wilson whom he sent out from the Berkeley Police Department and in Vollmer's getting professorships at the University of Chicago and California. The Chicago post came about through the patronage of Charles Merriam, while the appointment at Berkeley was a result of short-term support from Rockefeller money. However, the scholarly world did not really take him seriously, and in some semesters only one student signed up for his classes.[77] In time a school of criminology was founded at Berkeley with O. W. Wilson as dean, but it emphasized the bureaucratic more than the social work aspects of policing, and its scholarly impact was limited. In the 1950s the university sought to close the school, but political pressure and the appointment of a more academically oriented dean saved it for a time.*[78]

Until the late 1930s the police of California with the exception of Berkeley still followed the traditions of the past. In San Francisco under the regime of Mayor Rolph (1911–1931) and his successor Angelo Rossi (1931–1943), vice and violence continued but in a more subdued manner. In 1921 Captain Matheson, now chief of detectives, lent a hand to his fellow Scots Presbyterian, Donaldine Cameron, the Chinatown mission operator, by assigning Sergeant John Manion to head the Chinatown squad. "Chinatown Jack," a member of the Knights of Columbus, delighted Miss Cameron with his vigorous activity against the tongs.[79] Though Matheson was again passed over for Chief in 1928, the post going to William Quinn, he had better fortune the next year. After a scandal in the city treasurer's office, Mayor Rolph appointed the incorruptible Matheson to the post and he was periodically relected until his death in 1942.

During the interwar period, the San Francisco Police Department was a closed corporation run by a small group, and the cops themselves commonly referred to it as "the business."[80] The Rolph-Rossi administrations ruled for thirty-two years, during most of which the same faction held sway on the Board of Police Commissioners and police chiefs averaged the unusually long term of nine years in office. However, the real power lay with the McDonough brothers. As Jake Ehrlich, the city's most noted criminal lawyer, who was also attorney for the Police Association, described them:

---

* In the 1970s the school allegedly became dominated by radicals, and in 1976 it was closed.

From their grubby little office at Clay and Kearny streets, close enough to the Hall of Justice for the chief to wince if Pete McDonough raised his voice in anger, these Argus-eyed, squid-handed brothers supervised the many-splendored night life of San Francisco. They kept an eye on the nightly take of every hustling girl . . . and had the drawings on any burglary, con-game or safeblowing that happened *before* it happened—or it *didn't* happen.

The McDonoughs had lawyers and courtroom fixes—in all price categories—for sale. They created judges and uncreated them. They got city and county ordinances passed, defeated, amended and shelved. They bankrolled madams and assigned territories to bootleggers. They provided protection for pimps, dice hustlers, bookmakers, pickpockets, after-hours operations, lamsters and every stripe of fast-money specialist. They eliminated competition for their clients and acted as clearing house, chancellery and postoffice for the underworld. They performed special and vital functions at election time and they served as fiduciary agents for statesmen too high up to stoop to face-to-face collections. And . . . oh yes, they provided bail bonds.[81]

In 1934 the San Francisco cops applied massive and sometimes deadly force to break a strike of Harry Bridges's longshoremen. The police action polarized the city and made them many enemies.[82] The following year an IRS official casually noted at a luncheon that San Francisco police officers were paying income tax. Since local government employees were not required to pay federal income taxes on their salaries at the time, this was highly unusual. It suggested that the additional income came from graft. A grand jury was impaneled to look into the matter, and Edwin Atherton, a Los Angeles private detective with previous service in the FBI, was given $100,000 to conduct an investigation. His report identified 135 houses of prostitution, estimated the payoff from gambling and prostitution at 1 million dollars annually, accused the McDonough brothers of running the police department and serving as "the fountainhead of corruption," and named a number of officers as receiving payoffs.[83] Jake Ehrlich, defense attorney for the cops, challenged the accuracy of the report, indicating the take was over 4 million and the houses of prostitution numbered at least 300, indicating the situation was long established and sanctioned. One detective admitted banking over $800,000.[84] For a time it was like the good old days, with detectives trailing each other and bugging one another's offices, but though the McDonoughs' power was broken and three captains were indicted or forced to quit, the police department soon returned to normal.[85]

Fremont Older died in 1935 and the attempts of Paul Smith, liberal editor of the conservative *San Francisco Chronicle*, to play the crusading role did not catch fire. As in the rest of the nation, business and labor were beginning to cooperate, and perhaps neither group in San Francisco could see any advantage in a repeat of the graft trial or a revival of the passions which had been stirred by the Mooney case. In 1937 Bruce Smith was summoned to conduct a survey of the police department, but its findings had no real impact.

In Los Angeles more permanent results were attained as the result of a scandal. Through the '30s, the LAPD maintained a faithful anti-Red force headed by Captain Red Hines, whose squad broke up Communist and other radical meetings with gusto and spied on dissidents. One social reformer on the board of every leftist organization in town turned out to be a police spy. Often it was difficult to tell friend from foe. Upton Sinclair and Morris Hillquit had to call for Hines to protect them from rival leftists, while on occasion other police such as the Los Angeles sheriff's men or the Pasadena municipals evicted Hines's squad from meetings.[86] The chief of police during much of this period (1926–1929, 1933–1938) was a tough Texan, Jim Davis, noted for his strong law and order and antihomosexual attitudes. Chief Davis was a favorite of various California conservatives, and his reappointment in 1933 was part of a deal whereby the conservative Los Angeles Times agreed to back Mayor Frank Shaw. During the Depression, Davis even sent LA cops to patrol the state's borders and turn back unwanted Okies and Arkies.[87]

Despite Chief Davis's efforts, the vice problem and the radicals remained troublesome. In addition to the Red squad, the police department maintained a separate intelligence unit under Captain Earl Kynette, an experienced vice cop who undertook special investigations for Mayor Shaw and Chief Davis, including keeping an eye on alleged radicals such as State Assemblyman Sam Yorty.[88] An even greater challenge to the police were the antivice forces of the city led by Clifford Clinton, a restaurateur who was president of the Citizens Independent Vice Investigating Committee (CIVIC). Clinton, the son of missionary parents, allowed his restaurant customers to pay whatever they chose, and during the Depression many people ate free. Strangely, after he undertook his CIVIC responsibilities, Clinton's taxes rose, a number of patrons claimed food poisoning, and several suffered nasty falls on his premises. Clinton himself also became accident-prone as trick motorcyclists and stunt men ran into or fell under his car. In October 1937 Clinton's house was bombed. Many suspected that behind such events was the fine hand of the intelligence squad.[89]

Undaunted CIVIC hired an investigator, one Harry Raymond, who was as knowledgeable, if not as reputable, as any individual in the community. Formerly a Los Angeles city detective, police chief of Venice, California, and San Diego as well as a district attorney's investigator, he was invariably fired as a result of his involvement in vice scandals. In January 1938, a bomb wired to Raymond's car exploded, giving him twelve dozen shrapnel wounds, but it did not kill him. Eventually Captain Kynette was convicted of the crime and sentenced to prison.[90]

The fall of Kynette was actually a blow to some radicals, since he was in de facto possession of one of the hottest socialist movements around, the so-called "Ham and Eggs" or "$30 every Thursday" plan under which the state would pay old-age pensions of $30 a week to persons over fifty-five. While his task was to infiltrate and destroy such groups, the members' dues constituted big money, so the captain expanded the organization. Kynette's departure left the Ham and Eggs movement temporarily leaderless; then Gerald L. K. Smith stepped into the breach. In 1938, Ham and Eggs was narrowly defeated in a statewide referendum.[91]

The aftermath of the Raymond bombing brought Judge Fletcher Bowron, a former secretary to Governor Richardson, to the mayor's post and laid the foundation for the institution of police reform. Bruce Smith was summoned to conduct an exam to select a new chief of police, the Red squad was abolished, and gambler Guy McAfee moved to Las Vegas. In office, though, the reformers began using the same tactics of espionage that Chief Davis and company had employed, and Mayor Bowron and Clifford Clinton were themselves indicted but not convicted for wiretapping.[92]

By the middle '40s the system of vice payoffs was restored, leading to more scandals and the ouster of another police chief. Finally, in 1950, William H. Parker, former administrative assistant to Chief Davis, was appointed chief of police, and under his direction there developed the modern Los Angeles Police Department made so famous by "Dragnet" and other TV productions.

Mr. District Attorney

The success of Vollmer's Berkeley Police Department can be traced in part to the cooperation it received from the Alameda County District Attorney's Office. The key man in the office from 1920 to 1924 and the DA himself from 1925 to 1938 was Earl Warren. Like Vollmer, Warren was up from the ranks. His father had been a Debs railway union striker of 1894 and in an attempt to escape the blacklist had moved from Los Angeles to Bakersfield. Young Warren, an indifferent student at the University of California in college and law school, was happy to accept a political job as an assistant to the city attorney in Oakland, and then moved to a $150-a-month assistant district attorney post for the county. Throughout his prosecutorial career, Warren was a conservative rather than a Progressive Republican, and also, like Vollmer, a protégé of a powerful publisher, in Warren's case Joe Knowland of the *Oakland Tribune*. In 1925, Governor Richardson appointed him district attorney and the following year he was elected in his own right over Progressive opposition.

One of his first acts as DA was to warn the sheriff, a fellow Republican, to cut out his grafting, and, when the warning was ignored, to drive the man from office.[93] This was his usual pattern for corrupt cops or politicians, a warning first, which if ignored was followed by action. In 1930 he was reelected and was hailed by Raymond Moley as the best district attorney in the country.[94] Still, at forty, his salary was only $6,000 a year, compared with the $18,000 of the DA of San Francisco. Though the law permitted him to supplement his income with outside practice, Warren did not take advantage of it, preferring to spend his time serving as head of the State District Attorneys' Association and as counsel to both its sheriffs' and police chiefs' associations.

As district attorney, Warren was in a strategic position vis-à-vis the police, since he could refuse to prosecute persons they arrested if he felt the arrests were not in accord with law or proper procedure. Thus he could make the cops improve or, in effect, go out of business. He also had the power to prosecute policemen for their misdeeds. Warren himself noted that

> ... the district attorney has become the most powerful officer in local government; ... a powerful executive and legal officer who declares and determines the law enforcement standards of his county, and, through the exercise of quasi-judicial functions, determines, in the main, who shall be prosecuted and who shall not be subjected to our criminal procedure.[95]

Where Vollmer could only cajole non-Berkeley cops, Warren could give orders to police all over the county and ultimately beyond. For he expected to succeed to the post of state attorney general when the elderly incumbent, who had held the office since 1902, retired. In anticipation of this, Warren secured passage of a constitutional amendment making the attorney general the chief law enforcement officer of the state with authority over police in the sphere of criminal investigation. In addition, the AG was given control over police records and his own staff of investigators.[96] Upon assuming the office, Warren would become de facto chief of all California police.

While Warren labored in the professional sphere, he also found time to be state chairman of the Republican party, in which role he denounced Reds and socialists and condemned Tom Mooney. The political and professional roles sometimes collided. In 1936 the engineer of the freighter *Point Lobo* was found beaten to death. Warren's office convicted the killers, whom he identified as a Communist goon squad, but some questions were raised. Warren's detectives had obtained evidence via hidden microphones planted in a suspect's room. The judge had been sponsored for his post by Warren, and a later investigation revealed that one of the jurors was extremely close to the assistant DA who prosecuted the defendants.[97]

In 1938, Warren was elected attorney general, having been nominated by all three major parties. However, the Republicans lost the governorship to the liberal Democrat Culbert Olson, who pardoned Tom Mooney. Warren led the counterattack and as World War II drew near was a leading figure in warning of the dangers of Communists, Nazis, and Japanese. While the external threat occupied more of his time as attorney general, he continued his strong law and order activities, raiding a gambling ship beyond the territorial limits of California, an action that some local observers assessed as piracy.[98] After Pearl Harbor he was instrumental in securing the removal of Japanese to concentration camps outside the state. In 1942 Warren won the governorship, ousting Olson.

In his new post Warren could not concentrate solely on law enforcement, and, given the wider concerns of his office and national ambitions, he began to move to the center as a moderate progressive. In 1944 and 1948 he sought the presidential nomination, and in the latter year was defeated for Vice President as Governor Dewey's running mate. In 1953, he was appointed Chief Justice of the United States. His later career is beyond the scope of the present work, even though it had major significance for police. To many of his old law enforcement friends, such as O. W. Wilson, his behavior as Chief Justice was puzzling. However, in the first major criminal case considered by the Warren Court, *Irvine* v. *California*, the decision was not totally out of tune with Warren's career. California police had secured evidence to convict a major bookie via hidden microphones planted through surreptitious entry of the man's house. Warren voted to uphold the conviction but asked the Justice Department to investigate the case for possible violations of federal law with a view to prosecuting the policemen.[99] Once again he had given a warning to curb certain practices but it was not heeded, and once again, in a manner of speaking, he found it necessary to handcuff the sheriff.

In the post–World War II period the California style of professional policing emerged, first in Los Angeles, then in Oakland, San Diego, and other cities, with only San Francisco holding aloof. California's professional police departments would emphasize technical efficiency, vigorous law enforcement, and, most importantly, very astute public relations, particularly in terms of promoting their chiefs.* While the actual establishment of professional policing did not take place until the 1950s, the seeds were planted from 1905 onward, in the Berkeley Police Depart-

---

* From the 1920s to date seven California police chiefs have been elected president of the IACP. In the same period not one head of the New York, Boston, Philadelphia, or Chicago Police Department has been chosen.

ment and later in the Alameda County District Attorney's Office* and the Office of the California Attorney General.

Any objective analysis must attribute a larger influence to Earl Warren than to August Vollmer. While respected, Vollmer was still a small-town chief who had failed in the big city. Warren was a major office holder and politician with great power over the police and a record of political and personal success. For example, in the 1930s Vollmer urged a single state police force to supersede all local departments.[100] Warren, as an official of the state chiefs' and sheriffs' associations, with his eye on the attorney general's office, moved instead to ensure the primacy of the attorney general and local police. As a result the California State Highway Patrol was left to traffic duty and as late as the 1960s was not even considered a primary police agency.[101] Nor were Vollmer's social service ideas to become a part of postwar California policing.

More important than personalities, though, was the fact that administrative science, or "professionalism," made sense in California as it did not elsewhere. If New York politics was characterized by contests between regular and reformer, in Chicago by contests between the machine and organized crime, California's struggle pitted business elite against middle-class Progressives. In such an environment, what was required was a brand of policing which emphasized technical efficiency and educated cops (who presumably were less likely to embarrass their superiors) under a chief whose public relations astuteness meant he would respond to the dominant values whatever their ideological cast.

---

* Alameda County also pioneered in another area of criminal justice, appointing as the first female probation officer Anita Whitney, who later became a celebrity after her conviction for criminal syndicalism.

The Secret Agents
(1850–1945)

In the spring of 1898, United States Secret Service agents were engaged in the investigation of a Philadelphia engraving plant suspected of manufacturing plates for counterfeit bills. During the surveillance their attention was drawn to a fourteen-year-old cleaning boy who periodically did acrobatics on the fire escape. Two of the agents, a rookie and a veteran, conceived a scheme to use the boy to gain entrance to the plant. The rookie accosted the youngster on the street and offered him an opportunity to audition for vaudeville. Repairing to a nearby hotel the boy changed into an acrobat suit. While the youngster hurled himself across the room, the agents removed the keys from the boy's trousers and had them duplicated. Armed with the keys, they were able to enter the plant at will, and eventually the biggest counterfeiting ring in the United States was broken.[1]

The clever agents were officially commended, and both became stars of the service. The veteran, William J. Burns, was to become the most famous and controversial detective in America as head of his own agency and later director of the FBI. The rookie, Larry Richey (Ricci), became a confidential aide and lifelong intimate of President Herbert Hoover. When asked to suggest a replacement for Burns as FBI director, he would nominate another man named Hoover.

THE PRIVATE EYES

In the generation that followed the Civil War the patterns of American detective organization were firmly established. Each municipal police department of any size contained a detective branch whose personnel were increasingly drawn from the ranks of the uniformed force, although this was not a universal practice.* The federal government also established small detective forces with suboffices in major cities. Save for Inspector Byrnes in New York, however, until the twentieth century the publicly employed detectives were overshadowed in both numbers and importance by those in the service of private enterprise—a reflection of the larger society, where big business dominated small government.

There were many reasons for the preeminence of the private detectives in the post–Civil War era. Municipal governments were prevented from developing effective forces by their low quality of personnel, confinement to a single jurisdiction, and, most importantly, the political influence present in local police departments. Thus it was the private investigators who were called upon to deal with interstate crime, complex investigations, and secure the nation from its fears. In the late nineteenth century the most important of these businesses was the Pinkerton Agency, which occupied a position akin to that of the present-day FBI.

The founding father, Allan Pinkerton, was born in Scotland in 1819, the son of a Glasgow police constable. Pinkerton's career was surrounded by many legends, often self-generated to facilitate his own and his agency's success, one of them being that his father was killed in a riot, although no proof of this has been found. As a young man Pinkerton himself was active in the radical Chartist movement, participating in several street battles.[3] With a warrant for his arrest outstanding, he emigrated to America at the age of twenty-two, settling in Illinois. The newcomer gradually drifted into police work as a deputy sheriff and in 1849 became a Chicago detective. In the next few years Pinkerton developed his own agency, with railroads and express companies as primary customers. By 1860 the business was thriving.

From the start, Pinkerton's methods were those of the classic secret service. During an investigation it was standard procedure for his agents to infiltrate themselves into the lives of witnesses and suspects by any means possible. The porter who cleaned the suspect's room, the man who shared his cell, or the lady he made love to might be an agent. Pinkerton hired women detectives fifty years before the regular police

---

* As late as 1920, cities as large as Pittsburgh, Kansas City, Louisville, Memphis, and Birmingham were still appointing detectives directly from civilian life.[2]

undertook to do so, and used them exactly as he would any other agent, a practice that many police are still hesitant to follow. In fact, a major aspect of his success was his ability to recruit staff on a merit basis. The underworld philosopher Josiah Flynt observed:

> The Pinkertons hire men for what they can do, and not on account o' political pull or because they're Irishmen or niggers, and that's the reason they get such a lot of business.[4]

Another practice the Pinkertons employed was the planting of false information. For example, a detective might send an anonymous letter informing a suspect that his wife was carrying on with another man in the hope that the recipient would perform a rash act.

Though a business success, Pinkerton did not entirely abandon his legacy of radicalism. He was a strong supporter of the abolitionist movement, operating a station on the underground railroad over which runaway slaves fled to Canada. He was also a warm friend of John Brown, and is alleged to have sheltered him while he was a fugitive after a number of killings in Kansas. As Pinkerton wrote many years later, "I have always been a friend to the colored man and will do anything to secure him his rights."[5]

In 1861, at the outbreak of the Civil War, there arose the most famous case of Pinkerton's career. On his own initiative he undertook to protect President-elect Lincoln during the journey to Washington for his inauguration. In the course of these duties he claimed to have discovered a plot to assassinate the President-elect in Baltimore and arranged for him to slip through the city unobtrusively. In later years there would be dispute over who discovered the plot—the New York Metropolitan police claiming credit—or whether it was in fact ever in existence.[6] Certainly it made an exciting story: a band of terrorists led by an Italian barber had supposedly drawn straws for the honor of assassinating Lincoln. In 1858 Felice Orsini, an Italian terrorist, had been executed for throwing a bomb at Napoleon III outside the Paris Opera. The incident made the world conscious of Italian secret societies, and the Baltimore barber, Cypriano Ferrandini, was reputed to be a follower of Orsini.*

The legends of Pinkerton's Civil War service also assert that he was the first head of the United States Secret Service, though in fact, the agency was not founded until after the war. His actual work was intelligence or "secret service" activities for the Army of the Potomac, commanded by his lifelong hero, General George B. McClellan. The general,

---

* It is interesting that when the war began the federal government seized as security risks both the mayor of Baltimore and the local U.S. Marshal, but Ferrandini was allowed to go on cutting hair.[7]

a West Pointer, had been vice president of the Illinois Central Railroad, in which capacity he had dealt with Pinkerton. It is noteworthy that despite his alleged services to Lincoln in connection with the Baltimore incident, Pinkerton was offered a position not with the President, but with the man who became his chief rival.

The alleged spying exploits of Pinkerton's agents provided the basis for many postwar novels and dramas.[8] In his relationship with McClellan, Pinkerton essentially operated as a military analyst rather than an espionage agent, and in that capacity he was a failure, constantly overestimating enemy strength. This contributed to McClellan's reluctance to fight, and in 1862, when the general was dismissed, Pinkerton went with him. He did, however, continue to perform government work as a private detective and in 1866 was supposedly engaged by the White House to spy on Congress during the impeachment proceedings against President Johnson.[9]

Whatever the reality of Pinkerton's wartime services, the legends were widely believed and the association with Lincoln and the North's "holy crusade" afforded him considerable prestige which translated into increased business. Soon the agency's symbol, a watchful eye, became one of the nation's most prominent trademarks, giving rise to the term "private eye."

In one respect, Pinkerton could claim credit as the father of the Secret Service. The official agency was a small unit assigned to combat counterfeiting, with occasional investigations for other agencies. In a country with no major foreign enemies and few federal criminal statutes, its work was relatively insignificant until the end of the century. In contrast, Pinkerton was the prime defender of the economic and political theories which underlay the nation. In the post–Civil War era power resided with private entrepreneurs who controlled commerce and industry. Whoever threatened this arrangement menaced the national security. From 1865 on, such threats came from two sources—first, the discontented lower classes, the most prominent manifestations of whose discontent were labor and agrarian disorders; second, the skilled and mobile robbers, safecrackers, confidence men, and other criminals who were a product of the new economic system and its technical advancements such as the railroad network. Of course, it could be (and was) argued that the greatest threat to national security came from the monopolistic enterprises which employed the Pinkertons and that the latter were themselves a type of criminal conspiracy. But given the ascendancy of the industrial interests, this view would not become widespread until the beginning of the Progressive Era in the 1890s.

One of the first notable tasks of the agency was to combat the James Brothers robbery gang in Missouri. Jesse and Frank James had both served in a Confederate guerrilla force. Thus from one perspective they could be seen as continuing such activities by resisting the penetration of the commercial forces, particularly the railroads, into their agrarian homeland, a resistance which necessitated occasional "expropriations" from local banks. The James Boys were handsome, daring, and romantic in the tradition of Dick Turpin and Jack Sheppard. They were also of native stock and "good old Confederate boys." Thus the Pinkertons found themselves in the unpopular role of the thieftaker, Jonathan Wild, particularly after they bombed the James homestead, blowing off the mother's arm and killing a half-brother.

Two Pinkerton agents were killed in various skirmishes, including one who attempted to infiltrate the gang. Not until 1876 were the activities of the James Boys curtailed, as a result of losses sustained in an attempted bank robbery in Northfield, Minnesota, an event in which the Pinkertons were not involved. The James versus Pinkerton war was clearly a tactical and moral defeat for the agency, which was even blamed for a disgruntled gang member's bullet-in-the-back assassination of Jesse, with which the agency had no connection.

In the drive against bandits, it was publicity, not bullets, that ultimately counted. Criminals were easier to hunt down if they could be recognized and reported. Thus an obscure gang of train robbers became famous as Butch Cassidy and the Wild Bunch after Pinkerton agents circularized a group photo taken while the gang was on holiday at Fort Worth, Texas. As a result, Cassidy and the Sun Dance Kid were forced to flee to South America, but the Pinkertons followed with a batch of photos and eventually the outlaws were killed by local troops.[10] Publicity was also useful in shaping the image of bandits as evil men and "public enemies" rather than Robin Hood heroes. The James boys, who were thought of as the latter, were never caught by the Pinkertons, while people like the Reno gang and others who were seen as vicious killers were murdered by vigilante death squads even when in Pinkerton custody.* Such events, while officially deplored, did eliminate the possibility of acquittal by bribed, intimidated, or sympathetic judges and jurors.

In the 1870s the agency was called into the Pennsylvania coal fields to combat the industrial terrorism attributed to the Irish miners known as the Molly Maguires. The drive against the Mollies was another affair where alternative images could be projected. If the Mollies existed at all, they could be seen as an embittered proletariat fighting for justice or as a criminal conspiracy by a band of alien terrorists. The prevailing view was the latter, since the Irish evoked little sympathy beyond their own group because of their alien religion and culture. The successful resolution

---

* In 1868, three members of the Reno gang in the custody of six Pinkertons were lynched in Indiana. A few months later five more Renos whom the Pinkertons had arrested were taken from jail and lynched.[11]

of the case depended on standard secret service techniques. The Mollies were brought down by an Irish Catholic immigrant, James McParlan(d), who was able to infiltrate the group and secure the evidence which sent twelve of them to the scaffold.* Later, there were allegations that Mc-Parland was an agent provocateur or a perjurer. Whatever the truth, the infiltration of the Mollies not only was successful but served as a potent object lesson to others of like mind, since such groups could no longer feel sure of their own members.

After disposing of the Irish threat in the '70s, in the next decade the agency turned to the Italians. Although Allan Pinkerton suffered a paralyzing stroke in 1869, the work of his agency was unaffected, gradually passing into the hands of his sons, William and Robert, both experienced detectives. The two, operating out of Chicago and New York respectively, built up a network of contacts with police officials from Europe to California, and even August Vollmer had to consult them on cases.[12]

A close friend of the Pinkertons was David Hennessey, chief of police of New Orleans. In 1890 he was engaged in a struggle with Italian immigrant elements in that city who were allegedly responsible for a series of murders and extortions. In October he was fatally shot from ambush and before he died stated, "The Dagoes did it." The community was outraged, and nineteen Italians were jailed pending trial.** The case was weak, for there were no eyewitnesses to be found, and a confession or further evidence was needed. To this end, William Pinkerton made available Frank DiMaio, an Italian-speaking detective, who was imprisoned with the suspects in the guise of an arrested counterfeiter. According to the official version, DiMiao spent four months in jail, finally obtaining the necessary information, which he turned over to the local authorities. However, a jury, supposedly in fear of reprisal, acquitted the defendants.

The degree of community fear is problematic. When the nineteen were arrested, a local citizen entered the jail and shot one of them in an incident the press applauded under the heading "Assassination Attempt of . . . Dagoes." During the prisoners' incarceration, conditions in the jail were so bad that DiMaio himself became gravely ill. Finally, before the acquitted defendants could be released, a mob stormed the jail and killed ten of them, earning praise from the mayor. The incident provoked a diplomatic crisis and the temporary recall of the Italian Ambassador.[14]

After the events in New Orleans, Italians continued to be seen as a

---

* As noted earlier, eventually twenty Mollies were hanged; eight of the executions were a result of cases unrelated to McParland's investigation. (The detective's name was spelled both with and without a final "d" until, in later life, he settled on "McParland.")

** The murder so alarmed young August Vollmer's mother that it prompted her to leave the city for California, on the same train with Chief Hennessey's widow.[13]

threat, and in the '90s were lynched from West Virginia to Colorado.[15] Not surprisingly, the Pennsylvania mining districts were particularly virulent areas, and fear of the Italians was a major impetus to the formation of the Pennsylvania State Police in 1905. One such area was Lawrence County, particularly the town of Hillsville, known locally as "Hellsville," where murder and extortion were common. In the same year the state police were organized, the Pinkertons dispatched DiMaio, now head of a special "Italian" squad within the agency, to Hillsville to do battle with his countrymen. DiMaio infiltrated the local underworld and brought about the arrest and imprisonment of thirty-three miners and the execution of one for murder.[16]

In addition to their detective operations the Pinkertons supplied guards for industry and, when necessary, strikebreakers. As the '90s dawned, the activities of the Pinkertons were being included in the general criticism of big business, and the 1892 incident at Homestead (see Chapter 4) brought a Congressional investigation and loss of agency prestige. Out of Homestead arose a popular song of the '90s, "Father Was Killed by the Pinkerton Men." The agency name was increasingly pronounced with scorn.

The antilabor activities of the Pinkertons partially masked their important function as a national detective agency. Given the weakness of the local police, the agency often undertook investigations of major crimes. Two safecrackers who stole 1.25 million dollars from a Massachusetts bank were caught by Pinkertons, as was the state treasurer of South Dakota, who embezzled $300,000. America's best-known bank burglar, Langdon Moore, in one instance charged that the Pinkertons had attempted to kidnap him in Canada, and in another case he claimed that they had spent $10,000 (which they charged to the client) wining and dining him in an effort to get him to confess to the burglary of an express company. He even asserted they had offered him the Superintendency of their New York office. Since Moore rarely had favorable comments about police, his remarks probably reflect credit on the Pinkertons for making his life difficult.[17] The more objective Josiah Flynt paid a considerable tribute to the agency in reporting a conversation with another thief:

> "The pub[lic] doesn't hear of many good touches in New York, either," I could not help saying.
> "No, if you mean banks an' joolry places; but the Big Man's [the Pinkerton Detective Agency] protectin' mos o' them; 't ain't the Front Office [New York Police Detective Bureau]. The guns leave the Big Man's territory alone, if they can. If there was two banks standin' close together, an' one o' them was a member o' the Bankers' Association an' the other one wasn't, the guns 'ud tackle the other one first. The Big Man protects the Bankers' Association banks."[18]

In 1895, in the backwash of Homestead, the agency apprehended the man who may well have been the century's leading mass murderer, H. H. Holmes (also known as Herman Mudgett). Holmes was arrested for the murder of four members of a Philadelphia family, but the investigation disclosed that he had also slaughtered from eight to fifteen women in "Holmes castle" on Chicago's South Side.[19] In this instance the Pinkerton assertions were undisputed, and given the state of American police work at that time, the investigation probably could not have been conducted by any other body. Thus the agency's useful anticrime work in part offset the growing criticism of its antilabor activities.

In 1906, James McParland, now superintendent of the agency's Denver office, came back into the limelight in an attempt to repeat the glory of his youth. In December 1905 former Governor Frank Steunenberg of Idaho opened the front gate of his yard and was blown to bits. He had been elected governor in 1896 with strong support from the Western Federation of Miners, which later formed the nucleus of the IWW. The dominant figure of both groups was the one-eyed giant Bill Haywood, who constantly urged violence in the class struggle. Beginning in 1901, the miners under "Big Bill" fought a virtual civil war with the militia and law enforcement officers in the state of Colorado. During the struggle they made free use of dynamite and bullets, and the authorities, led by one of Theodore Roosevelt's former Roughriders, utilized even more force and the power of martial law.

In the late 1890s similar events had taken place in Idaho, and in 1899, after a mine was blown up, Governor Steunenberg requested federal troops. The army then proceeded to round up hundreds of miners and held them for months in a bull pen. The resulting bitterness was aggravated by the fact that some of the soldiers were black, and the miners thought they had been deliberately sent all the way from Brownsville, Texas, to add to their humiliation.[20] Afterward Steunenberg was a marked man.

The Pinkertons were engaged to investigate his assassination, with McParland in charge. A suspect, Harry Orchard, was already in custody, and under McParland's interrogation Orchard and an alleged accomplice confessed to being hired by Big Bill Haywood and two other mine union leaders. These three were arrested at union headquarters in Denver and spirited off to Idaho in an incident which supporters labeled a kidnapping. At the trial U.S. Senator William Borah led the prosecution and Clarence Darrow the defense. The prosecution was helped when President Theodore Roosevelt publicly referred to the defendants as "undesirable" citizens, but Darrow, aided when one of the bombers recanted his confession, was able to raise sufficient doubts in the jury's mind to win acquittal of Haywood and the other defendants.[21]

The Idaho case was a major victory for organized labor, though it would shortly be offset by the *Los Angeles Times* affair. For the Pinkertons it meant a serious loss of prestige, and they were replaced in favor by the William J. Burns Agency; the symbolic gesture of ascendancy came in 1909 when the American Bankers Association switched from Pinkerton to Burns. Robert Pinkerton died in 1907. William lived on until 1923, and the agency continued to prosper, though its importance in law enforcement was much less than it had been. In 1937 the Pinkertons came under heavy criticism from a Senate committee for their labor spying activities, and the agency head, Robert Pinkerton, great-grandson of the founder, Harvard polo captain and reluctant private detective chief, ordered an end to espionage against organized labor, noting that "it looks as if we were on the wrong side of the fence. Times have changed and we are out of step."[22]

It is fashionable to see the private eyes simply as goon squads, but for over fifty years they were virtually the only competent detectives available. Given a theory of government which placed the police function almost exclusively in the hands of ward politicians, murderers such as H. H. Holmes and burglars like Langdon Moore would have been virtually unchecked if it had not been for the Pinkertons. It should also be noted that in an era when physical torture to produce confessions was standard operating procedure, the private eyes eschewed such methods in favor of the gentler but more effective psychological ploys.

If the private detectives paid little attention to the law, they could hardly be seen as different from the Heneys, Rogerses, Darrows, Fallons, and other "hired guns" who attempted to influence juries, not to arrive at the truth, but to advance their clients' interests. In sum, the private detectives reflected many of the prevailing practices in the law and business worlds they served.

THE FEDS

From the earliest days of the Republic, the federal government employed detectives to investigate revenue violations, but their numbers were few and their jurisdiction limited. In 1865, Congress created the United States Secret Service within the Treasury Department to combat counterfeiting and fraudulent claims for war bounties. The former offense was a particularly appropriate target for a secret service, for counterfeiting had long been recognized as a crime that strikes at the heart of state security—the stability of its legal tender. Historically, it was treated as treason and punished by death and is one of the few crimes specifically mentioned in the United States Constitution. Periodically, operatives of the Service would be detailed to other government bureaus to assist in investigations calling for detective skills.

Until the 1890s, the Service numbered only thirty to forty men and was run in a casual patronage fashion. The first chief, William Woods, was a friend of Secretary of War Edwin Stanton, and before the Civil War, while an investigator assisting Stanton in a lawsuit, had falsified evidence in a major patent case.[23] In both the Mexican War and the Civil War he led guerrilla bands, and he had also been a Washington, D.C., jailkeeper. A gunman attempted to assassinate Allan Pinkerton during the hunt for the Reno gang and later, at his trial, claimed to have been acting on Chief Woods's orders.[24] The second chief was another guerrilla leader, 6'10" Herman Whitley. His career also ended under a cloud after he provided a burglar to crack a Washington, D.C., safe in an attempt to frustrate an investigation of corruption within the District of Columbia government.*[25]

Some of the later chiefs apparently ran private detective agencies on the side. William Flynn, appointed in 1912, accepted on the condition that he be allowed to remain in New York, and for five years he maintained this arrangement, occasionally commuting to Washington. In December 1917, in the midst of America's war effort, he quit to devote more time to the Flynn Detective Agency.[27]

During the Harding regime, the White House agents allegedly took sides in the dispute between the President and his wife, spying on one for the other.[28]

At the end of the nineteenth century, as the United States became a world power, it needed a real secret service. In 1898 Lyman Gage, Secretary of the Treasury in the McKinley administration, appointed a fellow Chicagoan, John E. Wilkie, to head the agency. Wilkie, then an editor of the staunch Republican *Chicago Tribune*, had been a foreign correspondent and businessman in London. He had no police experience save that as a reporter he had collaborated on a history of the Chicago Police Department. During the fifteen years of his tenure the Service became an important law enforcement agency.

The first important case of the new regime combined high politics, clever crooks, and famous detectives. In 1898–99 an investigation of a major counterfeiting operation involving two talented and respectable engravers utilized the talents of William Burns and Larry Richey. Burns, then forty, was a Columbus, Ohio, tailor who had investigated election fraud in his home town with such success that he became a private detective and, in 1891, an assistant operative of the Secret Service at $4 a

* The Washington, D.C., police underwent a similar scandal when it was revealed they spied on reporters and members of Congress and attempted to frame the chairman of a congressional investigating committee.[26]

day; eventually rising to full operative at $6, or about the salary of a New York City detective. Richey (Ricci), of Italian descent, had been a Philadelphia newsboy and had recently joined the Service as an assistant operative. Their trick on the cleaning boy mentioned at the opening of this chapter resulted in the conviction of the two engravers, but that was only the beginning.

So talented were the engravers that they continued their activities from a new shop in the Pennsylvania State Penitentiary until the Secret Service proved this fact, to the embarrassment of the state authorities. During the investigation the defense attorneys, one a former U.S. Attorney, the other a prospective federal judge, offered a Secret Serviceman $1,000 per month for information on the progress of the case. As a result the two attorneys became convicts despite character testimony provided by the governor of Pennsylvania and several congressmen and judges. One cannot help but note that for an attorney so knowledgeable regarding federal law enforcement to make such an offer suggests that there may have been some reason to suspect that it might have been accepted.[29]

The appointment of Wilkie as chief of the Service coincided not only with America's coming of age in the Spanish-American War but also with an intensification of class conflict. The internal upheavals of the post–Civil War era had involved the Service tangentially as a political intelligence unit. In the depression of 1893 an Ohio Civil War veteran, Jacob Coxey, had organized a group of unemployed for the purpose of marching on Washington. A march on the capital, so well known in Europe, was a new development in America, and the prospect frightened Washington in the same way that the Chartists did London in 1848. The Secret Service infiltrated the Coxey forces and sent periodic reports to headquarters estimating that they would arrive in Washington with 100,000 demonstrators. Actually, on May Day, 1893, approximately 500 showed up and were promptly arrested for demonstrating on the grounds of the United States Capitol. It was not the last occasion when political intelligence would overestimate a situation.

In addition to Coxey there were tough western railroad workers on the march under their own "generals." In view of the distances involved, an actual march from the West was impossible, and the government prevailed upon the railroads not to carry protesters. Undaunted, the various groups commandeered trains. Many of the railroads were in federal receivership, and United States marshals, armed with court orders, attempted to halt the protesters, with varying success. At Billings, Montana, for example, "General" Hogan's men routed a force of marshals.

Though there was militia available, the Justice Department under Attorney General Olney preferred to use the regular army. Its commander, General Schofield, was reluctant on both policy and legal grounds, doubting that the government could prevent citizens from coming to Washington. But the men of justice won out over the men of war, and the army was dispatched. Hogan and his men were sleeping on their train in the middle of a Montana prairie when another train raced up and disgorged soldiers, who arrested 331 Hoganites while hundreds more fled into the night.

In some places the Department of Justice men even contrived to create situations for intervention. In Oregon, for example, the U.S. Marshal left a train with steam up alongside one of the protest groups, which promptly seized it. When the army did arrest the protesters, usually they were brought back westward to the point at which the trains had been stolen, a tactic which often set them back 1,000 or 1,500 miles from their destination. As standard procedure, the prisoners were held for weeks in detention camps. Thus few of the western protesters ever got to Washington; nineteen-year-old Jack London, for example, who started from San Francisco with "Kelly's army," finally dropped off in Missouri.[30] The tactic of enforcing court orders with federal troops was noted by the Cleveland administration, so that when the Pullman strike erupted the following year, the strategy for breaking it was readily at hand.

In 1898, when war was declared against Spain, the Spanish naval attaché, Lieutenant Carranza, simply moved to Montreal and hired private detectives to conduct an espionage campaign. The Secret Service engaged auxiliary agents of their own and undertook a counteroffensive by the familiar tactic of burglarizing the attaché's quarters.[31] Since the war was brief and, from the American viewpoint, very successful, the Service was little tested.

From 1865 to 1901 three U.S. Presidents were assassinated. During the same period, Britain, Germany, Austria, and Spain did not suffer the loss of a ruler, and Italy, France, and even Russia lost but one.* In contrast to the Old World, the American Chief of State was not routinely protected by police and soldiers. Within the White House, security was an additional duty of the unarmed doorkeepers, and outside, the President was protected by local authorities and military escorts depending on the vagaries of person and locale.

In 1835, while President Andrew Jackson was returning from a funeral service, a demented housepainter attempted to fire two pistols at point-blank range, but they failed to discharge and the would-be assassin was seized by bystanders. In 1865, despite the fierce hatreds of the time, President Lincoln was guarded by a single officer stationed outside his box at Ford's Theater. The guard, a District of Columbia policeman,

* The Empress of Austria was assassinated in 1898, but she was not the Chief of State.

wandered away from his post, thus relieving the assassin of the necessity of killing him.* In 1881 President Garfield was shot in a Washington railroad station while unguarded. The assassin then surrendered to a nearby policeman.

In the 1890s, because of various threats, the Secret Service provided occasional guards for President Cleveland, but this practice was criticized, since there were no appropriations for it. Chief Wilkie ignored the criticism and assigned guards to McKinley on a sporadic basis, paying for them out of funds for counterfeiting investigations. Though this was illegal, he justified it on the grounds of various dangers; the Hearst press, for example, had suggested the desirability of assassinating the President. In 1900, after the murder of Governor Goebel of Kentucky, Hearst's *New York Journal* printed a poem:

> The bullet that pierced Goebel's breast
> Can not be found in all the West;
> Good reason, it is speeding here
> To stretch McKinley on his bier.[33]

When McKinley opened the Pan-American Exposition at Buffalo in 1901, he was guarded by three Secret Service men. Unfortunately, a member of the host committee displaced the man whose post was next to the President, where he might have been able to seize Leon Czolgosz's bandaged hand before he fired at McKinley.[34]

In 1903 assignment of the Secret Service guards was made permanent, though until 1914 the detail numbered only five men. In 1922 a uniformed guard force was also created. Until the late 1930s the agents were often older men, and a 1936 review of the Service found the agents out of shape and not proficient with firearms.[35] Thus it would not have been a particularly difficult task to kill the President. Theodore Roosevelt, as might be expected, carried his own gun, frequently entertaining walking companions by demonstrating how he would best an assassin and seemed almost to hope that one would leap out of the shadows.[36]

However, the protective force did in fact work. Whereas three Presidents had been shot in thirty-six years, there were no further casualties over the next sixty-two. It is likely that record can be attributed to preventive efforts. The Secret Service's principal function was to veto obviously unsafe procedures despite the desire of various VIPs to enhance their own position regardless of the danger to the President or others. In 1939 Grover Whalen, then acting as major domo for the New York World's Fair, stubbornly insisted that the visiting King and Queen

---

* The officer, John F. Parker, had a poor record prior to his assignment as a presidential guard. For some reason the police trial board absolved Parker of blame in the Lincoln assassination.[32]

of England be driven slowly down lower Broadway. Though World War II was only a few weeks off and two New York detectives were soon to be killed by a bomb exploding in the British Pavilion, the Secret Service chief was unable to overcome Whalen's insistence until Police Commissioner Valentine, who had no love for Whalen, lent his support.[37]

During Theodore Roosevelt's first administration the Department of the Interior was involved in major scandals over the disposition of government-owned timber lands in the western states. The first indications of fraud were provided when one faction of the grafters squealed on the other in an attempt to get them out of the way. As the dimensions of the scandal began to emerge, Secret Service men were detailed to the Interior Department to conduct the investigation. Larry Richey and several other agents went to Colorado, where one of them was murdered.

The most spectacular case, however, was in Oregon. William Burns, now the best-known and in his own opinion the most brilliant agent, was assigned to the investigation. Burns was fresh from arresting a well-connected official of the San Francisco mint for theft of silver, and his new assignment was in part to get rid of him and his propensity for publicity. In Oregon he teamed up with Special Prosecutor Francis Heney and U.S. Marshal Charles Reed, a prominent insurance agent who dabbled in Progressive politics. As a result of their efforts, United States Senator John Mitchell of Oregon was convicted of bribery, along with a Congressman, the United States Attorney, and other influential persons.* Later, during the Taft regime, a Department of Justice investigation under Attorney General George Wickersham would accuse the Heney-Burns forces of having rigged the juries to assure that they were packed with Mitchell's political enemies.[38]

The indictments of members of Congress in Oregon and similar investigations in Idaho, capped by the death of Senator Mitchell while

---

* From Oregon Burns moved on to the San Francisco graft trials, after which he resigned and entered the private detective business. In 1911 he won added renown by the arrest and conviction of the MacNamaras in the *Los Angeles Times* bombings. In 1912 he bested the Pinkertons when the two agencies were engaged on opposite sides of the Leo Frank murder trial in Atlanta, Georgia. The defendant, who was Jewish and a native New Yorker, was accused of the rape-murder of fifteen-year-old Mary Phagan, an employee in the mill where Frank was the manager. The ethnic and ideological aspects of the case contributed to both the rebirth of the Ku Klux Klan and the founding of the Anti-Defamation League. Though he was convicted, Frank's death sentence was commuted by the governor of Georgia on the latter's last day in office. Whether the governor acted out of genuine concern that the defendant had not received a fair trial or because he was a business associate of the defense counsel was a matter of dispute. In any event, the Ku Klux Klan overruled the governor by lynching Frank. The Pinkertons' role for the prosecution was generally deplored, while Burns was again a hero for his efforts on behalf of Frank, which led to the near lynching of Burns himself at the hands of a mob. Interestingly, the Pinkertons were brought into the case by the Frank defense and Burns by the authorities, after which each agency switched sides.[39]

fighting to reverse his conviction, brought great unhappiness on Capitol Hill. This and the fact that President Theodore Roosevelt appeared to be using the Service to investigate legislators caused Congress to insert a rider in an appropriations bill forbidding the Service to undertake investigations beyond its statutory duty. This left the Department of Justice without an investigating arm, so Attorney General Charles Bonaparte, grandnephew of Emperor Napoleon I, proposed the creation of a Bureau of Investigation. Congress refused, decrying the need for a secret police of the type employed under Bonaparte's French relatives. Despite the refusal, President Theodore Roosevelt created such an agency by executive order a few days after Congress adjourned in June 1908.*

In the first few months the Bureau's activities were less than spectacular, centering on antitrust investigations. But in 1910 the passage of the Mann Act to control white slavery provided an ideological mission. One of the first raids took place in the Chicago Levee when W. C. Dannenberg and Larry Richey arrested several of Colisimo's brothel keepers.

For many years the Mann Act was a major preoccupation of the Bureau and was enforced against a variety of private sinners, despite the fact that the law had been meant to counter commercial vice. One of the first persons snared was Jack Johnson, the black man who reigned as heavyweight champion of the world. Johnson had taken up with a white woman who formerly worked in the Everleigh bordello in Chicago. An even more important catch was young Drew Caminetti, who with his girl friend had gone from Sacramento, California, to Reno, Nevada, for a weekend of fun and was arrested by Bureau agents. What made the case most interesting was that Caminetti's father was the United States Commissioner of Immigration. Congressman Mann and his fellow Republicans pointed out that entrusting such an individual to guard the gates of entry to the land of the free and home of the brave was a mistake, his son's predicament seeming to confirm their worst fears about the moral turpitude of foreigners. Young Caminetti was sentenced to eighteen months, and on appeal the U.S. Supreme Court upheld his conviction.[40] The Bureau continued to enforce the law against noncommercial sinners until the Supreme Court reversed itself in the 1940s. The supervision of private morals also provided a legal basis for the collection of many interesting dossiers which could not help but make some prominent persons reluctant to incur Bureau disfavor.

The creation of the FBI alongside the Secret Service provided the basis for an army-navy type of rivalry in federal law enforcement. Inevitably the two agencies would step on each other's toes. In 1909 President Taft was scheduled for an exchange of visits with President Diaz of Mexico at El Paso. At the time Mexico seethed with revolutionary ten-

---

* The title Federal Bureau of Investigation was not adopted until 1935; however, for clarity the agency henceforth will be referred to as the FBI.

sions which the following year were to drive Diaz from office. Prior to the meeting, the FBI notified Secret Service Chief Wilkie that an informant had made the Bureau aware of a plot to assassinate Taft. The resulting joint investigation was hampered because of the secrecy the FBI insisted upon maintaining, but the plot's outlines were finally revealed. Apparently a band of revolutionaries had drawn lots to see who would be the assassin. The story must have had a familiar ring, since it was the old Baltimore plot. The alleged plan could not be verified, and nothing came of it, but it did attract attention to the Bureau.[41] In the future the thrilling business of political intelligence would have to be shared between the two agencies until the FBI finally shoved the Secret Service aside.

Radicals and the Great Crusade

The municipal police departments also were aware of the dangers from anarchists and other radical un-American groups. In 1906, the New York police formed an anti–Black Hand, or "Italian," squad under Lieutenant Joseph Petrosino. The unit worked closely with the federal authorities, and Secret Service man Larry Richey was sent undercover into New York's Little Italy.[42] Since many of the Black Handers were immigrants, an investigation was undertaken in Italy and Sicily to determine if they had lied about their criminal backgrounds when they entered the country, in which case they could be deported. In 1909, during the course of the investigation, Lieutenant Petrosino was assassinated in Sicily, but the following year the police department and the Secret Service convicted a number of alleged Black Handers on various charges. Later, in 1919, Petrosino's successor, Detective Mike Fiaschetti, was loaned out to work undercover in Akron, Ohio, where a local Italian gang had killed four policemen. This was a sign of the progress of municipal detectives; a generation earlier such an assignment would have gone to a private investigator.[43]

The New York police also formed special squads to watch various radicals in the city. In the days of Inspector Byrnes, they arrested Emma Goldman after her lover Alexander Berkman had shot Henry Frick. According to Goldman, Byrnes suggested that she become an informer but she refused.[44]

In fact, until World War I it was the local police who comprised the greatest deterrent to radicals. In December 1882 Johann Most arrived in New York after completing the British prison sentence awarded him following his arrest by Howard Vincent's CID. Soon he was publishing manuals on bomb making. In 1887 New York detectives arrested Most for a speech in which he condemned the Haymarket trial, and he received a year in jail. Most frequently went on drinking bouts, and in such situations it was necessary to fill space in his anarchist newspaper with reprints. One standby was "Murder Against Murder," an article from the 1850s by another German radical, in which he urged the assassination of rulers. On September 5, 1901, Most reprinted this article, and the following day President McKinley was shot. Most immediately attempted to recall the paper, but the New York City police department, faithful readers, retained their copy and prosecuted Most, who received another year in prison; he died shortly after his release.[45] The following year the New York Legislature passed a criminal anarchy statute making it a felony to advocate the overthrow of the government.

In Chicago, after McKinley's assassin, Czolgosz, had admitted to being influenced by her ideas, the local police seized Emma Goldman. Cops and media now advanced the appealing and plausible theory of a red queen who sent her lovers out to assassinate prominent men. Deputy Chief Herman Schuettler strove mightily to obtain proof, but Police Chief Francis O'Neill was less sure. Since he had started an investigation of graft, he wondered if the whole thing was intended to detract attention from the corruption investigation, and eventually Goldman was released.[46]

Chicago was also the birthplace and center of the IWW, and the movement was kept under tight surveillance by the police Red squad, led for nearly half a century by Lieutenant Make Mills, a Polish immigrant.* One of the IWW's best speakers, a tough Irishman called Mac, was revealed to be a city detective named McDonough when a member of the party found his book of streetcar passes. Mac then switched to open attendance at IWW meetings, where he took copious notes. When the Wobbly goon squad attempted to seize the notes, Mac held them off at gunpoint until his detective partner could make his way into the hall and settle the dispute with a blackjack.[48]

Prior to World War I the American radicals had mixed success. In the 1880s the execution of the Haymarket defendants and the imprisonment of Most put the movement into decline. In the hard times of the '90s radicalism recovered, but the Pullman strike and Homestead battle, including Berkman's attempted assassination of Frick, turned most Americans away from violence to the more acceptable doctrines of populism espoused by William Jennings Bryan.

The wild foreigners like the Haymarket defendants, the grotesquely deformed Most, and the freeloving Russian Jews Berkman and Goldman were easy for the authorities to defeat in the war of public relations. But the native American radicals of the twentieth century, such as Eugene Debs, Bill Haywood, John Reed, the Harvard-educated son of

---

* Make Mills (1871–1956) joined the CPD in 1896 and was shortly assigned to antisubversive investigations. Despite a law mandating compulsory retirement at sixty-three, Mills was kept on until he was seventy-six.[47]

Charles Reed, U.S. Marshal of Oregon, and a New York Irish girl, Elizabeth Gurley Flynn, could not be put down so easily, and they frequently received sympathetic support from such rich and powerful persons as Mrs. A. H. Belmont, Mrs. J. Borden Harriman, and Walter Lippmann. Indeed, the radical movement became chic in many circles. As Emma Goldman said, "Bohemianism was sort of a narcotic to help them to endure the boredom of their lives,"[49] and certainly some of the so-called "radicals" were faddists and poseurs.

Jack Reed, even as an undergraduate, had enjoyed battling authority, and as a reporter in New York, protégé and roommate of Lincoln Steffens, he continued his ways by baiting cops who bothered prostitutes. Sent to cover the IWW-led Paterson, New Jersey, silk strike, he promptly got into an altercation with a policeman and was jailed. Yet he looked so clean-cut that his cellmate, the famous anarchist Carlo Tresca, at first refused to have anything to do with him, fearing he was a secret agent.[50] To bolster the strikers' cause, Reed and his Greenwich Village friends arranged a great show at Madison Square Garden. Though the appearance of the workers tugged at hearts, the performance actually lost money and the strike soon collapsed.

Another movement character was Ben Rietman, a Chicago doctor who called himself "King of the Hoboes." Rietman became Emma Goldman's lover and manager, promoting her as a superstar of the left. Ben was not a popular figure with other radicals, however; Elizabeth Gurley Flynn called him an "insufferable baboon," and Bill Haywood detested him. When superpatriotic vigilantes branded Rietman's behind with the letters "I.W.W.," the Wobblies actually cheered.[51] Rietman was noted for pocketing the take from Goldman's speeches and was on very good terms with Chief Schuettler and the Chicago cops. Always a lover of publicity, in 1908 he tipped off the press that Emma intended to speak in Chicago. Predictably, a large police detail responded, and as soon as Goldman opened her mouth, a police captain dragged her off the stage.[52]

Like the Progressives and reformers, the radicals were a varied group, with anarchists, Communists, socialists, and proponents and opponents of violence, frequently clashing over doctrine and personality. For fifty years after their husbands were hanged for inspiring the Haymarket bombing, Lucy Parsons and Nina Spies would not even speak from the same platform.[53] The Wobblies, led by Haywood, were usually violent in speech and deed. The socialists under Debs believed in working within the system, while Emma Goldman and Alexander Berkman (who was released from prison in 1906) stood for a type of philosophical anarchism. On the fringes of the various movements were so-called "parlor radicals" such as Clarence Darrow. Ego played a role; Darrow, for example, refused to allow Debs to assist in the Steunenberg murder trial because he did not want to share the spotlight.[54]

Alongside the social revolutionaries were the nationalists, particularly the Irish. While the police were resolute in opposition to the leftists, many cops were active partisans of Irish freedom. In the 1880s, a Chicago detective was convicted of arranging the murder of a prominent Irish-American doctor, Patrick Henry Cronin, who had been accused of being a British spy.* In New York, prominent men such as Judge Goff and Colonel Murphy, the first police commissioner, were openly active in preaching anti-British violence. Chicago's Chief O'Neill was a strong advocate of Irish culture, filling the force with Gaelic singers and musicians.[56] The cops, like most Americans, were usually supportive of national revolutionaries whether Irish, Polish, Czech, or East Indian, in this respect following the traditions of their own history. But the social revolutionaries who talked of abolishing property, family, and government were another matter. Occasionally, an Irish revolutionary such as Marxist labor leader Jim Larkin, who was a fugitive from Ireland, was able to transmit information from his police contacts to other leftists.[57] World War I would further split the radicals; some supported it, others were silent, and many vociferously opposed it. At the end of the war, the Bolshevik Revolution would occasion more division.

When World War I began in Europe, President Wilson on his own authority removed restrictions on the Secret Service and the FBI and gave them counterespionage tasks. In 1915 Secret Service Agent Frank Burke, trailing Dr. Heinrich Albert, commercial attaché of the German Embassy, saw the suspect leave his briefcase on an elevated train. Burke seized it and outran the victim in a foot race. The contents helped to establish Germany's espionage and sabotage campaign, and the government released the contents to the *New York World* to stir up anti-German sentiment. Dr. Albert, now known by his colleagues as the minister without portfolio, could only grumble that the United States did nothing about British espionage.

While the seizure of the briefcase became a legend, the affair was amateurish. The agents assigned to the surveillance of German officials did not speak German, although the New York City Police Department utilized German-speaking detectives for the same tasks. It might also

---

* A British secret service agent mentioned Dr. Cronin in testimony before the commission which investigated charges that the Irish Nationalist leader C. S. Parnell was involved in the Phoenix Park murders. The agent, Thomas Beach (alias Henri LeCaron) was assigned in the 1860s by Robert Anderson to infiltrate the American wing of the Fenians. Officer Dan Coughlin was the "man" or personal detective of Captain Mike Schaack, the scourge of the Haymarket anarchists. When suspicion fell on Coughlin, Shaack covered up out of loyalty to his subordinate, while Herman Schuettler, the other star detective in the Haymarket case, helped to unmask Coughlin. As a result Schaack was fired and Schuettler promoted. It is entirely possible that the British secret service deliberately sought to create dissentions in the Irish nationalist movement. If so, the unintended result was to split the Chicago police anti-anarchist forces.[55]

have been wiser to photograph the documents in the briefcase surreptitiously by a quiet "inspection" (burglary) of Albert's office—an action no more unlawful than the briefcase theft, but one which might have permitted further surveillance of the spy network.[58]

As in the Spanish-American War, both sides, the Germans and the Allies, retained American private detectives and other persons to advance their interests. For example, the papers stolen from Dr. Albert included a letter to ex-prosecutor William Travers Jerome.* A former chief of detectives for the Southern Pacific Railroad undertook to organize bombings in the state of Washington and elsewhere until an accomplice squealed and he and his German bosses were indicted. In July 1916 German agents blew up millions of dollars' worth of munitions at Black Tom Island, New Jersey, in New York Harbor, the blast breaking every window in Jersey City. At the time the munitions were being guarded by private detectives from an agency in the employ of the Russian government, though it was alleged that the Germans bribed some of the guards. The Germans also utilized various anti-British nationalists such as Irish and Indian revolutionaries. The British secret service countered by bringing pressure on the U.S. government, so that Jim Larkin was jailed until 1923, when Governor Al Smith pardoned him, and a group of Indian nationalists were brought to trial in San Francisco on subversion charges. In the fashion of that city, one of them shot a suspected informer dead in the courtroom and was himself killed by a marshal.[59]

In 1917, Congress passed the Espionage Act, making it a crime to convey false statements to interfere with the war effort. In 1918, the Sedition Act made it a crime to utter "disloyal" statements. Depending on how various judges would construe such laws, it might be very dangerous to criticize any aspect of American life. In a test case Justice Holmes, speaking for the U.S. Supreme Court, upheld the Espionage Act, proposing a test whereby the words must constitute a "clear and present danger." In the key case involving the sedition law Holmes thought that the prosecution did not prove a clear and present danger, though the majority of the Court upheld the conviction.[60]

During the war the FBI, with the assistance of volunteers from the American Protective League, conducted activities of dubious legality, including highly publicized "slacker" raids where agents and police picked thousands of suspected draft evaders off the streets and held them until they could produce their identity. Not surprisingly, the radicals who agitated against the war were the prime targets of government activity.

---

* The letter referred to $10,000 paid to Jerome in a "delicate" matter. Jerome himself refused to discuss the incident.

A coalition of antiwar activists attempted to stage a national conference; they were rejected by a number of cities, then Big Bill Thompson allowed them to meet in Chicago, promising that the police would not interfere. Governor Frank Lowden, George Pullman's son-in-law, warned that troops would be sent to break up the meeting. Unfortunately for the governor, the nearest militia units were some that were training in Springfield while they awaited induction into the federal service. As the conference opened, the troops entrained for Chicago. The circumstances caused socialist leader Morris Hillquit to remark that this was a radical meeting unusually "ready to cut out discussion and eager to settle down to practical work," spurred on as it was by periodic bulletins on the progress of the troop train.*

Since Chicago was the center of IWW activities, the government proceeded to indict the radical antiwar movement in the Federal District Court of that city. In September 1917 Wobblies were seized throughout the United States and shipped to Chicago for trial. As a patriotic gesture the debutantes of the North Shore offered to haul prisoners from IWW headquarters to the county jail in their limousines; the latest in 1917 chic was a pretty girl in mink driving her limousine with handcuffed Wobblies under armed guard chained in the back.[62]

The choice of Chicago also put the defendants before one of the most erratic judges in the nation, Kenesaw Mountain Landis, later the baseball commissioner. Landis was famous for running his court with an iron hand and theatrical gestures.** The defendants requested the services of Clarence Darrow, but he declined on the grounds that he was in Washington "doing war work"; some of the Wobblies heard a rumor that he had in fact written the espionage law under which they were indicted.[64] Ninety-nine of the defendants were convicted, receiving terms

---

* The convention concluded with a cheer for Thompson's police, but Captain William Russell (later commissioner of police, 1928–1930) refused the praise and lectured the radicals on patriotism. Hillquit reported that as the radicals departed, a previously arranged wedding party replaced them, but was shortly disrupted by a regiment of black soldiers who, unaware the radicals had departed, stormed the hall.[61]

** Kenesaw Mountain Landis (1866–1944) was the son of an Ohio doctor who lost a leg at the Battle of Kenesaw Mountain during the Civil War. As a lawyer he was a protégé of his father's old regimental commander, Walter Gresham, U.S. Secretary of State (1893–1895) and a Federal appeals judge in Chicago. Appointed to the bench by Theodore Roosevelt in 1905, Landis turned his courtroom into a theater, causing Heywood Broun to remark that "his career typifies the heights to which dramatic talent may carry a man in America if only he has the foresight not to go on the stage." In one instance Landis called John D. Rockefeller into court and fined Standard Oil 29 million dollars, though an appeals court reversed the decision. In bankruptcy cases, Landis more than once noted the petitioner's wife sitting in court with an expensive coat and diamond rings and ordered her to be stripped of them and the baubles given to creditors.[63]

in the ten-to-twenty-year range, and most went to Leavenworth Prison, though Bill Haywood eventually jumped bond and fled to Russia, where he lived in exile until his death.

Eugene Debs, now sixty-three, deliberately sought prosecution via antiwar speeches but was ignored until June 1918, when in an open-air meeting in Canton, Ohio, he denounced the draft and was indicted. Debs was convicted and sentenced to ten years in Atlanta. In this instance, Darrow offered to defend him, but Debs refused to accept defense from a supporter of the war.[65]

If the war was difficult for the radicals, the aftermath was more so. Prior to America's entry into the war, President Wilson told the *New York Wold*'s Frank Cobb:

> Once lead this people into war, and they'll forget there ever was such a thing as tolerance. To fight you must be ruthless and brutal, and ruthless brutality will enter into the very fiber of our national life, infecting Congress, the Courts, the policeman on the beat, the man in the street.[66]

Of course, the President was himself a major contributor to such attitudes with his own intolerance to opposition. In 1919, when Wilson was largely concerned with making the peace, the home front was in convulsion. It was the year when, in February, a general strike in Seattle was crushed by Mayor Ole Hansen, who summoned troops. It was the year when, in April, bombs were mailed to many prominent persons—Mayor Hansen, J. P. Morgan, John D. Rockefeller, Justice Holmes, Immigration Commissioner Caminetti (an ardent antiradical), Judge Landis, Attorney General Palmer, and others. One exploded in the home of a United States Senator, injuring his wife and a maid. On May Day riots broke out in Boston, Cleveland, and New York. In June there were more bombs, and an explosion killed a man carrying a device up the steps of Attorney General Palmer's home in Washington. On July 4 a national demonstration was planned for Tom Mooney, but it fizzled. In that same month there was a race riot in Chicago, and in September the Boston police struck and a race riot occurred in Washington. September also saw the beginning of a steel strike, with major disturbances in Pennsylvania and Indiana. In the latter state, General Leonard Wood led the regular army into Gary and ruled by martial law.[67] The bombings and strikes, not the least of which was the Boston police strike, and the rhetoric and action of many radicals produced widespread fear and antiradical sentiment. Such feelings were bound to result in government excesses.

In September 1919 the President collapsed with a stroke, leaving the government leaderless, though his control of domestic affairs had hardly been significant before that. Throughout 1919 the forces of law and order grew increasingly active. In February the Secret Service rounded up Wobblies in New York. In June the FBI, assisted by gray-clad troopers of the New York State Police, raided a headquarters of some Russian-born socialists in New York City. So frightened were some of the radicals of the troopers, whom they thought were Cossacks, that they tried to jump out the window to their deaths and had to be restrained.[68]

At this point leadership in the anti-Red drive was in the hands of Attorney General A. Mitchell Palmer, a Pennsylvania Quaker and liberal reformer who had fought the Republican state machine in a manner Mark Sullivan could hardly have faulted. In 1913, he had turned down the post of Secretary of War on the grounds that he was a man of peace. Palmer placed the FBI under the direction of former Secret Service Chief William Flynn, and its General Investigations Division, which directed the anti-Red activities, under a twenty-four-year-old lawyer named J. Edgar Hoover.

At the end of 1919 Flynn and Hoover moved quickly to round up alien agitators, and in December 249 of them were deported to Russia on the so-called Soviet Ark, the U.S. Army transport *Buford*. Among the deportees were Emma Goldman and Alexander Berkman; their departure was the answer to a generation of conservative prayers. Even Hoover and Flynn came down to the dock to wave goodbye to the fist-shaking Emma. Unlike Reed and Haywood, the two anarchists did not find Russia to their liking and soon left, having been branded as Czarist agents. Throughout the postwar period they would attempt to expose Bolshevism, but formerly friendly American leftists and publications such as *The Nation* and *The New Republic* were now hostile.[69]

The following month the so-called "Red scare" reached its height with mass raids across the United States on January 2, 1920, in which 4,000 persons were seized for possible deportation. The raiding parties were composed of federal agents, local authorities, and military personnel. Nonaliens were turned over to state authorities for prosecution under anarcho-syndicalism laws. In Chicago the flavor was taken off the raids because the locals, eager as always, made their own raids on January 1.[70] The massive illegality of this action (most prisoners were released for lack of evidence) finally turned public opinion against such tactics, and they tapered off—although, of course, so too did the radical activities, because those who might have engaged in them were in jail, exile, or hiding.

In 1921 the Harding administration pardoned Debs and dismissed Flynn as director of the FBI, replacing him with William J. Burns, now sixty-two, wealthy and famous, and an old Ohio friend of Attorney General Harry Daugherty. The assistant directorship went to young J. Edgar Hoover. Burns applied his familiar aggressive tactics to FBI operations. Among his new agents was Gaston B. Means. In 1914 Means, a well-born North Carolinian, joined the Burns Agency and secured the account of the German Ambassador, Count Von Bernstorff. In 1917, after leaving Burns, Means was tried for murder and attempting to file a false will following the gunshot death of a rich widow he was courting, but he was not convicted. When Means's past record was revealed in the press, Burns switched him from agent to paid informant status. Still later, Means served prison sentences for violation of the Volstead Act and mail fraud before he was finally sent away permanently for his role in the Lindbergh case.[71]

Among other bureau agents were Ned McLean, wealthy publisher of the *Washington Post* and well-known alcoholic man about town, who served without pay, and Jess Smith, alleged collector for Harding's "Ohio gang," who committed suicide or in some way sustained a fatal gunshot wound after the Teapot Dome scandal broke.

The death of Harding and the revelations of official corruption in leasing the Teapot Dome oil reserves brought major changes in the Department of Justice. Harding's friend Attorney General Daughtery resigned, and Coolidge appointed Columbia Law School Dean Harlan Fiske Stone in his place. One of Stone's first acts was to dismiss Burns, who promptly resumed his private detective duties on behalf of the Teapot Dome defendants. Since the Department of Justice was itself suspect, Secret Service agents were assigned to assist in a Senate investigation and were themselves trailed by Burns operatives. Later, the Burns Agency was fined for shadowing jurors and William Burns was given a jail sentence for contempt of court, though it was never served.[72]

Attorney General Stone also cast about for an FBI head, canvassing his fellow cabinet member Commerce Secretary Herbert Hoover. Hoover, in turn, solicited advice from his aide Larry Richey, and he suggested his friend, twenty-nine-year-old J. Edgar Hoover, who as assistant director had been untouched by the various scandals.[73] Stone appointed him acting director, and within a short time the "acting" was dropped. For nearly a decade Hoover's Bureau would remain a relatively obscure backwater, its three hundred agents engaged in routine investigations of auto theft and bank embezzlements spiced with a bit of white slavery. In the 1920s the real focus of national law enforcement was the Treasury.

The T-Men

In 1920, with the adoption of national Prohibition, enforcement authority was lodged in the Bureau of Internal Revenue of the Treasury Department. Eventually, the number of Prohibition agents would swell to a massive 4,000—a previously unheard-of size for a federal detective force. The staff was appointed outside of civil service, and for practical purposes the Bureau was run by the Anti-Saloon League. Prohibition would serve as the ultimate struggle over morality, Parkhurst versus Tammany on a national scale. As Walter Lippmann wrote:

> The evil that the old fashioned preachers ascribe to the Pope, to Babylon, to atheists, and to the devil, is simply the new urban civilization, with its irresistible scientific and economic and mass power. The Pope, the devil, jazz, the bootleggers, are a mythology that expresses symbolically the impact of a vast and dreaded social change. The change is real enough. . . . The defense of the Eighteenth Amendment has, therefore, become much more than a mere question of regulating the liquor traffic. It involves a test of strength between social orders and when that test is concluded, and if, as it seems probable, the Amendment breaks down, the fall will bring down with it the dominion of the older civilization. The Eighteenth Amendment is the rock on which the evangelical church militant is founded, and with it are involved a whole way of life and an ancient tradition. The overcoming of the Eighteenth Amendment would mean the emergence of the cities as the dominant force in America, dominant politically and socially as they are already dominant economically.[74]

Prohibition enforcement would demonstrate that the federal government could be as corrupt and incompetent as any other. At the beginning, liquor stocks then in existence were stored in government warehouses. Anyone who could obtain a legal permit to withdraw a portion for medicinal, industrial, or other lawful purposes possessed a valuable commodity. A gallon of whiskey worth 62 cents at the government warehouse could be sold to a bootlegger for $8, cut, and resold to the public for three times that amount. Not surprisingly, some $165-per-month Prohibition agents were able to make $200,000 a year and come to work in chauffeured limousines. Between 1920 and 1928, when the Treasury shifted the Prohibition Bureau to the Department of Justice, 706 agents were fired for theft and 257 prosecuted. At one time, the chief of the New York office asked his men to put their hands on the table and summarily fired everyone wearing a diamond ring, thereby losing half his staff. A Commissioner of Internal Revenue and a Congressman were indicted for violation of Prohibition laws.[75]

Nor were the Prohibition men particularly restrained in their enforcement activities. Occasionally, innocent bystanders would be shot during the spectacular raids which soon became a feature of the roaring twenties. In Chicago, in 1927, a local chief agent gained much newspaper attention and praise with his aggressive tactics until he shot an innocent person, and then the press demanded his indictment. To avoid local prosecution, he had to take shelter in the federal building for several days, eating and sleeping in the U.S. Attorney's office until he could be spirited out of the state.[76]

While the Prohibition agents received public attention, strutting about the stage, a much more important Treasury unit appeared quietly in the background. World War I had created a host of new rich, many of whom neglected to pay their appropriate income and war profits taxes. Traditionally American governments do not object to grafting as long as the grafter spreads it around—the stern injunction "Cut it up or cut it out" is understood from the Tenderloin precinct to Capitol Hill. Therefore, in 1919 the Treasury formed a 100-man Intelligence unit, not to explore why the war killed some people while enriching others, but to make sure the latter included Uncle Sam in the take.

The new chief of Intelligence was a Virginia postal inspector named Elmer Irey, a Horatio Alger of the Civil Service who started as a nineteen-year-old stenographer in 1907 and worked his way up to become an $1,800-a-year sleuth. Irey leaped at the chance to earn the $2,500 a year which his new job paid. He would become the Treasury's foremost agent in the interwar years, but unlike his predecessors and contemporaries, he would not form a private detective agency or become a national idol. Perhaps this is what caused William Burns to remark, "Irey of the Intelligence Unit, bah, that's a misnomer."[77]

In 1921 the Intelligence squad prosecuted a South Carolina bootlegger who appealed his conviction on the grounds that the profits from an illegal business were not taxable. The courts disagreed, and the U.S. government was provided with a major new weapon to use against grafters, particularly those who offended Washington. Tax evasion cases did not lend themselves to dramatic raids, blazing gun battles, or quick arrests. Where an open saloon or bordello was obvious to a twelve-year-old and the people who operated such places were often from the wrong side of the tracks, the proof of tax evasion was usually hidden in volumes of bound ledgers and the perpetrators were occasionally found in the social register. The ideal tax agent was someone like Frank Wilson, a Buffalo policeman's son who was so nearsighted that he was discharged from the World War I army and always did poorly on the pistol range. In the 1920s Wilson was assigned to check the work of a woman accountant whose wizardry enabled Hollywood stars to pay very little on their huge incomes. When Wilson was finished, the woman was in prison and various idols of the screen, including Tom Mix, cowboy symbol of American virtue, had to plead guilty to federal charges.[78]

In 1929 Irey was ordered to "get" Al Capone. Intelligence agents believed the order arose from an incident in a Florida hotel. Allegedly, while President-elect Herbert Hoover was checking in, he noticed another guest receiving more attention. Larry Richey was dispatched to determine the identity of the rival celebrity and reported it was Capone, whereupon Hoover tersely ordered, "Get him." Many years later ex-President Hoover assured Irey that the story was false, but it was believed at the time, an impression heightened by Treasury Secretary Andrew Mellon of Pittsburgh, who daily informed Irey that the President had inquired, "Have you got that fellow Capone yet?" Naturally (as Irey later recounted), the federal agents were not going to let some lawyer's "hocus pocus" stop them.[79] When Frank Wilson learned that one underworld figure with considerable knowledge of Capone's doings had a deadly fear of insects, he persuaded a federal judge to set a high bond and throw the man in a maggoty cell, whereupon he became a government informer.[80] The "get Capone" drive was also aided by $75,000 from a group of Chicago businessmen known as "the secret six"—a throwback to the tradition of rich reformers' hiring of private detectives.[81]

Another figure in the Capone investigation was Eliot Ness, a twenty-six-year-old Prohibition agent who was assigned to supervise a squad of "untouchables," i.e., men who would not take graft. After graduation from the University of Chicago in 1925 Ness had worked as a credit investigator, then joined the Prohibition Bureau. His assignment on the Capone case was arranged by his brother-in-law, a former FBI man who was chief investigator for the secret six.[82] In 1931, Capone was convicted of tax violations and sentenced to eleven years in prison. In 1932 Irey and Wilson were assigned to assist in the Lindbergh kidnapping, and they, in effect, broke the case by their insistence on paying the ransom in distinguishable gold certificates whose serial numbers had been recorded.

The Lindbergh and Capone cases brought prestige to Treasury Intelligence, though in later years Eliot Ness claimed major credit for Capone and a popular TV series portrayed him as an FBI man with a roving commission to exterminate gangsters. Deception was enhanced by the engagement of FBI press agent Walter Winchell as narrator. Irey's memoirs ignore Ness but lionize Wilson; Wilson's memoirs ignore not only Ness but the deceased Irey as well. Perhaps the biggest winner in the Capone case was Dwight Green, the federal attorney who prosecuted Capone, since he eventually became the governor of Illinois.

Curiously, an undercover T-man referred to as Pat O'Rourke turns up in virtually all the major cases of the day. Apparently, O'Rourke was a great master of disguise, since he could arrest gangsters in the capacity of an agent and then live for months with the same groups without being recognized.[83]

Under FDR, the "get" squads, that is, the uptown version of the strong arms, would be kept busy getting such figures as Nucky Johnson, boss of Atlantic City, New Jersey,* Boss Tom Pendergast of Kansas

---

* In the Johnson case the T-men first employed the famous tactic of counting towels sent to the laundry from local brothels. From the number of towels was determined the number of patrons, thence the income to the house and on to the estimated payoffs to the machine.

City, James Michael Curley of Boston, and Huey Long of Louisiana. Although in the case of the last named, someone else got Huey with bullets, leaving the feds to jail his lieutenants. All these men were, of course, thorns in the side of FDR. In the instance of friendly bosses like New Jersey's Frank Hague or Chicago's Kelly and Nash, the criminal sanction was not invoked; instead Treasury settled for payment of a few thousands of the bosses' millions.

Of course, the tax weapon so useful against White House enemies could occasionally backfire. In 1944 one of FDR's aides, Eugene Casey, was subjected to an investigation. In 1932 Casey, then a Maryland plumber, had been broke. A decade later he was worth 2.5 million dollars. Casey had been stingy with the U.S., paying less than $14,000 in taxes in one two-year period when he should have paid ten times that amount. The Commissioner of Internal Revenue (later jailed himself) attempted to intervene to kill the investigation, but Treasury Secretary Henry Morgenthau refused to acquiesce, and a case was prepared and sent to the Department of Justice. Casey had offended some Democrats by his role in FDR's purges, and unfortunately for him the President died in April 1945.* Irey's accounts of the handling of the case provides insight into the processes by which federal justice was dispensed in such matters:

> During those two years it was interesting to watch the forces of politics grinding grimly to keep Casey out of jail for the good of the party and to put him in jail to repay old political scores. The possibility of his guilt or innocence didn't seem to enter the matter at all. The party leaders wanted Casey to escape the ignominy of jail, but some of the party powers remembered Casey's enthusiastic support of FDR's abortive "purge" campaign of 1938. I'm afraid it was just as bald as that.[84]

The G-Men

As Capone departed for Alcatraz and the Prohibition era ended, many ex-bootleggers and the dispossessed of the Depression turned to spectacular crimes such as bank robbery or kidnapping. Organized in gangs and moving from state to state, such groups were beyond the control of the local police, but neither were they organized vice purveyors or defrauders of the type the Treasury Department was used to dealing with. FDR and his new Attorney General, Homer Cummings, a

---

* Eventually, Casey was brought to trial and offered the defense that he was too busy helping FDR win the war to bother with his tax returns. The first trial ended in a hung jury, but at the second the government was prepared to prove that his returns had been incorrect for many years before the war. Casey pleaded no contest and received six months in jail and a $30,000 fine. He was also forced to pay the government an additional half-million dollars in back taxes.

former crusading prosecutor from Connecticut, pledged federal action. The assault on banks and wealthy individuals was seen as a type of subversion, though contemporary filmmakers have tended to portray Dillinger, Bonnie and Clyde, et al. as romantic proletarian heroes.

The ideal force to combat this new menace was a revival of the Pinkerton methods used against Jesse James, Butch Cassidy, and the Renos—that is, a mobile force of detectives to hunt down the "public enemies." However, in 1933 the task could not be turned over to a private agency. Given the restrictions on the Secret Service, the body assigned to undertake such an effort was the FBI, although at first glance this was a dubious choice. Generally, Bureau agents did not carry arms or have arrest powers greater than ordinary citizens. In the first twenty-five years of its existence only one agent had been slain in the line of duty—killed by a car thief in that most predictable of locations, Chicago. Nor was J. Edgar Hoover, who had never made an arrest, thought of as a real policeman. Some consideration was given to employing the army, which would have meant the creation of a national gendarmerie. Another proposal was to put a cop in Hoover's place, and Val O'Farrell, then conducting quiet investigations for the White House, was considered but rejected.* By default Hoover and his Bureau got the job.

As in the Pinkerton days, the first prerequisite to defeating the "public enemies" was to win the battle of publicity. The image of the Prohibition bootleggers was mixed. Some were thought of as daring individuals who performed a service, others like Capone were seen as sinister aliens, subversive of American life. Most of the bank robbers and kidnappers of the early '30s seemed to be plain American folks off the farms, people such as Dillinger, Pretty Boy Floyd, Bonnie and Clyde, and Ma Barker and her boys. In Depression-ridden America a large portion of the population did not grieve too greatly over an attack on a bank or the kidnapping of a millionaire.

In this respect two crimes helped to promote the public enemy image. The 1932 kidnapping and murder of the Lindbergh baby, besides its innate cruelty, was a blow at the public's number one hero. The perpetrator's identity as a German ex-convict would not be made known until the fall of 1934, and in the interim the underworld was widely blamed.

---

* Valerian O'Farrell (1876–1934), a boyhood friend of Al Smith, joined the NYPD in 1900 after graduating from college. He served until 1912, when he resigned to set up his own agency. As a private eye he catered to wealthy clients including the Broadway crowd, and among those who retained him were the British government, the Vanderbilts, Arnold Rothstein, and Charley Becker. In the 1920s he was employed by an American leftist to investigate the death of President Friedrich Ebert of Germany. O'Farrell also analyzed major crimes for a New York paper with the assistance of a ghost writer, but his deductions were reportedly so inept that the ghost writer substituted his own for the detective's. O'Farrell's chief supporter for FBI head was Democratic Party Chairman Jim Farley.[85]

The other event was the Kansas City Massacre, and here the central figures, at least on the surface, were native types.

Kansas City in the 1930s was about as wide-open and corrupt as any city in America. A young reporter named Edward R. Murrow, writing at the time, expressed the opinion that Kansas City had more vice than Paris.[86] The Treasury Department considered it to be a major drug center. The local political boss was an Irish-American named Thomas J. Pendergast. The chief of police was a puppet of a gangster named John Lazia, and the department was full of Lazia appointees.[87]

In 1930 a prisoner named Frank Nash escaped from the federal penitentiary in Leavenworth, Kansas. Nash, though a robber and murderer, was a popular figure in the underworld, and after escaping he roamed about openly in the mob-dominated city of Hot Springs, Arkansas. In June 1933, FBI agents, assisted by a respected Oklahoma lawman, seized Nash and transported him by car and train to Kansas City for return to Leavenworth. The feds were well aware that an attempt might be made to free the prisoner; therefore they arranged for additional agents and Kansas City detectives to be present at the railroad station to assist them in the motor trip to Leavenworth.

Their plans were leaked to the underworld by Lazia-dominated police, and a plot was laid to free Nash. The leader of the endeavor, Verne Miller, had been a hero in World War I and upon his return to his South Dakota home was elected sheriff. Though a fearless lawman, he was sent to the penitentiary for embezzling county funds. After his release he became a bootlegger, bank robber, and gunman operating throughout the Midwest. Miller, supposedly suffering from paresis, undertook the assignment to rescue Nash and recruited Charlie "Pretty Boy" Floyd and Adam Richetti, to assist. On the morning of June 17, while Nash was being transferred to an automobile at the Union Station, the three hoodlums attacked with machine guns, killing two Kansas City detectives, the Oklahoma lawman, an FBI agent, and Frank Nash himself. Two other agents were wounded.

If the transfer had been handled properly, the attackers would have had no chance at all. A constabulary type of organization like the New Jersey State Police, for example, would have deployed a detail at strategic locations before the arrival so that the streets would have been full of troopers with shotguns and the roofs covered by sharpshooters with high-powered rifles. In the face of this even Verne Miller and company would have fallen back. As it was, the lawmen were sitting ducks grouped together.*

Like the Valentine Massacre, the Kansas City slaughter shocked the

---

* The Kansas City detectives assigned to assist the federal officers were chosen because their vehicle was equipped with automatic weapons, but the weapons were mysteriously removed on the morning of the 17th.

country because of the number of casualties and the boldness of a day-light assault in the heart of the city. Within a few months a Treasury squad arrested Lazia for tax violations, and the underworld murdered him. Verne Miller was also killed by gangsters, while Pretty Boy Floyd was killed by the FBI in Ohio and Adam Richetti was captured, convicted, and executed.[88] And as a result of these spectacular crimes Congress passed the Lindbergh law, making kidnapping a federal crime, and authorized FBI men to carry guns, effect arrests, and pursue bank robbers and interstate fugitives.

The chief antigangster fighter of the Bureau was the agent in charge of the Chicago office, Melvin Purvis, a South Carolina lawyer who had joined up in 1927. It was his roving squad that had killed Pretty Boy Floyd. Earlier they had brought down the top prize of all, John Dillinger. In fact, it was Purvis whose career most resembled that of the figure presented on "The Untouchables" on TV. In 1934 Dillinger had been captured in Arizona and returned to the Lake County jail in Indiana to await trial for robbery and the murder of a police officer. Dillinger, though a small-time hoodlum, had caught the imagination of the nation with his daring bank robberies, and his return to the custody of a female sheriff was greeted with the attention accorded a visiting President, or Al Capone. Predictably, Dillinger escaped from the jail. Because he drove a car across a state line, the FBI was formally enabled to enter the case.

The first battle of the war went badly for the Bureau. In April 1934 Purvis in Chicago was notified that Dillinger and company were staying at the Little Bohemia Lodge in northern Wisconsin. The FBI men flew to the nearest airport, rented cars, and drove to the lodge. En route, some of the cars broke down, and the last several miles were accomplished with agents hanging on the running boards through the frozen night. As they approached the lodge, three local citizens came out and were promptly gunned down by the Bureau men, one of them receiving fatal wounds. The Dillinger gang then shot their way past the G-men. Agents dispatched to find a telephone bumped into Baby Face Nelson (Lester Gillis), who killed one and made his escape. A few months later, Nelson would kill two more agents who crossed his path, in the encounter receiving fatal wounds himself.[89]

At the same time as the FBI men were flying, driving, and stumbling through the wilds of Wisconsin, en route to massacre some of the local residents while losing one of their own number, the New Jersey State Police were prowling about the wilds of New York City attempting to trace various ransom notes in pursuit of Bruno Hauptman. To a detached observer it might have appeared more productive for Purvis and his college-educated agents to work on the Lindbergh kidnapping, while if the State of Wisconsin had a police force like New Jersey's, its officers would have been on the scene at Little Bohemia with reliable autos, knowledge of the territory and, perhaps, the ability to tell locals from gangsters. A quasi-military type of force like the New Jersey State Police was the ideal body to conduct a raid on a rural lodge, and the FBI was ideal to trace ransom money.

Given their shortcomings, the G-men were fated to repeat many of the mistakes the Pinkertons made in their war with the James boys. In August 1934 the East Chicago, Indiana, police induced an informer, the famous "woman in red," to set up Dillinger's capture, and he walked into a trap at the Biograph Theater in Chicago. There Purvis and company killed him, wounded two bystanders, and came near to a shootout with city police summoned to the scene by a report of suspicious men lurking in the neighborhood. In St. Paul, agents shot and killed a Dillinger associate, and, when he was found unarmed, there was criticism. In New York in 1936, agents attacked a Manhattan flat where a bank robber was hiding out. As *Newsweek* described the story:

> [A] sharp clatter of gunfire echoed through the placid neighborhood.... [l]ater, a tear-gas bomb set fire to the apartment and brought fire engines screaming to the scene.... Amid the hubbub, a flustered G-man poked a sub-machine gun at a husky fireman. "Damn it, can't you read?" growled the fireman, pointing at his helmet. "If you don't take that gun out of my stomach, I'll bash your head in." For 35 minutes the shooting continued. Then a lull. "Give up or we'll shoot," shouted a G-man—as if they had been throwing spitballs up to then.[90]

Police Commissioner Valentine attacked "melodramatic raids," claiming that the Bureau had broken an agreement with New York detectives to make a joint arrest.

Even incidents which did not end in violence were hardly textbook models of police procedure. Up to 1936 Hoover had not made an arrest personally, and various critics chided him on his lack of qualifications and bullet-proof career while young agents fell before gangster guns. To combat this, Hoover undertook to personally arrest the current public enemy number one, Alvin Karpis. When FBI men located him in a New Orleans flat, Hoover flew to the scene and led his men as they seized Karpis coming out of a building. Hoover then gave the familiar movie command, "Put the cuffs on him," but none of the agents had any handcuffs, so a necktie was pressed into service. Undaunted, Hoover barked, "To headquarters." After a period of aimless driving it turned out that the agent driver, flown in to assist in the capture, did not know where headquarters was. Luckily the cooperative Karpis did.[91]

The Bureau might have been helped by working more closely with the local police, but in many cases this was an invitation to betrayal, as the Kansas City Massacre had demonstrated. A more practical expedient which the Bureau employed was to hire non-college graduates directly from the ranks of local police departments. This policy was not acknowledged, though, since Hoover always perpetuated the fiction that all his agents were lawyers or accountants, even though the accounting experience of some consisted of counting the notches on their guns.

The well-publicized exploits of Hoover's G-men were a reversal of the previous policy of federal law enforcement agencies which had deliberately sought anonymity. Herman Moran, chief of the Secret Service from 1917 to 1936, for example, felt that publicizing anticrime activities helped criminals.[92] Treasury subordinates such as Burns fell into disfavor for their public relations activities, while Irey declared that the first rule of government service was "Don't stick your neck out."[93] For many years Hoover too kept a low profile, but in the early 1930s he switched completely, encouraging movies, books, and articles about the Bureau and its director, although he disliked personal publicity for his subordinates, exhibiting great displeasure when Purvis quit to write a book and participate in a movie. The Bureau's massive public relations campaign brought major dividends to Hoover and the FBI, as well as the Roosevelt administration, and the director became a national hero in high favor at the White House.

Treasury Coordination

The growth of the FBI had not passed unnoticed at the Treasury. In 1936, Secret Service agents began a quiet investigation of FBI shooting incidents, but when Hoover found out and complained, the personnel involved were demoted.[94] In that same year Treasury Secretary Morgenthau proposed a unification of the several Treasury enforcement agencies (Customs, Narcotics, Intelligence, Secret Service, and Alcohol and Tobacco Tax), into one force, but his plan was rejected. He then appointed Irey as coordinator of all Treasury enforcement and retired the seventy-two-year-old Herman Moran as chief of the Secret Service. Moran, a fifty-five-year veteran, had been kept on by presidential waiver of age but was now permitted to enjoy his $100-a-month pension.[95] As a replacement Frank Wilson was brought over from Treasury Intelligence. For the once preeminent Secret Service it was a bitter blow. Not only had it been outstripped by the very junior FBI, but it was superseded within the Treasury itself by an Intelligence agent as coordinator and another one as chief of the Service.

According to Wilson, the Secret Service was in bad shape. The White House detail was over age and couldn't shoot straight; the field agents were untrained and counterfeiting was out of hand. He quickly installed younger men in the White House, set up Treasury training schools, and established a massive public relations campaign, engaging Lowell Thomas to acquaint the public with means of spotting counterfeit currency.[96]

Within the Treasury another agency was growing in importance. In 1914 a Hague Conference had provided for international action against illicit narcotics and the United States Congress passed the Harrison Act, making the distribution of nonmedicinal drugs a federal crime. Enforcement was placed in the hands of the Internal Revenue Service. In 1920 it was moved to the Prohibition Bureau, and in 1930 a separate Narcotics Bureau was established in the Treasury Department.

The drive for an independent bureau to carry on a vigorous antidrug campaign was largely a result of the efforts of the socially prominent Mrs. Hamilton Wright, a most formidable lady who had Congressmen hiding under their desks in fear of her onslaughts. She was not successful, though, in naming the agency head, since her choice, Admiral Mark Bristol, was out of favor at the Hoover White House. But Mrs. Wright, who had fought opium for thirty years beginning with her China missionary days, was determined to ensure that the new chief, a former U.S. consul named Harry Anslinger, took his job seriously.[97] He was not to disappoint her. Through the '30s Anslinger would campaign vigorously to alert the nation to the dangers of even one puff of a marijuana cigarette. Soon the Bureau of Narcotics took its place as a premier law enforcement agency.

In one instance, the Narcs fought the Secret Service through the Treasury hierarchy to the Attorney General over who would have control of an informer possessing information useful in both drug and counterfeiting cases. Narcotics got first chance, promising to turn the man over to the Secret Service, but in the meantime he was murdered. The Bureau of Narcotics also borrowed many Pinkerton tactics, making extensive use of undercover operatives and hiring on a merit basis, being one of the first federal agencies with a significant number of Negro agents. In the world of drugs, mystery was the rule. In an international case the Treasury awarded a medal to a Mexican policeman for his assistance, but the whole affair had to be kept quiet. In the classic espionage tradition, the officer received a secret medal for a secret operation. Thus while white slavery and liquor faded out as important menaces, drugs moved in, though they would not reach their full bloom until after World War II.[98]

Despite the fact that the Treasury agents conducted the bulk of federal criminal investigations, from 1936 on the FBI was clearly the number one federal law enforcement agency. Most Treasury officials realized that this was irreversible, though Irey, for one, attacked the G-men and the Department of Justice every chance he got.[99] Within the Treasury, Intelligence, with its list of severed heads of the mighty, was the premier unit in the '30s, though the Secret Service would regain a bit of prestige with its wartime role in protecting the President and notable visitors like Winston Churchill. In the postwar period the glamour squad would be Narcotics, but no T-men would approach the prestige of the FBI.

Federal to Local

The success of the G-men (a term which in the public mind often included all federal agents) was contrasted with the failure of the local police. In 1935, the FBI opened a National Academy where state and local law enforcement officials could receive FBI training. Inflated by the Bureau's public relations machine to "the West Point of Law Enforcement,"—the thirteen-week course for experienced police officers could hardly be compared with a four-year college course for pre-service cadets—it would provide a useful experience; but since the Bureau's basic operations were quite different from those of municipal police, its value was limited. Perhaps its real utility was in enabling the Bureau to build up a network of local police contacts who had been indoctrinated in the FBI's concepts and subject to its screening. Indeed, some of the graduates were so eager to embrace the Bureau's mystique that throughout the remainder of their careers they would seek bureaucratic and political advancement on the basis of their "FBI training." The Bureau's ascendancy over local police was further heightened by its control of the best crime laboratory in the country and the national identification records. Some might wonder why the Bureau, which comprised but 10 percent of all federal law enforcement activity and a fraction of 1 percent of the national total, was so favored, but it was, and local police were well advised to cooperate or risk the consequences. Cities whose chiefs displeased Hoover were denied an opportunity to send officers to the National Academy, and their crime figures might be rejected as false even though they were no more preposterous than those from other locales not out of favor.

Naturally it occurred to many city fathers that federal agents might be the new supermen to clean up their local force, and in fact a number of them did become state and municipal police chiefs, with varying degrees of success. One such was Lear B. Reed, a minister's son, lawyer, and ex-captain of Marines, who joined the FBI in 1924 and rose to special agent in charge of the St. Louis office. Reed was not an office supervisor, though. One subordinate remembered him as "a turbulent personality . . . thorough extrovert, impatient for action . . . quick to anger . . . a man of strong likes and dislikes."[100]

Reed's autobiographical account of his career relates several shooting incidents, including one in St. Louis in 1934 where he was indicted for manslaughter in the death of a woman during a raid, although he attributed the blame for this to the local police.[101] Reed, a country boy, took a dim view of cities and their police. Recounting an investigation in the Chicago stockyards district, he wrote:

> We were in a neighborhood where an officer was as welcome as a skunk at a lawn party. From that section one might come back alive or one might be brought back dead or dying. . . .
>   About an hour later one of the officers left his post. He wanted to smoke, he had to have a sandwich, and his feet hurt him. He stumbled over a clothes line. Dogs began barking, windows flew open, and again police officers began running over each other.[102]

Eventually Reed was assigned to Kansas City, Missouri, where the machine run by Tom Pendergast had absolute control of the city and county governments and virtually everything was for sale. It was, in fact, a western Jersey City, and Boss T. J. Pendergast's career paralleled that of his contemporary Frank Hague. Born in St. Joseph, Missouri, in 1872, he had followed his political brother to the city in the 1890s and served briefly as a constable. As a young man, T. J. was a brawler, frequently including cops among his opponents. By World War I, he was a local power, by 1925 a czar.[103]

In 1926 the reformers brought about a city manager form of government, and, like Hague with the commission plan, T. J. took over the system and made it work for him. On one occasion his handpicked city manager, Henry McElroy, made his acceptance speech to the City Council before that body had gone through the formality of electing him, causing his daughter Mary to break up with laughter. One thorn in T. J.'s side was state control of the police department, but in 1932 that was removed and a Pendergast man was installed, although the real chief was John Lazia. However, 1933 was a bad year; local hoodlums had the effrontery to kidnap Mary McElroy. One of the kidnappers became the first man executed under the Lindbergh law. Another was spared the death penalty when Mary testified that she had fallen in love with him.[104] The massacre at the Union Station also shook the police-politics-crime alliance. In '34 Lazia's murder and a violent election in which a number of middle-class reformers were slugged caused Pendergast to appoint a Kansas City newsman as director of police, although according to Elmer Irey he was suspected of murder. As Irey described local law enforcement,

> You could buy all the morphine or heroin you could lift in Kansas City; and the man who wanted to keep his job as a police captain in Kansas City had better keep his prostitute file correct and up to the minute so

Tom's machine would be certain no girl practiced her ancient art without paying full tribute.[105]

The outcry after the 1934 troubles was so severe that a number of prominent Democrats turned down the chance to be T. J.'s candidate for the U.S. Senate. The designation went to a minor official whom the boss had previously refused to slate for county collector.[106] The designee, Harry Truman, defeated Jake Milligan in the primary and went on to be elected to the Senate. The only effective opposition to the machine came from the United States Attorney, Maurice Milligan (brother of Jake), who conducted an investigation of vote fraud in federal elections using Reed's G-men as investigators. As a result a number of municipal officials were convicted.

In the late '30s Pendergast's handpicked governor turned against him and in an alliance with Roosevelt and Maurice Milligan mounted a campaign which eventually sent the boss, City Manager McElroy, the police director, and others to the penitentiary for income tax evasion. The fall of the machine came as a blow to its loyal supporters. Mary McElroy committed suicide, and Senator Truman faced almost certain defeat in the 1940 primary. However, both the governor and U.S. Attorney Milligan ran against him, splitting the field, and Truman went back to the Senate. In 1945, in one of his first official acts as President— "He had hardly set the Bible aside," according to Elmer Irey—Truman fired Milligan.[107] Truman's action was seen by some as a blow to federal law enforcement, but it could be pointed out that the Milligan family was not exactly neutral politically. In 1948 Truman, a product of Boss Pendergast and Vice President thanks to bosses Kelly, Hague, et al., met the great reform prosecutor, Tom Dewey, in the ultimate struggle, and, as often happened, the public picked the warm man of the people over the cold-blooded prosecutor.

With the demise of the machine in Kansas City an old expedient was introduced to reform the police. In 1939 the Legislature removed the department from municipal control and substituted a gubernatorially appointed Board of Commissioners. In July the board appointed Lear Reed as chief of police. According to the new chief, he turned down $147,500 in bribes in the first five weeks. Indeed, the Reed regime resembled the marshalship of Dodge City more than a major-city police administration. Reed had a simple answer for bribery offers:

> At first these lavish offers made me want to fight. They fired the indignation of a country boy raised on honesty, the Golden Rule and patriotism. One alleged promoter of nefarious operations lost some teeth and his hat, between my desk and the door, in his hurried departure. He unwittingly confided in one of my confidants that he never thought a person could

get so mad when offered some money, and that I should enter the ring with Joe Lewis [sic]. If my fist made that impression, he should have sampled my blackjack.[108]

When persuasion failed, shots were fired at Reed, who shot right back, though both sides missed. Next the county prosecutor indicted him for oppression. In 1941 Reed tired of the battle and resigned, stating his case in a book titled *Human Wolves: Seventeen Years of War on Crime*. In it he warns of the menace of Communism, drugs, sex perversion, and racial integration.

If Reed represented the overt, activist facet of federal law enforcement, the career of Eliot Ness in Cleveland represented the clandestine investigation facet. Cleveland, like New York, was a city that experienced periodic reform efforts. In 1901, Tom Johnson, a millionaire disciple of single taxer Henry George, had been elected mayor and brought with him a brand of municipal socialism. In 1903, he chose Fred "Golden Rule" Kohler, a tough career cop, to be chief of police. Kohler alternated between permissiveness and crackdowns. His policy of releasing minor offenders without charge, in accord with the Golden Rule, won him a national reputation. Within the department he kept the cops in turmoil, since he represented an anti-Irish clique. Nevertheless, like Devery or Enright, Kohler was a man of native intelligence and driving energy, with a social sensitivity akin to the mayor's. Theodore Roosevelt called him the best chief in the country. His civil service rating permitted him to remain in office even after Johnson's defeat, but in 1912 Kohler delivered a speech to an IACP meeting in which he decried the failure of the correctional system to rehabilitate. Unfortunately, his recitation of this ancient refrain was found to be plagiarized and the chief was embarrassed. In 1913 he was caught in an extramarital affair and dismissed by another reformer, Mayor Newton D. Baker, later Wilson's Secretary of War.

In 1921, Kohler was elected mayor, serving until 1923. In 1920 the chief justice of the municipal court was indicted for participating in a gangland murder, and the public furor resulted in a survey headed by a galaxy of national experts, including Dean Roscoe Pound and Professor Felix Frankfurter of Harvard Law School, Raymond Moley of Columbia, and Raymond Fosdick.[109] The survey urged the usual administrative changes but was ignored. After a term as mayor Kohler later became sheriff, and when he died a decade later, he left half a million dollars in his safe-deposit box. The police department continued its loose operations, the chief internal issue being the struggle between the Masons and the Catholics.[110]

In 1935 the new Republican mayor, Harold H. Burton, later U.S. Senator and Supreme Court Justice, decided to appoint Eliot Ness, now head of the Treasury's Alcohol and Tobacco Tax unit (ATU) for northern Ohio, as safety director, thus outflanking the civil service police chief. Ness was a clever public relations manipulator, not a town marshal type like Reed—in essence, a true secret agent. Cleveland was corrupt, and he set out to destroy the corruption by amassing evidence and winning the battle of public opinion. His first target was a vice squad captain whom the press exposed as having a personal fortune in excess of $100,000. Ness brought charges and the captain and members of his squad were indicted, convicted, and sentenced to prison. Next came a precinct commander on the model of Clubber Williams, a tough cop who ran his territory as a fiefdom, defying headquarters and making no secret of his corruption, while amassing over $200,000. The man fought Ness bitterly, hiring women to lure witnesses to bugged apartments. Finally, he threw in the towel and sought to retire on a disability, but Ness would not accept a compromise and the captain ended up in prison.[111]

In 1941 Ness resigned to take over vice control for the armed forces, playing the same role in World War II that Raymond Fosdick had in World War I. He died in obscurity at fifty-four, shortly before his name was to become a household word as a result of the TV series.

Both Reed and Ness neglected fundamental changes in favor of short-term effects; Reed enjoyed shootouts at high noon, while Ness actually jailed many of the opposition. Whatever the method, the federal men who came to head American police departments rarely had much impact after the initial clean-up of the scandal which brought them, but their public relations were usually dramatic.

HOOVER AND THE BUREAU: AN ASSESSMENT

Under J. Edgar Hoover, the FBI became a major American institution bulwarked by what a Brookings Institution study called "remarkable propaganda,"[112] which created a number of myths, some mild puffery, and some serious distortions. One long-continued inaccuracy related to agent quality, particularly the claim that all agents were either lawyers or accountants. It is not clear what percentage of the staff actually were during the '30s, although several individuals who began their careers at that time and later rose to high rank were neither attorneys or accountants.* In some instances, they were not even college graduates.

* A 1937 article reported 60 percent of the agents had "legal training" and 16 percent were graduate accountants. What legal training meant was not clear, but apparently something less than a lawyer. A contemporary account places the number of lawyers and accountants at 22 percent and 9 percent respectively.[113]

The agents were doubtless far better educated than the other American law enforcement personnel—as late as 1958, only about half of all new Treasury agents had bachelors' degrees[114]—but the Bureau always felt the need to puff their credentials. On the other hand, the FBI was unique among federal law enforcement agencies in not operating under civil service rules, preferring a type of merit system which left sole discretion regarding hiring, firing, promotion, and assignment in the hands of the director, who many critics alleged was not unmindful of an applicant's political affiliation, particularly if such connections were on Capitol Hill. Finally, several agents who have chosen to write memoirs admit to failing their draft physicals.[115] In comparison with the rigid civil service requirements of some state and local police departments, the FBI was clearly less stringent.

A second major myth concerns the unblemished record of the Bureau in terms of misconduct. It is frequently proclaimed that no agent ever disgraced the organization by succumbing to the various temptations of law enforcement. Despite the Bureau's ability to wash its dirty linen privately, accounts of FBI men charged with crimes do exist, and agents were, in fact, dismissed for a variety of offenses. A particular troublesome area was the interrogation of women involved in Mann Act cases.[116] Again, though it is very likely that the FBI has been the cleanest of all the law enforcement agencies, it has not been perfect.

A third myth was the Bureau's claims for success in its day-to-day work, citing 95 percent conviction rates. Interestingly, a 1937 study of federal law enforcement by the Brookings Institution found conviction rates in criminal cases ranging from 71.5 to 82.6 percent. The FBI at 72.5 percent managed to edge out the Customs Bureau for sixth place. Brookings also found that the Bureau, which continually urged local police to report their arrest figures, did not bother to report its own. However, a study of terminated cases showed a total of 5,335 defendants produced by the Bureau in one year, or about one-sixth of the Treasury total. With approximately 800 agents its was obvious that the typical FBI man was not exactly filling the jails, half a dozen arrests per year constituting an average performance. Indeed, many arrests for crimes such as auto theft, the largest source of Bureau cases, were made by local cops who turned the prisoner over to the Bureau for prosecution. Often the thieves were youngsters who had taken a joy ride from the Bronx to Bridgeport, Connecticut, or from Chicago to Gary, Indiana. The Brookings Institution also noted that the FBI annual report claimed 117 convictions in 120 bank robbery cases, whereas the Attorney General showed 114 cases, 53 of which resulted in conviction, 31 acquittal, and the others were not disposed of.[117]

Finally, the Bureau sought to hold itself out as a model of restrained law enforcement, though its shooting affrays sometimes brought embarrassment. The director also liked to declare his aversion to wiretapping; as late as 1940, he reiterated this in the prestigious *Harvard Law Review*. Again the facts were somewhat different. On several occasions in the '30s it became public knowledge that the Bureau did in fact employ this technique.[118]

The cumulative total of the myths presented the vision of a near-perfect FBI which always got its man, through strictly legal means, of course, never missed a shot, and never suffered any scandal. Since the average citizen never saw an FBI man, the contrast between the mythical Bureau and his all too human local police department was painful. The slightest failure of local policing brought the complaint "Why can't our officers be like the G-men?"—a variation on the theme that life should be more like the movies.

In the late 1930s the FBI was again propelled into the antisubversive field. In 1936, President Roosevelt ordered it to undertake investigations of various fascist and Communist groups in the United States,[119] and again, this would lead to controversy. In January 1940 the Bureau brought charges against an alleged pro-Nazi group in New York and the America Firsters were unhappy. In February agents in Detroit arrested alleged Communists, who were veterans of the Spanish Civil War, for violating U.S. neutrality laws. Immediately the left was in an uproar. Both cases failed of prosecution, the Attorney General dismissing the Communist case, while in New York the teenage FBI informer admitted supplying weapons and otherwise encouraging the embryo storm troopers.

While these cases caused major criticisms of the Bureau, their genesis at a higher level was obvious. During the time when the raids were made, Hitler and Stalin were allied and the war in Europe was under way. Both of the raided groups were or had been engaged in military training. Also, not least important, 1940 was an election year and both Reds and fascists were opposing President Franklin Roosevelt.* Thus many reasons existed for the federal action, and FDR went out of his way to defend Hoover publicly.[121] In the war that soon followed, the Bureau quickly seized most dangerous aliens, and to Hoover's great credit he was the leading opponent of the expulsion of Japanese-Americans from the West Coast.

J. Edgar Hoover was one of the most controversial men of the twentieth century. To some he was on a plane with Washington or Lincoln.

---

* More serious blows at the suspected Reds and Nazis were struck by the New York City police, whose detectives infiltrated both groups. The strong-arms were also employed, and Bobby McAllister, "the flying cop," routed a horde of Christian Fronters in a Bronx riot. As a turnabout both Communists and Christian Fronters also had their men in the police department.[120]

To others he was evil incarnate. If one considers the undisputed facts of his career in the period up to and including World War II, it is possible to make an assessment of his role. Had FDR dismissed the virtually unknown Hoover in 1933, no unfavorable political consequences would have resulted. Probably as late as 1940 the President could have fired him without suffering significant negative effects. After that, American Presidents apparently did not wish to take him on, despite later bold assertions by some of their lieutenants as to what the President might have done had he won the next election.

Why did Hoover remain in his obscure post for nine years prior to 1933? No doubt his appointment as director when he was but twenty-nine was a career boost, but after a few years' service no further gains accrued. Unlike Irey, who was happy to work for $2,500 a year, Hoover was a lawyer of sufficient talent to be given responsible tasks by a succession of Attorneys General including Harlan Fiske Stone, dean of Columbia Law School and later Chief Justice of the United States, who remained to the end of his days a great Hoover admirer. With this sort of recommendation, Hoover no doubt would have been well received in a New York, Philadelphia, or Washington law office of the late 1920s when men were getting rich quickly. His critics would respond that Hoover wanted not money but the power to control people's lives, but there was little power in the FBI until 1933. A power seeker might have sought to align himself with a great man, as Larry Richey had done with Herbert Hoover, or founded a detective agency like William Burns. Of course, it could be argued that Hoover was simply biding his time, waiting for his day to arrive. If Hoover in the '20s foresaw the Depression, New Deal, gangster era, war, and cold war, then one must look respectfully at the view of him as an omniscient god-like figure and take seriously his other predictions regarding the fate of the Republic. In fact, his early career suggests very strongly that he was a dedicated public servant who, like his father and brother, found satisfaction in a modest bureaucratic career.

In line with this hypothesis, few have disputed Hoover's skill as a bureaucrat. He knew how to please his superiors and how to make his will felt among his subordinates. After 1933 successive Attorneys General, Congress, and most importantly FDR strongly supported Hoover. It was no wonder that the President did so, for Hoover provided him with a series of public relations triumphs in the "war on crime." As historian Arthur Schlesinger, Jr., has pointed out, Roosevelt was a man with a limited respect for the Constitution when he wanted something done and he encouraged aggressiveness by Bureau chiefs.[122] Hoover was also very helpful in smashing some of the President's opponents and providing both important and amusing tidbits of intelligence regarding

FDR's friends and foes. Indeed, a major function of an intelligence service is to provide such information, and FDR was not the only President who liked to chuckle over Senator Jones's bedroom problems.* Thus the modern FBI was in large part created by the demands of the New Deal government, itself a product of its time and place.

Since Congress and the President were pleased with the Bureau, the only possible check was the media. Here, too, Hoover provided what was wanted—sensational news and heroes for the public to worship. Not all the media loved the Bureau all the time, but in general they went along with the image of the dedicated, intelligent, law enforcement officer. Indeed, the myths had much truth, and it is notable that the FBI did not use third-degree tactics and provided warnings against self-incrimination thirty years prior to their being required by the Supreme Court. More fundamentally, much of what the Bureau did was necessary in its time. If the FBI had not stopped the gangsters and Nazis, then some other group would have, probably the military or vigilantes, with excesses on a scale greater than those of the Civil War or World War I era.

A more basic question is whether Hoover and the Bureau were ultimately a beneficial influence on the American political process and the development of law enforcement. A complete answer would carry one into considerations beyond the time frame of the present study, since the Hoover era continued into the 1970s. Many Americans object to the massive public relations, secret files, and clandestine activities of the FBI. Yet as has been pointed out, public support is essential to a police agency, and unlike community model forces detectives must rely upon their media images, as very few citizens actually encounter them. Similarly, covert activities, often of questionable ethics, historically have been the standard operating procedures of detectives. Whether various techniques can appropriately be characterized as propaganda or dirty tricks is often based upon situational factors external to the acts in question. Very few Americans would criticize Secret Service Agent Burke's theft of Dr. Albert's briefcase and the subsequent leaking of its contents to the *New York World*, because in restrospect the German saboteurs stand condemned. Thus assessments of Hoover and company are likely to change over time.

Again, considering only the period to the end of World War II, the passage of time permits some evaluation of the FBI *in that era*. In the 1940s, the Bureau was not so predictable ideologically as it later

* P. J. Stead, an English expert on the French police, has noted: "As one turns the pages of the voluminous reports compiled by the inspectors of police in the 18th century, . . . it is obvious that they were as concerned to amuse as they were to inform . . . entertainment rather than intelligence seems to have been the result."[123]

became. In the prewar era, conservative stalwarts such as Westbrook Pegler and the *New York Daily News* were frequent critics,*[124] while leaders of the American Civil Liberties Union were often complimentary. For a long time after World War II, the Bureau rode the wave of political consensus. It was inevitable that when the consensus ended, the FBI would suffer. Though the storm was long delayed, Hoover and his Bureau, like the Pinkertons and William Burns, would reap the whirlwind.

---

* *The Daily News* attacked the Christian Front raids and publicized accounts of agents involved with prostitutes, though in part this was a reaction to Hoover's close ties to Walter Winchell of the rival *New York Mirror*.

Conclusion:
The Passing Parade

At the end of a narrative which has stretched from eighteenth-century London to twentieth-century California it is time to return to the questions posed in the Introduction. Police administration, as the parade metaphor implies, is dramatic, colorful, and to a large extent repetitive, and clearly it is not simply a technical specialization. Rather, it is centrally related to the processes of governance and struggles over wealth, power, and prestige, with control of the police frequently determining which values shall be stressed and which groups shall receive advantages. To state the foregoing still leaves unanswered questions of what constitutes the essence of policing and what are the mechanics by which police are controlled.

THE NATURE OF POLICING

Role

Our analysis makes it clear that modern policing is a product of the complexity and impersonality of urban industrial society. It is a formal, structured system designed to replace the relatively unstructured, informal social control of the rural village. At the elemental level, the London-model police force constituted a type of civil army characterized by the beat system of organization and the goal of preventing crime and disorder rather than dealing with it after the fact. This was largely achieved, since urban life became safer and more orderly. However, the success of the police was dependent upon other societal improvements and vice versa. Effective policing provided a climate of law and order permitting abolition of barbarous punishments. More importantly, it permitted social and political reforms, since as the fear of mob violence abated, greater liberty was extended to proponents of change. In this respect it is notable to contrast the relatively mild Trafalgar Square Riot of 1887 with the Gordon Riots a century earlier.

A similar situation prevailed in the United States after the adoption of a modern police system. The overall crime rate appeared to decline,[1] and mob violence became less common. As in Britain, social reform *plus* police effectiveness lead to a situation where an ever larger portion of the population supported law and order.

American cities, however, never achieved the levels of order and safety of British cities. Viewed in the broadest context, two perennial problems faced American police—vice and gangs. The term "vice" embraces efforts to regulate or suppress gambling, prostitution, liquor, drugs, and other indulgences. During the early years of the twentieth century, there was massive pressure to suppress liquor and prostitution culminating in federal enactment of the Volstead and Mann Acts. Yet by midcentury one was repealed and the other had become relatively unimportant. While liquor and prostitution suppression was at its height, drug enforcement remained a minor police concern despite the assertions of prominent men such as Arthur Woods and Raymond Fosdick that a quarter of a million addicts resided in New York City alone. In midcentury, however, drugs became a major law enforcement priority.

The problem of "gangs" carries one into a discussion of the supposed difference between crime and public order offenses, a dichotomy which is largely false. In virtually any city, the number of common predatory crimes such as robbery or assault is usually such that the average citizen is not likely to personally suffer violence. Yet, as in eighteenth-century London, the fear of violence is frequently high. In part, this can be explained by what might be termed "symbolic" assaults and muggings, i.e., public disorder, which alarms many citizens. For example, very few women are raped in a city, but many experience fear and humiliation from taunts and gestures. A lesser proportion of the male population is mugged, but a significant number are elbowed, eyed, or accosted by tough-looking characters.

By far the largest percentage of both predatory crimes and public order offenses has invariably, though far from exclusively, emanated from young (under twenty-five) low-income males. Groups ranging from the apprentice boys of London to the corner gang of an American neighborhood are frequently seen as a menace. When they are organized in well-known gangs such as the Dead Rabbits, Whyos, Ragen Colts, and Gustins, or represent some particular ethnic group which is itself the subject of negative stereotypes, the fear becomes magnified. Thus a central task of police has been to control the gangs. As Henry George observed:

> [L]et the policeman's club be thrown down or wrested from him, and the fountains of the great deep are opened, and quicker than ever before chaos comes again. Strong as it may seem, our civilization is evolving destructive forces. Not desert and forest, but city and slums and country roadsides are nursing the barbarians who may be to the new what Hun and Vandal were to the old.[2]

At a higher level, the problem of gangs, i.e. predatory crime, moves into the sphere of organized racketeers and professional criminals who poison the political and economic life of the society. A young Monk Eastman or Dion O'Bannion threatens the peace and order of the neighborhood. The mature Arnold Rothstein or Al Capone poses a menace to the national welfare. As the criminals have their hierarchy from corner tough to gang boss, so do the police from beat cop to federal detective chief, and each must counter its opposite number.

In some periods of American history the police have also been caught up in antisubversive activities. Here too, as with vice, viewpoints change rapidly. In the years just before World War I, Eugene Debs drew a respectable vote for President and Emma Goldman lectured to large audiences and was received in fashionable circles. A few years later one was in prison and the other in exile. And yet a decade after World War I radicalism was back in style, only to fade out and then reappear.

Thus police activity can be seen as a symbolic reaction to the fears of society. While the struggle to maintain order against the "gangs"— i.e., predatory criminals—seems to be rooted in perennial reality, from a long-range perspective activities undertaken to control vice or subversion appear to be less so, since the menace so threatening to one generation is often ignored by another.

Organization

The primary vehicle of controlling crime and disorder has been the London-style police force, or, in contemporary terms, the community service model. As James Q. Wilson has written:

> In the community service model . . . the essential idea is to assign a team of patrolmen and supervisors to a small area . . . to learn about the neigh-

borhood. This approach is based on the assumption that if officers are encouraged to become familiar with the neighborhoods in which they work and to take larger responsibilities for following through on citizens' requests for assistance as well as on complaints of crime, they will win the confidence of those whom they are to protect and thereby elicit more cooperative assistance from the public and better intelligence about criminal activities. . . .

[In contrast] the "crime attack" model . . . is based on the assumption that the best use of patrolmen is to place them as close as possible, not to the citizens, but to the scene of a potential crime in ways that will enable them to apprehend the criminal in the act, or at least cut short his crime almost as soon as it begins.[3]

In effect, crime attack is based on the patrol-type policing that was in existence in eighteenth-century Paris and Munich. Other types of crime attack forces are the constabulary and detective models. Within municipal police the community service versus crime attack debate can be seen as perennial, with chiefs such as New York's Walling and Boston's Savage arguing for the primacy of the uniform force and quasi-social-service techniques against Inspector Byrnes's stress on detectives and crime repression methods. At the extreme level there was always available the repressive capabilities of the constabulary model.

Interestingly, American municipal police in the post-World War II era, under the leadership of California professionalism, moved away from the beat system and community relations in favor of roving patrols emphasizing apprehension of criminals—in effect the crime attack model. In the '60s, when confronted with massive civil disorder, many even took on the appearance of a constabulary force.* This was further heightened by the practice of some communities of employing large numbers of nonresidents whose social characteristics were frequently quite different from those of the population being policed, thus giving rise to charges that they constituted an army of occupation. Whether the generally perceived increase in the level of postwar crime and disorder has been at least partially a result of this change in police operations, or whether the change is itself a response to the changing nature of the community, or both, is an interesting question beyond the scope of the present study.

* Given their stress on efficiency, the professionalized forces lacked the manpower to maintain the beat system even if they had so desired. While Commissioner O'Meara's Boston Police Department, circa 1915, and Chief Parker's LAPD of the '60s each had about 2.5 officers per 1,000 population, the Boston cops worked seventy to eighty hours a week, so that there were more on duty at any given time. This and the greater population density of Boston meant O'Meara's police could be assigned small foot beats whereas Parker's men could not. The latter, operating motor vehicles over wide areas, were thus denied close contact with the citizenry, a situation aggravated by the transient nature of the community.

Viewed from a long-term perspective, then, the key to policing is the task of social control by symbolic means. In community-type policing, arrests are less important than day-to-day contacts between policeman and public in which the former by his actions and bearing persuades the latter to accept the rules of society and join him in resisting those who will not. In effect, the sheriff achieves victory by forming a posse and pursuing the "bad man." By this action the community rallies to the side of legitimate authority and the criminal accepts his status as an outlaw. Thus the actual capture is relatively unimportant; it is necessary only that the criminal be caught and punished in enough instances to make the sanctions credible. Indeed, for some offenders the outlaw status alone may be sufficient to discourage further misconduct.

Even in noncriminal instances, the symbolic importance of the community policeman is significant. To the lower class he is, in Max Weber's words, "the representative of God on earth,"[4] which means that for a large segment of the population the police are the government. Again, the contrast between the London-model beat police and other forms is notable. The community force can only exist when it has the support of the majority of the populace. That is, where a moral consensus has been achieved and needs only to be implemented or extended. In contrast, the creation of a militarized constabulary type force is an indication of the failure of consensus and a situation where the police can only enforce the rule of the strong. In carrying out their role as moral preceptors, the community police have the advantage of close contact with the public while the constabulary, detective, and crime attack forces do not, and must therefore emphasize repression more than prevention.

CONTROLLING THE CONTROLLERS

Law, Administration, and Politics

How do police decide which values to project and which to ignore or deny? The foregoing chapters have suggested three mechanisms for control of the police: the law, administration, and politics. Politics, as used in the present work, implies the direct assertion of individual or group self-interest. Obviously, both law and administration can serve to further political ends, but in theory, they manifest a degree of detachment from narrow concerns in favor of the broader public interest. Between law and administration there is the difference illustrated by the contrast between the due process and crime control models. Administration generally seeks to define the public interest in the judgment of certified experts, with efficiency a major value. Law, on the other hand, adheres to a body of rules and often poses barriers to administrative efficiency. In societies where the law embodies a moral consensus, a community type police operates most effectively when it is used in the *service* of the law rather than as a *force* at the disposal of political or administrative heads.

The practical differences among the three mechanisms of control may be illustrated by the vice problem. In deciding on the appropriate posture toward a Canfield-style gambling operation, a political police chief need only note the balance of forces, meaning essentially that if the machine is stronger than the reformers, Canfield's can operate. When the balance is reversed, the axes are then employed and the gambling is temporarily stopped. An administrative chief might start enforcement via legal means, but if this proved frustrating the law might be "bent" by such tactics as stationing policemen at the entranceway to photograph (and thus intimidate) customers. In any event Canfield's would be suppressed. A legalistic chief would seek to close the operation if, and only if, it could be lawfully done. In practice this might well mean that the police would have to accept defeat.

In our narrative not only the Tim Sullivans and Abe Ruefs, but the Reverend Parkhursts and Fremont Olders could be viewed as politicians in that they vigorously pursued their own values in an unrestrained fashion. The Woods, Fosdicks, and Vollmers, as proponents of administrative science, attempted to substitute expert judgment for the passions of the bosses on one side and the reforming zealots on the other. Adherents of legality such as O'Meara, Gaynor, and Altgeld favored due process, so that unlike the administrators they were willing to accept less than maximum efficiency in the achievement of social control.

In assessing systems of police control, legality can be dealt with rather easily. The American police generally could not look for guidance to the law. Virtually all interest groups consistently ignored it or shaped it for their own purposes. Unfortunately, the bar and its leaders often set the worst examples. Defense attorneys such as Fallon, Rogers, or Darrow were matched in their excesses by prosecutors like Heney and Jerome and even the highest officials such as Attorneys General Olney and Palmer. Nor was ideology a guide to an individual or group's adherence to the rule of law. The few who unhesitatingly stood for legality varied in political faith from the conservative O'Meara to the liberal Altgeld. Until the late 1930s liberals were more distrustful of the courts than conservatives, and liberal leaders like Theodore and Franklin Roosevelt frequently ignored the law. Often the worst violations occurred under progressive governments, such as the Palmer Red raids, during the Wilson Presidency, or the wiretapping of priests by Mayor Mitchell's police.

Even committed civil libertarians were often willing to waive other persons' rights. Ernest Jerome Hopkins, for instance, made a career of supporting Tom Mooney's innocence and published a popular account of the Wickersham Commission's investigation of police abuses entitled *Our Lawless Police*. Yet as late as 1932 he argued that the San Francisco Preparedness Day parade should have been banned because of threats made against it.[5]

Almost never was the lesson learned that a worthy end could not be justified by an unlawful means. Frequently, the very persons who taught the police to use the questionable techniques were hoist by their own petard. As Professor Vern Countryman of the Harvard Law School has observed:

> The trouble I have is that many people ... can't get too alarmed about getting informants and surveillants into the Klan. So we tell the law-enforcement agency it's alright. But the law-enforcement agency can't see any difference between the Klan and the Communist Party. They've been told time and again by courts and others that the Communist Party advocates forcible overthrow of the government. If it's justified in one place, it's justified in the other.
>
> Then, from the law enforcement agency's point of view, there is no real difference between the Communist Party and what they regard as fellow traveller groups sympathetic to the Party.
>
> It seems to me that when we open the door in one place for all practical purposes we've opened it across the board. Law enforcement agencies will not make these nice distinctions.[6]

Legality also failed to solve real-world problems—for example, how a city administration could deal with gang violence without loosing the strong-arm squad, with rampant vice without harassing raids, and with crooked cops without shoeflies. More often than not, the individual who most often broke the law or used dirty tricks profited by winning the trial or the election. Had Fremont Older not maneuvered as he did, the Ruef machine would have continued to rule San Francisco. So Older "bribed or did anything to serve justice," although, as Older ultimately came to realize, justice could not be secured in that way.

Administrative systems proved a more effective means of controlling police than law, though despite the vast attention paid to administrative science, it had limited impact. America adopted the London model of policing but retained local political control over it. Thus reformers attempted to remove police from the political machine and put it under strong chiefs of moral character and expert knowledge. However, until well into the twentieth century, it could be argued that the call for administrative reform was simply an attempt by an upper-class minority to secure control over police administration regardless of the will of the electorate—in effect, a disguised politics.

In the mid-twentieth-century the elite largely came to terms with the political machines and police administration saw no more of the Theodore Roosevelts, Woods, or Fosdicks. Instead, under the leadership of the Enrights and Vollmers (though the two were personally quite different) the move for professional police administration came to mean competent career officers in the top posts, a more modest objective and to some extent a negative one. In general, the most able police chiefs in our narrative were not technically trained, but individuals of general competence who could understand the broad dimensions of policing. Not surprisingly, some of the best, such as Roosevelt, Woods, or O'Meara, possessed journalistic experience which enabled them to present their own views in a persuasive manner. Despite the rhetoric of reform, the career chiefs, whether New York bureaucrats or California professionals, were often required to be more political than civilians because in the event of dismissal, they usually had no resources to fall back on. Therefore, they had to constantly maneuver to secure their positions. Vollmer, for example, was almost as much a politician as Hiram Johnson.*

From a long-range standpoint, the ascendancy of the Enrights and even Vollmers over the Woodses and O'Mearas also meant that the police would have no spokesmen in the upper worlds. The Harvard workshop or the weekend party at a Long Island estate could be expected to include a civil liberties lawyer, a liberal professor, and even an occasional radical to present their versions of the problems of urban crime and disorder. But there would be no one to represent the police view. Similarly, the police chiefs' association would be directed by men little different from their rank and file, and their viewpoints would be narrowly professional. It is noteworthy that Vollmer and his protegés never underwent the kind of growth experienced by Earl Warren when he moved away from professional law enforcement.

Even when able police administrators did come to the fore, they tended to falter on real-world obstacles. The institution of a European-style police administration in Boston ultimately failed despite the talents of O'Meara. Though he was able to hold the balance between Yankee and Irish and establish a regime of law, the very divorcement of police administration from politics led to the strike and collapse of the force. Nor was the czar-like commissioner an unmixed blessing. The career of Frank Hague could be seen as the opposite side of the coin of an all-powerful chief. Even a constabulary-type force such as the New Jersey State Police, under a strong chief like Schwartzkopf, suffered defeat when confronted with political reality. Finally, even so astute an individual as Theodore Roosevelt could not solve the vice problem, since he was trapped by the moral ambivalence of the larger society.

---

* Indeed, if the military careers of Generals Smedley Butler and Leonard Wood constitute a gauge, the most tightly structured uniformed bureaucracies frequently seem to produce highly political leaders.

Thus whether police chiefs tried to stand above politics like O'Meara, pretend it did not exist like Schwartzkopf, or fight it like Roosevelt, they ultimately failed; throughout our narrative the dominant form of control of the police was politics. Indeed, as our study pointed out, quite often the real control of policing was not found in the mayor's chambers or in the chief's office, but in the political headquarters of New York's Croker or Sullivan or Chicago's Kenna or Coughlin, the California parsonages of the Reverend Shuler or Father Caraher, the editorial offices of the *Los Angeles Times* or the *New York World*, or bail bond firms such as that of Skidmore of Chicago or that of the Mc-Donoughs of San Francisco.

Group Images

When discussing police, many writers portray them as servants of the rulers. In the United States the rulers versus ruled dichotomy is a very difficult one to sustain. As our analysis has described, control of the police has been the object of various elites. If America had a single ruling class, such as bankers and industrialists, the Tammany cops would never have existed and there would not have been a strike in Boston in 1919. The Haymarket defendants and Tom Mooney would not have been pardoned. Thus it is perhaps useful to view American politics in terms of clashing groups, motivated by a variety of interests beyond simply economics. As Joseph Gusfield has noted:

> On behalf of which ethnic, religious, or other cultural group is this gov-
> ernment and this society being carried out? We label these as *status is-*
> *sues* precisely because what is at issue is the position of the relevant
> groups in the status order of this society. Such issues polarize the society
> along lines of status group differentiation, posing conflicts between diver-
> gent styles of life. They are contrasted with *class issues*, which polarize
> the society along lines of economic interests.[7]

Based on our analysis, status issues would appear more common in policing than those of class.

This book has noted the existence of five major interest groups who significantly effect the police. For purposes of this discussion they will be referred to as the social elite, the business elite, the Progressives, the blue-collar or working class, and the radicals.*

The American social elite composed of persons of inherited wealth or prestige, was usually of WASP background, and included such individuals and groups as the Roosevelts and the Beacon Hill Brahmins. Usually, they held conservative to moderate views on basic social and economic questions, though they frequently attacked the excesses of the

---

* The following discussion generally ignores rural politics.

nouveau riche represented by the robber barons. The social elite was the closest American approach to a British-style governing class whose members believed in their own fitness and duty to rule.

In contrast, the business elite was generally composed of the most successful entrepreneurs, whose power rested ultimately on money. For such men as Jay Gould and General Otis, government was an adjunct to their business, and they often preferred to deal with party bosses in a straightforward fashion. A Pat Calhoun, despite his aristocratic background, was a member of the business elite because of his adherence to the power of money, while John D. Rockefeller, Jr., managed to move from the business to the social elite not only by the passage of time but by undertaking good-government and social betterment efforts.

The Progressives were upper-middle-class individuals, predominantly WASP, college-educated, and often of a puritan heritage. Their most notable characteristic was a concern for self-reformation. Often, the Progressives and the social elite made common cause against the business elite or the working class. At other times the Progressives were badly divided. During World War I, Newton Baker, Arthur Woods, John P. Mitchell, Clarence Darrow, and Raymond Fosdick generally followed the social elite in supporting the war, while Rudy Spreckels, Anita Whitney, Jane Addams, Hiram Johnson, and Fremont Older were opposed.

The working classes were usually composed of the foreign-born or their children, their religion was often other than Protestant, and their strength lay in the cities. Normally they supported political machines, bosses, and, indirectly, organized crime in their desire for a personalized government over a disinterested one. Their heroes were men like Governor Al Smith of New York and Mayor Curley of Boston, and they supported the more conservative labor unions such as the AFL.

The radicals dealt with in the present study were frequently foreign-born, and their leaders were usually intellectuals. They rarely participated in politics of the two major parties or in conventional unionism, preferring socialism or anarchism or unions such as the Western Miners and the New York Garment Workers. Among this group were Johann Most, Emma Goldman, Bill Haywood, and Eugene Debs. Usually they could agree on what they were against, but not what they were for, and they often fought among themselves. Occasionally, progressives such as Darrow or Steffens would move into the radical camp; but in the ultimate test, the willingness to go to prison (as differentiated from a short symbolic jail term), they would depart from the radicals. Unlike other groups, the radicals did not achieve power in any American community,*

---

* Occasionally, a moderate socialist would be elected to office, as in Milwaukee, where socialist mayors and congressmen served long terms.

but they were influential if only in the negative sense as foils and targets for other groups.

In general, the social elite and progressives were strong supporters of police reform of the administrative science or professionalization variety, while the working class was the bulwark of the political machines which dominated local policing. The business elite vacillated between the contending forces, sometimes supporting the machine bosses and other times opposing them.

It should not be assumed, however, that the police themselves were totally passive. Most American police during the period surveyed here were employed by cities, and almost inevitably they were drawn from the working class. Therefore they were imbued with what has been described as "the spirit of Tammany," a preference for personalized government of the favor-seeking variety.* Thus, to comprehend the nature of the dominant strain of American police administration, it is necessary to look at the values which underlay the political machines.

What follows is perhaps the best account of this spirit that has been encountered during the present research. It was provided by John Landesco of the University of Chicago in the Illinois Crime Survey of 1929. It is excerpted from a description of a political meeting in the stockyards district of Chicago in 1928, but similar scenes could be portrayed in lower Manhattan, South Boston, West Philadelphia, San Francisco's North Beach, or hundreds of other blue-collar urban neighborhoods at any time from the 1870s to World War II:

> A testimonial banquet to John (Dingbat) Oberta, by the William J. Nellis Post of the Veterans of Foreign Wars, brings together a representation of all the phases of life of the stockyards district and an expression of its complex psychology. . . .
>
> Family life is the cardinal virtue. You may know another Dingbat Oberta, but they know the "Johnnie" whose sisters sit at the main table. By his efforts he has supported his widowed mother and raised his orphaned sisters. There is the emancipated woman too, Kitty Mulhall, City Hall attache, frequently seen in the office of the Chief of Police helping out stockyards friends. . . . as vivacious as an Irish colleen can be. . . .
>
> One thousand hands and five hundred voices render a storm of ovation to the big Pollack, Joe Saltis, as he enters to take the seat across from Tim Murphy. . . .
>
> Patriotism, with flags, fife and drum, with oratory and song, is the sweeping motif of the feast. . . .
>
> Tim Murphy is the leading speaker of the evening. . . . There is the one-sided smile that comes from a mouth battered crooked back in the days when knuckles counted in the stockyards district.

---

* Obviously not all cops behaved alike. There were always a few Costigans, Valentines, Nootbars, and Goffs who were willing to battle the politicians openly.

"I'm glad to be back here with you where I was raised, around Halsted and forty-seventh, back here where a man is a man, where I know all of you. . . . I don't care what the newspapers say about me or Joe Saltis or Johnnie Oberta, we never done any harm to anybody around the stockyards. You probably know us from the newspapers. I have been picked up, many's the time for, 'funny' larceny and concealed 'ideas.'" (Great Applause). "I even served three years in Uncle Sam's boarding house." (Overwhelming applause.) "And I want to tell you that even there the men are ninety percent good."

Tim knows the vernacular of the stockyards, although his business associations have carried him high into the sphere of proper English and he now lives in Rogers Park. He is genuinely popular; his humor, aided by his own hearty laugh, produces great merriment. And after all, most of his "rough stuff" involved the organization of unskilled labor to get raises in pay and to insure greater security in their jobs to neighborhood wage-earners. What if he did hold up a United States mail train—with so confusing a spectacle as the due process of law, who knows whether they had the right man? Certainly a great many "wrong" men are free and a great many "right" men are in prison. . . .*

A priest rises to say a few words and the hall is in perfect silence. He does what the clergy can do in a community where there is a great deal of what is bad—he lauds as exemplary the good deeds of Oberta

Four leading sentiments color the morality of the stockyards; family solidarity, revolutionary labor heroism, patriotic national heroism, and unconditional mutual aid without hesitant criticism or question, against any danger, whether it be constituted authority or from rival gang interests. As for the law, it is believed to be often an ally of the exploiter or a tool of the enemy gang. The "racketeer" is the example of success under grim conditions. He retains his popularity because he is loyal to the neighborhood's morals. In industrial relations, as in bootlegging, or "racketeering," he promotes the interests of himself and his fellows "by every means, in any manner."[8]

To some it might seem unusual to group family solidarity and national patriotism with revolutionary labor heroism as key traits. In America, though, the working class saw no conflict between supporting labor violence, robbing a mail train, and respect for patriotism, law, and order, however maddening such an assortment of sentiments might be to both doctrinaire radicals and conservatives. The social elite and Progressives who feared the lawless foreigners in the turn-of-the-century industrial cities and Pennsylvania mining districts would no doubt have been surprised by our recent national history where the "hard hats" took over the championship of law and order.

---

* To add to the confusion, the postal inspector who captured Big Tim was himself later sent to prison for masterminding a mail train robbery. Three months after the night's festivities Big Tim was assassinated. So too, somewhat later were Saltis and Oberta.

Given the confusing and highly fluid nature of American politics, how, then, is one to view the political machines which have controlled and set the moral tone for most American police—state troopers, federal agents, and some California cops excepted? At least two contrasting images can be presented. In times of national unity or when machines served the elite, such as under Franklin Roosevelt in the 1940s, the bosses are seen as benign, All-American symbols of the melting pot. In this view, there are good bosses such as Ed Flynn of the Bronx or Mayor Daley (circa 1960), or at least lovable rogues such as Big Tim Sullivan, Mayor Curley, or Jimmy Walker. In similar vein, cops like Inspector Byrnes or Johnny Broderick are hailed by the press, and gangsters like Colisimo and Rothstein become Damon Runyan characters whose company is sought by persons of wealth and standing. In contrast, reformers are viewed as hypocrites or nuisances. Thus Charles Whitman's drinking, William Travers Jerome's womanizing, and Francis Heney's violent temper are highly publicized. In his biography of Al Smith, even Oscar Handlin, the foremost American urban historian, dismisses the Reverend Parkhurst as a minor annoyance and describes the typical reformer as

> . . . the type of man in his cutaway coat and with "a big, long shoelace on his eyeglasses," who rose to worry over the fate of migratory birds and fish [but] did not extend his concern to women and children. Smith and [Robert] Wagner were not surprised to find in the Auburn factory of Thomas Mott Osborne [the criminal justice reformer and prison warden], leader of the Progressive Democrats, "the vilest and most uncivilized conditions of labor in the state."[9]

William Whyte, writing shortly before World War II, found positive value in the policy of strategic leniency toward vice. In his view police corruption, like the big-city politics it served, constituted a stabilizing force:

> There are prevalent in society two general conceptions of the duties of the police officer. Middle-class people feel that he should enforce the law without fear or favor. [Lower-class] people and many of the officers themselves believe that the policeman should have the confidence of the people in his area so that he can settle many difficulties in a personal manner without making arrests. These two conceptions are in a large measure contradictory. The policeman who takes a strictly legalistic view of his duties cuts himself off from the personal relations necessary to enable him to serve as mediator of disputes in his area. The policeman who develops close ties with local people is unable to act against them with the vigor prescribed by the law.[10]

The foregoing can be seen as a refrain on William Allen White's approval of the role of Croker's Tammany in stemming radicalism in New

York. In times of discontent, however, machines are seen as predatory, reactionary, or un-American. Bosses like Croker, Hague, and Daley (circa 1968) are deplored, and cops of the likes of Charlie Becker, Clubber Williams, or Red Hines become symbols of evil. Gangsters such as Jerome Bassity or Al Capone are excoriated, and reformers like Parkhurst, Whitman, or Heney are portrayed in heroic terms.

Thus it is as difficult to reach a conclusion on the police-politics-vice alliance as it is to assess, at the other end of the spectrum, the extensive Rockefeller involvement in various police reform projects; is the latter a conspiracy to set up administrative systems to frustrate the majority of the electorate, or an honest effort to provide disinterested public service in the classic justification of great wealth as enabling its holder to do good for society?

It is clear, however, that the graft which flowed inevitably from the machine control of the police partially negated their role as the expressers of prevailing moral values. Despite the prevalence of corruption in America, its practice violated one of the most important value premises of the society. The clash between morality and politics trapped the American police in an ambivalent posture which ultimately reduced their effectiveness. Their adoption of the code of the machine facilitated the maintenance of order in some areas but made it impossible for other sections of the society to view the police as a moral force.

Given the compromises and ambivalencies of American police administration, no standard model of policing developed. Instead, representative types arose based on various local configurations of power. In New York, the police were constantly caught in the struggle between regulars and reformers, but beginning with Enright and increasingly under Valentine, they gradually developed a means of remaining aloof from both by turning inward and institutionalizing bureaucracy. In time, it became clear that an officer's career from patrolman to commissioner depended more upon his adherence to bureaucratic routine than on political connections or a reformist posture.

In California, where the political struggle was generally between Progressives and business elites, the police (with the exception of San Francisco) opted for a model of efficiency equally adaptable to the conservatism of General Otis and the progressivism of Fremont Older. Thus the California style of technically efficient, professionalized police, with a publicity-conscious chief at their head, became a leading model of American police administration.

In Chicago, where the business and social elite abdicated civic responsibility and reformers like Darrow, Addams, and Merriam, though world-famous, were powerless, the real struggle was usually between the political machine and organized crime. Thus the police were at best servants of their politician masters.

The Lost Opportunity

In summing up the blue parade, we might lament what might have been. Obviously the society would have been better served had it placed a higher value on adherence to law, though a sophisticated argument could no doubt be advanced that such adherence would have retarded the economic growth of the country. However, legality is but a component of justice. In this respect, we might compare the perspectives of Jacob Riis and Lincoln Steffens. Though they were friends and allies as New York reporters in the era of Theodore Roosevelt, they were fundamentally different. Steffens, of middle-class origin, was as perceptive and humane as Riis but was essentially a cynic, insisting that nothing short of utopia could improve conditions. Not surprisingly, the equally cynical Bill Devery was his favorite cop. In contrast, Riis, a poor immigrant, was always hopeful that urban life could be dramatically improved by relatively minor reforms. Despite all the national shortcomings he so movingly reported, he chose to entitle his autobiography *The Making of an American*, while Steffens might well have entitled his *The Unmaking* of one since he ended his career by invoking Stalinist Russia as the hope of the future.

Riis's technique was to educate the various elites to the conditions of the less well-off, and his favorite policeman was Inspector Byrnes, though he was under no illusions about the great detective's faults. Byrnes was a doer, a man of action who was the scourge of the hoodlum gangs which Riis, despite his sympathy with the underdog, saw as destructive to urban life. However, Byrnes, unlike Riis, was blind to the less fortunate New Yorkers, preferring to serve only the wealthy and powerful and to perpetuate myths while suppressing reality.

Despite the insoluble conflict between the ideal police role as moral preceptor and the reality of political dominance, there were opportunities for American police, like journalists, to serve as educators of their masters. Had Inspector Byrnes chosen, like Riis, to utilize his skill and upperworld contacts to convey to the upper classes the inequities of New York life, i.e., to make the police moral preceptors for the elite as well as the humble, he might have better served the community. That this opportunity was not grasped is perhaps the greatest regret in surveying the blue parade. As William Westley has written, "Our police are precious to us and we need policemen whom we can trust and respect, who will act in ways giving us confidence in the . . . democracy of our community."[11]

Notes

INTRODUCTION (pp. vii–x)

1. Arthur Millspaugh, *Crime Control by The National Government* (Washington, D.C.: Brookings, 1937), pp. 2–3.
2. Joseph Gusfield, *Symbolic Crusade: Status Politics and the American Temperance Movement* (Urbana: University of Illinois Press, 1963), p. 5.
3. Raymond B. Fosdick, *American Police Systems* (Montclair, N.J.: Patterson Smith, 1969; orig. 1920), pp. 344–45.
4. Josiah Stamp, *Some Economic Factors in Modern Life* (London: P. S. King & Sons, 1929), p. 258.

Chapter 1 (pp. 1–37): GREAT BRITAIN: THE NEW URBAN SOCIETY (1748–1890)

1. There are accounts of the riots in T. A. Critchley, *The Conquest of Violence* (London: Constable, 1970), pp. 81–87, and George Rude, *Hanoverian London 1714–1808* (Berkeley: University of California Press, 1971), pp. 222–24.
2. Discussions of the changing meaning of the word "police" are found in Roger Lane, *Policing the City: Boston 1822–1858* (Cambridge, Mass.: Harvard University Press, 1967), pp. 3, 247; Sir Leon Radiznowciz, *A History of English Criminal Law and Its Administration from 1750*, 4

vols. (London: Stevens & Sons, 1948–68), vol. III, pp. 1–8; Charles Reith, *The Blind Eye of History* (London: Faber & Faber, 1952), pp. 9–10; and T. A. Critchley, *A History of Police in England and Wales*, 2nd ed. (Montclair, N.J.: Patterson Smith, 1972), 25, 35.

3. This description of a thousand years of British policing obviously omits many nuances and complexities. A short but comprehensive account is contained in, Captain W. L. Melville-Lee, *A History of Police in England and Wales* (London: Methuen, 1901) chpts. I–VIII.

4. Henry Fielding, *Amelia*, vol. I (London: 1751), p. 6.

5. On the quality of these Parish Forces see Anthony Babington, *A House in Bow Street: Crime and the Magistracy in London 1740–1881* (London: McDonald, 1969), p. 38 Radzinowicz, *op. cit.*, vol. II, pp. 194–201.

6. On London population see J. J. Tobias, *Crime and Industrial Society in the 19th Century* (London: B. T. Batsford, 1967), p. 35, and Rude, *op. cit.*, chap. 1.

7. On economic growth see Rude, *op. cit.*, chap. 2.

8. Luke O. Pike, *A History of Crime in England*, 2 vols. (Montclair, N.J.: Patterson Smith, 1962, orig. 1873–76), vol. II, p. 409.

9. Rude, *op. cit.*, p. 82–83.

10. Melville-Lee, *op. cit.*, p. 133, and Pike, *op. cit.*, pp. 240–41.

11. Henry Fielding, *An Enquiry into the Causes of the Late Increase in Robbers* (London: 1751), p. 1. (Reprinted, New York: AMS Press, 1975).

12. Quoted in F. Homes Dudden, *Henry Fielding: His Life, Work, and Times* (Oxford: Clarendon Press, 1952), vol. II, p. 759.

13. *Ibid.*, p. 760.

14. *Ibid.* Patrick Pringle, *Hue and Cry* (London: Morrow, 1965), p. 90.

15. Dudden, *op. cit.*, p. 734–35, and Babington, *op. cit.*, p. 76.

16. Rude, *op. cit.*, p. 97.

17. Patrick Colguhoun, *A Treatise on the Police of the Metropolis*, 7th ed. (Montclair, N.J.: Patterson Smith, 1969; orig. 1806, preface, p. 4.

18. Pike, *op. cit.*, pp. 240–41, 337, 370–71, 468–70. A similar conclusion is reached in Dorothy Gorge, *London Life in the Eighteenth Century* (New York: Capricorn Books, 1965; orig. 1926), pp. 16–17.

19. Radzinowicz, *op. cit.* vol. I, p. 148.

20. *Ibid.*, pp. 708–09.

21. Rude, *op. cit.*, p. 91, and Radzinowicz, *op. cit.*, vol. I, p. 400.

22. Quoted in Melville-Lee, *op. cit.*, pp. 144–45.

23. Reith, *op. cit.*, p. 49.

24. Quoted in Rude, *op. cit.*, p. 86.

25. George Rude, *The Crowd in History* (New York: Wiley, 1964) p. 51, 215.

26. Radzinowicz, *op. cit.*, vol. I, p. 400.

27. On fear versus concern see Frank Furstenberg, Jr., "Public Reaction to Crime in the Streets," *American Scholar*, 40, 1971, p. 603.

28. Radzinowicz, *op. cit.*, vol. I, p. 2.

29. Fielding, *Enquiry*, pp. 3–4.

30. Quoted in Tobias, *op. cit.*, p. 182–83. See also Babington, *op. cit.*, p. 19.

31. Tobias, *op. cit.*, pp. 238–41.

32. Quoted in Dudden, *op. cit.*, p. 759.

33. Radzinowicz, *op. cit.*, vol. I, pp. 79–94.

34. Pike, *op. cit.*, p. 80.

35. *Ibid.*, and Melville-Lee, *op. cit.*, p. 133.

36. Fielding, *Enquiry*, p. 76.

37. Tobias, *op. cit.*, pp. 57–58.

38. Melville-Lee, *op. cit.*, pp. 272–73, 406–07.

39. On rewards see Radzinowicz, *op. cit.*, vol. II, chap. 3.

40. On the life of Wild see Howson, *op. cit.* Fielding's *Life of Jonathan Wild the Great* is actually a thinly disguised satire of Sir Robert Walpole.

41. Cited in Pringle, *op. cit.*, p. 45.

42. *Ibid.*, p. 23.

43. Radzinowicz, *op. cit.*, vol. IV, p. v.

44. Philip J. Stead, *The Police of Paris* (London: Staples, 1957), pp. 45–48.

45. On the career of Count Rumsford se Egon Larsen, *An American in Europe* (London: Rider & Co., 1953), esp. pp. 57–67, 79.

46. Melville-Lee, *op. cit.*, pp. 152–53.

47. On Beccaria and Bentham see Herman Manheim, *Pioneers in Criminology*, 2nd ed. (Montclair, N.J.: Patterson Smith, 1973), pp. 36–68.

48. From "A Detective Police Party," *Household Words*, vol. 18, 1850, p. 409, cited in Radzinowicz, *op. cit.*, vol. II, p. 263.

49. See Patrick Colquhoun, *A Treatise on the Commerce and Police of the River Thames* (Montclair, N.J.: Patterson Smith 1972; orig. 1800).

50. On Peterloo see Donald Read, *Peterloo: The Massacre and Its Background* (Manchester: Manchester University Press, 1958). On threats to the yeomanry see Joyce Marlow, *The Peterloo Massacre* (London: Rapp & Whiting, 1969), pp. 168–70.

51. See, for example, J. M. Hart, *The British Police* (London: George Allen & Unwin, 1951), p. 27–28.

52. Radzinowicz, *op. cit.*, vol. IV, p. 156.

53. Critchley, *Violence*, p. 122.

54. Samuel Beer and Adam Ulam, *Patterns of Government: The Major Political Systems of Europe*, 2nd ed., rev. (New York: Random House, 1962), pp. 161–62.

55. Quoted in Melville-Lee, *op. cit.*, p. 333.

56. Norman Gash, *Mr. Secretary Peel* (Cambridge, Mass.: Harvard University Press, 1961), p. 502.

57. Radzinowicz, *op. cit.*, vol. III, p. 541.

58. Raymond B. Fosdick, *European Police Systems* (Montclair, N.J.: Patterson Smith, 1969; orig. 1915), p. 201.

59. *Ibid.*, p. 210. On British Army height, Barbara Tuchman, *The Proud Tower* (New York: Bantam ed., 1967) p. 417.

60. Belton Cobb, *The First Detectives* (London: Faber & Faber, 1967), p. 51.

61. Charles Reith, *A New Study of Police History* (London: Oliver & Boyd, 1956), p. 147.
62. On riot see Gavin Thurston, *The Clerkenwell Riot* (London: George Allen & Unwin, 1967).
63. Critchley, *Violence,* p. 140.
64. *Ibid.,* p. 166.
65. Melville-Lee, *op. cit.,* p. 242.
66. Stead, *op. cit.,* pp. 120–21.
67. See, for example, William Booth, *In Darkest England and the Way Out* (Montclair, N.J.: Patterson Smith, 1974; orig. 1890); James Greenwood, *The Seven Curses of London* (London: Stanley Rivers, 1869); and Henry Mayhew, *London Labour and the London Poor,* vol. IV (London: Frank Cass, 1967; orig. 1861–62).
68. Pike, *op. cit.,* p. 480.
69. Melville-Lee, *op. cit.,* pp. 405–06.
70. Tobias, *op. cit.,* p. 236. For an account of mid-nineteenth-century burglars which illustrates their fear of apprenhension, see Mayhew, *op. cit.,* pp. 354–55.
71. On burglary sentences, Tobias, *op. cit.,* pp. 217–18. On the prison population, Sir Basil Thomson, *The Story of Scotland Yard* (New York: Doubleday, Doran, 1936), p. 100.
72. Sir William Nott-Bower, *Fifty-two Years a Policeman* (London: Edward Arnold, 1926), pp. 149–53.
73. Melville-Lee, *op. cit.,* pp. xxviii–xxix.
74. Geoffrey Gorer, *Exploring English Character* (New York: Criterion Books, 1955), pp. 294–96 and app. I.
75. Sir Ronald Howe, *The Story of Scotland Yard* (London: A. Barker, 1965), p. 38.
76. Fosdick, *op. cit.,* p. 374.
77. Radzinowicz, *op. cit.,* vol. IV, pp. 180–83, and Thurston, *op. cit.,* pp. 173–74.
78. Seamus Breatnach, *The Irish Police* (Dublin: Anvil Books, 1974), p. 45; Sir Arthur Hezlet, *The B-Specials* (London: Tom Stacey, 1972), pp. 3, 25; and Robert B. McDowell, *The Irish Administration 1801–1914* (Westport, Conn.: Greenwood, 1976), p. 140.
79. Cited in Breatnach, *op. cit.,* p. 45.
80. Nott-Bower, *op. cit.,* pp. 30–31, 76.
81. Reith, *Blind Eye,* p. 147.
82. Melville-Lee, *op. cit.,* p. 394.
83. Galen Broeker, *Rural Disorder and Police Reform in Ireland* (London: Routledge & Kegan Paul, 1970), p. 239.
84. Sir Charles Jeffries, *The Colonial Police* (London: Max Parish, 1952), pp. 30–32.
85. Nott-Bower, *op. cit.,* p. 167.
86. General Sir Neville Macready, *Annals of an Active Life,* 2 vols. (London: Hutchinson, 1924), vol. II, p. 179.

87. J. F. Moylan, *Scotland Yard and the Metropolitan Police* (London: Putnam, 1929), p. 150.

88. For early development of detectives see Cobb, *op. cit.*

89. Melville-Lee, *op. cit.*, p. 192, and Babington, *op. cit.*, p. 233.

90. Critchley, *History of Police*, p. 43.

91. Critchley, *Violence*, pp. 110–12.

92. Thomson, *op. cit.*, p. 105, and Thurston, *op. cit.*, pp. 53, 76.

93. Howe, *op. cit.*, p. 33, and Radzinowicz, *op. cit.*, vol. IV, pp. 185–86.

94. Pike, *op. cit.*, p. 465.

95. See Philip J. Stead, *Vidocq: Picaroon of Crime* (London: Staples, 1953).

96. Belton Cobb, *Critical Years at the Yard* (London: Faber & Faber, 1961), p. 127.

97. Greenwood, *op. cit.*, p. 194–95.

98. Tobias, *op. cit.*, pp. 102–04, and Babington, *op. cit.*, p. 192.

99. On scandal see Cobb, *Critical Years*, pp. 139–78.

100. Babington, *op. cit.*, p. 235.

101. Melville-Lee, *op. cit.*, pp. 366–67.

102. S. H. Jeyes and F. D. How, *The Life of Sir Howard Vincent* (London: George Allen, 1912), pp. 76–81, and Cobb, *Critical Years*, pp. 195–202.

103. Cobb, *Critical Years*, pp. 218–22.

104. Jeyes and How, *op. cit.*, pp. 87–90.

105. Sir Melville Macnaghten, *Days of My Years* (London: Edward Arnold, 1915), p. 78.

106. Morris Hillquit, *Loose Leaves from a Busy Life* (New York: Macmillan, 1934; Da Capo reprint, 1971), p. 120.

107. Jeyes and How, *op. cit.*, pp. 87–90.

108. See "Sir Patrick Quinn, M.V.O.," *British Police Journal*, October 1965, pp. 472–76.

109. Winston Churchill, *A Roving Commission* (New York: Scribner, 1930), p. 313.

110. Critchley, *Violence*, pp. 149–58.

111. For accounts of the case see Tom Cullon, *Autumn of Terror* (London: Bodley Head, 1965), and Daniel Farson, *Jack the Ripper* (London: Sphere Books, 1973).

112. Jeffries, *op. cit.*, p. 31.

113. Fosdick, *op. cit.*, pp. 21–23.

Chapter 2 (pp. 38–87): NEW YORK: THE NEW WORLD (1845–1913)

1. Account based on Lothrop Stoddard, *Master of Manhattan: The Life of Richard Croker* (New York: Longmans, Green, 1931), p. 3.

2. "Report of the Select Committee appointed to examine into the condition of tenant houses in New York and Brooklyn," transmitted to the Legislature, Albany, N.Y., March 9, 1857, pp. 11–12. Quoted in Charles N. Glaab, *The American City: A Documentary History* (Homewood, Ill.: Dorsey, 1963), p. 269.

3. Jacob Riis, *How the Other Half Lives* (New York: Hill and Wang, 1957; orig. 1890), pp. 2, 15.

4. *Ibid.*, p. 8, and Augustine Costello, *Our Police Protectors* (Montclair, N.J.: Patterson Smith, 1972; orig. 1885), p. 525.

5. Charles Dickens, *American Notes* (London: Oxford University Press, 1957; orig. 1842), p. 88–89.

6. James F. Richardson, *The New York Police: Colonial Times to 1901* (New York: Oxford University Press, 1970), pp. 37–38.

7. George Walling, *Recollections of a New York Chief of Police* (Montclair, N.J.: Patterson Smith, 1972; orig. 1887), pp. 28–29.

8. James Gerard, *My First 83 Years in America* (Garden City, N.Y.: Doubleday, 1951), p. 8.

9. Walling, *op. cit.*, pp. 47–48.

10. Richardson, *op. cit.*, p. 66.

11. *Ibid.*, p. 52.

12. Frank J. Goodnow and Frank G. Bates, *Municipal Government* (New York: Century, 1919; orig. 1909), p. 293.

13. Accounts of the riot and its aftermath in Costello, *op. cit.*, pp. 141–42; Walling, *op. cit.*, pp. 54–61; and Herbert Asbury, *The Gangs of New York* (New York: Capicorn, 1970; orig. 1927), pp. 108–11.

14. On the Dead Rabbits see Asbury, *op. cit.*, chap. 6.

15. *Ibid.*, p. 104, and Walling, *op. cit.*, p. 48.

16. Asbury, *op. cit.*, p. 119.

17. M. R. Werner, *It Happened in New York* (New York: Coward-McCann, 1957), p. 221.

18. Alexis de Tocqueville, *Democracy in America* (New York: Knopf, 1945; orig. 1835), pp. 289–90.

19. James Bryce, *The American Commonwealth*, 3 vols. (New York: AMS Press, 1973; orig. 1888), vol. II, pp. 281, 288.

20. Richardson, *op. cit.*, pp. 126–27.

21. Costello, *op. cit.*, pp. 123–24.

22. Adrian Cook, *The Armies of the Streets* (Lexington: University Press of Kentucky, 1974), pp. 194–95 and app. I.

23. Accounts of riots in *ibid.*; Asbury, *op. cit.*, chaps. 7 and 8; Costello, *op. cit.*, chaps. 8 and 9; and Walling, chap. VI.

24. Stoddard, *op. cit.*, chap. 6, and M. R. Werner, *Tammany Hall* (New York: Doubleday, Doran, 1928), p. 310.

25. Quoted in Werner, *It Happened in New York*, p. 230.

26. Costello, *op. cit.*, pp. 311, 477–78.

27. William A. White, "Croker," *McClure's Magazine*, February 1901, p. 324.

28. Asbury, *op. cit.*, p. 177. There are many versions of Williams's words, but all agree on the essence.

29. *Ibid.*, p. 228.

30. Jacob Riis, *The Making of an American* (New York: Macmillan, 1901), pp. 239–40.

31. *Ibid.*, pp. 72–74, 231–32.

32. *Ibid.*, pp. 237–38.

33. Costello, *op. cit.*

34. The payoff system is described in Josiah Flynt (Willard), *The World of Graft* (New York: McClure, Phillips, 1901). See also Langdon Moore, *His Own Story* (Boston: by author, 1893), esp. pp. 497–98.

35. On Tukey see Roger Lane, *Policing the City: Boston 1822–1885* (Cambridge, Mass.: Harvard University Press, 1967), chap. 3; on Nelson see John J. Flinn and John E. Wilkie, *History of the Chicago Police* (Montclair, N.J.: Patterson Smith, 1973; orig. 1887), pp. 104–06.

36. Accounts of Byrnes in Riis, *Making of an American*, pp. 339–44; Lincoln Steffens, *Autobiography* (New York: Harcourt, Brace, 1931), pp. 164–82; and Arthur Carey, *Memoirs of a Murder Man* (New York: Doubleday, Doran, 1930), pp. 27–36. See also Byrnes's own book *Professional Criminals of America* (New York: 1886) and his article "How to Protect a City from Crime," *North American Review*, July 1894, pp. 100–07.

37. Walling, *op. cit.*, pp. 589–90.

38. Asbury, *op. cit.*, p. 54.

39. From Philip Dunne, *Mr. Dooley Remembers: The Informal Memoirs of Finley Peter Dunne*, cited in Gerald Astor, *The New York Cops: An Informal History* (New York: Scribner, 1971), pp. 96–97.

40. Noel F. Busch, *The Story of Theodore Roosevelt and His Influence on Our Times* (New York: Reynal, 1963), pp. 77–78, 96.

41. Arthur Woods, *Policemen and Public* (Montclair, N.J.: Patterson Smith, 1975; orig. 1919), p. 113.

42. Steffens, *op. cit.*, p. 219.

43. Asbury, *op. cit.*, p. 272.

44. *Ibid.*, pp. 234–35; Costello, *op. cit.*, p. 233.

45. Asbury, *op. cit.*, pp. 258–59.

46. On Williams see Asbury, *op. cit.*, pp. 235–37; Costello, *op. cit.*, pp. 364–67; and obituary, *New York Times*, March 26, 1917, p. 11.

47. See *Report and Proceedings of the Senate Committee Appointed to Investigate the Police Department of the City of New York* (Lexow Committee), 1895, pp. 4518–32.

48. Cornelius Willemse, *Behind the Green Lights* (New York: Knopf, 1931), p. 34.

49. Riis, *Making of an American*, pp. 224–25.

50. *Ibid.*, p. 341.

51. Richardson, *op. cit.*, p. 235.

52. Heywood Broun and Margaret Leech, *Anthony Comstock: Roundsman of the Lord* (New York: Boni, 1927), p. 206.

53. Steffens, *op. cit.*, p. 161, and Harold Syrett, ed., *The Gentleman and the Tiger: Autobiography of G. B. McClellan Jr.* (Philadelphia: Lippincott, 1956), p. 58.

54. Werner, *It Happened in New York,* p. 116.

55. On Comstock, Broun and Leech, *op. cit.*

56. Werner, *It Happened in New York,* p. 50.

57. Charles H. Parkhurst, *Our Fight with Tammany* (New York: Scribner, 1895), p. 95.

58. Asbury, *op. cit.*, pp. 174–75.

59. Cornelius Willemse, *A Cop Remembers* (New York: Knopf, 1933), p. 87.

60. Werner, *It Happened in New York,* pp. 57–59.

61. *Ibid.*, p. 62.

62. Parkhurst, *op. cit.*, p. 249.

63. Asbury, *op. cit.*, p. 305, and Steffens, *op. cit.*, p. 194.

64. The Lexow Committee report contains over 5,000 pages. Among the highlights are the testimony of Captain Schmittberger, pp. 5311–84, Inspector Williams, pp. 5431–5578, and Superintendent Byrnes, pp. 5709–58.

65. Busch, *op. cit.*, p. 85.

66. *Ibid.*, p. 116.

67. Morton Prince, M.D., in *New York Times,* Mar. 24, 1912, pt. VI, p. 12.

68. R. W. Stallman, *Stephen Crane* (New York: Braziller, 1968), pp. 218–36.

69. H. F. Pringle, *Theodore Roosevelt* (New York: Harcourt, Brace, 1931), p. 139.

70. Theodore Roosevelt, *Autobiography* (New York: Scribner, 1924), pp. 186–87.

71. Richardson, *op. cit.*, p. 259.

72. Steffens, *op. cit.*, pp. 226–30.

73. Stoddard, *op. cit.*, p. 154.

74. Theodore Roosevelt, *American Ideals* (New York: AMS Press, 1969; orig. 1897), p. 182.

75. Steffens, *op. cit.*, p. 330.

76. Alexander Gardiner, *Canfield* (Garden City, N.Y.: Doubleday, 1930), p. 122.

77. On the need for a plumber, Steffens, *op. cit.*, p. 335. On Devery in general, pp. 327–36.

78. Werner, *Tammany,* p. 408.

79. William L. Riordan, *Plunkitt of Tammany Hall* (New York: McClure, Phillips, 1905), pp. 3–10.

80. Asbury, *op. cit.*, pp. 274–78.

81. *Ibid.*, pp. 273–74.

82. George Kibbe Turner, "Tammany Control of New York by Professional Criminals," *McClure's Magazine,* June 1909, pp. 117–34.

83. Stoddard, *op. cit.*, p. 231.

84. Werner, *Tammany*, pp. 504–06; *New York Times*, Sept. 14, 1913, pt. II, p. 2.

85. Flynt, *op. cit.*, pp. 49–50.

86. *New York Times*, March 9, 1900, pp. 1–2.

87. Stoddard, *op. cit.*, pp. 241–46; *New York Times*, Sept. 18, 1901, p. 1.

88. New York Assembly, *Finally Report of Special Committee to Investigate the Public Offices and Departments of the City of New York* (Mazet Committee), 1900.

89. Richard O'Connor, *Courtroom Warrior: The Combative Career of William Travers Jerome* (Boston: Little, Brown, 1963), pp. 69–71.

90. Werner, *Tammany*, pp. 487–97.

91. Woods, *op. cit.*, p. 147.

92. On Canfield, see Gardiner, *op. cit.* On the "Canfield crowd," *New York Times*, March 9, 1900, pp. 1–2.

93. Turner, *op. cit.*, p. 132.

94. Gardiner, *op. cit.*, pp. 87–88.

95. O'Connor, *op. cit.*, pp. 99–109.

96. Andy Logan, *Against the Evidence: The Becker-Rosenthal Affair* (New York: McCall Publishing Co., 1970), p. 89, and Lately Thomas, *The Mayor Who Mastered New York: The Life and Opinions of William J. Gaynor* (New York: Morrow, 1969), p. 119.

97. See William J. Gaynor, "Lawlessness of the Police in New York," *North American Review*, January 1903, pp. 19, 24–25, and, by same author, "A Government of Laws Not of Men," *North American Review*, February 1903, pp. 282–83. See also rebuttal by Howard Gans, assistant DA of New York, "In the Matter of the Lawlessness of the Police: A Reply to Justice Gaynor," *North American Review*, February 1903, pp. 287–96.

98. W. T. Stead, *Satan's Invisible World Displayed* (New York: R. F. Fenno, 1897), p. 172. Walling, *op. cit.*, pp. 196, 601.

99. William McAdoo, *Guarding a Great City* (New York: Harper, 1906), pp. 265–66.

100. See Carey, *op. cit.*

101. Raymond B. Fosdick, *Chronicle of a Generation* (New York: Harper, 1958), pp. 58–60.

102. Frank Marshall White, "When Clubs Were Trumps," *Outlook*, Apr. 7, 1915, p. 480, and *New York Times*, Sept. 17, 1903, p. 8.

103. Asbury, *op. cit.*, pp. 279–82.

104. *Ibid.*, pp. 282–83, and Werner, *Tammany*, pp. 506–07.

105. Asbury, *op. cit.*, pp. 285–86.

106. *New York Times*, Feb. 3, 1904, p. 16.

107. Asbury, *op. cit.*, pp. 295–98.

108. Craig Thompson and Allan Raymond, *Gang Rule in New York* (New York: Dial, 1940), pp. 360–63.

109. Thomas, *op. cit.*, pp. 145–51.

110. George W. Aler, "Mayor Gaynor and the Police," *Outlook*, Jan. 1, 1910, p. 30.

111. Thomas, *op. cit.*, pp. 254–67.

112. Fosdick, *op. cit.*, p. 92.

113. Gardiner, *op. cit.*, p. 186.

114. E. J. Kahn, *The World of Swope* (New York: Simon & Schuster, 1965), p. 136.

115. Logan, *op. cit.*, p. 114.

116. Jonathan Root, *One Night in July* (New York: Coward-McCann, 1961), pp. 41–42.

117. Henry Curran, *Pillar to Post* (New York: Scribner, 1941), p. 159.

118. *Report of the Special Committee of the Board of Aldermen of the City of New York to Investigate the Police Department* (Curran Committee), 1913, p. 14.

119. Root, *op. cit.*, pp. 13–20.

120. *Ibid.*, pp. 49–61.

121. *Ibid.*, p. 61.

122. Harlan Phillips, *Felix Frankfurter Reminisces* (New York: Reynal, 1960), pp. 45–46.

123. *Report of Board of Aldermen.*

124. Logan, *op. cit.*, pp. 50, 96, 230–31; Root, *op. cit.*, p. 102.

125. Root, *op. cit.*, p. 17.

126. Logan, *op. cit.*, pp. 173–74.

127. Recent accounts are Root, *op. cit.* (anti-Becker), and Logan, *op. cit.* (pro).

128. Harold Zink, *City Bosses in the United States* (Durham, N.C.: Duke University Press, 1930), pp. 94–99.

129. *New York Times*, Sept. 14, 1913, pt. II, p. 1, and Sept. 16, 1913, p. 5.

130. Kahn, *op. cit.*, p. 122.

Chapter 3 (pp. 88–120): BOSTON: EUROPE IN AMERICA (1854–1943)

1. Calvin Coolidge, *Autobiography* (New York: Cosmopolitan Book Corp., 1929), p. 49, and William Allen White, *A Puritan in Babylon: The Story of Calvin Coolidge* (New York: Macmillan, 1938), pp. 29–31.

2. Raymond B. Fosdick, *European Police Systems* (Montclair, N.J.: Patterson Smith, 1969, orig. 1915).

3. Donal E. J. MacNamara in introduction to *ibid.*

4. Raymond B. Fosdick, *Chronicle of a Generation* (New York: Harper, 1958), p. 128.

5. Henri Souchon, "Alphonse Bertillon" in P. J. Stead, ed., *Pioneers in Police Went on Strike* (London: Weidenfeld Nicholson, 1968), app. 2.

6. On strike see Gerald W. Reynolds and Anthony Judge, *The Night the Police Went on Strike* (London: Weidenfeld Nichloson, 1968), app. 2.

7. Sir Basil Thomson, *The Story of Scotland Yard* (New York: Doubleday, Doran, 1936), p. 190. Sir Melville MacNaghten, *Days of My Years* (London: Edward Arnold, 1915), p. 62.

8. Richard Deacon, *A History of the British Secret Service* (New York: Taplinger, 1969), pp. 241–43.

9. See Donald Rumbelow, *The Houndsditch Murders: The Siege of Sidney Street* (London: Macmillan, 1973), and Bernard Leeson, *Lost London* (London: Stanley Paul, 1934), pp. 158–74.

10. Deacon, *op. cit.*, pp. 128–31, 173.

11. On dissension in Metropolitan Police see Reynolds and Judge, *op. cit.*, chap. 3.

12. On high reputation of Washington, D.C., police see Leonhard F. Fuld, *Police Administration* (New York: Putnam, 1910), p. 181.

13. On Boston Brahmins see Cleveland Amory, *The Proper Bostonians* (New York: Dutton, 1947), chap. 2.

14. Lincoln Steffens, *Autobiography* (New York: Harcourt, Brace, 1931), p. 607.

15. Roger Lane, *Policing the City: Boston 1822–1885* (Cambridge: Harvard University Press, 1967), pp. 29–33.

16. Raymond B. Fosdick, *American Police Systems* (Montclair, N.J.: Patterson Smith, 1969, orig. 1920), pp. 122–23.

17. On Tukey, Lane, *op. cit.*, chap. 5.

18. On Chief Savage, *ibid.*, pp. 116, 157–58, 168–69, 201. See also Edward H. Savage, *Police Records and Recollections or Boston by Daylight and Gaslight* (Montclair, N.J.: Patterson Smith, 1971; orig. 1873).

19. S. H. Jeyes and F. D. How, *The Life of Sir Howard Vincent* (London: George Allen, 1912), p. 153.

20. Lane, *op. cit.*, pp. 75–78.

21. Josiah Flynt (Willard), *World of Graft* (New York: McClure Phillips, 1901), pp. 57–85.

22. On O'Meara see obituary, *Boston Globe*, Dec. 14, 1918, p. 1, and *Report of Boston Police Commissioner, 1919*.

23. Fosdick, *American Police Systems*, pp. 293–95.

24. *Report of Boston Police Commissioner, 1915*, p. 21

25. On the pre-1919 Boston Police Department, Richard L. Lyons, "The Boston Police Strike of 1919," *New England Quarterly*, XX, July 1947, pp. 148–49, and George H. McCaffrey, "The Boston Police Department," *Journal of the American Institute of Law and Criminology*, January 1912.

26. Quoted in *Holiday Magazine*, March 1964, p. 90.

27. *Boston Herald*, Sept. 10, 1919, p. 6.

28. William McAdoo, *Guarding a Great City* (New York: Harper, 1906), p. 72.

29. Kenneth Alfers, *Law and Order in the Capital City: A History of the Washington Police, 1800–1886* (Washington, D.C.: George Washington University Press, 1976), pp. 38–39.

30. *Report of Boston Police Commissioner, 1909,* p. 20, and *1910,* p. 47.

31. Amory, *op. cit.,* 328–31.

32. Fosdick, *Chronicle,* pp. 144–47.

33. On the white slave Legend see Walter Reckless, *Vice in Chicago* (Montclair, N.J.: Patterson Smith, 1969, orig. 1933), chap. 2.

34. Alexander Gardiner, *Canfield* (Garden City, N.Y.: Doubleday, 1930), pp. 203–04.

35. M. R. Werner, *Tammany Hall* (New York: Doubleday, Doran, 1928), p. 407.

36. A relevant discussion is Robt. E. Riegel, "Changing American Attitudes Toward Prostitution (1800–1920)," *Journal of the History of Ideas,* July–September 1968, pp. 437–52.

37. *Report of Boston Police Commissioner, 1910,* pp. 34–36.

38. *Report of Boston Police Commissioner, 1909,* p. 16.

39. *Report of Boston Police Commissioner, 1910,* pp. 37–38.

40. *Report of Boston Police Commissioner, 1911,* p. 68.

41. *Report of Boston Police Commissioner, 1910,* p. 44.

42. National Commission on Law Observance and Enforcement (Wickersham Commission), #11, *Report on Lawlessness in Law Enforcement,* 1931, pp. 104–07.

43. Leonard V. Harrison, *Police Administration in Boston* (Cambridge, Mass.: Harvard University Press, 1934), p. 23.

44. On acclaim for Boston police see Fosdick, *American Police Systems,* pp. 121–22.

45. *Ibid.,* pp. 137, 201.

46. John Henry Cutler, *"Honey Fitz": Three Steps to the White House* (Indianapolis: Bobbs-Merrill, 1962), pp. 31–32.

47. Amory, *op. cit.,* p. 324.

48. Cutler, *op. cit.,* p. 145.

49. On Lomasney, Steffens, *op. cit.,* pp. 615–27, and Harold Zink, *City Bosses in the United States* (Durham: University of North Carolina Press, 1930), pp. 69–84.

50. Cutler, *op. cit.,* pp. 215–16.

51. *Ibid.,* p. 81.

52. Edwin O'Connor, *The Last Hurrah* (Boston: Little, Brown, 1956), p. 152.

53. Francis Russell, *A City in Terror* (New York: Viking, 1975), p. 39.

54. White, *op. cit.,* p. 145.

55. *Ibid.,* p. 151.

56. On Curtis, Russell, *op. cit.,* pp. 43–46.

57. On Peters, *ibid.,* pp. 70, 226–27.

58. Cutler, *op. cit.,* pp. 215–16.

59. *Ibid.,* p. 138, and Amory, *op. cit.,* pp. 34, 193.

60. *Report of Citizens Committee Appointed by the Mayor to Consider the Police Situation,* Boston, 1919.

61. On Coolidge, White, *op. cit.*

62. On 1919 see Robert K. Murray, *Red Scare* (New York: McGraw-Hill, 1964).

63. *Boston Globe,* May 2, 1919, p. 1.

64. *Boston Herald,* Aug. 25, 1919, p. 2.

65. On McInnes *Boston Globe,* Sept. 8, 1919, p. 1.

66. Scenes in stations, *Boston Herald,* Sept. 10, 1919, pp. 4, 6.

67. *Report of Boston Police Commissioner, 1919,* p. 16.

68. On Crowley, see *Boston Globe,* Aug. 22, 1933, p. 1.

69. *Boston Herald,* Sept. 10, 1919, p. 6.

70. James Michael Curley, *I'd Do It Again* (Englewood Cliffs, N.J.: Prentice-Hall, 1957), p. 121, and Joseph Dineen, *The Purple Shamrock* (New York: Norton, 1949), pp. 100–01.

71. Curley, *op. cit.,* p. 117, and Dineen, *op. cit.,* p. 100.

72. Curley, *op. cit.,* p. 139.

73. On volunteers, *Boston Herald,* Sept. 10, 1919, p. 6, and *Boston Globe,* Sept. 9, p. 1, and Sept. 10, p. 4.

74. *Boston Herald,* Sept. 11, 1919, pp. 4–5.

75. *Ibid.,* p. 2.

76. *Ibid.,* pp. 2, 4.

77. *Boston Globe,* Sept. 11, 1919, pp. 1, 5.

78. *Ibid.,* pp. 1, 6.

79. *Boston Globe,* Sept. 12, 1919, p. 1.

80. Amory, *op. cit.,* p. 337.

81. Nevil Macready, *Annals of an Active Life,* 2 vols. (London: Hutchinson, 1924), vol. I, pp. 65–66, 152.

82. Martin Gilbert, *Winston S. Churchill,* vol. III, *The Challenge of War* (Boston: Houghton Mifflin, 1971), pp. 695–97.

83. On the 1918 strike, Reynolds and Judge, *op. cit.,* chaps. 4 and 5.

84. Macready, *op. cit.,* vol. II, p. 403.

85. On 1919 strike, Reynolds and Judge, *op. cit.,* chap. 10.

86. *Ibid.,* p. 193.

87. Cutler, *op. cit.,* pp. 235–36.

88. Alfred Steinberg, *The Bosses* (New York: Macmillan, 1972), p. 184.

89. Dixon Wecter, *When Johnny Comes Marching Home* (Cambridge, Mass.: Houghton Mifflin, 1944), p. 375.

90. Dineen, *op. cit.,* p. 233, and, for his own version, Curley, *op. cit.,* pp. 279–82.

91. Russell, *op. cit.,* pp. 230–31.

92. William F. Whyte, *Street Corner Society,* 2nd ed. (Chicago: University of Chicago Press, 1955), pp. 123–39.

93. *Newsweek,* Apr. 19, 1943, p. 42.

94. On indictments, *Boston Globe,* Mar. 28, 1943, pp. 1, 17. Ultimately all defendants were acquitted.

95. See *Time,* Nov. 1, 1943, p. 42.

96. On Saltonstall, Amory, *op. cit.,* pp. 41, 73.

97. *Ibid.*, p. 73; Steinberg, *op. cit.*, pp. 184–85.

98. *Boston Herald*, Nov. 25, 1943, pp. 1, 17.

99. On Bushnell, *Newsweek*, April 19, 1943, pp. 42, 44, and obituary, *New York Times*, Oct. 24, 1949, p. 23.

100. Harrison, *op. cit.*, p. 23.

Chapter 4 (pp. 121–153): PENNSYLVANIA AND NEW JERSEY: THE AMERICAN CONSTABULARY (1905–1940)

1. *New York Times*, Apr. 21, 1917, p. 11.

2. The vulnerability of small-town banks is a major theme in the autobiography of nineteenth-century Americas most famous burglar. See Langdon Moore, *His Own Story* (Boston: by author, 1893).

3. A modern account of the Commune is Alistair Horne, *The Fall of Paris* (New York: St. Martins, 1965).

4. Theodore Ropp, *War in the Modern World* (Chapel Hill, N.C.: Duke University Press, 1962), p. 175.

5. On Baltimore, Robert V. Bruce, *1877: Year of Violence* (Indianapolis: Bobbs-Merrill, 1959; Quadrangle ed., 1970), chap. 6.

6. On Pittsburgh, *ibid.*, chaps. 7, 8, 9.

7. *Ibid.*, pp. 185–86.

8. *Ibid.*, pp. 241–42, 247.

9. *Ibid.*, pp. 180, 212–13.

10. *Ibid.*, p. 265, and Alpheus Mason, *Brandeis: A Free Man's Life* (New York: Viking, 1956), pp. 47–48.

11. For an example of white soldiers' neglect of duty see Elliot M. Rudwick, *Race Riot in East St. Louis, July 2, 1917* (Carbondale: University of Southern Illinois Press, 1964).

12. Bruce, *op. cit.*, p. 309.

13. Wayne Broehl, *The Molly Maguires* (Cambridge, Mass.: Harvard University Press, 1964).

14. Leon Wolff, *Lockout: The Story of The Homestead Strike* (New York: Harper & Row, 1965).

15. Emma Goldman, *Living My Life*, 2 vols. (New York: Da Capo Press, 1970; orig. 1931), vol. I, pp. 83–107.

16. Anonymous (Mark Sullivan), "The Ills of Pennsylvania," *Atlantic Monthly*, October 1901, pp. 558–65.

17. Samuel Pennypacker, *The Autobiography of a Pennsylvanian* (Philadelphia: John C. Winston, 1918), p. 426.

18. *Ibid.*, p. 378.

19. Victor Hurley, *Jungle Patrol: The Story of the Philippine Constabulary* (New York: Dutton, 1939), pp. 74–75.

20. *Ibid.*, p. 54.

21. *New York Times,* Apr. 15, 1902, p. 3.
22. Quoted in Hurley, *op. cit.,* p. 35.
23. *Ibid.,* pp. 67–68.
24. On Garwood, *ibid.,* pp. 88–93.
25. Katherine Mayo, *Justice to All: The Story of the Pennsylvania State Police,* 5th ed., rev. (Boston: Houghton Mifflin, 1920), pp. 5–6.
26. *Ibid.,* p. 32.
27. *Ibid.,* p. 25.
28. *Ibid.,* pp. 91–92, and Katherine Mayo, *The Standard Bearers* (Boston: Houghton Mifflin, 1918), p. 126.
29. Mayo, *Justice to All,* pp. 37–39.
30. *Ibid.,* p. 42.
31. Pennypacker, *op. cit.,* p. 423. Account of strike in *Philadelphia Inquirer,* May 1, 2, 3, 1906.
32. *Philadelphia Inquirer,* Aug. 23, 1909, pp. 1–2.
33. Hurley, *op. cit.,* p. 383.
34. Mayo, *Justice to All,* pp. 75, 181, and *Philadelphia Inquirer,* Feb. 20–25, 1910.
35. *Annual Report of Pennsylvania State Police 1916,* pp. 24–32.
36. M. Nelson McGeary, *Gifford Pinchot: Forester Politician* (Princeton, N.J.: Princeton University Press, 1960), pp. 304–05.
37. Bruce Smith, *The State Police* (Montclair, N.J.: Patterson Smith, 1969; orig. 1925), pp. 16–17.
38. Leo J. Coakley, *Jersey Troopers* (New Brunswick, N.J.: Rutgers University Press, 1971), pp. 17–18.
39. Mayo, *Justice to All,* pp. xiii–xvi.
40. Coakley, *op. cit.,* p. 10.
41. Augustine Costello, *History of the Police Department of Jersey City* (Jersey City, N.J.: by author, 1891), p. 220.
42. On Hague, Alfred Steinberg, *The Bosses* (New York: Macmillan, 1972), pp. 10–71; see also Coakley, *op. cit.,* pp. 23–24.
43. Steinberg, *op. cit.,* pp. 11, 27–28, 125, and Dayton McKean, *The Boss* (Boston: Houghton Mifflin, 1940), pp. 208–09.
44. Steinberg, *op. cit.,* p. 29.
45. *The Municipal Year Book 1940,* pp. 427–30.
46. McKean, *op. cit.,* p. 210.
47. *Ibid.,* pp. 78–80, and Steinberg, *op. cit.,* pp. 61–62.
48. *Ibid.,* p. 51.
49. *Ibid.,* p. 56.
50. Coakley, *op. cit.,* pp. 30–35.
51. *Ibid.,* pp. 37–49.
52. *Ibid.,* pp. 74–76.
53. *New York Times,* Sept. 29, 1926, pp. 1, 16, and Nov. 7, pp. 22–23.
54. August Vollmer and Alfred Parker, *Crime and the State Police* (Berkeley: University of California Press, 1935), p. 92.

55. Coakley, *op. cit.*, pp. 71, 80.

56. On Smedley Butler see Lowell Thomas, *Old Gimlet Eye: The Adventures of Smedley Butler* (New York: Farrar & Rinehart, 1933), and obituary, *New York Times,* June 22, 1940, p. 34; on Thomas Butler, obituary, *New York Times,* May 27, 1928, p. 3.

57. Jules Archer, *The Plot to Seize the White House* (New York: Hawthorn Books, 1973), pp. 57–58.

58. On Waller see obituary, *New York Times,* July 14, 1926, p. 21.

59. Thomas, *op. cit.*, p. 195.

60. Frank Freidel, *Franklin D. Roosevelt: The Apprentice Years* (Boston: Little, Brown, 1952), pp. 279–83.

61. Archer, *op. cit.*, p. 69.

62. Allen F. Davis and Mark H. Haller, eds., *The Peoples of Philadelphia* (Philadelphia: Temple University Press, 1973), pp. 3–11.

63. Lincoln Steffens, *The Shame of the Cities* (New York: Hill and Wang, 1970; orig. 1904), p. 134.

64. Raymond B. Fosdick, *Chronicle of a Generation,* New York: Harper, 1958), p. 146.

65. Raymond B. Fosdick, *American Police Systems* (Montclair, N.J.: Patterson Smith, 1969; orig. 1920), p. 343.

66. Vice conditions, Archer, *op. cit.*, pp. 82–87; Pinchot criticisms, McGeary, *op. cit.*, pp. 306–07.

67. On the Philadelphia machine, McGeary, *op. cit.*, pp. 277–78, 353. See also (Boss) William B. Vare, *My 40 Years in Politics* (Philadelphia: Roland Swain, 1933).

68. Thomas, *op. cit.*, p. 260.

69. Butler's career in Philadelphia is discussed in *ibid.*, pp. 264–75. An excellent summary is found in Fred D. Baldwin, "Smedley D. Butler and Prohibition Enforcement in Philadelphia, 1924–5," *Pennsylvania Journal of History and Biography,* pp. 352–68. Butler was also fully covered by the Philadelphia papers and the *New York Times* particularly in the hectic first weeks of his office, Jan. 7–15, 1924, and at the time of his departure, Dec. 22–31, 1925.

70. For highlights of the Williams incident see the *New York Times* for the following dates in 1926: Mar. 11, p. 3; Mar. 12, pp. 1 and 2; Mar. 13, p. 4; Mar. 14, p. 1; Mar. 26, p. 7; Apr. 29, p. 5; May 22, p. 19; and Oct. 2, p. 1. See also Butler's version, Thomas, *op. cit.*, pp. 276–86.

71. For Butler's post-Marine career see Archer, *op. cit.*

72. On the crime see George Waller, *Kidnap: The Story of the Lindbergh Case* (New York: Dial, 1961). The state police perspective is presented in Coakley, *op. cit.*, pp. 99–138. A recent book attacking the official version of the case is Anthony Scaduto, *Scapegoat: The Lonesome Death of Bruno Richard Hauptman* (New York: Putnam, 1977).

73. Elmer L. Irey and William J. Slocum, *The Tax Dodgers* (New York: Garden City Publishing, 1948), pp. 72–73.

74. Fletcher Pratt, *The Cunning Mulatto and Other Cases of Ellis Parker, American Detective* (New York: Smith & Hass, 1930), p. 12.

75. Waller, *op. cit.*, pp. 530–40.

76. On Schwartzkopf's later career see obituary, *New York Times*, Nov. 27, 1958, p. 29.

77. Coakley, *op. cit.*, pp. 189–91.

78. On the Philippines see Katherine Mayo, *The Isles of Fear* (New York: Harcourt, Brace, 1925). A summary of the criticism of *Mother India* is contained in H. G. Dalway Turnbull, "Miss Mayo and Her Critics," *Fortnightly Review*, vol. CXXV, 1929, pp. 355–69.

79. For Ms. Mayo's obituary see *New York Times*, Oct. 10, 1940, p. 25; account of the funeral Oct. 12, p. 17.

80. Accounts of state police reluctance to confront politically protected gambling: concerning the New York State Police, *Kefauver Committee Report on Organized Crime* (New York: Didier, 1951), pp. 87–90, and, concerning Pennsylvania State Police, John A. Gardiner and David J. Olson, "Wincanton: The Politics of Corruption," in President's Commission on Law Enforcement and Administration of Justice, *Task Force Report: Organized Crime* (Washington, GPO, 1967), p. 63.

Chapter 5 (pp. 154–187): NEW YORK: THE FINEST AND THE FALL OF THE HALL (1914–1945)

1. Gene Fowler, *Beau James: The Life and Times of Jimmy Walker* (New York: Viking, 1949), pp. 5–8.

2. *New York Times*, Aug. 8, 1912, p. 2.

3. Frank Freidel, *Franklin D. Roosevelt: The Apprentice Years* (Boston: Little, Brown, 1952), pp. 197–201.

4. Jane Dahlberg, *The New York Bureau of Municipal Research: Pioneer in Government Administration* (New York: New York University Press, 1966), p. 54.

5. Raymond B. Fosdick, "The Police Scandal and the Good Old Days," *Outlook*, Oct. 19, 1912, p. 348. *Report of the Special Committee of the Board of Aldermen of the City of New York to Investigate the Police Department* (Curran Committee), 1913, p. 2.

6. Cleveland Foundation, *Criminal Justice in Cleveland* (Cleveland: 1922), p. vii.

7. Raymond B. Fosdick, *American Police Systems* (Montclair, N.J.: Patterson Smith, 1969; orig. 1920), pp. 4–27, 358.

8. *Ibid.*, p. 56.

9. *Outlook*, Jan. 1, 1910, p. 15.

10. Edwin A. Lewinson, *John Purroy Mitchell: The Boy Mayor of New York* (New York: Astra Books, 1965), pp. 118–20.

11. See Herbert L. Packer, "Two Models of the Criminal Process," *University of Pennsylvania Law Review*, 113, November 1964, pp. 1–68, and *The Limits of the Criminal Sanction* (Stanford, Calif.: Stanford University Press, 1968), synthesized in Jerome H. Skolnick, *Justice Without Trial: Law Enforcement in a Democratic Society* (New York: Wiley, 1967), pp. 182–83.

12. *Weeks v. U.S.*, 232 U.S. 383 (1914).

13. Arthur Woods, *Crime Prevention* (Princeton, N.J.: Princeton University Press, 1918), p. 74.

14. Arthur Woods, *Policemen and Public* (Montclair, N.J.: Patterson Smith, 1975; orig. 1919), pp. 94–95.

15. Lowell J. Limpus, *Honest Cop: Lewis J. Valentine* (New York: Dutton, 1939), p. 61.

16. *Ibid.*, pp. 67–70.

17. *New York Times*, Feb. 22, 1914, pt. II, p. 3.

18. Wallace Sayre and Herbert Kaufman, *Governing New York City* (New York, Russell Sage Foundation, 1960), pp. 432–35.

19. Raymond B. Fosdick, *Chronicle of a Generation* (New York: Harper, 1958), p. 84.

20. On charity fight and wiretapping, Lewinson, *op. cit.*, chap X, and pt. 5, *Minutes and Testimony of Joint Legislative Committee to Investigate the Public Service Commissioners* (Albany, N.Y.: J. B. Lyon, 1916).

21. Woods's statement, *ibid.*, pp. 99–111. Woods's appearances were reported in the *New York Times*, May 9, 1916, p. 22; May 18, pp. 1, 8; May 20, p. 1.

22. Lewinson, *op. cit.*, introduction, p. 13.

23. Francis Russell, *The Great Interlude* (New York: McGraw-Hill, 1964), pp. 7–20.

24. Lewinson, *op. cit.*, p. 237.

25. Leon Stein, *The Triangle Fire* (Philadelphia: Lippincott, 1962).

26. *Ibid.*, pp. 144–45.

27. Warren Moscow, *What Have You Done for Me Lately? The Ins and Outs of New York City Politics* (Englewood Cliffs, N.J.: Prentice-Hall, 1961), pp. 180–81.

28. Fosdick, *Chronicle*, pp. 142–43.

29. Lewinson, *op. cit.*, p. 255, and Grover Whalen, *Mr. New York: The Autobiography of Grover Whalen* (New York: Putnam, 1955), p. 34.

30. On Fosdick's later career see Fosdick, *Chronicle*.

31. W. A. Swanberg, *Citizen Hearst* (New York: Scribner, 1961), pp. 317, 319–20, 344–46, 361–62, 366, 370, 372.

32. Whalen, *op. cit.*, pp. 35–38.

33. Limpus, *op. cit.*, pp. 89–90.

34. *New York City Police Department Annual Report, 1923*, p. 24.

35. Craig Thompson and Allan Raymond, *Gang Rule in New York* (New York: Dial, 1940), p. 184.

36. Assertions of Rothstein's cheating in Fowler, *op. cit.*, p. 208, and Leo Katcher, *The Big Bankroll: The Life and Times of Arnold Rothstein* (New Rochelle, N.Y.: Arlington House, 1958), p. 106.

37. Fowler, *op. cit.*, p. 223. Biographies of Rothstein are Katcher, *op. cit.*, and Donald H. Clarke, *In the Reign of Rothstein* (New York: Vanguard, 1929).

38. Katcher, *op. cit.*, pp. 151–56; Clarke, *op. cit.*, pp. 34–40.

39. The police raid and the troubles of Inspector Henry are contained in Katcher, *op. cit.*, pp. 156–64, and Clarke, *op. cit.*, pp. 40–54. The raid and the events which ensued were covered extensively in the *New York Times* in the years 1919 through 1921. See especially *New York Times*, May 15, 1920, p. 2, on the slacker raids, and June 11, 1920, p. 26, on running the Jews out of the Tenderloin.

40. Michael Fiaschetti, *You Gotta Be Rough* (New York: Doubleday, Doran, 1930), pp. 179–93, esp. 181.

41. Thompson and Raymond, *op. cit.*, p. 21; Katcher, *op. cit.*, p. 175; Clarke, *op. cit.*, pp. 1–6. Also Gene Fowler, *The Great Mouthpiece: The Life Story of William J. Fallon* (New York: Covici, Friede, 1931), pp. 248–49. pp. 248–49.

42. F. Scott Fitzgerald, *The Great Gatsby* (New York: Scribner, 1925), p. 74.

43. Fowler, *Great Mouthpiece*, p. 339.

44. Moscow, *op. cit.*, p. 169.

45. For a detailed account of Smith's family background with reference to official city records, see Matthew Josephson, *Al Smith: Hero of the Cities* (Boston.: Houghton Mifflin, 1969). Smith's paternal grandmother came from Germany. His maternal grandfather was Irish and his maternal grandmother English. Most biographers and Smith himself are either silent or vague on the subject of his background. Since there was no mystery or scandal about his ancestry, it is obvious that the subject was avoided because it did not fit the legend.

46. *Ibid.*, pp. 176, 253–54, and Oscar Handlin, *Al Smith and His America* (Boston: Little, Brown, 1958), pp. 149–50.

47. Josephson, *op. cit.*, pp. 74, 387.

48. *Ibid.*, p. 322, and Moscow, *op. cit.*, p. 158.

49. Fowler, *Beau James*, p. 113.

50. Handlin, *op. cit.*, p. 52.

51. A friendly biography of Walker is Fowler, *Beau James*. See also George Walsh, *Gentleman Jimmy Walker: Mayor of the Jazz Age* (New York: Praeger, 1974).

52. Cornelius W. Willemse, *Behind the Green Lights* (New York: Knopf, 1931), and *A Cop Remembers* (Knopf, 1933).

53. Robert McAllister, *The Kind of Guy I Am* (London: Hammond and Hammond, 1959), p. 103.

54. Profile, *New Yorker*, Sept. 5 and 12, 1953.

55. Thompson and Raymond, *op. cit.*, pp. 70, 229.

56. On Broderick see obituary, *New York Times*, Jan. 18, 1966, p. 37; profile, *New Yorker*, Dec. 26, 1931; and Fowler, *Beau James*, pp. 236–37.

57. *New Yorker*, Oct. 17, 1936, p. 39.

58. Clarke, *op. cit.*, pp. 284–90, and Katcher, *op. cit.*, pp. 1–7, 328–33.

59. John Henry Cutler, *"Honey Fitz": Three Steps to the White House* (Indianapolis: Bobbs-Merrill, 1962), p. 133.

60. Frederick Lewis Allen, *Only Yesterday* (New York: Harper, 1957; orig. 1931), pp. 222–23.

61. Fowler, *Beau James*, p. 233.

62. *New York Times*, Dec. 30, 1928, pp. 1, 6.

63. Whalen, *op. cit.*, pp. 150–53.

64. Thompson and Raymond, *op. cit.*, p. 103.

65. Herbert Mitgang, *The Man Who Rode the Tiger: The Life and Times of Judge Samuel Seabury* (Philadelphia: Lippincott, 1963), pp. 94, 221, 253.

66. A very favorable account of the investigation is William B. and John B. Northrop, *The Insolence of Office* (New York: Putnam, 1932).

67. Thomas E. Dewey, *Twenty Against the Underworld*, Rodney Campbell, ed. (Garden City, N.J.: Doubleday, 1974), pp. 82–93.

68. Mitgang, *op. cit.*, pp. 180–215.

69. *Ibid.*, p. 267.

70. Moscow, *op. cit.*, pp. 24–25.

71. On La Guardia see Charles Garrett, *The La Guardia Years: Machine and Reform Politics in New York City* (New Brunswick, N.J.: Rutgers University Press, 1961).

72. Limpus, *op. cit.*, pp. 169–70.

73. "Nineteen Thousand Cops," *Fortune*, July 1939, p. 168.

74. *New Yorker*, Oct. 17, 1936, p. 3.

75. Lewis J. Valentine, *Nightstick* (New York: Dial, 1947), pp. 190–92; Garrett, *op. cit.*, p. 160; *New York Times*, Jan. 27, 1935, p. 1.

76. *New York Times*, Jan. 2, 1934, p. 1.

77. Garrett, *op. cit.*, p. 162; Moscow, *op. cit.*, pp. 90–91; and Fred J. Cook, *The Secret Rulers* (New York: Duell, Sloan & Pearce, 1966), p. 129.

78. Dewey, *op. cit.*, pp. 192–93, 324–25, 384.

79. *Ibid.*, chaps. xxviii, xxxii, and xxxiii.

80. Moscow, *op. cit.*, pp. 169–93, 171, 173–76.

Chapter 6 (pp. 188–223): CHICAGO: THE TOWN THEY COULD NOT SHUT DOWN (1857–1945)

1. Accounts of riot are in Henry David, *The History of the Haymarket Affair*, 2nd ed. (New York: Russell, 1958; orig. 1936), and John J. Flinn and John E. Wilkie, *History of the Chicago Police* (Montclair, N.J.: Patterson Smith, 1973; orig. 1887).

2. Arthur E. Sutherland, *The Law at Harvard* (Cambridge, Mass.: The Belknap Press, 1967), pp. 272–73.

3. Bruce Smith, *Police Systems in the U.S.*, 2nd rev. ed. (New York: Harper, 1960; orig. 1940), p. 27.

4. On Smith see O. W. Wilson, "Bruce Smith," *Journal of Criminal Law, Criminology and Police Science*, vol. 47, 1956–57, pp. 235–37, and profile, *New Yorker*, Feb. 27, 1954.

5. Smith, *op. cit.*, p. 5.

6. Virgil W. Peterson, *Barbarians in Our Midst: A History of Chicago Crime and Politics* (Boston: Little, Brown, 1952), p. 150.

7. Lloyd Lewis and Henry Justin Smith, *Chicago: A History of Its Reputation* (New York: Harcourt, Brace, 1929), p. 113.

8. Ray Ginger, *Altgeld's America* (Chicago: Quadrangle Books, 1965; orig. 1958), p. 19.

9. *Ibid.*, p. 281.

10. Lloyd Wendt and Herman Kogan, *Lords of the Levee* (Indianapolis: Bobbs-Merrill, 1943), p. 274.

11. *The Complete Poems of Carl Sandburg* (New York: Harcourt Brace Jovanovich, 1970), p. 3.

12. Elizabeth Gurley Flynn, *The Rebel Girl* (New York: International Publishers, 1955), p. 79.

13. Peterson, *op. cit.*, p. 29.

14. *Ibid.*, pp. 82–83.

15. On McDonald, Herbert Asbury, *Gem of the Prairie: An Informal History of the Chicago Underworld* (Garden City, N.Y.: Knopf, 1942), pp. 144, 149–50, 153.

16. *Chicago Record Herald*, Dec. 3, 1911, quoted in *ibid.*, p. 162.

17. On Kenna and Coughlin see Wendt and Kogan, *op. cit.*

18. *Ibid.*, p. 327.

19. Asbury, *op. cit.*, pp. 247–60.

20. Wendt and Kogan, *op. cit.*, p. 319.

21. *Ibid.*, p. 268.

22. On Stead, Barbara Tuchman, *The Proud Tower* (New York: Macmillan, 1966), pp. 245–47.

23. On Lucy Gaston, Asbury, *op. cit.*, pp. 254–55; on Bloom, Stephen Longstreet, *Chicago 1860–1919* (New York: McKay, 1973), p. 354.

24. Asbury, *op. cit.*, pp. 281–84.

25. Wendt and Kogan, *op. cit.*, pp. 270–71.

26. Asbury, *op. cit.*, p. 260.

27. Wendt and Kogan, *op. cit.*, p. 182.

28. *Ibid.*, pp. 103–04.

29. Ginger, *op. cit.*, p. 302.

30. Asbury, *op. cit.*, p. 207.

31. Longstreet, *op. cit.*, p. 445.

32. Carter Harrison, *Stormy Years* (Indianapolis: Bobbs-Merrill, 1935), pp. 297, 310.

33. On Schuettler, *Chicago Tribune*, Jan. 11, 1917, p. 2.

34. On Nootbar see *Chicago Tribune* July 21, 1914, pp. 1–2, and obituary, June 10, 1939, p. 12; and Donald Culross Peattie, "The Most Unforgettable Character I've Met" (Max Nootbar), *Reader's Digest*, January 1944, pp. 77–82.

35. On Heitler and West Side investigation, see Peterson, *op. cit.*, pp. 90–91, 94, 101, 247.

36. On Levee clean-up, Wendt and Kogan, *op. cit.*, chap. 26.

37. On Thompson, Lloyd Wendt and Herman Kogan, *Big Bill* (Indianapolis: Bobbs-Merrill, 1953).

38. *Ibid.*, pp. 70–71.

39. Illinois Association for Criminal Justice, *The Illinois Crime Survey* (Chicago: 1929), pp. 1025–27 (reprinted by Patterson Smith, Montclair, N.J., 1968).

40. Walter Reckless, *Vice in Chicago* (Montclair, N.J.: Patterson Smith, 1969; orig. 1933), p. 72.

41. On O'Bannions, Illinois Association for Criminal Justice, *op. cit.*, pp. 1013–15, 1025–32.

42. *Ibid.*, pp. 916–17.

43. On Collins, Mark H. Haller, "Civic Reformers and Police Leadership: Chicago 1905–1935," in Harlan Hahn, ed., *Police in Urban Society* (Beverly Hills, Calif.: Sage Publications, 1971), p. 47; on Sportsmen's Club, Peterson, *op. cit.*, p. 100.

44. Illinois Association for Criminal Justice, *op. cit.*, p. 901.

45. Asbury, *op. cit.*, pp. 341–42.

46. Illinois Association for Criminal Justice, *op. cit.*, p. 914.

47. Peterson, *op. cit.*, pp. 113, 136.

48. Wendt and Kogan, *op. cit.*, *Big Bill*, pp. 50–51.

49. Citizens Police Committee, *Chicago Police Problems* (Chicago: University of Chicago Press, 1931), p. 8.

50. On Lingle case see John Boettinger, *Jake Lingle* (New York: Dutton, 1931).

51. On Cermak see Alex Gottfried, *Boss Cermak of Chicago* (Seattle: University of Washington Press, 1962).

52. Peterson, *op. cit.*, p. 155.

53. *Ibid.*, p. 160.

54. Harold F. Ickes, *The Autobiography of a Curmudgeon* (New York: Reynal & Hitchcock, 1943), p. 256.

55. Peterson, *op. cit.*, pp. 164, 191.

56. *Ibid.*, pp. 261–64.

57. Allan A. Grimshaw, ed., *Racial Violence in the United States* (Chicago: Aldine, 1969), p. 285.

58. Frederic M. Thrasher, *The Gang* (Chicago: University of Chicago Press, 1927), pp. 20–22.

59. Gerald G. Eggert, *Richard Olney: Evolution of a Statesman* (University Park: Pennsylvania State University Press, 1974), p. 143.

60. See FBI, *Uniform Crime Reports*, 1930 and later years.

61. On Annenbergs see John T. Flynn, "Smart Money," *Colliers*, Jan. 13–Feb. 3, 1940, in 4 parts.

62. *People v. Scalisi*, 324 Ill. 131.

63. Peterson, *op. cit.*, p. 151.

64. Langdon Moore, *His Own Story* (Boston: by author, 1893), p. 501.

65. Illinois Association for Criminal Justice, *op. cit.*, pp. 606, 610.

66. *Chicago Tribune* Nov. 22, 1875, quoted in Hary Barnard, *Eagle Forgotten: The Life of John Peter Altgeld* (Indianapolis: Bobbs-Merrill, 1938; Charter ed., 1962), p. 45.

67. Barnard, *op. cit.*, pp. 56, 108.

68. Lewis and Smith, *op. cit.*, p. 152.

69. On Parsons, Barnard, *op. cit.*, p. 90; Pinkerton statement, Ginger, *op. cit.*, pp. 37–38; see also Robt. V. Bruce, *1877: Year of Violence* (Indianapolis: Bobbs-Merrill, 1959; Quadrangle ed., 1970), p. 246.

70. Flinn and Wilkie, *op. cit.*, pp. 198–99.

71. Barnard, *op. cit.*, p. 80.

72. Willis J. Abbot, *Watching the World Go By* (Boston: Little, Brown, 1935), p. 64.

73. Barnard, *op. cit.*, pp. 45–46.

74. On McCormick incident, Flinn and Wilkie, *op. cit.*, pp. 274–78, and David, *op. cit.*, pp. 189–91.

75. Flinn and Wilkie, *op. cit.*, pp. 234–49.

76. Accounts of bombing, *ibid.*, chaps. 14 and 15, and David, *op. cit.*, chap. IX.

77. Capture of Linge, Flinn and Wilkie, *op. cit.*, pp. 377–78; police dissension, Captain Michael J. Schaack, *Anarchy and the Anarchists* (Chicago: F. J. Schulte & Co., 1889), pp. 183–205.

78. Barnard, *op. cit.*, p. 201.

79. *Ibid.*, p. 116.

80. Ginger, *op cit.*, p. 42.

81. Richard Drinnon, *Rebel in Paradise* (Boston: Beacon Press, 1961), p. 47.

82. Barnard, *op. cit.*, p. 189.

83. On Altgeld see *ibid.* and Ginger, *op. cit.*

84. John P. Altgeld, "Reasons for Pardoning Fielden, et al.," quoted in Bernard Kogan, *The Chicago Haymarket Riot* (Boston: Heath, 1959), p. 107.

85. *New York Times*, June 28, 1893, cited in Barnard, *op. cit.*, p. 245.

86. Barnard, *op. cit.*, p. 241.

87. On Olney, see Eggert, *op. cit.*

88. On the strike see Almont Lindsay, *The Pullman Strike* (Chicago: University of Chicago Press, 1971; orig. 1942).

89. Barnard, *op. cit.*, pp. 317, 328; Lindsay, *op. cit.*, p. 190.

90. Barnard, *op. cit.*, p. 385.

91. *Ibid.*, pp. 414–15.

92. Ginger, *op. cit.*, pp. 263–64.

93. *Ibid.*, pp. 268–69.

94. On Memorial Day incident see Irving Bernstein, *Turbulent Years* (Boston: Houghton Mifflin, 1970), pp. 485–90.

95. Harold F. Gosnell, *Negro Politicians: The Rise of Negro Politics in Chicago* (Chicago: University of Chicago Press, 1967; orig. 1935), p. 248.

96. Flinn and Wilkie, *op. cit.*, pp. 414–15.

97. William Tuttle, Jr., *Race Riot: Chicago in the Red Summer of 1919* (New York: Atheneum, 1970), pp. 113, 117.

98. *Ibid.*, pp. 102–03.

99. Illinois Commission on Race Relations, *The Negro in Chicago* (Chicago: University of Chicago Press, 1922), pp. 3, 122–33.

100. On Ragens, Illinois Association for Criminal Justice, *op. cit.*, pp. 1001–07.

101. On Thompson and blacks see Gosnell, *op. cit.*; see also Tuttle, *op. cit.*, pp. 188–207.

102. On San Juan Hill riot, see Citizens Protective League, *Story of the Riot* (New York: Arno, 1969; orig. 1900).

103. In addition to Tuttle, *op. cit.*, and Illinois Commission on Race Relations, *op. cit.*, the riot was extensively covered in the press. For accounts of police activity see, for example, *Chicago Tribune*, July 27–31, 1919.

104. Illinois Commission on Race Relations, *op. cit.*, pp. 59–64.

105. Gosnell, *op. cit.*, p. 251.

106. Third degree in Chicago, National Commission on Law Observance and Enforcement (Wickersham Commission), #11, *Report on Lawlessness in Law Enforcement*, 1931. On Franks and Degnan cases, Peterson, *op. cit.*, pp. 218–20.

107. Ginger, *op. cit.*, pp. 339–40.

Chapter 7 (pp. 224–254): CALIFORNIA: THE NEW BREED (1901–1942)

1. Leo Katcher, *Earl Warren: A Political Biography* (New York: McGraw-Hill, 1967), p. 19, and John D. Weaver, *Warren: The Man, the Court, the Era* (Boston: Little, Brown, 1967), pp. 23–25.

2. George E. Mowry, *The California Progressives* (Berkeley: University of California Press, 1951; Quadrangle ed., 1963), p. 12.

3. Herbert Asbury, *The Barbary Coast: An Informal History of the San Francisco Underworld* (Garden City, N.Y.: Knopf, 1933), p. 76. *In Re Neagle*, 135 U.S. 1 (1889).

4. Katcher, *op. cit.*, p. 138.

5. Asbury, *op. cit.*, pp. 150–52.

6. Police Department, City and County of San Francisco, *The History of the San Francisco Police Department* (San Francisco, 1972), p. 4.

7. *Ibid.*, pp. 198–99.

8. Walton Bean, *Boss Ruef's San Francisco* (Berkeley: University of California Press, 1967), p. 49.

9. J. W. Ehrlich, *A Life in My Hands* (New York: Putnam, 1965), p. 87. (Excerpts reprinted by permission of G. P. Putnam's Sons. Copyright © 1965 by J. W. Ehrlich.)

10. On career of Ruef see Bean, *op. cit.*, and Lately Thomas, *A Debonair Scoundrel* (New York: Holt, Rinehart and Winston, 1962).

11. Description of Bassity, *San Francisco Bulletin*, May 14, 1910, cited in Asbury, *op. cit.*, p. 236.

12. Bean, *op. cit.*, pp. 81–82.

13. On Caraher see Asbury, *op. cit.*, pp. 260–74, and on Cameron see pp. 183–84, as well as Carol Wilson, *Chinatown Quest* (Palo Alto, Calif.: Stanford University Press, 1931).

14. Mowry, *op. cit.*, p. 97.

15. *Ibid.*, p. 112.

16. Fremont Older, *My Own Story* (San Francisco: Call Publishing Co., 1919), pp. 41–46.

17. Bean, *op. cit.*, p. 67.

18. *Ibid.*, p. 44.

19. Accounts of the Heney shooting incident in *ibid.*, pp. 68–70, and Thomas, *op cit.*, pp. 44–46. Steffens's account has it exactly the opposite, with Heney's assailant being the one who had a gun; Lincoln Steffens, *Autobiography* (New York: Harcourt, Brace, 1931), pp. 545–46.

20. Don Whitehead, *The FBI Story* (New York: Random House, 1956), pp. 18–19.

21. The best account is Bean, *op. cit.* Others are Thomas, *op. cit.*, also Steffens, *op. cit.*, chaps. 28–29. For a contemporary account highly favorable to the prosecution, see Franklin Hichborn, *The System: The San Francisco Graft Prosecution* (Montclair, N.J.: Patterson Smith, 1969; orig. 1915).

22. Bean, *op. cit.*, p. 167.

23. Thomas, *op. cit.*, pp. 107–08.

24. Bean, *op. cit.*, p. 201.

25. "Ruef, a Jew Under Torture," *Overland Monthly*, November 1907, pp. 516–19.

26. Bean, *op. cit.*, p. 190.

27. Adela Rogers St. Johns, *Final Verdict* (Garden City, N.Y.: Doubleday, 1962), pp. 305–06.

28. Bean, *op. cit.*, p. 286.

29. *The Nation*, July 1, 1909, quoted in Bean, *op. cit.*, p. 286.

30. Asbury, *op. cit.*, p. 293.

31. Carey McWilliams, *Southern California Country* (New York: Duell, Sloan & Pearce, 1946), p. 167.

32. For an explanation of Southern California economic facts, see *ibid.*, pp. 274–75.

33. Morrow Mayo, *Los Angeles* (New York: Knopf, 1933), p. 152.

34. William J. Burns, *The Masked War* (New York: George H. Doran and Co., 1913), p. 147.

35. On Darrow's brother-in-law and the disappearance of the witness see Irving Stone, *Clarence Darrow for the Defense* (New York: Doubleday, Doran, 1941), pp. 283–84. On the office bugging see Robert Cleland, *California in Our Time* (New York: Knopf, 1947), p. 84. For Darrow's own account see Clarence Darrow, *The Story of My Life* (New York: Charles Scribner, 1932), chaps. 21, 22.

36. Steffens, *op. cit.*, pp. 570–89.

37. Lewis Adamic, *Dynamite* (Gloucester, Mass.: Peter Smith, 1963; orig. 1931), p. 235.

38. Cleland, *op. cit.*, p. 86.

39. McWilliams, *op. cit.*, pp. 290–91.

40. David Taylor, *The Life of James Rolph, Jr.* (San Francisco: by author, 1934), p. 110.

41. Ernest Jerome Hopkins, *What Happened in the Mooney Case?* (New York: Brower, Warren and Putnam, 1932; Da Capo reprint, 1970), p. 11.

42. Richard H. Frost, *The Mooney Case* (Stanford, Calif.: Stanford University Press, 1968), pp. 50–51.

43. *Ibid.*, p. 31.

44. Hopkins, *op. cit.*, pp. 38–39.

45. Frost, *op. cit.*, p. 99.

46. Hopkins, *op. cit.*, p. 46.

47. *Ibid.*, p vii.

48. Curt Gentry, *Frame-up* (New York: Norton, 1967), pp. 146, 354.

49. Frost, *op. cit.*, pp. 445–46.

50. *Ibid.*, pp. 313–17.

51. *Ibid.*, p. 218.

52. Gentry, *op. cit.*, p. 206.

53. *Ibid.*, p. 280.

54. Frost, *op. cit.*, pp. 341–43.

55. *Ibid.*, pp. 89, 309–10. For leftist disappointment with Older see *The Nation*, Nov. 28, 1936, pp. 636–38.

56. Gentry, *op. cit.*, p. 256.

57. Frost, *op. cit.*, pp. 375–76.

58. *Ibid.*, p. 480.

59. *Ibid.*, p. 489.

60. Mowry, *op. cit.*, pp. 137–38; deal with San Francisco groups, p. 218; Hughes incident, pp. 261–73; refusal to resign as governor, p. 278.

61. Accounts of Vollmer have been drawn from Alfred E. Parker, *August Vollmer: Crime Fighter* (New York: Macmillan, 1961), and Gene E. and Elaine H. Carte, *Police Reform in the United States: The Era of August*

Vollmer (Berkeley: University of California Press, 1975). The first is exceedingly adulatory; the second is more objective.

62. Albert Deutsch, *The Trouble with Cops* (New York: Crown Press, 1954), p. 124.

63. Parker, *op. cit.*, p. 123.

64. John P. Kenney, *The California Police* (Springfield, Ill.: Charles C Thomas, 1964), p. 55.

65. Carte, *op. cit.*, pp. 52–53.

66. Rhodri Jeffreys-Jones, *American Espionage: From Secret Service to CIA* (New York: Free Press, 1977), p. 69.

67. Duncan Matheson, "The Technique of the American Detective," *Annals of the American Academy of Political and Social Science*, November 1929, p. 217.

68. Carte, *op. cit.*, p. 74.

69. Joseph Woods, *The Progressives and the Police: Urban Reform and the Professionalization of the Police*, unpublished dissertation, UCLA, Los Angeles, 1973, pp. 46–47.

70. *Ibid.*, p. 141.

71. Kenneth T. Jackson, *The Ku Klux Klan in the City* (New York: Oxford University Press, 1970), p. 190.

72. Carte, *op. cit.*, p. 102.

73. Woods, *op. cit.*, p. 170.

74. Leslie T. White, *Me Detective* (New York: Harcourt, Brace, 1936), pp. 125–26; Woods, *op. cit.*, p. 277.

75. Los Angeles Police Department, *Annual Report*, 1924, p. 174.

76. National Commission on Law Observance and Enforcement (Wickersham Commission), #14 *Report on Police*, and #11, *Report on Lawlessness in Law Enforcement*, 1931.

77. Alfred E. Parker, *The Berkeley Police Story* (Springfield, Ill.: Charles C Thomas, 1972), p. xii.

78. Kenney, *op. cit.*, p. 92–93.

79. Wilson, *op. cit.*, pp. 212–29, 246.

80. Ehrlich, *op. cit.*, p. 86.

81. *Ibid.*, pp. 87–88.

82. Irving Bernstein, *Turbulent Years* (Boston: Houghton Mifflin, 1970), pp. 259–298.

83. *Newsweek*, June 6, 1936, p. 9; *Literary Digest*, Apr. 3, 1937, pp. 3–4.

84. Ehrlich, *op. cit.*, p. 97; *San Francisco Chronicle*, June 2, 1936, p. 1.

85. An account of the case from the perspective of the defense is contained in Ehrlich, *op. cit.*, pp. 84–114.

86. On the social reformer spy, McWilliams, *op. cit.*, p. 291. On the police evicted, Woods, *op. cit.*, pp. 293–96.

87. Woods, *op. cit.*, p. 343.

88. *Ibid.*, p. 361.

89. *Ibid.*, pp. 350, 362.

90. *Ibid.,* pp. 357–58.
91. McWilliams, *op. cit.,* p. 305.
92. Woods, *op. cit.,* p. 388.
93. Katcher, *op. cit.,* pp. 52–65.
94. *Ibid.,* p. 62.
95. Weaver, *op. cit.,* p. 45.
96. Kenney, *op. cit.,* chap. IV.
97. Katcher, *op. cit.,* pp. 96–99, 119–20, Weaver, *op. cit.,* pp. 84–91.
98. Katcher, *op. cit.,* p. 130.
99. *Irvine v. California,* 347 U.S. 128 (1954).
100. August Vollmer and Alfred Parker, *Crime and the State Police* (Berkeley: University of California Press, 1935), p. 208, and Carte, *op. cit.,* pp. 75–80.
101. Kenney, *op. cit.,* p. 29.

Chapter 8 (pp. 255–298): THE SECRET AGENTS (1850–1945)

1. Based on Gene Caesar, *Incredible Detective* (Englewood Cliffs, N.J.: Prentice-Hall, 1961), pp. 61–62; Don Wilkie and Mark Luther Lee, *American Secret Service Agent* (New York: Frederick A. Stokes, 1934), pp. 107–08.
2. Raymond B. Fosdick, *American Police Systems* (Montclair, N.J.: Patterson Smith, 1969; orig. 1920), p. 328.
3. Most accounts of Pinkerton's career simply report the myths. Even the *Dictionary of American Biography* accepts the account of Pinkerton's father's being killed in a Chartist riot while serving as a Glasgow police sergeant. Other accounts are bitter tirades against the agency, such as Charles Siringo (a longtime Pinkerton agent), *Two Evil Isms: Pinkertonism and Anarchism.* The most carefully researched account is James D. Horan, *The Pinkertons* (New York: Crown, 1967). Background of Pinkerton is taken from this, pp. 4–12.
4. Josiah Flynt (Willard), *World of Graft* (New York: McClure Phillips, 1901), pp. 182–83.
5. Horan, *op. cit.,* p. 327.
6. An article which questions the Pinkerton version is Edward S. Lanis, "Allan Pinkerton and the Baltimore Assassination Plot Against Lincoln," *Maryland Historical Magazine,* XLV, March 1950, pp. 1–13.
7. *Ibid.,* p. 12.
8. On alleged wartime exploits see Allan Pinkerton, *Spy of the Rebellion* (New York: G. W. Carleton, 1883).
9. George F. Milton, *The Age of Hate: Andrew Johnson and the Radicals* (New York: Coward-McCann, 1930), pp. 411, 732.
10. Horan, *op. cit.,* p. 386.
11. *Ibid.,* chap. 20.

12. Alfred E. Parker, *The Berkeley Police Story* (Springfield, Ill.: Charles C Thomas, 1972), p. 8.

13. Gene E. Carte and Elaine H. Carte, *Police Reform in the United States: The Era of August Vollmer* (Berkeley: University of California Press, 1975), p. 20.

14. On New Orleans, Horan, *op. cit.,* chap. 34.

15. John Higham, *Strangers in the Land: Patterns of American Nationalism* (New Brunswick, N.J.: Rutgers University Press, 1963), pp. 90–91, 169, 184–85, 264–68.

16. On DiMaio in Pennsylvania, Horan, *op. cit.,* chap. 35.

17. Langdon Moore, *His Own Story* (Boston: by author, 1893), pp. 296, 325–33.

18. Flynt, *op. cit.,* p. 47.

19. On Holmes, Horan, *op. cit.,* chap. 32.

20. William Haywood, *Autobiography* (New York: International Publishers, 1929), p. 87.

21. Accounts of the case in *ibid.,* chaps. XII and XIII; Horan, *op. cit.,* chaps. 36–38; Louis Adamic, *Dynamite* (Gloucester, Mass.: Peter Smith, 1963; orig. 1931), chaps. 12–16; and Irving Stone, *Clarence Darrow for the Defense* (New York: Doubleday, Doran, 1941), chap. VII.

22. Horan, *op. cit.,* p. 509.

23. Walter S. Bowen and Harry E. Neal, *The United States Secret Service* (Philadelphia: Chilton, 1960), pp. 12–13.

24. Horan, *op. cit.,* p. 172.

25. Bowen and Neal, *op. cit.,* p. 15.

26. Kenneth Alfers, *Law and Order in the Capital City: A History of the Washington Police, 1800–1886* (Washington, D.C.: George Washington University Press), 1976, pp. 38–39.

27. Bowen and Neal, *op. cit.,* pp. 161–63.

28. On Hardings, Francis Russell, *The Shadow of Blooming Grove: Warren G. Harding in His Times* (New York: McGraw-Hill, 1968), p. 451.

29. On Philadelphia case, Caesar, *op. cit.,* pp. 56–84, and Wilkie and Lee, *op. cit.,* chaps. IX, X, XI.

30. See Donald L. McMurray, *Coxey's Army* (Seattle: University of Washington Press, 1929, reprint 1968), and Gerald G. Eggert, *Richard Olney: Evolution of a Statesman* (University Park: Pennsylvania State University Press, 1974), chap. 8.

31. Wilkie and Lee, *op. cit.,* pp. 18–22.

32. Alfers, *op. cit.,* p. 29.

33. *New York Journal,* Feb. 4, 1900, cited in W. A. Swanberg, *Citizen Hearst* (New York: Scribner, 1961), p. 181.

34. Wilkie and Lee, *op. cit.,* pp. 11–12.

35. Frank J. Wilson and Beth Day, *Special Agent* (New York: Holt, Rinehart, and Winston, 1965), pp. 95–100.

36. Wilkie and Lee, *op. cit.,* pp. 143–44.

37. Wilson and Day, *op. cit.,* p. 11.

38. Don Whitehead, *The FBI Story* (New York: Random House, 1956), p. 18.

39. On Phagan see Leonard Dinnerstein, *The Leo Frank Case* (New York: Columbia University Press, 1966).

40. *Caminetti v. U.S.*, 242 U.S. 470 (1917). See also Edward H. Levi, *An Introduction to Judicial Reasoning* (Chicago: University of Chicago Press, 1961), pp. 42–47, and Max Lowenthal, *The Federal Bureau of Investigation* (Westport, Conn.: Greenwood Press, 1950, p. 18.

41. Wilkie and Lee, *op. cit.*, pp. 155–65.

42. Arthur Carey, *Memoirs of a Murder Man* (New York: Doubleday, Doran, 1930), p. 112.

43. Michael Fiaschetti, *You Gotta Be Rough* (New York: Doubleday, Doran, 1930), pp. 135–46.

44. Emma Goldman, *Living My Life* (New York: Da Capo Press, 1970; orig. 1931), vol. I, pp. 125–27.

45. Morris Hillquit, *Loose Leaves from a Busy Life* (New York: Macmillan 1934; Da Capo reprint, 1971), pp. 120–29.

46. Goldman, *op. cit.*, pp. 298–311.

47. On Mills, obituary, *Chicago Tribune*, Sept. 25, 1956, sec. IV, p. 11.

48. On McDonough, Ralph Chaplin, *Wobbly* (Chicago: University of Chicago Press, 1948, Da Capo reprint, 1972), pp. 174–75, 181–82, 214.

49. Goldman, *op. cit.*, p. 463.

50. Robert A. Rosenstone, *Romantic Revolutionary: John Reed* (New York: Knopf, 1975), pp. 120–21.

51. Chaplin, *op. cit.*, p. 151; Elizabeth Gurley Flynn, *The Rebel Girl* (New York: International Publishers, 1955), p. 50.

52. On Reitman and Schuettler, Goldman, *op. cit.*, p. 421, on Chicago speech, pp. 417–23, and Richard Drinnon, *Rebel in Paradise* (Boston: Beacon Press, 1961), p. 122.

53. Chaplin, *op. cit.*, pp. 364–65.

54. Haywood, *op. cit.*, p. 207.

55. On Cronin case see Henry M. Hunt, *The Crime of the Century: The Assassination of Dr. Patrick Henry Cronin* (Chicago: H. & D. Kochersperger, 1889), and Richard Deacon, *A History of the British Secret Service* (New York: Taplinger, 1969), chap. 11. For Beach's own story see Henri LeCaron (Thomas Beach) *Twenty-five Years in the Secret Service: The Recollections of a Spy* (London: Heinemann, 1892).

56. *Irish Echo*, Mar. 26, 1977, p. 13.

57. Curt Gentry, *Frame-up* (New York: Norton, 1967), p. 70.

58. Bowen and Neal, *op. cit.*, chap. 10.

59. On German espionage during World War I, see Henry Landau, *The Enemy Within* (New York: Putnam, 1937).

60. The case testing the Espionage Act was, *Schenck v. U.S.* 249 U.S. 47 (1919), and that testing the Sedition Act was, *Abrams vs. U.S.*, 250 U.S. 616 (1919).

61. On antiwar meeting, Hillquit, *op. cit.*, pp. 176–79, and *Chicago Tribune*, Sept. 1–3, 1919, esp. Sept. 3, p. 3.

62. Chaplin, *op. cit.*, pp. 227–28.

63. On Landis see Henry Pringle, "A Grandstand Judge," in Pringle's *Big Frogs* (New York: Vanguard, 1938), pp. 73–91.

64. Chaplin, *op. cit.*, pp. 225–26.

65. Ray Ginger, *Eugene V. Debs: The Making of an American Radical* (New York: Macmillan, 1949), p. 372, and Clarence Darrow, *The Story of My Life* (New York: Scribner, 1932), p. 69.

66. William Allen White, *Woodrow Wilson* (Boston: Houghton Mifflin, 1924), pp. 355–56.

67. On 1919 see Robert K. Murray, *Red Scare* (New York: McGraw-Hill, 1964).

68. Murray, *op. cit.*, p. 101.

69. Drinnon, *op. cit.*, pp. 241–42.

70. Murray, *op. cit.*, p. 216.

71. On Means, Russell, *op. cit.*, pp. 517–20, Whitehead, pp. 57–58, 94–96; George Waller, *Kidnap: The Story of the Lindbergh Case* (New York: Dial, 1961), pp. 38–42.

72. On Burns in Teapot Dome, Bowen and Neal, *op. cit.*, chap. 11.

73. Whitehead, *op. cit.*, pp. 66–67.

74. Quoted in Richard Schwartz and Jerome Skolnick, *Society and the Legal Order* (New York: Basic Books, 1970), p. 86.

75. Elmer L. Irey and William J. Slocum, *The Tax Dodgers* (New York: Garden City Publishing, 1948), pp. 4–12.

76. *Ibid.*, p. 20.

77. *Ibid.*, p. XI.

78. Wilson and Day, *op. cit.*, p. 55.

79. Irey and Slocum, *op. cit.*, pp. 25–26, 35–36, 50.

80. Wilson and Day, *op. cit.*, p. 48.

81. Andrew Tully, *Treasury Agent* (New York: Simon & Schuster, 1958), p. 40; Eliot Ness with Oscar Fraley, *The Untouchables* (New York: Messner, 1957), chap. 1.

82. Ness with Fraley, *op. cit.*, p. 12.

83. On O'Rourke (real name Mike Malone), Irey and Slocum, *op. cit.*, chap. 2; Wilson and Day, *op. cit.*, p. 33; Tully, *op. cit.*, pp. 32–50.

84. Quoted in Irey and Slocum, *op. cit.*, p. 213; full account of case, pp. 209–14.

85. On O'Farrell as possible FBI chief, profile (Hoover), *New Yorker*, Nov. 2, 1937, p. 25. O'Farrell obituary, *New York Times*, Oct. 8, 1934.

86. Alfred Steinberg, *The Bosses* (New York: Macmillan, 1972), p. 379.

87. *Ibid.*, pp. 341–44.

88. Accounts of massacre, Melvin Purvis, *American Agent* (New York: Garden City Publishing, 1938), chap. III, Maurice Milligan, *Missouri Waltz* (New York: Scribner, 1948), pp. 111–34, and Merle Clayton, *Union Station Massacre* (Indianapolis: Bobbs-Merrill, 1975).

89. Purvis, *op. cit.*, chap. I.

90. *Newsweek,* Dec. 26, 1936, pp. 16–17.

91. Whitehead, *op. cit.,* pp. 108–09.

92. Bowen and Neal, *op. cit.,* p. 165.

93. Irey and Slocum, *op. cit.,* p. 3.

94. Whitehead, *op. cit.,* p. 111.

95. Bowen and Neal, *op. cit.,* p. 170.

96. Wilson and Day, *op. cit.,* pp. 95–100.

97. Harry J. Anslinger with Dennis J. Gregory, *The Protectors* (New York: Farrar, Straus & Giroux, 1964), pp. 17–20, 39.

98. *Ibid.,* pp. 68–69.

99. See Irey and Slocum, *op. cit.,* pp. 119, 152, 253.

100. Louis Cochran, *FBI Man: A Personal History* (New York: Duell, Sloan & Pearce, 1966), pp. 27–28, 35. Biographical data on Reed, *Kansas City Star,* July 11, 1939, p. 1.

101. Lear B. Reed, *Human Wolves: 17 Years of War on Crime* (Kansas City, Mo.: Brown-White, Lowell Press, 1941), pp. 107–15.

102. *Ibid.,* pp. 124–25.

103. Steinberg, *op. cit.,* pp. 307–360.

104. *Ibid.,* pp. 334, 343.

105. Irey and Slocum, *op. cit.,* p. 226, on police chief, p. 243.

106. Steinberg, *op. cit.,* p. 347.

107. Irey and Slocum, *op. cit.,* p. 228.

108. Reed, *op. cit.,* p. 184. For an overview of Kansas City reform see Stanley High, "Kansas City Has Its Chin Up," *National Municipal Review,* October 1941, pp. 561–64.

109. Cleveland Foundation, *Criminal Justice in Cleveland,* 1922.

110. On Kohler and Cleveland Police Department see James F. Richardson, *Urban Police in the United States* (Port Washington, N.Y.: Kennikat Press, 1974), pp. 54, 77–83, 95.

111. A highly sensational account of Ness in Cleveland is contained in Oscar Fraley, *Four Against the Mob* (New York: Popular Library, 1961). See also Stanley High, "Cleveland vs. the Crooks," *Current History,* October 1938, pp. 22–29.

112. Arthur Millspaugh, *Crime Control by The National Government,* Washington, D.C.: Brookings, 1937), p. 79.

113. Profile (Hoover), *New Yorker,* Oct. 2, 1937, p. 22; Pat Watters and Stephen Gillers, eds., *Investigating the FBI* (Garden City, N.Y.: Doubleday, 1973), p. 95.

114. Tully, *op. cit.,* p. 30.

115. For physical defects of FBI men see Frederick Ayer, Jr., *Yankee G-Man* (Chicago: Regnery, 1957), p. 2, and Norman Ollestad, *Inside the FBI* (New York: Lyle Stuart, 1967), p. 20.

116. See, for example, *New York Daily News,* Sept. 11, 1941, p. 2.

117. Millspaugh, *op. cit.,* pp. 250–58.

118. Lowenthal, *op cit.,* pp. 19–20; Watters and Gillers, *op. cit.,* pp. xxv, 315–16; *Harvard Law Review,* 53, 1940, p. 870, note 53.

119. Watters and Gillers, *op. cit.*, pp. 292–94.

120. McAllister incident, John Roy Carlson (Arthur Derounian), *Undercover* (New York: Dutton, 1943), pp. 87–89, infiltration of NYCPD, pp. 426–33; on Communist infiltration, *New York Times*, July 15–31, 1953; on police lieutenant the Party was grooming for commissioner, Charles Thomson, "New York City's Communist Cop." *Saturday Evening Post*, Mar. 20, 1954, pp. 142–44.

121. An account of the Detroit case favorable to the FBI is contained in Whitehead, *op. cit.*, chap. 19; a similar account of the New York case is in Carlson, *op. cit.*, chap. VI. Accounts of the cases unfavorable to the FBI are found in Lowenthal, *op cit.*, chap. 29, and Fred J. Cook, *The FBI Nobody Knows* (New York: Macmillan, 1964), pp. 240–57.

122. Watters and Gillers, *op. cit.*, pp. 293–94.

123. Philip J. Stead, *The Police of Paris* (London: Staples, 1957), p. 49.

124. Watters and Gillers, *op. cit.*, p. 9.

CONCLUSION (pp. 299–313): THE PASSING PARADE

1. A study which supports the view that urban crime rates have significantly decreased over the period from the middle of the nineteenth century to approximately World War II is Theodore N. Ferdinand, "The Criminal Patterns of Boston since 1849," *American Journal of Sociology*, July 1967, pp. 84–99.

2. Henry George, *Social Problems* (New York: 1883), p. 12.

3. James Q. Wilson, *Thinking about Crime* (New York: Basic Books, 1967), pp. 90–91.

4. H. H. Gerth and C. Wright Mills, *From Max Weber: Essays in Sociology* (New York: Oxford Press, 1958), p. 213.

5. Ernest Jerome Hopkins, *What Happened in the Mooney Case?* (New York: Brower, Warren and Putnam, 1932; Da Capo reprint 1970), p. 12.

6. Pat Watters and Stephen Gillers, eds., *Investigating the FBI* (New York: Doubleday, 1973), p. 203.

7. Joseph Gusfield, *Symbolic Crusade: Status Politics and the American Temperance Movement* (Urbana: University of Illinois Press, 1963), p. 173.

8. Illinois Association for Criminal Justice, *The Illinois Crime Survey* (Chicago: 1929; Reprinted by Patterson Smith, Montclair, N.J., 1968), pp. 1008–1010.

9. Oscar Handlin, *Al Smith and His America* (Boston: Little, Brown, 1958), pp. 58–59.

10. William F. Whyte, *Street Corner Society*, 2nd ed. (Chicago: University of Chicago Press, 1955), p. 36.

11. William A. Westley, *Violence and the Police: A Sociological Study of Law Custom and Morality* (Cambridge, Massachusetts: MIT Press, 1970), pp. 192–193.

Bibliography

GENERAL

Books

ADAMIC, LOUIS. *Dynamite*. Gloucester, Mass.: Peter Smith, 1963. (Original 1931.)

ALLEN, FREDERICK LEWIS. *Only Yesterday*. New York: Harper, 1957. (Original 1931.)

BERNSTEIN, IRVING. *Turbulent Years*. Boston: Houghton Mifflin, 1970.

BRYCE, JAMES. *The American Commonwealth*. 3 vols. London: Macmillan, 1888. (AMS reprint 1973.)

DARROW, CLARENCE. *The Story of My Life*. New York: Scribner, 1932.

DRINNON, RICHARD. *Rebel in Paradise*. Boston: Beacon Press, 1961.

EGGERT, GERALD G. *Richard Olney: Evolution of a Statesman*. University Park: Pennsylvania State University Press, 1974.

FLYNT (WILLARD), JOSIAH. *World of Graft*. New York: McClure Phillips, 1901.

FOSDICK, RAYMOND B. *American Police Systems*. Montclair, N.J.: Patterson Smith, 1969. (Original 1920.)

———. *Chronicle of a Generation*. New York: Harper, 1958.

———. *European Police Systems*. Montclair, N.J.: Patterson Smith, 1969. (Original 1915.)

GOLDMAN, EMMA. *Living My Life*, 2 vols. New York: Da Capo Press, 1970. (Original 1931.)

GOODNOW, FRANK J., and BATES, FRANK G. *Municipal Government.* New York: Century, 1919. (Original 1909.)

GRAPER, ELMER D. *American Police Administration.* Montclair, N.J.: Patterson Smith, 1969. (Original 1921.)

GUSFIELD, JOSEPH. *Symbolic Crusade: Status Politics and the American Temperance Movement.* Urbana: University of Illinois Press, 1963.

HOFSTADTER, RICHARD. *The Age of Reform.* New York: Knopf, 1955.

JACKSON, KENNETH T. *The Ku Klux Klan in the City.* New York: Oxford University Press, 1970.

KEFAUVER, ESTES. *Crime in America.* Garden City, N.Y.: Doubleday, 1951.

MOORE, LANGDON. *His Own Story.* Boston, Mass.: by the author, 1893.

RICHARDSON, JAMES F. *Urban Police in the United States.* Port Washington, N.Y.: Kennikat Press, 1974.

SCHWARTZ, RICHARD, and SKOLNICK, JEROME. *Society and the Legal Order.* New York: Basic Books, 1970.

SMITH, BRUCE. *Police Systems in the U.S.* 2nd rev. ed. New York: Harper, 1960. (Original 1940.)

STEAD, PHILIP J. *Pioneers in Policing.* Montclair, N.J.: Patterson Smith, 1977.

STEFFENS, LINCOLN. *Autobiography.* New York: Harcourt, Brace, 1931.

————. *The Shame of the Cities.* New York: Hill and Wang, 1970. (Original 1904.)

STEINBERG, ALFRED. *The Bosses.* New York: Macmillan, 1972.

STONE, IRVING. *Clarence Darrow for the Defense.* New York: Doubleday, Doran, 1941.

SWANBERG, W. A. *Citizen Hearst.* New York: Scribner, 1961.

WIEBE, ROBERT H. *The Search for Order: 1877–1920.* New York: Hill and Wang, 1967.

ZINK, HAROLD. *City Bosses in the United States.* Durham, N.C.: Duke University Press, 1930.

Articles

"Crime in the United States." *Annals of the American Academy of Political and Social Science,* September 1941.

"Modern Crime, Its Prevention and Punishment." *Annals of the American Academy of Political and Social Science,* May 1926.

"The Police and the Crime Problem." *Annals of the American Academy of Political and Social Science,* November 1929.

Reports

National Commission on Law Observance and Enforcement (Wickersham Commission). #11, *Report on Lawlessness in Law Enforcement.* 1931.

National Commission on Law Observance and Enforcement (Wickersham Commission). #14, *Report on Police.* 1931.

Chapter 1 (pp. 1–37): GREAT BRITAIN: THE NEW URBAN SOCIETY (1748–1890)

Books

BABINGTON, ANTHONY. *A House in Bow Street: Crime and the Magistracy in London 1740–1881.* London: McDonald, 1969.

BOOTH, WILLIAM. *In Darkest England and the Way Out.* Montclair, N.J.: Patterson Smith ed., 1974. (Original 1890.)

BREATNACH, SEAMUS. *The Irish Police.* Dublin: Anvil Books, 1974.

BROEKER, GALEN. *Rural Disorder and Police Reform in Ireland.* London: Routledge & Kegan Paul, 1970.

COATMAN, JOHN. *Police.* London: Oxford University Press, 1959.

COBB, BELTON. *Critical Years at the Yard.* London: Faber & Faber, 1961.

———. *The First Detectives.* London: Faber & Faber, 1967.

COLQUHOUN, PATRICK. *A Treatise on the Commerce and Police of the River Thames.* Montclair, N.J.: Patterson Smith, 1969. (Original 1800.)

———. *A Treatise on the Police of the Metropolis,* 7th ed. London: 1806. (Patterson Smith reprint, 1969.)

CRITCHLEY, T. A. *The Conquest of Violence.* London: Constable, 1970.

———. *A History of Police in England and Wales,* 2nd ed. Montclair, N.J.: Patterson Smith, 1972.

CULLON, TOM. *Autumn of Terror.* London: Bodley Head, 1965.

DUDDEN, F. HOMES. *Henry Fielding: His Life, Work and Times.* 2 vols. London: Oxford University Press, 1952.

FARSON, DANIEL. *Jack the Ripper.* London. Sphere Books, 1973.

FIELDING, HENRY. *An Enquiry into the Causes of the Late Increase in Robbers.* New York: AMS Press, 1975. (Original, 1751.)

FITZGERALD, PERCY. *Chronicles of Bow Street.* Montclair, N.J.: Patterson Smith, 1972. (Original 1888.)

GARROW-GREEN, G. *In the Royal Irish Constabulary.* London: J. Blackwood, 1905.

GASH, NORMAN. *Mr. Secretary Peel.* Cambridge, Mass.: Harvard University Press, 1961.

GORER, GEOFFREY. *Exploring English Character.* New York: Criterion Books, 1955.

GREENWOOD, JAMES. *The Seven Curses of London.* London: Stanley Rivers, 1869.

HART, J. M. *The British Police.* London: George Allen & Unwin, 1951.

HEZLET, SIR ARTHUR. *The B-Specials.* London: Tom Stacey, 1972.

HOWE, SIR RONALD. *The Story of Scotland Yard.* London: A. Barker, 1965.

HOWSON, GERALD. *The Thief-Taker General: The Rise and Fall of Jonathan Wild.* London: Hutchinson, 1970.

JEFFRIES, SIR CHARLES. *The Colonial Police.* London: Max Parish, 1952.

JEYES, S. H., and How, F. D. *The Life of Sir Howard Vincent*. London: George Allen, 1912.

MacNAGHTEN, SIR MELVILLE L. *Days of My Years*. London: Edward Arnold, 1915.

McDOWELL, ROBERT. *The Irish Administration: 1801–1914*. Westport, Conn.: Greenwood Press, 1976.

MARLOW, JOYCE. *The Peterloo Massacre*. London: Rapp & Whiting, 1969.

MAYHEW, HENRY. *London Labour and the London Poor*. Vol. IV. London: Frank Cass, reprint, 1967. (Original 1861–62.)

MELVILLE-LEE, CAPTAIN W. L. *A History of Police in England*. London: Methuen, 1901.

MOYLAN, J. F. *Scotland Yard and the Metropolitan Police*. London: Putnam, 1929.

NOTT-BOWER, SIR WILLIAM. *Fifty-two Years a Policeman*. London: Edward Arnold, 1926.

PIKE, LUKE O. *A History of Crime in England*. 2 vols. Montclair, N.J.: Patterson Smith, 1962. (Original 1873–76.)

PRINGLE, PATRICK. *Hue and Cry*. London: Morrow, 1965.

RADZINOWICZ, SIR LEON. *A History of English Criminal Law and Its Administration from 1750*. 4 vols. London: Stevens & Sons, 1948–68.

READ, DONALD. *Peterloo: The Massacre and Its Background*. Manchester: Manchester University Press, 1958.

REITH, CHARLES. *The Blind Eye of History*. London: Faber & Faber, 1952.

———. *A New Study of Police History*. London: Oliver and Boyd, 1956.

RUDE, GEORGE. *The Crowd in History*. New York: Wiley, 1964.

———. *Hanoverian London 1714–1808*. Berkeley: University of California Press, 1971.

RUMBELOW, DONALD. *I Spy Blue: Police and Crime in the City of London from Elizabeth I to Victoria*. London: Macmillan, 1971.

STEAD, PHILIP J. *The Police of Paris*. London: Staples, 1957.

THOMSON, SIR BASIL. *The Story of Scotland Yard*. New York: Doubleday, Doran, 1936.

THURSTON, GAVIN. *The Clerkenwell Riot*. London: George Allen & Unwin, 1967.

TOBIAS, J. J. *Crime and Industrial Society in the 19th Century*. London: B. T. Batsford, 1967.

WADE, JOHN. *A Treatise on the Police and Crimes of the Metropolis*. Montclair, N.J.: Patterson Smith reprint, 1972. (Original 1829.)

WEBB, SIDNEY and BEATRICE. *The Development of English Local Government 1689–1835*. London: Oxford University Press, 1963.

Articles

"Sir Patrick Quinn, M.V.O." *The British Police Journal*, October 1965, pp. 472–76.

Chapter 2 (pp. 38–87): NEW YORK: THE NEW WORLD (1845–1913)

Books

ASBURY, HERBERT. *The Gangs of New York.* New York: Knopf, 1927. (Capricorn ed. 1970.)

BROUN, HEYWOOD, and LEECH, MARGARET. *Anthony Comstock: Roundsman of the Lord.* New York: Boni, 1927.

BUSCH, NOEL F. *The Story of Theodore Roosevelt and His Influence on Our Times.* New York: Reynal and Co., 1963

COOK, ADRIAN. *The Armies of the Streets.* Lexington: University Press of Kentucky, 1974.

COSTELLO, AUGUSTINE. *Our Police Protectors.* Montclair, N.J.: Patterson Smith, 1972. (Original 1885.)

CURRAN, HENRY H. *Pillar to Post.* New York: Scribner, 1941.

DICKENS, CHARLES. *American Notes.* London: Oxford University Press, 1957. (Original 1842.)

GARDINER, ALEXANDER. *Canfield.* Garden City, N.Y.: Doubleday, 1930.

GERARD, JAMES. *My First 83 Years in America.* Garden City, N.Y.: Doubleday, 1951.

KAHN, E. J. *The World of Swope.* New York: Simon & Schuster, 1965.

KLEIN, HENRY H. *Sacrificed.* New York: Isaac Goldman, 1927.

LOGAN, ANDY. *Against the Evidence: The Becker-Rosenthal Affair.* New York: McCall Publishing Co., 1970.

McADOO, WILLIAM. *Guarding a Great City.* New York: Harper, 1906.

O'CONNOR, RICHARD. *Courtroom Warrior: The Combative Career of William Travers Jerome.* Boston: Little, Brown, 1963.

PARKHURST, CHARLES H. *Our Fight with Tammany.* New York: Scribner, 1895.

PRINGLE, H. F. *Theodore Roosevelt.* New York: Harcourt, Brace, 1931.

RICHARDSON, JAMES F. *The New York Police: Colonial Times to 1901.* New York: Oxford University Press, 1970.

RIIS, JACOB. *How the Other Half Lives.* New York: Hill and Wang, 1957. (Original 1890).

————. *The Making of an American.* New York: Macmillan, 1901

RIORDAN WILLIAM L. *Plunkitt of Tammany Hall.* New York: McClure Phillips, 1905.

ROOSEVELT, THEODORE. *American Ideals.* New York: AMS Press, 1969. (Original 1897.)

————. *Autobiography.* New York: Scribner, 1924.

ROOT, JONATHAN. *One Night in July.* New York: Coward-McCann, 1961.

STEAD, W. T. *Satan's Invisible World Displayed.* New York: R. F. Fenno, 1897.

STODDARD, LOTHROP. *Master of Manhattan: The Life of Richard Croker.* New York: Longmans Green, 1931.

SYRETT, HAROLD, ed. *The Gentleman and the Tiger: Autobiography of G. B. McClellan Jr.* Philadelphia: Lippincott, 1956.

THOMAS, LATELY. *The Mayor Who Mastered New York: The Life and Opinions of William J. Gaynor.* New York: Morrow, 1969.

WALLING, GEORGE. *Recollections of a New York Chief of Police.* Montclair, N.J.: Patterson Smith ed., 1972. (Original 1887.)

WERNER, M. R. *It Happened in New York.* New York: Coward-McCann, 1957.

————. *Tammany Hall.* New York: Doubleday, Doran, 1928.

Articles

ALER, GEORGE W. "Mayor Gaynor and the Police." *Outlook,* Jan. 1, 1910, pp. 27–30.

BROOKS, SYDNEY. "The Problems of the New York Police." *The 19th Century and After,* pp. 687–700.

BYRNES, THOMAS. "How to Protect a City from Crime." *North American Review,* July 1894, pp. 100–07.

CROKER, RICHARD. "Tammany Hall and Democracy." *North American Review,* February 1892, pp. 225–30.

FOSDICK, RAYMOND B. "The Police Scandal and the Good Old Days." *Outlook,* Oct. 19, 1912, pp. 346–49.

GANS, HOWARD S. "In the Matter of the Lawlessness of the Police: A Reply to Mr. Justice Gaynor." *North American Review,* February 1903, pp. 287–96.

GAYNOR, WILLIAM J. "A Government of Laws Not of Men." *North American Review,* February 1903, pp. 282–86.

————. "The Lawlessness of the Police in New York." *North American Review,* January 1903, pp. 10–26.

TURNER, GEORGE KIBBE. "Tammany Control of New York by Professional Criminals." *McClure's Magazine,* June 1909, pp. 117–34.

WHITE, WILLIAM A. "Croker." *McClure's Magazine,* February 1901, pp. 317–26.

Reports

New York Assembly. *Final Report of Special Committee to Investigate the Public Offices and Departments of the City of New York* (Mazet Committee). 5 vols., 1900.

New York City Police Department. *Annual Reports.*

Report and Proceedings of the Senate Committee Appointed to Investigate the Police Department of the City of New York (Lexow Committee). 5 vols., 1895.

Report of the Special Committee of the Board of Aldermen of the City of New York to Investigate the Police Department (Curran Committee). 1913.

Newspapers

The New York Times.

Chapter 3 (pp. 88–120): BOSTON: EUROPE IN AMERICA (1854–1943)

Books

AMORY, CLEVELAND. *The Proper Bostonians.* New York: Dutton, 1947.

COOLIDGE, CALVIN. *Autobiography.* New York: Cosmopolitan Book Corp., 1929.

CURLEY, JAMES MICHAEL. *I'd Do It Again.* Englewood Cliffs, N.J.: Prentice-Hall, 1957.

CUTLER, JOHN HENRY. *"Honey Fitz":* Three Steps to the White House. Indianapolis: Bobbs-Merrill, 1962.

DEACON, RICHARD. *A History of the British Secret Service.* New York: Taplinger, 1969.

DINEEN, JOSEPH. *The Purple Shamrock.* New York: Norton, 1949.

HARRISON, LEONARD V. *Police Administration in Boston.* Cambridge, Mass.: Harvard University Press, 1934.

LANE, ROGER. *Policing the City: Boston 1822–1885.* Cambridge, Mass.: Harvard University Press, 1967.

LEESON, BERNARD. *Lost London.* London: Stanley Paul, 1934.

LITT, EDGAR. *The Political Culture of Massachusetts.* Cambridge, Mass.: MIT Press, 1965.

MACREADY, NEVIL. *Annals of an Active Life.* 2 vols. London: Hutchinson, 1924.

O'CONNOR, EDWIN. *The Last Hurrah.* Boston: Little, Brown, 1956.

REYNOLDS, GERALD W., and JUDGE, ANTHONY. *The Night the Police Went on Strike.* London: Weidenfeld & Nicholson, 1968.

RUMBELOW, DONALD. *The Houndsditch Murders: The Siege of Sidney Street.* London: Macmillan, 1973.

RUSSELL, FRANCIS. *A City in Terror.* New York: Viking, 1975.

SAVAGE, EDWARD H. *Police Records and Recollections or Boston by Daylight and Gaslight.* Montclair, N.J.: Patterson Smith, 1971. (Original 1873.)

WHITE, WILLIAM ALLEN. *A Puritan in Babylon: The Story of Calvin Coolidge.* New York: Macmillan, 1938.

WHYTE, WILLIAM F. *Street Corner Society.* 2nd ed. Chicago: University of Chicago Press, 1955.

Articles

LYONS, RICHARD L. "The Boston Police Strike of 1919." *New England Quarterly* XX, July 1947, pp. 147–68.

McCAFFREY, GEORGE H. "The Boston Police Department." *Journal of the American Institute of Law and Criminology,* January 1912, pp. 672–90.

RIEGEL, ROBERT E. "Changing American Attitudes Towards Prostitution (1800–1920)." *Journal of the History of Ideas,* July–September, 1968, pp. 437–52.

Reports

Report of Citizens Committee Appointed by the Mayor to Consider the Police Situation. Boston, 1919.

Boston Police Department. *Annual Reports.*

Newspapers

The Boston Globe.
The Boston Herald.

Chapter 4 (pp. 121–153): PENNSYLVANIA AND NEW JERSEY: THE AMERICAN CONSTABULARY (1905–1940)

Books

ARCHER, JULES. *The Plot to Seize the White House.* New York: Hawthorn Books, 1973.

BROEHL, WAYNE. *The Molly Maguires.* Cambridge, Mass.: Harvard University Press, 1964.

BRUCE, ROBERT V. *1877: Year of Violence.* Indianapolis: Bobbs-Merrill, 1959. (Quadrangle ed., 1970.)

COAKLEY, LEO J. *Jersey Troopers.* New Brunswick, N.J.: Rutgers University Press, 1971.

COSTELLO, AUGUSTINE. *History of the Police Department of Jersey City.* Jersey City, N.J.: by the author, 1891.

DAVIS, ALLEN F., and HALLER, MARK H., eds. *The Peoples of Philadelphia.* Philadelphia: Temple University Press, 1973.

FREIDEL, FRANK. *Franklin D. Roosevelt: The Apprentice Years.* Boston: Little, Brown, 1952.

HURLEY, VICTOR. *Jungle Patrol: The Story of the Philippine Constabulary.* New York: Dutton, 1939.

McGEARY, M. NELSON. *Gifford Pinchot: Forester Politician.* Princeton, N.J.: Princeton University Press, 1960.

McKEAN, DAYTON. *The Boss.* Boston: Houghton Mifflin, 1940.

MAYO, KATHERINE. *Justice to All: The Story of the Pennsylvania State Police.* 5th ed., rev. Boston: Houghton Mifflin, 1920.

———. *Mounted Justice.* Boston: Houghton Mifflin, 1922.

———. *The Standard Bearers.* Boston: Houghton Mifflin, 1918.

MONROE, DAVID G. *State and Provincial Police.* Evanston, Ill.: International Association of Chiefs of Police and Northwestern University Traffic Institute, 1941.

PENNYPACKER, SAMUEL. *The Autobiography of a Pennsylvanian.* Philadelphia: John C. Winston, 1918.

PRATT, FLETCHER. *The Cunning Mulatto and Other Cases of Ellis Parker, American Detective.* New York: Smith & Haas, 1930.

ROPP, THEODORE. *War in the Modern World.* Chapel Hill, N.C.: Duke University Press, 1962.

SHALLOO, J. P. *Private Police: With Special Reference to Pennsylvania.* Philadelphia: American Academy of Political and Social Science, 1933.

SMITH, BRUCE. *The State Police.* Montclair, N.J.: Patterson Smith, reprint 1969. (Original 1925.)

THOMAS, LOWELL. *Old Gimlet Eye: The Adventures of Smedley Butler.* New York: Farrar & Rinehart, 1933.

VARE, WILLIAM B. *My 40 Years in Politics.* Philadelphia: Roland Swain, 1933.

VOLLMER, AUGUST, and PARKER, ALFRED. *Crime and the State Police.* Berkeley: University of California Press, 1935.

WALLER, GEORGE. *Kidnap: The Story of the Lindbergh Case.* New York: Dial, 1961.

WARNER, SAM B., JR. *The Private City: Philadelphia in Three Periods of Its Growth.* Philadelphia: University of Pennsylvania Press, 1968.

WOLFF, LEON. *Lockout: The Story of the Homestead Strike.* New York: Harper & Row, 1965.

Articles

ADAMS, MAJOR LYNN G. "The State Police." *Annals of the American Academy of Political and Social Science,* November 1929, pp. 34–40.

Anonymous (Mark Sullivan). "The Ills of Pennsylvania." *Atlantic Monthly,* October 1901, pp. 558–65.

BALDWIN, FRED D. "Smedley D. Butler and Prohibition Enforcement in Philadelphia, 1924–5." *The Pennsylvania Journal of History and Biography,* pp. 352–68.

Reports

New Jersey State Police. *Annual Reports.*
Pennsylvania State Police, *Annual Reports.*
Philadelphia Police Department. *Annual Reports.*

Newspapers

The Philadelphia Inquirer.

Chapter 5 (pp. 154–187): NEW YORK: THE FINEST AND THE FALL OF THE HALL (1914–1945)

Books

CAREY, ARTHUR. *Memoirs of a Murder Man.* New York: Doubleday, Doran, 1930.

CLARKE, DONALD H. *In the Reign of Rothstein.* New York: Vanguard, 1929.

DAHLBERG, JANE. *The New York Bureau of Municipal Research: Pioneer in Government Administration.* New York: New York University Press, 1966.

DEWEY, THOMAS E. *Twenty Against the Underworld.* Rodney Campbell, ed. Garden City, N.Y.: Doubleday, 1974.

FIASCHETTI, MICHAEL. *You Gotta Be Rough.* New York: Doubleday, Doran, 1930.

FOWLER, GENE. *Beau James: The Life and Times of Jimmy Walker.* New York: Viking, 1949.

———. *The Great Mouthpiece: The Life Story of William J. Fallon.* New York: Covici, Friede, 1931.

FULD, LEONHARD F. *Police Administration.* New York: Putnam, 1910.

GARRETT, CHARLES. *The La Guardia Years: Machine and Reform Politics in New York City.* New Brunswick, N.J.: Rutgers University Press, 1961.

HANDLIN, OSCAR. *Al Smith and His America.* Boston: Little, Brown, 1958.

HYLAN, JOHN F. *Autobiography.* New York: Rotary Press, 1922.

JOSEPHSON, MATTHEW. *Al Smith: Hero of the Cities.* Boston: Houghton Mifflin, 1969.

KATCHER, LEO. *The Big Bankroll: The Life and Times of Arnold Rothstein.* New Rochelle, N.Y.: Arlington House, 1958.

LEWINSON, EDWIN A. *John Purroy Mitchell: The Boy Mayor of New York.* New York: Astra Books, 1965.

LIMPUS, LOWELL J. *Honest Cop: Lewis J. Valentine.* New York: Dutton, 1939.

McALLISTER, ROBERT. *The Kind of Guy I Am.* London: Hammond and Hammond, 1959.

MITGANG, HERBERT. *The Man Who Rode the Tiger: The Life and Times of Judge Samuel Seabury.* Philadelphia: Lippincott, 1963.

MOSCOW, WARREN. *What Have You Done for Me Lately? The Ins and Outs of New York City Politics* (Englewood Cliffs, N.J.: Prentice-Hall, 1961).

NORTHROP, WILLIAM B., and NORTHROP, JOHN B. *The Insolence of Office.* New York: Putnam, 1932.

REYNOLDS, QUENTIN. *Headquarters.* New York: Harper, 1955.

SAYRE, WALLACE, and KAUFMAN, HERBERT. *Governing New York City.* New York: Russell Sage Foundation, 1960.

THOMPSON, CRAIG, and RAYMOND, ALLAN. *Gang Rule in New York.* New York: Dial, 1940.

VALENTINE, LEWIS J. *Nightstick.* New York: Dial, 1947.

WHALEN, GROVER. *Mr. New York: The Autobiography of Grover Whalen.* New York: Putnam, 1955.

WILLEMSE, CORNELIUS W. *Behind the Green Lights.* New York: Knopf, 1931.

———. *A Cop Remembers.* New York: Knopf, 1933.

WOODS, ARTHUR. *Crime Prevention.* Princeton, N.J.: Princeton University Press, 1918.

———. *Policemen and Public.* Montclair, N.J.: Patterson Smith, 1975. (Original, Yale Press, 1919.)

Articles

"Nineteen Thousand Cops." *Fortune,* July 1939, pp. 101–106, 167–68.
Profile (John Broderick). *The New Yorker,* Dec. 26, 1931.
Profile (John Cordes). *The New Yorker,* Sept. 5, 12, 1953.
Profile (Commissioner Edward Mulrooney). *The New Yorker,* Oct. 24, 1931.
Profile (Lewis J. Valentine). *The New Yorker,* Oct. 3, 10, and 17, 1936.
Profile (Grover Whalen). *The New Yorker,* July 14, 21, 1951.
WHITE, FRANK MARSHALL. "A Man Who Achieved the Impossible." *Outlook,*
    Sept. 26, 1917, pp. 124–26.
———. "When Clubs Were Trump." *Outlook,* Apr. 7, 1915, p. 480.

Reports

Wiretapping in New York City, volume V of *The Minutes and Testimony of
    the Joint Legislative Committee to Investigate the Public Service Commis-
    sioners.* Albany, 1916.
New York City Police Department. *Annual Reports.*

Newspapers

The New York Times.

Chapter 6 (pp. 188–223): CHICAGO: THE TOWN THEY COULD NOT SHUT DOWN (1857–1945)

Books

ADDAMS, JANE. *Twenty Years at Hull House.* New York: Macmillan, 1923.
———. *The Second Twenty Years at Hull House.* New York: Macmillan, 1930.
ASBURY, HERBERT. *Gem of the Prairie: An Informal History of the Chicago
    Underworld.* Garden City, N.Y.: Knopf, 1942.
BARNARD, HARRY. *Eagle Forgotten: The Life of John Peter Altgeld.* Indianapolis:
    Bobbs-Merrill, 1938. (Charter ed., 1962.)
BOETTINGER, JOHN. *Jake Lingle.* New York: Dutton, 1931.
Citizens Police Committee (Bruce Smith, director). *Chicago Police Problems.*
    Chicago: University of Chicago Press, 1931.
DAVID, HENRY. *The History of the Haymarket Affair.* 2nd ed. New York:
    Russell, 1958. (Original 1936.)
DAVIS, ALLEN F. *American Heroine: The Life and Legend of Jane Addams.*
    New York: Oxford University Press, 1973.
FARIS, ROBERT E. L. *Chicago Sociology 1920–32.* San Francisco: Chandler, 1967.
FLINN, JOHN J., and WILKIE, JOHN E. *History of the Chicago Police.* Montclair,
    N.J.: Patterson Smith, 1973. (Original 1887.)

GINGER, RAY. *Altgeld's America.* Chicago: Quadrangle Books, 1965. (Original 1958.)

GOSNELL, HAROLD F. *Negro Politicians: The Rise of Negro Politics in Chicago.* Chicago: University of Chicago Press, 1967. (Original 1935.)

GOTTFRIED, ALEX. *Boss Cermak of Chicago.* Seattle: University of Washington Press, 1962.

GRIMSHAW, ALLEN A., ed. *Racial Violence in the United States.* Chicago: Aldine, 1969.

HARRISON, CARTER. *Stormy Years.* Indianapolis: Bobbs-Merrill, 1935.

ICKES, HAROLD F. *The Autobiography of a Curmudgeon.* New York: Reynal & Hitchcock, 1943.

LEWIS, LLOYD, and SMITH, HENRY JUSTIN. *Chicago: A History of Its Reputation.* New York: Harcourt, Brace, 1929.

LINDSAY, ALMONT. *The Pullman Strike.* Chicago: University of Chicago Press, 1971. (Original 1942.)

LINN, JAMES WEBER. *James Keely, Newspaperman.* Indianapolis: Bobbs-Merrill, 1937.

MERRIAM, CHARLES E. *Chicago: A More Intimate View of Urban Politics.* New York: Macmillan, 1929.

PETERSON, VIRGIL W. *Barbarians in Our Midst: A History of Chicago Crime and Politics.* Boston: Little, Brown, 1952.

RECKLESS, WALTER. *Vice in Chicago.* Montclair, N.J.: Patterson Smith, 1969. (Original 1933.)

SCHAACK, MICHAEL J. *Anarchy and the Anarchists.* Chicago: F. J. Schulte & Co., 1889.

STEAD, WILLIAM T. *If Christ Came to Chicago.* Chicago: Laird & Lee, 1894.

THRASHER, FREDERIC M. *The Gang.* Chicago: University of Chicago Press, 1927.

TUTTLE, WILLIAM, JR. *Race Riot: Chicago in the Red Summer of 1919.* New York: Atheneum, 1970.

WENDT, LLOYD, and KOGAN, HERMAN. *Big Bill.* Indianapolis: Bobbs-Merrill, 1953.

———— and ————. *Lords of the Levee.* Indianapolis: Bobbs-Merrill, 1943.

Articles

FLYNN, JOHN T. "Smart Money." *Colliers,* Jan. 13–Feb. 3, 1940, in 4 parts.

HALLER, MARK H. "Civic Reformers and Police Leadership: Chicago 1905–1935." In Harlan Hahn, ed., *Police in Urban Society.* Beverly Hills, Calif.: Sage Publications, 1971.

————. "Urban Crime and Criminal Justice." *Journal of American History,* December 1970, pp. 619–635.

PEATTIE, DONALD CULROSS. "The Most Unforgettable Character I've Met" (Max Nootbar). *Reader's Digest,* January 1944, pp. 77–82.

Profile (Bruce Smith). *The New Yorker,* Feb. 27, 1954.

WILSON, O. W. "Bruce Smith." *The Journal of Criminal Law, Criminology and Police Science,* vol. 47, 1956–57, pp. 235–37.

Reports

Chicago Police Department. *Annual Reports.*
Illinois Commission on Race Relations. *The Negro in Chicago.* Chicago: The University of Chicago Press, 1922.
Illinois Association for Criminal Justice. *The Illinois Crime Survey.* Chicago: Illinois Association for Criminal Justice, 1929.

Newspapers

The Chicago Tribune.

Chapter 7 (pp. 224–254): CALIFORNIA: THE NEW BREED (1901–1942)

Books

ASBURY, HERBERT. *The Barbary Coast: An Informal History of the San Francisco Underworld.* Garden City, N.Y.: Knopf, 1933.
BEAN, WALTON. *Boss Ruef's San Francisco.* Berkeley: University of California Press, 1967.
BURNS, WILLIAM J. *The Masked War.* New York: George H. Doran and Co., 1913.
CARTE, GENE E. and ELAINE H. *Police Reform in the United States: The Era of August Vollmer.* Berkeley: University of California Press, 1975.
CLELAND, ROBERT. *California in Our Time.* New York: Knopf, 1947.
DEUTSCH, ALBERT. *The Trouble with Cops.* New York: Crown Press, 1954.
EHRLICH, J. W. *A Life in My Hands.* New York: Putnam, 1965.
FROST, RICHARD H. *The Mooney Case.* Stanford, Calif.: Stanford University Press, 1968.
GENTRY, CURT. *Frame-up.* New York: Norton, 1967.
HICHBORN, FRANKLIN. *The System: The San Francisco Graft Prosecution.* Montclair, N.J.: Patterson Smith, 1969. (Original 1915.)
HOPKINS, ERNEST JEROME. *What Happened in the Mooney Case?* New York: Brower, Warren and Putnam, 1932. (Da Capo reprint, 1970.)
KATCHER, LEO. *Earl Warren: A Political Biography.* New York: McGraw-Hill, 1967.
KENNEY, JOHN P. *The California Police.* Springfield, Ill.: Charles C Thomas, 1964.
McWILLIAMS, CAREY. *Southern California Country.* New York: Duell, Sloan & Pearce, 1946.
MAYO, MORROW. *Los Angeles.* New York: Knopf, 1933.
MOWRY, GEORGE E. *The California Progressives.* Berkeley: University of California Press, 1951. (Quadrangle ed., 1963.)
OLDER, FREMONT. *Growing Up.* San Francisco: Call-Bulletin Publishing, 1931.
———. *My Own Story.* San Francisco: Call Publishing, 1919.

PARKER, ALFRED E. *August Vollmer: Crime Fighter*. New York: Macmillan, 1961.

———. *The Berkeley Police Story*. Springfield, Ill.: Charles C Thomas, 1972.

ST. JOHNS, ADELA ROGERS. *Final Verdict*. Garden City, N.Y.: Doubleday, 1962.

THOMAS, LATELY. *A Debonair Scoundrel*. New York: Holt, Rinehart and Winston, 1962.

VOLLMER, AUGUST, and PARKER, ALFRED E. *Crime, Crooks and Cops*. New York: Funk & Wagnalls, 1937.

WEAVER, JOHN: *Warren, the Man, the Court, the Era*. Boston: Little, Brown, 1967.

WELLS, EVELYN. *Fremont Older*. New York: Appleton-Century, 1936.

WHITE, LESLIE T. *Me Detective*. New York: Harcourt, Brace, 1936.

WILSON, CAROL. *Chinatown Quest*. Palo Alto, Calif.: Stanford University Press, 1931.

Articles

MATHESON, DUNCAN. "The Technique of the American Detective." *Annals of the American Academy of Political and Social Science*. November 1929, pp. 214–18.

"Portrait: Edward Atherton." *Literary Digest*, Apr. 3, 1937.

Reports

Los Angeles Police Department. *Annual Reports*.

National Commission on Law Observance and Enforcement (Wickersham Commission). *Mooney-Billings Report*, 1931.

San Francisco Police Department. *Annual Reports*.

Unpublished

WOODS, JOSEPH. *The Progressives and the Police: Urban Reform and the Professionalization of the Police*. UCLA, Los Angeles, 1973.

Newspapers

The Los Angeles Times.
The San Francisco Chronicle.

Chapter 8 (pp. 255–298): THE SECRET AGENTS (1850–1945)

Books

ALFERS, KENNETH. *Law and Order in the Capital City: A History of the Washington Police 1800–1886*. Washington, D.C.: George Washington University Press, 1976.

ANSLINGER, HARRY J., with GREGORY, DENNIS J. *The Protectors.* New York: Farrar, Straus & Giroux, 1964.

BOWEN, WALTER S., and NEAL, HARRY EDWARD. *The United States Secret Service.* Philadelphia: Chilton, 1960.

CAESAR, GENE. *Incredible Detective.* Englewood Cliffs, N.J.: Prentice-Hall, 1961.

CARLSON, JOHN ROY (Arthur Derounian). *Undercover.* New York: Dutton, 1943.

CHAPLIN, RALPH. *Wobbly.* Chicago: University of Chicago Press, 1948. (Da Capo reprint, 1972.)

CLAYTON, MERLE. *Union Station Massacre.* Indianapolis: Bobbs-Merrill, 1975.

COOK, FRED J. *The FBI Nobody Knows.* New York: Macmillan, 1964.

COCHRAN, LOUIS. *FBI Man: A Personal History.* New York: Duell, Sloan & Pearce, 1966.

DETOLEDANO, RALPH. *J. Edgar Hoover: The Man in His Time.* New Rochelle, N.Y.: Arlington House, 1973.

FLYNN, ELIZABETH GURLEY. *The Rebel Girl.* New York: International Press, 1955.

FRALEY, OSCAR. *Four against the Mob.* New York: Popular Library, 1961.

GINGER, RAY. *Eugene V. Debs: The Making of an American Radical.* New York: Macmillan, 1949.

HAYWOOD, WILLIAM. *Autobiography.* New York: International Publishers, 1929.

HILLQUIT, MORRIS. *Loose Leaves from a Busy Life.* New York: Macmillan, 1934. (Da Capo reprint, 1971.)

HORAN, JAMES D. *The Pinkertons.* New York: Crown, 1967.

HUNT, HENRY M. *The Crime of the Century: The Assassination of Dr. Patrick Henry Cronin.* Chicago: H. & D. Kochersperger, 1889.

IREY, ELMER L., and SLOCUM, WILLIAM J. *The Tax Dodgers.* New York: Garden City Publishing, 1948.

JEFFREYS-JONES, RHODRI. *American Espionage: From Secret Service to CIA.* New York: Free Press, 1977.

LANDAU, HENRY. *The Enemy Within.* New York: Putnam, 1937.

LOWENTHAL, MAX. *The Federal Bureau of Investigation.* Westport, Conn.: Greenwood Press, 1950.

McMURRAY, DONALD L. *Coxey's Army.* Seattle: University of Washington Press, 1929. (Reprint 1968.)

MILLIGAN, MAURICE. *Missouri Waltz.* New York: Scribner, 1948.

MILLSPAUGH, ARTHUR. *Crime Control by the National Government.* Washington, D.C.: Brookings, 1937.

MURRAY, ROBERT K. *Red Scare.* New York: McGraw-Hill, 1964.

NESS, ELIOT, with FRALEY, OSCAR. *The Untouchables.* New York: Messner, 1957.

OTTENBERG, MIRIAM. *The Federal Investigators.* Englewood Cliffs, N.J.: Prentice-Hall, 1962.

PURVIS, MELVIN. *American Agent.* New York: Garden City Publishing, 1938.

REED, LEAR B. *Human Wolves: Seventeen Years of War on Crime.* Kansas City, Mo.: Brown-White, Lowell Press, 1941.

ROSENSTONE, ROBERT A. *Romantic Revolutionary: John Reed.* New York: Knopf, 1975.

RUSSELL, FRANCIS. *The Shadow of Blooming Grove: Warren G. Harding in His Times.* New York: McGraw-Hill, 1968.

TULLY, ANDREW. *Treasury Agent.* New York: Simon & Schuster, 1958.

WATTERS, PAT, and GILLERS, STEPHEN, eds. *Investigating the FBI.* Garden City, N.Y.: Doubleday, 1973.

WHITEHEAD, DON. *The FBI Story.* New York: Random House, 1956.

WILKIE, DON, and LUTHER, MARK LEE. *American Secret Service Agent.* New York: Frederick A. Stokes, 1934.

WILSON, FRANK J., and DAY, BETH. *Special Agent.* New York: Holt, Rinehart and Winston, 1965.

Articles

HIGH, STANLEY. "Cleveland vs. the Crooks." *Current History,* October 1938, pp. 22–29.

———. "Kansas City Has Its Chin Up." *National Municipal Review,* October 1941, pp. 561–64.

Profile (J. Edgar Hoover). *New Yorker,* Sept. 25, Oct. 2, Oct. 9, 1937.

LANIS, EDWARD S. "Allan Pinkerton and the Baltimore Assassination Plot Against Lincoln." *Maryland Historical Magazine,* XLV, March, 1950, pp.1–13.

Reports

Cleveland Foundation. *Criminal Justice in Cleveland.* 1922.

U.S. Congress, Committee on Education and Labor, 76th Congress, 1st Session. Report 6, *Private Police Systems.* Washington, D.C., 1939.

Newspapers

The Kansas City Star.

CONCLUSION: THE PASSING PARADE (pp. 299–313)

Books

WESTLEY, WILLIAM. *Violence and the Police: A Sociological Study of Law, Custom and Morality.* Cambridge, Mass.: MIT Press, 1970.

WILSON, JAMES Q. *Thinking About Crime.* New York: Basic Books, 1976.

Articles

FERDINAND, THEODORE. "The Criminal Patterns of Boston Since 1949," *American Journal of Sociology,* July 1967, pp. 84–99.

Index